RUBI

Readers are invited to view and download
the supplementary Instructor's Guide for *Human
Resources Management for Public and Nonprofit
Organizations,* Second Edition.

The Instructor's Guide is available FREE on-line.

If you would like to download and print out an
electronic copy of the Guide, please visit
www.josseybass.com/go/pyneshr

Thank you,

Joan E. Pynes

Human Resources Management for Public and Nonprofit Organizations

Consulting Editor
James L. Perry
Indiana University

Human Resources Management for Public and Nonprofit Organizations

Second Edition

Joan E. Pynes

JOSSEY-BASS
A Wiley Imprint
www.josseybass.com

Published by Jossey-Bass
A Wiley Imprint
989 Market Street, San Francisco, CA 94103-1741   www.josseybass.com

Jossey-Bass books and products are available through most bookstores. To contact Jossey-Bass directly call our Customer Care Department within the U.S. at 800-956-7739, outside the U.S. at 317-572-3986, or fax 317-572-4002.

Jossey-Bass also publishes its books in a variety of electronic formats. Some content that appears in print may not be available in electronic books.

Library of Congress Cataloging-in-Publication Data
Pynes, Joan.
  Human resources management for public and nonprofit organizations /
Joan E. Pynes.—2nd ed.
      p. cm.
  Includes bibliographical references and index.
  ISBN 0-7879-7078-6 (alk. paper)
  1. Public administration–United States—Personnel management.
  2. Nonprofit organizations—United States—Personnel management. I. Title.
  HF5549.2.U5P96 2004
  352.6'0973—dc22

                                                                2004011530

Printed in the United States of America
SECOND EDITION
HB Printing   10 9 8 7 6 5 4 3

Contents

Tables, Figures, and Exhibits

Tables

Figures

Exhibits

Preface

The conceptual foundation of the first edition of this book was strategic human resources management (SHRM). SHRM is the integration of human resources management with the strategic mission of the organization. It adapts human resources policies and practices to meet the challenges faced by agencies today, as well as those they will face in the future. What was written then and is even more important today is the necessity that human resources departments take a proactive role in guiding and supporting agency efforts to meet the changing demands of their environments.

Government and nonprofit organizations are facing many challenges. They are confronted with tight budgets brought about by tax cuts provided in the early 2000s, the loss of approximately 2.6 million private sector jobs since 2001, concerns over terrorism, and the war and subsequent obligations in Iraq. Reductions in public dollars and private donations have led public and nonprofit organizations to lay off staff even as demands for services are increasing. These changes have occurred simultaneously with increasing demands for efficient and effective services.

The new public service has become more diverse. Changing demographics have resulted in an increase in the numbers of employees who are women, members of ethnic and racial minorities, and persons with disabilities. Graduates of schools of public policy and administration are likely to take jobs in the nonprofit sector and show a greater interest in seeking employment opportunities in the private sector. Today's graduates are moving across the three sectors, looking for challenging work and the opportunity to learn new skills. The challenge for public and nonprofit organizations is to design a human resources management (HRM) system that keeps them motivated and able to make a difference through their work.

Changes in information technology and automation led to the restructuring of many public and nonprofit agencies. Advances in technology have enabled employees to work from their homes, provided opportunities for more flexible work hours, and increased the employment options for disabled individuals. Computer networks and videoconferencing have changed communication patterns. Information technology is being used not only to automate routine tasks but also increasingly to restructure and integrate service delivery procedures and programs.

Organizations must do more than just adapt to internal changes. They must also seek better ways to meet the expectations of citizens, clients, funding sources, foundations, elected officials, boards of directors, interest groups, and the media.

The public sector is becoming less involved in direct service delivery. Government at all levels is increasingly relying on nonprofit and private sector organizations to provide services. Government work is being implemented through a network of contracting, intergovernmental grants, vouchers, tax credits, regulations, and other indirect administrative approaches. While the federal government in particular is reducing the number of individuals it employs directly, it continues to need a sizable "shadow" to accomplish its mission (Light, 1999). These employees are part of the shadow that is created when public goods and services are provided through private, nonprofit, or state and local entities. According to Paul Light, many of the nation's most challenging public service jobs are now found outside the federal government, not inside (1999, pp. 3–4). Donald Kettl (2002, p. 120) notes the following:

> Government has come to rely heavily on for-profit and nonprofit
> organizations for delivering goods and services ranging from
> antimissile systems to welfare reform. These changes have scarcely
> obliterated the role of Congress, the president and the courts. State
> and local governments have become even livelier. Rather, these
> changes have layered new challenges on top of the old ones, under
> which the system already mightily struggles. New process-based
> problems have emerged as well: How can hierarchical bureaucracies,
> created with the presumption that they directly deliver services,
> cope with services increasingly delivered through multiple (often
> nongovernmental) partners? Budgetary control processes that
> work well for traditional bureaucracies often prove less effective

in gathering information from nongovernmental partners or in shaping their incentives. Personnel systems designed to insulate government from political interference have proven less adaptive to these new challenges, especially in creating a cohort of executives skilled in managing indirect government.

Declining revenues combined with demographic changes, changes in employees' values, and the need to retain effective workers are some of the forces that have compelled public and nonprofit organizations to become concerned with their survival. These changes require a more flexible and more skilled workforce. To survive, organizations need employees with new skills. *Hard Truths/Tough Choices* (National Commission on the State and Local Public Service, 1993) identified five skill areas that are needed by the new public manager: competency in team building, competency in communication, competency in involving employees, commitment to cultural awareness, and commitment to quality. These skills have HRM implications for employee recruitment, selection, and training. Public and nonprofit sector jobs are increasingly professional in nature, requiring higher levels of education. At the same time, there has been a decrease in jobs that are physically demanding. Employees in public and nonprofit agencies often deal with a variety of people, many of whom have a stake in the agency. Taxpayers, clients, customers, elected officials, donors, contractors, board members, and special interest groups are just some of the stakeholders concerned about agency performance. Employers must ask themselves how to meet the public's objectives and satisfy the organization's stakeholders.

More recently, there has been an emphasis on human capital, recognizing that employees are an agency's most important organizational asset. Workers define its character, affect its capacity to perform, and represent the knowledge base of the organization. Despite this acknowledgment, little strategic human capital management is being conducted in federal agencies. Reports indicate that the following activities are lacking: (1) leadership, continuity, and succession planning; (2) strategic human capital planning and organizational alignment; (3) acquiring and developing staffs whose size, skills, and use meet agency needs; and (4) creating results-oriented organizational cultures. All have been identified as challenges facing the federal government (General Accounting Office, 2001a, 2001c, 2002b). State and local governments and nonprofit and for-profit organizations are facing these same human capital challenges as well (Beatty, Craig, & Schneier, 1997; Hays & Kearney, 2001; Hinden & Hull, 2002; Light, 1998, 2000a, 2000b; Ulrich, 1997, 1998; Walters, 2000b).

To be strategic partners, HRM departments must possess high levels of professional and business knowledge. HRM must establish links to enhancing organizational performance and be able to demonstrate on a continuing basis how HRM activities contribute to the success and effectiveness of the organization.

Public and nonprofit agencies must be flexible and attuned to the needs of society. They must seek to improve the quality of their services by engaging in strategic human resources management. Recruitment and selection strategies must be innovative, career development opportunities must be provided, work assignments must be flexible, and policies must reward superior performers and hold marginal employees accountable. These policies must be developed and administered according to the principles of equity, efficiency, and effectiveness. Performance standards must be designed to promote the goals and values of organizations.

Historically, HRM has been seen as a Cinderella—on the periphery, not integrated into the core of agency functions. Fitz-enz (1996, p. 3) notes that historically, personnel departments were either dumping grounds for "organizational casualties"—likable employees who were not proficient at other tasks—or were staffed with employees from line functions, neither of whom had any formal education in personnel administration. He also attributes the peripheral relationship of HRM departments to other functional departments to the fact that for years it was believed that organizations could not measure or quantify what the HRM department accomplished or contributed to the organization's bottom line. HRM departments did not speak in financial terms, the common denominator of business language, nor were they very good at communicating the relationship between successful HRM programs and organizational success. As a result, most HRM departments were denied access to the organization's strategic planning processes and forced into reactive activities instead of being allowed to collaborate with the other management teams to formulate policies and determine future objectives. This approach has been a mistake. Research in the private sector has found that returns on wise HRM policies can surpass returns from other resources (Cascio, 2000; Fitz-enz, 1996, 2000). In the public and nonprofit sectors, where 60 to 80 percent of expenditures are for personnel, SHRM is even more important than in the private sector.

Purpose and Audience

This book addresses HRM issues that arise in nonprofit and public agencies. Although there are many textbooks on public personnel management, none address the nonprofit sector, thus omitting a significant partner that provides services that benefit society. Topics such as recruiting and managing volunteers or working with a board of directors have not been addressed. There are other omissions as well, such as a discussion of nonprofit labor relations. For example, nonprofit labor relations are governed by the amended National Labor Relations Act (the Labor-Management Relations Act), while most federal employees fall under the Federal Service Labor-Management Relations Statute (Title VII of the Civil Service Reform Act of 1978), and state and local government employees are guided by their respective public employee relations statutes. In the public sector, an applicant's or employee's religion is irrelevant, and discrimination because of religion is prohibited. However, religiously affiliated nonprofits that provide services of a religious nature may in special circumstances discriminate against applicants or employees on the basis of their religion.

Because service provider nonprofits are typically the recipients of government contracts and grants, a new intergovernmental environment has emerged as nongovernment organizations have increasingly been used to implement public policy. Kramer and Grossman (1987) and Salamon (1995, 1999) refer to this new interorganizational environment as the "new political economy," the "contract state," or "nonprofit federalism," while Light (1999) refers to it as "shadow government."

The emphasis in this book will be on nonprofits that are closely associated with providing a public benefit or service or with solving a problem on behalf of the public interest. It will focus on non-profits that are responsible for delivering health care, social services, education, arts, and research. The objectives of these nonprofits often parallel those of many government agencies in terms of the individual and community services they provide.

Public organizations and nonprofits are similar in that they define themselves according to their missions or the services they offer. These services are often intangible and difficult to measure. The clients receiving public or nonprofit services and the professionals delivering them make very different judgments about the quality of those services. Both sectors are responsible to multiple constituencies: nonprofits are responsible to supporters, sponsors, clients, and government sources that provide funding and impose regulations; and public agencies are responsible to their respective legislative and judicial branches and to taxpayers, cognate agencies, political appointees, clients, the media, and other levels of government (Kanter & Summers, 1987; Starling, 1986). Lipsky and Smith (1989–1990) comment that public and private service organizations share many characteristics: the need to process clients through systems of eligibility and treatment, the need to maintain a competent staff to be effective, and the need to account for financial expenditures. These organizations are also expected to be fair (equitable), to accommodate likely and unanticipated complexities (responsive), to protect the interests of sponsors in minimizing costs (efficient), to be true to their mandated purposes (accountable), and to be honest (fiscally honorable) (pp. 630–631).

The conceptual foundation of this book is strategic human resources management. SHRM is the integration of human resources management with the strategic mission of the organization. It adapts human resources policies and practices to meet the challenges agencies face today, as well as those they will face in the future. Human resources departments must take a proactive role in guiding and supporting agency efforts to meet the changing demands of their environments. The information provided in this book is to be used to improve the effectiveness of HRM activities.

In many organizations, HRM policies and practices develop on an ad hoc basis, with little integration of the organization's future needs. Often policies are developed to solve an immediate problem, with no thought to their long-term implications. Such policies and practices lock the agency into inflexible modes of operation, leaving them unable to see that other strategies might be more appropriate.

This book emphasizes the importance of HRM functions, revealing them as major contributors to the accomplishment of the agency's mission both in the present and as the agency changes. The purpose of the book is to provide practitioners, policymakers (such as elected officials), and board members of local, state, federal, and nonprofit organizations with an understanding of the importance of SHRM in managing change. It provides the guidance necessary to implement effective HRM strategies.

The book was also written to be a textbook for use in public administration and nonprofit management graduate programs that offer courses in personnel administration, human resources management, strategic planning, and nonprofit management. Although the literature on nonprofit management has increased in recent years, little of that information addresses nonprofit HRM concerns. This book should help fill that void. As more public administration programs offer a specialization in nonprofit management, it is important that resources be available that target the challenges faced by both the public and nonprofit sectors.

Overview of the Contents

Part One introduces the context and environment of human resources management. Chapter One discusses how society and workplaces have changed and the HRM implications of those changes. Chapter Two explains why SHRM and human resources planning are imperative if agencies are going to remain competitive and be able to accomplish their missions; it also discusses how the role of human resource specialists have to change as well. Chapter Three discusses strategic human management and information technology. Chapter Four presents the legal environment of equal employment opportunity, and Chapter Five discusses the importance of valuing and managing diversity if organizations expect to prosper. The importance of managing volunteers and how SHRM practices can assist in making the volunteer experience productive for the agency and satisfying to the volunteers are discussed in Chapter Six.

Part Two presents the techniques and functional areas of human resources management. Examples are provided in each chapter. Chapter Seven explains the importance of job analysis before executing HRM policies or developing job descriptions, performance appraisal instruments, training and development programs, and recruitment and selection criteria. A variety of job analysis techniques are discussed. In Chapter Eight, recruitment and selection techniques are explained. Drug testing, physical ability tests, psychological examinations, and other selection techniques used in the public and nonprofit sectors are summarized. At the end of the chapter, important psychometric concepts are explained. New to this edition is the introduction of practical intelligence, emotional intelligence, adaptability, multiple intelligences, and organizational citizen performance behaviors. Performance management and evaluating employees' performance is the focus of Chapter Nine. Different performance appraisal techniques are explained, and their strengths and weaknesses are identified. The importance of rater training and documentation is noted. Ethical issues in performance appraisal are discussed, as are merit pay and 360-degree evaluations. Chapter Ten identifies the internal and external factors that influence compensation policies and practices. The techniques used to develop pay systems are discussed. Examples of job evaluation systems are provided, and nontraditional pay systems are explained. In Chapter Eleven, employer-provided benefits and pensions are discussed.

The focus of Chapter Twelve is training and development activities. Changes in technology and demographics and the development of new responsibilities and expectations have made training and career development more important than ever. Identifying training needs, developing training objectives and the curriculum, and the evaluation of training are explored. Different training formats are summarized. The chapter concludes with examples of management training and career development programs. Chapter Thirteen discusses collective bargaining in the public and nonprofit sectors. The legal environment of labor-management relations for nonprofit, federal, state, and local employees is explored. Definitions and explanations are provided for concepts such as unit determination, union security, unfair labor practices, management rights, impasse resolution, and grievance arbitration. The reasons that unions exist in the public and non-profit sectors are examined. The final chapter provides an overall conclusion. It summarizes the key lessons presented in the book, which I hope will have convinced public and nonprofit adminis-trators of the importance of strategic HRM.

Tampa, Florida   Joan E. Pynes
May 2004

Acknowledgments

A number of people have made valuable contributions to this book. I would like to thank Allison Brunner and Johanna Vondeling at Jossey-Bass as well as James L. Perry and the anonymous reviewers for their helpful comments and suggestions.

As in the fist edition, friends, colleagues, and students provided assistance by contributing workplace examples and reviewing chapters. I would like to thank Anne Goldych Dailey, Liberty Resources; Patricia Goldstein, Neuse Mental Health Center; Patricia Murray, New York State Office of Children and Family Services; and graduate students from the University of South Florida, who address and implement HRM responsibilities on a regular basis. Special acknowledgment goes to my husband, Mike McNaughton, for his sense of humor, editorial assistance, and time spent preparing and revising the tables and exhibits.

I would also like to express my appreciation to my mother, my sister Robyn, and my husband for their support and encouragement. Like the first edition, this book is dedicated to my mother, who has always inspired me to do my best.

—J.E.P.

The Author

Joan E. Pynes is professor of public administration and director of the public administration program at the University of South Florida. She received her B.A. degree (1979) in public justice from the State University of New York at Oswego and her M.P.A. degree (1983) and Ph.D. degree (1988) in public administration from Florida Atlantic University. She is the author of articles and chapters on public and nonprofit human resources management. Her article "Are Women Underrepresented as Leaders of Nonprofit Organizations?" was named the best article published in *Review of Public Personnel Administration* for 2000 by the American Society for Public Administration's Section on Personnel and Labor Relations (SPLAR).

Human Resources Management for Public and Nonprofit Organizations

Part One

Human Resources Management in Context

Public and nonprofit organizations are finding themselves having to confront a variety of economic, technological, legal, and cultural changes with which they must cope effectively if they are to remain viable. The key to viability is well-trained and flexible employees. To be responsive to the constantly changing environment, agencies must integrate their human resources management (HRM) needs with their long-term strategic plans. This part of the book consists of six chapters that explain how society and workplaces have changed and what the HRM implications of these changes are for organizations.

Chapter One reviews some of the external factors that affect the internal operations of an organization, such as changes in economic conditions and the financial uncertainty that such changes can bring to an agency, and the social and cultural changes affecting the demographic composition of the workforce. Most organizations today have a more diverse group of employees than ever before, bringing new expectations into the organization. The legal environment must always be monitored for change. Equal employment opportunity, labor relations, and compensation and benefits are all regulated by law.

There is also an emphasis on accountability and performance management in public and nonprofit organizations. Staff need critical knowledge, skills, abilities, and other characteristics (KSAOCs) to perform specific jobs, and they also need to be flexible and willing to deal with rapid and unstructured change. To make this possible, HRM needs to be more closely integrated with the organization's objectives and mission.

Chapter Two addresses the strategic side of HRM and the importance of strategic human resources and human resources planning. It explains why strategic human resources management (SHRM) and human resources planning are critical if agencies are going to accomplish their missions. SHRM believes that realistic planning is not possible unless strategic planning takes into consideration information on current and potential human resources. Human resources planning requires the assessment of past trends, evaluation of the present situation, and projection of future events. The external and internal environments must be scanned, and changes that might affect an organization's human resources must be anticipated if organizations wish to remain viable.

The effect of information technology on strategic human resources management is presented in Chapter Three. Technological changes such as the increased use of computers, information systems, databases, telecommunications, and networking have changed the way agencies are structured and work is organized and managed. Organizations need to recruit and hire people who have the skills and orientation to fit the new culture.

Chapter Four focuses on the federal laws governing equal employment opportunity. Equal employment opportunity requires that employers not discriminate in the administration and execution of all HRM practices, such as recruitment, selection, promotion, training, compensation, career development, discipline, and labor-management relations. To understand the legal environment of equal employment opportunity, one must be familiar with the laws and regulations that govern its implementation.

Chapter Five is devoted to exploring the issues of managing a diverse workforce. As already noted, the composition of public and nonprofit workforces has changed. Women, racial and ethnic minorities, and older, disabled, and homosexual workers are more visible in today's workplace and may not always be accepted by other employees and managers. This diversity must be understood if organizations want to deal effectively with all employees regardless of their different characteristics. When diversity is well managed, all employees are supported, valued, and included. A supportive work environment enables employees to achieve their fullest potential.

Chapter Six, the last chapter in Part One, discusses the use of volunteers in the public and nonprofit sectors. Volunteers are used by public and nonprofit organizations to provide a range of services. Some volunteers serve as board members for nonprofit organizations or on local government commissions or boards. Other volunteers provide assistance where needed in cultural, social service, health care, and educational agencies. Still other volunteers are used to supplement paid staff in professional roles.

Chapter One

Human Resources Management in a Dynamic Environment

Many external and internal environmental factors affect an organization's human resources management (HRM). The public and nonprofit sectors continue to be influenced by external factors that affect the internal operations of the organization. Economic factors, social and cultural changes, technological changes, and legal changes all present HRM challenges. This chapter reviews some of the challenges that nonprofit and public agencies face and then briefly addresses how proactive HRM practices can make a difference in helping organizations achieve their missions despite these changes.

Economic Changes

Public and nonprofit organizations are confronting serious economic challenges. By the end of January 2003, thirty-six of the fifty U.S. states were projecting a combined budget gap of $25.7 billion for the current fiscal year. Most states are in fiscal crisis. They have laid off employees, enacted across-the-board cuts, reorganized programs, and used early retirements to save money (National Governors Association & National Association of State Budget Officers, 2002). Contributing factors include the decline in the national economy, stock market declines, downturns in manufacturing and high-technology industries, and rising health care costs. The $2.3 trillion federal budget proposed by President George W. Bush has been criticized by the National Conference of State Legislatures, which notes that the proposed budget fails to provide the billions of dollars needed for education, homeland security, and election reform or to provide enough help to offset the soaring costs of Medicaid (Janofsky, 2003; "States Plunging into Red," 2003).

The fiscal conditions in America's cities are also declining. The decline is being exacerbated by slower-than-expected growth in revenues from sales tax, income taxes, and tourist-related revenues such as restaurant and hotel taxes. At the same time, there are increases in public spending on safety and education and rising health care costs (Pagno, 2002). The fiscal crisis in the state of Connecticut has prompted local governments to send property tax bills to nonprofit organizations. A state supreme court ruling in December 2002 allowing the city of Bridgeport to tax a homeless shelter has reverberated throughout other local communities. Stamford is asking the YMCA, the Jewish Community Center, the Italian Center, St. Luke's Community Services, and Stamford Hospital to justify their current exempt status. New Haven is taxing an agency that provides emergency and transitional shelter for women and children, Hartford is taxing a halfway house, and Windham is taxing a substance abuse rehabilitation center (Santaniello, 2003).

Hunger and homelessness are on the rise in twenty-five major U.S. cities. Requests for emergency food assistance increased an average of 19 percent in 2001. The increases in hunger and homelessness are attributed to high housing costs, low-paying jobs, unemployment, and the economic downturn (U.S. Conference of Mayors, 2002).

More than 23 million people received emergency hunger relief from the America's Second Harvest network of charities. A survey of its affiliates found that 86 percent have seen an increase in requests for food assistance. New York City's soup kitchens and food pantries fed 45 percent more people in 2003 than in 2000. The Greater Chicago Food Depository, which provides food to six hundred agencies, estimates that the food bank will distribute 42 million pounds this year to about ninety-one thousand families a week. The Greater Boston Food Bank has also seen the amount of food it distributes increase. Since October 2002, the amount it has distributed increased from 350,000 pounds of food a week to between 500,000 to 600,000 pounds a week ("Hunger and Homelessness," 2003).

Public and nonprofit agencies and employees are not the only workers facing an uncertain future. The economy has lost more than two million jobs since the most recent recession began in March 2001. The number of companies cutting jobs has spiked since November, with AOL Time Warner, Boeing, Dow Jones, Eastman Kodak, Goodyear, McDonalds's, Merrill Lynch, Sara Lee, and Verizon all announcing new layoffs. The airlines, brokerage firms, and makers of clothing and textiles each cut at least a tenth of their workforces. The manufacturers of durable goods such as computers, furniture, and steel have eliminated the most positions, with one of every nine jobs eliminated since early 2001 (Leonhardt, 2003).

There has also been an increase in the shift from full-time employment to contingent or part-time employment. Data from the U.S. Bureau of Labor Statistics reports that from February 1999 to February 2001, there were 5.4 million contingent workers; 52 percent of these workers would have preferred a permanent job. Contingent workers were more likely to be women and to be black or Hispanic (U.S. Bureau of Labor Statistics, 2001). Contingent, part-time, and temporary employees often work two jobs and live in poverty, and many of them require assistance from public and nonprofit agencies.

Uncertain financial times place additional stress on public and nonprofit organizations. Increased unemployment often requires the expansion of financial assistance, medical aid, and job training or retraining services. These services are typically provided by the public and nonprofit sectors, which must absorb an increase in demand for services without increasing staff and possibly facing layoffs themselves.

Nonprofit and public agencies are affected by economic uncertainty in other ways. Individuals who have been or might be laid off are less inclined to spend money on cultural activities than more securely employed people. They are also likely to reduce the level of their contributions to charitable nonprofits or to services such as National Public Radio or the Public Broadcasting Service, exacerbating the financial pressures on these already stressed agencies. Chicago public television station WTTW laid off fifteen employees in late May 2002. Management blamed the reduction on significant decreases in underwriting that created a $3 million budget shortfall. WTTW is not alone when dealing with reduced underwriting and membership revenues. Layoffs have occurred at several public television and radio stations, including Oregon Public Broadcasting, Maryland Public Television, KERA in Dallas, Pacifica Radio, and National Public Radio's Performance Today. All cited the rough economy and reduced corporate sponsorship revenue (Carpenter, 2002).

In New York City, cultural institutions are taking financial hits. Driven by a weak economy, a drop in tourism, city budget cuts, and a decline in private contributions, museums, theaters, concert halls, opera companies, public gardens, and zoos through the five boroughs are cutting performances, exhibitions, days of operation, and staff. For example, the Bronx Museum of Arts canceled two exhibitions last year and has eliminated four management positions. "Last year we killed programs," said Jenny Dixon, the executive director. "This year we're killing people" (Pogrebin, 2003). The American Museum of Natural History has closed on Saturday nights, cut its $130 million budget by $14 million, reduced the number of entrances to two from seven, and through attrition reduced its 1,700-member staff by 200. The Staten Island Historical Society, an outdoor living history site, recently announced a 20 percent pay cut and reduction in work hours for its employees and is contemplating closing completely. "I'm holding off as long as I can," said John W. Guild, the executive director (Pogrebin, 2003).

The Roman Catholic Archdiocese of Los Angeles, which cut sixty jobs and pared programs in an effort to bridge a $4.3 million budget gap, released figures showing that its deficit had more than tripled. From 2001 to 2002, the archdiocese's assets fell from $643.7 to $626.4 million. Much of the decrease was in investments that lost value or were sold to cover operating expenses. Pledges were down about $7.6 million, and insurance and pension costs increased. "The church is subject to the same market forces as other nonprofit organizations," said Tod Tamberg. "Economic conditions have not been good and are unlikely to improve in the near-term." The budget covers the church headquarters and finances departments that provide pastoral support to parishes, school, and seminaries (Whitaker, 2003).

There is a greater emphasis on social enterprise and social entrepreneurship activities. Nonprofits are expected to diversify their revenue streams and eliminate their reliance on public monies or foundation grants. The leadership of nonprofit organizations must understand, supervise, and implement finance strategies and social marketing.

Uncertain financial times cause citizens to focus more on the performance of the public and nonprofit sectors. People with less money to spend want assurances that their tax dollars are spent wisely and without waste. This is especially true given the revelations of how some of the money raised by the American Red Cross after the terrorist attacks of September 11, 2001, was diverted to funds not related to those events; the guilty plea entered by the vice president for finance at the United Way in Lansing, Michigan, who embezzled $1.9 million and spent the money by purchasing quarter horses; and the money spent by various Catholic archdioceses around the country for settlements dating back many years to settle allegations of sexual abuse. Tough financial times provoke greater scrutiny of the performance outcomes of both sectors. More and more citizens are demanding a voice in the way monies are allocated.

Social and Cultural Changes

The demographic composition of American society is changing. Hispanics (who can be of any race) are now the largest minority in the United States, at approximately 37 million. The growth has resulted from higher birthrates and from the wave of immigration that has taken place in the last decade. The 2000 census forms allowed respondents to choose more than one race when identifying themselves. The number of Americans who declared themselves black in combination with one or more other races is now 37.7 million, slightly higher than the overall figures for Latinos, indicating a growing multiculturalism in America (U.S. Census Bureau, 2003b). Not only will there continue to be an increase in Hispanics in the workforce, but there will also be an increase in the number of persons of color. The increase in the number of women will continue along with an increase in foreign-born or immigrant workers. Employers face new issues arising from the diverse workforce. They must offer more flexible work schedules to accommodate training, education, and family needs. Employers must also provide greater opportunities for work-based learning to prepare future workers and to continually upgrade the skills of current workers. The increased diversity of our workforce poses new challenges for the systems that educate and train workers. These systems must accommodate ethnic and cultural differences, provide for the needs of working families and individuals with disabilities, and address gaps in literacy and job skills among some immigrant populations. This will require increased investments in adult literacy and English as a Second Language programs, more opportunities for continuous learning to stay competitive, and expanded access to work supports to sustain labor force participation. Employers need to manage a diverse workforce. They will need to ensure that agency rewards such as promotional opportunities and compensation are determined by job performance, initiative, or special skills, not by racism or sexism.

There has been a shift in the attitudes and values of employees. Employees are seeking a balance between their personal and work lives. They are demanding more leisure time to spend with their families. There has also been a change in what constitutes a family; a father, mother, and two children is no longer the norm. Nontraditional families are now prevalent. Divorce, death, domestic partners, and different generations of the same family living together have become commonplace. The number of children being raised by grandparents has increased 30 percent since 1990. Because of the increase in single-parent families, families in which both parents work, employees taking care of elderly parents and young children, and children living with caregivers instead of their parents, organizations need to provide employees with more flexibility and options in choosing work schedules and benefits. Issues such as day care, elder care, assistance with family problems, and spousal involvement in career planning have become important.

Attitudes toward work have also changed; a greater number of employees want challenging jobs and the opportunity to exercise discretion in the performance of their tasks. Improving the quality of work life has become important. Empowerment, teamwork, quality improvement, job design, labor-management cooperation, and participative management are expected. Organizational culture will need to be changed if organizations wish to attract, motivate, and retain a competent workforce.

Technological Changes

A major challenge to U.S. economy in the twenty-first century is the shortage of skilled workers. The Bureau of Labor Statistics projects that by 2020, there will be a 22 percent increase in the number of jobs requiring some postsecondary education. Yet during the next two decades, we will lose 46 million skilled workers as baby boomers retire (National Governors Association, 2002, p. 11). Specific industries crucial to our growth, including education, health care, and information technology, will continue to suffer disproportionately large shortages of skilled workers as job openings go unfilled. As we continue the transition from the Industrial Age to the Knowledge Age, people are the key factor in attaining and maintaining a competitive posture.

Changes in technology have had a tremendous impact on many nonprofit and public organizations. The introduction of "e-government" is changing the way organizations are structured and how work is organized and managed. The Center for Technology in Government defines e-government as "the use of information technology to support government operations, engage citizens, and provide government services" (Cook, La Vigne, Pagano, Dawes, & Pardo, 2002, p. 3). Within the definition are four dimensions that reflect the functions of government itself:

- *E-services*—the electronic delivery of government information, programs, and services over the Internet
- *E-management*—the use of information technology to improve the management of government and to streamline business processes to improve the flow of information within government offices
- *E-democracy*—the use of electronic communication vehicles, such as e-mail and the Internet, to increase citizen participation in the public decision-making process
- *E-commerce*—the exchange of money for goods and services over the Internet, as when citizens pay taxes and utility bills, renew vehicle registrations, and pay for recreation programs

or when governments buy office supplies and auction off surplus equipment

In December 2002, President Bush signed the E-Government Act of 2002 (P.L. 107-347) into law. The legislation formalizes a structure to support e-government efforts across the federal government. As a result of this law, the U.S. Department of Labor (DOL) has developed an e-government framework to guide its ability to (1) build the customer relationship and improve customer value; (2) establish e-government management structures and management e-government portfolios; (3) ensure that technology is managed in the way that best serves the mission, goals, and objectives of the DOL; and (4) ensure that transactions with the DOL are secure and that appropriate privacy protections are in place.

Computers and automation play a major role in the redesign of traditionally routine jobs. The child support Web site that is part of New Mexico's Child Support Enforcement Division gives parents more control over their cases. New Mexico parents can use the site to communicate electronically with Child Support Enforcement staff, deposit child support payments directly into their bank accounts, monitor payment status and account balances, provide change-of-employer and new-address information, apply for services, review recent actions taken by the agency on their cases, authorize automatic withdrawals from their bank accounts, and provide information regarding the location of a noncustodial parent (Newcombe, 2002).

A geographic information system (GIS) called the School Partnership Resource Locator has helped the Charlotte-Mecklenburg School district in North Carolina match school needs with volunteers and businesses willing to provide support services. Using the GIS program, schools can be matched with businesses and resources in the community that might assist the schools with their needs. Likewise, GIS is being used by nonprofits to map the membership data of Boys and Girls Clubs against census information to show the percentages of young people involved in club activities and by food banks to see whether or not emergency food pantries are located where they are most needed. Information technology is being used not only to automate routine tasks but also increasingly to restructure and integrate service delivery procedures and programs.

Rocheleau (1988, p. 165) posed the following questions in regard to the changes introduced by computer technology:

How well does the new information technology mesh with the old structures?

How do existing structures have to be modified, and what structures have to be created in order to manage the new information technology?

How does the degree of centralization within organizations affect the implementation of the new information technology?

Does the new information technology spur centralization or decentralization?

Perry and Kramer (1993) noted that most of the changes necessary to accommodate greater use of information technology will need to occur in personnel systems. "High demand in many technological specialties will necessitate rapid assessment and hiring of applicants. This is likely to require streamlining government hiring practices and shifting merit system controls from input practices (for example, testing) to post audit" (p. 240). Thus information technology is creating new challenges for HRM systems.

Organizations need to recruit and hire people with a new set of skills and orientations to fit the new culture. Key challenges facing organizations will be the ability to attract and hire qualified applicants and to provide training for incumbent employees so that the benefits of technology can be realized.

The Legal Environment

Public and nonprofit agencies must comply with federal, state, and local laws, with executive orders, and with the rules and regulations promulgated by administrative agencies such as the Equal Employment Opportunity Commission, as well as with federal and state court decisions. Equal employment opportunity, labor relations, and employer contributions to benefits such as retirement plans and pensions, worker's compensation, and unemployment are regulated by law. The legal environment must be monitored because it is always changing. Two recent U.S. Supreme Court decisions, *Kimmel* v. *Florida Board of Regents* (528 U.S. 62, 2000) and *Board of Trustees of the University of Alabama* v. *Garrett* (531 U.S. 356, 2001), held that state employees may not sue their employer (state governments) for violation of the Age Discrimination in Employment Act (ADEA) and the Americans with Disabilities Act (ADA). The Supreme Court ruled that the application of New Jersey's public accommodation law to the Boy Scouts violated the organization's First Amendment right of expressive association (*Boy Scouts of America and Monmouth Council et al.* v. *James Dale*, 530 U.S. 640, 2002). The Boy Scouts argued successfully that as a private organization, it has the right to determine criteria for membership. Therefore, it is lawful for the Boy Scouts to discriminate on the basis of sexual orientation when selecting scout leaders.

President Bush, through the use of executive orders, is promoting faith-based initiatives. He wants to make sure that faith-related organizations have a chance to compete with secular nonprofits or for-profits for government grants and contracts. One issue that has not been resolved to the satisfaction of many Americans is whether faith-based organizations that receive public monies should be able to discriminate on the basis of religion for nonministerial positions.

Privatization and Contracting Out Services

Privatization or contracting-out occurs when public sector agencies contract with nonprofit, private, or other public agencies to provide specific services. A typical privatization agreement specifies that a private or nonprofit entity is responsible for providing particular services. The public employer chooses the service level and pays the amount specified in the contract but leaves decisions about provision methods to the contracted firm. From an administrative perspective, privatization is often viewed as a way to save tax dollars, reduce the public payrolls, minimize government spending, and boost productivity. Supporters claim that contracting out government programs will lead to greater efficiency and more effective operations. They maintain that competition and fewer restrictions allow the contractors to be more cost-efficient and responsive and that cost savings can be achieved through the economies of scale used by one vendor to provide services to many communities and organizations. It is believed that nonprofit and private firms, not hampered by bureaucratic rules and regulations, can be more innovative than public sector ones.

President Bush has announced plans to let the private sector compete for as many as 425,000 federal government jobs through "competitive sourcing." Some of the positions targeted for privatization are three thousand air traffic controllers; Internal Revenue Service employees who are involved in the collection, control, and disbursements of federal funds; and seventeen hundred employees of the National Park Service, including scientists, archaeologists, museum curators, electricians, plumbers, gardeners, historians, and the fee collectors who greet park visitors (Long, 2003; Tremain, 2003; Wald, 2003a, 2003b; Walsh, 2003a, 2003b). State governments tend to contract out social services, community, and health and mental health services (Ewoh, 1999). The state of Florida has contracted with Aramark, a food services company, to manage the food service in most of the state's prisons; with Accenture for computerizing the licensing and information functions of the state Department of Business and Professional Regulation; and with Convergys Corporation to take over most state personnel functions (Murphy, 2002). Florida also contracts for the provision of foster care and adoption services to a variety of nonprofit and for-profit agencies, responsibilities that previously fell to state employees working for the Department of Children and Family Services (DCF).

Privatization is controversial. It often results in job loss, invokes the ire of public unions, in some cases has led to poorer service, and establishes the need for oversight responsibilities and monitoring of the contractee's performance. In the public sector, elected officials are still responsible to the citizens for the provision of efficient and quality services. After a snowstorm, for instance, snow needs to be removed in a timely manner, whether it be by public employees or a contracted firm. As a result of the *Columbia* disaster, an investigation is under way to determine whether privatization has undermined NASA procedures and rules (Murphy, 2003). The Philadelphia school district changed course and is allowing Edison Schools, a for-profit school management company, to run only 32 of the city's 264 schools, less than originally planned (Caruso, 2003; Henriques, 2003).

When public services are contracted out, the employees who used to provide them may be adversely affected. They must be transferred to different departments or hired by the contractor, usually at lower salaries and with fewer benefits. Needless to say, contracting out is typically opposed by public sector unions. The job security of union members is put at risk, as well as the union's survival. If agencies decide to privatize, they should attempt to make the transition fair to employees. If the contractee will not hire incumbent employees, the incumbents should be provided with severance packages and retraining. An adversarial shift to privatization will spill over to other areas of governance. Other employees will view the administration with suspicion and feel insecure about their positions. Agencies planning to privatize must make sure they do so in a humane manner.

As with most decisions, there are pluses and minuses to privatization. For privatization to be effective, certain conditions must be present. Competition is a necessity, because without competition, there is little reason to be efficient. Monitoring is critical; government must provide oversight and hold the contractee accountable for poor service. Finally, the public's interest should be a priority (Hass, 1993; Van Slyke, 2003). Some services are best left in house. Praeger (1994) cites as an example the services provided by an emergency hospital. It may be cost-efficient to contract out emergency services, but what if the contractee left the community or was forced to close its doors due to financial hardship? The community would be left without a care provider. Likewise, Avery (2000) cautions about the privatization of public health laboratory services, noting that the core mission of public health laboratories differs from that of private laboratories. Public health revolves around the detection, prevention, treatment, control, intervention, surveillance, and assessment of health threats in a population, whereas private sector laboratories focus on the diagnoses and treatment of individual patients. Prior to contracting or privatizing services, Avery suggests an agency or department should evaluate six factors (p. 333):

- The impact on the agency's core mission
- The availability, stability, and reliability of private sector service providers
- The relative costs of internal and external (public or private sector) service providers
- The potential impact on regulatory enforcement
- The ability to monitor the performance of external providers
- Potential conflicts of interest

The decision to privatize should not be capricious; instead, it should be the result of a thoughtful and comprehensive decision-making process. The reactions of employees, clients, citizens, and the public interest, as well as the financial implications and quality of services, must all be considered.

The New Public Service

Recent graduates of schools of public policy and administration were twice as likely as members of earlier classes to take first jobs in the nonprofit sector and have shown an interest in working for the private sector. The nonprofit sector is attractive to the graduates because they are motivated to serve and believe that they will find more challenging work and the opportunity to learn outside of government. As a result, government trails the private and nonprofit sectors in competing for new graduates, and once they are outside of government, they are likely to remain there because government offers few opportunities to enter at the middle and senior levels (Light, 2003).

Strategic Human Resources Management

To meet the challenges just identified, public and nonprofit agencies must be flexible and attuned to the needs of society. They must seek to improve the quality of their services by engaging in strategic human resources management (SHRM). Recruitment and selection strategies must be innovative, career development opportunities must be provided, work assignments must be flexible, and policies must reward superior performers and hold marginal employees accountable. Performance standards must be designed to promote the goals and values of organizations.

The reinvention movement at the federal level—see, for example, *Creating a Government That Works Better and Costs Less* (National Performance Review, 1993); *Leadership for America: Rebuilding the Public Service* (National Commission on the Public Service, 1989); *Revisiting Civil Service, 2000: New Policy Direction Needed* (Office of Personnel Management, 1993); and *The State of Merit in the Federal Government* (Ingraham & Rosenbloom, 1990)—and at the state and local levels—see *Final Report: Recommendation for Change in Illinois* (Governor's Human Resources Advisory Council, 1993); *Hard Truths/Tough Choices: An Agenda for State and Local Reform* (National Commission on the State and Local Public Service, 1993); and *New York City Solutions II: Transforming the Public Personnel System* (Columbia University, 1993)—acknowledged the need to redesign and reinvigorate the public service. According to Hays and Kearney (2001), the recommendations address every HRM technique and every personnel office responsibility. Overall, the HRM recommendations sought to (1) enhance management discretion in personnel management, (2) increase the flexibility and responsiveness of public personnel systems, (3) improve public sector performance, and (4) adopt private sector staffing techniques (p. 586).

While the reinvention movement has emphasized efficiency and market-based reforms, Wise (2002) reminds us that the practice of public management is still influenced by alternative values. She provides evidence that public management remains influenced by the demand for greater social equity, the demand for democratization and empowerment, and the humanization of the public service. Likewise, *Hard Truths/Tough Choices* (National Commission on the State and Local Public Service, 1993) identified four skill areas that are needed by today's managers: competency in team building, competency in involving employees, commitment to cultural awareness, and commitment to quality.

It is not just public agencies that have to deal with change. Nonprofits, dependent on government for most of their revenue, must compete with other nonprofits, government agencies, and for-profits for shrinking dollars. Facing the same changes that are confronting public organizations, nonprofits must demonstrate they are capable of providing cost-effective professional services.

The nature of work has changed, and like public agencies, non-profit organizations require their employees to have more professional and technical skills. In both sectors, there is a greater reliance on technology. Advances in technology call for advanced education, continuous training, and the addition of new benefits, such as educational leaves or tuition reimbursement. Jobs may have to be redesigned to take advantage of employee skills and to enhance job satisfaction. Job rotation, job enlargement, and job enrichment have become HRM components.

Public and nonprofit administration must meet the challenge of changing social needs and priorities, new directions in public policy, demands for greater citizen involvement in the decision-making process, and pressures for increased accountability and productivity. A recent article in the *Harvard Business Review* suggests that nonprofits could save $100 billion a year by eliminating inefficiencies, reducing funding costs, distributing holdings faster, reducing program service costs, trimming administrative expenses, and improving the nonprofit sector's effectiveness (Bradley, Jansen, & Silverman, 2003). There is a bipartisan bill in the U.S. House of Representatives to require foundations to distribute a true 5 percent of their assets each year (presently, foundations can count their own salaries and administrative expenses as part of the 5 percent).

Nonprofit social service agencies are already competing with for-profit social service agencies such as Lockheed Martin IMS, Maximus, and Youth Services International. As government is striving for greater efficiency and improved performance, nonprofits are expected to do so as well (Ryan, 1999). No longer are nonprofits the only beneficiaries of government contracts; they must compete not only with other nonprofits but also with for-profit agencies.

Agencies must be prepared to adapt quickly to changes in their external and internal environments. As a result, organizations must think strategically as never before, and they must translate their insights into effective strategies for meeting future challenges. Human resources functions must be active components in these responses. Strategic planning and HRM activities must be integrated and work together so that agencies can confront and manage impending challenges and change. Problems need to be diagnosed, and strategies need to be implemented. HRM departments must be linked with the strategy of the organization, and HRM activities must be integrated into the everyday work of line managers and employees.

In many agencies, human resources management departments are thought to be concerned with only the tasks or functions of human resources management, such as staffing, evaluation, training, and compensation. Or they are perceived as regulators and enforcers, concerned with compliance to rules and regulations. Very rarely are they perceived as partners willing and able to work with line managers and staff to make public agencies more effective. Human resources management departments need to expand their scope of activities beyond their typical tasks and emphasis on enforcing regulations and instead link their activities into the everyday work of managers and employees.

HRM departments need to expand their scope of activities beyond being just functional specialists concerned with staffing, evaluation, training, and compensation. Instead, they need to be concerned with how the organizations can be more competitive and more effective. By soliciting ideas from employees and managers and by listening to their concerns, HRM departments can become valuable members of the management team.

Summary

An uncertain external environment, coupled with changing needs for organizational skills, has facilitated a shift in the importance of HRM functions. Organizations need individuals with the right technical knowledge, skills, abilities, and other characteristics, but they also need people who are flexible and willing to deal with rapid and unstructured changes. Public and nonprofit jobs are becoming ever more professional, requiring higher levels of education. At the same time, the number of jobs requiring manual labor is decreasing. Employees in public and nonprofit agencies need to be able to deal with a variety of people, many of whom have a stake in the agency. Taxpayers, clients, customers, elected officials, foundations, donors, contractors, board members, and special interest groups are just some of the stakeholders concerned about agency performance. HRM specialists should be team players working with line managers to identify such employees. Together they should identify any political, technological, financial, and social changes affecting the organization and assist current employees in adapting to those changes.

Chapter Two demonstrates how strategic human resources management can prepare today's organizations for the challenges they will be confronting tomorrow. It will also address the changing role of HRM practitioners and the role of HRM specialists in organizations.

Questions and Exercises

1. Identify how the human resources challenges discussed in the chapter are evident in a current or past employer.
2. How well do you think human resources as a profession responds to the social and workplace trends affecting human resources today?
3. Why is it important for HRM to evolve from an administrative and operational role to a strategic one?
4. Visit the Bureau of Labor Statistics' Web page (http://www. bls.gov), and review "Occupation Outlooks and Demographics Data." What additional workforce changes do you believe might take place in the next five to ten years?
5. Visit the Monthly Labor Review Online (http://www.bls.gov/ opub/mlr/mlrhome.htm). Review the two most recent editions. Select two articles from each edition. What topics are discussed, and why do the authors think they are important? Explain.

Strategic Human Resources Management and Planning

These are challenging times for public and nonprofit organizations. As the Preface and Chapter One illustrate, public and nonprofit administration must meet the challenge of revenue shortfalls and financial cutbacks, new directions in service delivery, changing social needs and priorities, changes in public policy, demands for greater citizen involvement in the decision-making process, and pressures for increased accountability. Agencies must be prepared to adapt quickly to changes in their external and internal environments.

Strategic human resources management (SHRM) is based on the belief that to be effective and able to adapt to changes quickly, agencies need realistic information on the capabilities and talents of their current staff—in essence, their *human resources*. For example, in New York City, firefighters are retiring at more than double the usual rate. The percentage of the senior command staff retiring is approximately 60 percent higher than in previous years. At a time when the fire department needs to improve its planning and training for major emergencies, it is losing its most experienced personnel (Baker, 2002). It has been estimated that by 2006, state governments could lose more than 30 percent of their workforce, resulting in a loss of expertise and experience (Carroll & Moss, 2002). The assets of the David and Lucile Packard Foundation have declined 63 percent since 1999. Grants to help charities operate more effectively have been reduced, as has funding for environmental programs, population control projects, and programs that serve children and families (Whelan, 2003). This reduction of funding has human resources management (HRM) implications for the recipients of Packard Foundation grants.

SHRM refers to the implementation of human resources activities, policies, and practices to make the necessary ongoing changes to support or improve the agency's operational and strategic objectives. Agency leaders need to understand how their workplaces will be affected by impending changes and must prepare for the changes accordingly. Agency objectives should be formulated after relevant data on the quantity and potential of available human resources have been reviewed. Are human resources available for short- and long-term objectives? To be competitive, organizations must be able to anticipate, influence, and manage the forces that affect their ability to remain effective. In the service sector, this means that they must be able to manage their human resources capabilities. All too often, agencies have relied on short-term service requirements to direct their HRM practices without giving much thought to long-term implications. By invoking SHRM, agencies are better able to match their human resources requirements with the demands of the external environment and the needs of the organization. The human resources focus is not just an individual employee issue; it also focuses on integrating human resources into the organization's strategy. It becomes part of the visionary process. Strategic planning, budgeting, and human resources planning are linked in SHRM. SHRM is the integrative framework that matches human resources management activities with strategic organizational needs. This chapter discusses strategic planning, SHRM, human resources planning, and the changing role of HRM and illustrates the importance of all these concerns to organizational vitality and success.

Strategic Planning

Strategic planning is a process that enables public organizations to guide their future activities and the use of their available resources. It assists elected officials, funders, foundations, citizens, business partners, and public administrators in determining organizational purposes and objectives. The strategic planning process permits the external forces that affect the organization and the people in it to be identified. These forces may include workforce patterns, economic conditions, competition, regulation, social values, and technological developments. After the external factors have been assessed, the internal strengths and weaknesses of the organization's incumbents must be identified. Factors to include in an internal assessment are current workforce skills, retirement patterns, demographic profiles, and employee capabilities. The agency's vision, mission, and measurable goals and objectives drive the identification of future functional requirements. Those requirements drive the analysis and elements of the workforce plan. The question to ask is "What key functions need to be performed to move in the direction set out in the strategic plan?" This may include many current functions, in addition to forecasting important future functions and activities. This information can be used to forecast the organization's capabilities to confront its future opportunities and threats. The ultimate feasibility of strategic planning depends on the people who make it operational.

Strategic Human Resources Management

In *The Case for Transforming Public-Sector Human Resources Management,* the National Academy of Public Administration (2000, pp. 14–17) identified five steps that were imperative in aligning human resources management to an agency's mission:

Step 1: Include human resources in strategic plans. HRM strategies needed to address agency goals must be discussed, and the resources needed to implement those strategies must be identified.

Step 2: Define human resources requirements. Workforce planning requires that line managers and HRM experts work as partners to identify gaps that exist in the current workforce when compared to future requirements. A workforce planning system must be in place that enables the agency to understand the competency gaps to be addressed so that the agency can achieve its strategic goals. The assessment process will typically include documenting workforce demographics, calculating the current and projected attrition rates for key occupations, assessing the efficacy of primary sources of labor supply in both qualitative and quantitative terms, developing strategies for building the human capital needed to attain future mission goals, and evaluating progress, making midcourse corrections, and fixing accountability for achieving the desired outcomes.

Step 3: Develop an action plan for implementing human resources strategies. An action plan should establish accountability for implementing the plan and identify the resources needed to complete the plan. The plan should also provide solutions to close any competency gaps that have been identified. To what extent is the agency able to attract and retain the expertise it needs to accomplish its strategic goals? Does the agency have the right people to meet mission and strategic goals?

Step 4: Evaluate progress. It is important to determine progress, make midcourse corrections, and assign accountability for achieving the desired outcomes. An evaluation provides a regular flow of information about how well HRM strategies are working. Information should be provided on a regular basis so that informed decisions can be made about an agency's staff. Information about recruitment, retention, morale, and training and development should be analyzed.

Step 5: Manage the change process. Top management and human resources professionals work together to develop a successful change process. Top management identifies the desired change, the reason for change, the expected benefits of the change, and the impact the change will have on employees. The leadership of the agency provides the necessary resources and allows time for the changes to occur but holds staff accountable for performance.

Human Resources Planning

In an effort to be proactive, the Washington State Department of Personnel (2000) developed the *State of Washington Workforce Planning Guide: Right People, Right Jobs, Right Time.* Washington, like many other states, is facing the retirement of a significant portion of its workforce. As of 2002, more than 50 percent of state employees were age forty-five or older. Facing impending retirements and the loss in workforce skills and knowledge, the workforce planning guide was developed to assist agencies in preparing workforce plans to ensure necessary staff levels and competencies to carry out agency missions. Some benefits of workplace planning articulated in the guide include the following (p. 3):

1. Human resources planning allows more effective use of employees through accurate, efficient alignment of the workforce with strategic objectives.
2. Planning helps ensure that replacements are available to fill important vacancies. This is especially critical as agencies face increased turnover, labor market shortages, and limited compensation levels.
3. Planning provides realistic staffing projections for budget purposes.
4. Planning ensures that recruitment resources are used more efficiently and more effectively.
5. Planning permits a better-focused investment in training and retraining, development, career counseling, and productivity enhancement.
6. Planning helps maintain or improve the agency's diversity profile.

Human resources planning is a critical component of strategic planning and SHRM. It is the process of analyzing and identifying the need for and availability of human resources to meet the organization's objectives. Forecasting is used to assess past trends, evaluate the present situation, and project future demand and events. Forecasting and planning are complementary in that forecasts identify expectations while plans establish concrete goals and objectives.

Forecasting has become increasingly important as a large segment of the public workforce is inching toward retirement. Forty-two percent of the 15.7 million individuals working for state and local government in 1999 were between the ages of forty-five and sixty-four years old. Two-fifths of state and local government employees will be eligible to retire in the next fifteen years (Newcombe, 2001; Walters, 2000a). In Iowa, 33 percent of the state's twenty-one thousand employees will be able to retire over the next ten years, and 70 percent of the state's supervisors are over forty-five years old. Surveys conducted by the Annie E. Casey Foundation, CompassPoint, and the Maryland Association of Nonprofit Organizations found that between 15 and 35 percent of nonprofit executives plan to leave their current positions within two years and that 61 to 78 percent are planning to leave within five years (Hinden & Hull, 2002).

Agencies must consider how to allocate people to jobs over long periods. Attempts must be made to anticipate expansions or reductions in programs or other changes that may affect the organization. Based on these analyses, plans can be made for the recruitment and selection of new employees, the shifting of employees to different programs or units, or the retraining of incumbent employees.

A *demand forecast* anticipates the workforce that will be needed to accomplish future functional requirements and carry out the mission of the organization. In this step, a visionary staffing assessment against future functional requirements is conducted. The result is a forecast of the type of competencies, numbers, and locations of employees needed in the future. An important part of the demand forecast is examining not only what work the agency will do in the future but also how that work will be performed. Some things to consider include the following:

How will jobs and workload change as a result of technological advancements, economic, social, and political conditions?

What are the consequences or results of these changes?

What will the reporting relationships be?

How will divisions, work units, and jobs be designed?

How will work flow into each part of the organization?

Once these questions have been answered, the next step is to identify the competencies employees will need to carry out that work. The set of competencies provides management and staff with a common understanding of the skills and behaviors that are important to the agency. Competencies play a key role in decisions on recruiting, employee development, personal development, and performance management.

A few years ago, confronted with a shortage of workers with information technology (IT) skills, the state of Nebraska developed a six-month, full-time training program for state employees. The program is a partnership with Southeast Community College and is designed to train employees in PC, server, network, and data communication skills. During training, the employees remain classified at their current levels and earn their regular pay and benefits. At the conclusion of the training program, the employees are moved into IT positions, and their job classification and pay are adjusted to reflect their new responsibilities (Schock, 1998–1999). Other states responded differently to the loss of IT workers. The Texas legislature passed a bill that allows state workers who have retired to return to the public sector workforce and earn full pay while also receiving their retirement annuity. (Previously, returning workers could work only nine months of the year and had their salary capped at $60,000.) In Iowa, the need for workers with special skills forced it to outsource IT services. Texas and Iowa created new compensation and classification systems that were more consistent with the private sector (Newcombe, 2001). As a result of the 2001 recession, the collapse of dot-com organizations, and layoffs in the financial services industry, public and nonprofit organizations are in a better position to recruit and retain IT professionals and individuals with specialized skills who previously sought employment in the private for-profit sector. Despite a greater availability of IT and accounting and finance professionals, public and nonprofit agencies still need to anticipate vacancies and recruit for newly created positions.

Forecasting human resources requirements involves determining the number and types of employees needed by skill level. First, agencies need to audit the skills of incumbent employees and determine their capabilities and weaknesses. Positions must also be audited. In most organizations, there are likely to be jobs that are vulnerable and that technology or reengineering are ready to replace. Job analyses must be conducted to provide information on existing jobs. The basic requirements of a job should be defined and converted to job specifications that stipulate the minimum knowledge, skills, abilities, and other characteristics (KSAOCs) necessary for effective performance. The skill requirements of positions do change, so any changes that occur must be monitored and reflected in the job specifications. It is not enough to monitor changes in positions; organizations must also keep abreast of the skills that their employees possess. Human resources planning uses data inventories to integrate the planning and utilization functions of SHRM. Data inventories compile summary information, such as the characteristics of employees, the distribution of employees by position, employees' performance, and career objectives. Specific data that are typically catalogued are age, education, career path, current work skills, work experience, aspirations, performance evaluations, years with the organization, and jobs for which one is qualified. Expected vacancies due to retirement, promotion, transfer, sick leave, relocation, or termination are also tracked. Using a computerized human resources information system (HRIS) to compile these data makes the retrieval of information readily available for forecasting workforce needs.

When forecasting the availability of human resources, agencies need to consider both the internal and the external supply of qualified candidates. The internal supply of candidates is influenced by training and development and by transfer, promotion, and retirement policies. Assessing incumbent staff competencies is crucial. Agencies should undertake an assessment of employees' competency levels. This will provide information for determining the number of people available for and capable of fulfilling future functional requirements. It will provide salient information as to what recruitment, training, and other strategies need to be deployed to address workforce gaps and surpluses. Washington State recommends using a checklist of the future desired competencies identified through a demand forecast and assigning ratings of "advanced," "intermediate," "beginning," and "none." Once this information has been obtained, the agency can develop strategies for training and succession planning.

A *succession analysis* should be prepared that forecasts the supply of people for certain positions. Succession plans should be used to identify potential personnel changes, to select backup candidates, and to keep track of attrition. The external supply of candidates is also influenced by a variety of factors, including developments in technology, the actions of competing employers, geographical location, and government regulations. San Diego County, California, examined succession planning for its executive positions. The county put together a talent bank listing incumbent employees' current skills and areas of expertise, job preferences, and possible new skills the employees may need in order to be promoted. Succession planning becomes more important as the labor supply tightens and the unemployment rate hits low levels.

SHRM attempts to match the available supply of labor with the forecasted demand in light of the strategic plan of the organization. A gap analysis is the process of comparing the workforce demand forecast with the workforce supply projection. The expected result is the identification of gaps and surpluses in staffing levels and competencies needed to carry out future functional requirements of the organization. A gap occurs when the projected supply is less than the forecasted demand. It indicates a future shortage of needed employees. Strategies such as recruitment, training, and succession planning will need to be developed and implemented. A surplus is when the projected supply is greater than forecasted demand. This indicates future excess in some categories of employees that may also require action to be taken. The surplus data may represent occupations or skill sets that will no longer be needed in the future or will be needed to a lesser degree. Retraining, transfers, or separation incentives may need to be implemented to deal with surplus situations.

SHRM involves the development of strategies to address future gaps and surpluses. A variety of factors will influence which strategy or which combination of strategies should be used. Washington State has identified some of the factors:

Time. Is there enough time to develop staff internally for anticipated vacancies or new competency needs, or is special, fast-paced recruitment the best approach?

Resources. The availability of adequate resources will likely influence which strategies are used and to what degree, as well as priorities and timing.

Internal depth. Do existing staff demonstrate the potential or interest to develop new competencies and assume new or modified positions, or is external recruitment needed?

"In-demand" competencies. How high the competition is for the needed future competencies may influence whether recruitment or internal development and succession is the more effective strategy, especially when compensation levels are limited.

Workplace and workforce dynamics. Whether particular productivity and retention strategies need to be deployed will be influenced by such factors as workplace climate, employee satisfaction levels, workforce age, diversity, and personal needs.

Job classifications. Do the presently used job classifications and position descriptions reflect future functional requirements and competencies? Does the structure of the classification series have enough flexibility to recognize competency growth and employee succession in a timely fashion? Does it allow compensation flexibility?

If necessary skills do not exist in the present workforce, employees will need to be trained in the new skills or otherwise external recruitment must be used to bring those skills to the organization. The employer must identify where employees with those skills are likely to be found, and recruitment strategies must be developed.

The state of Pennsylvania studied the age patterns among its employees to see what skills the state will lose in the next five to ten years and began targeting recruitment toward acquiring those skills. The state has gone on direct recruiting campaigns to hire employees with accounting, budgeting, personnel administration, and computer technology skills. Those candidates are then placed in special state-run classes designed to develop their expertise (Walters, 2000a).

Implementing Strategic Human Resources Management

To implement an SHRM system, it is important for human resources management departments to expand their scope of activities beyond the traditional HRM tasks and functions and to enter partnerships with managers and employees. Working together gives managers and employees a better understanding of HRM issues. Likewise, HRM staff become more informed about the needs of the employees and departments.

SHRM is a process that must be implemented throughout the organization. The goal is to make the SHRM process the template for organizational change and innovation.

To facilitate the partnership, HRM departments should establish a human resources planning task force composed of managers and staff from a variety of departments and staff from the HRM department who are responsible for identifying the trends and challenges that will affect the agency. The task force should involve other employees, seeking their input and observations. This can be done through the use of surveys, focus groups, agency publications, or a needs assessment instrument. After the task force has received this information, it should prioritize the most critical issues. HRM staff should be directed to develop strategies, solutions, and alternatives to address the issues.

Questions that should be investigated and planned for include the following:

Is the top administration committed to quality and excellence?

Are changes necessary?

How can we meet employees' perceptions and concerns?

Which employees will be affected?

What barriers might there be to successful implementation of SHRM?

Once program cost estimates have been developed, will funding be provided for training and development?

Who will be responsible for the implementation of SHRM?

Who will evaluate and adjust the planning process?

Once these questions have been answered, authority and resources must be assigned to the person or persons responsible for the planning and implementation of SHRM. Failing to put human and financial resources into SHRM will render it just another fad. Organizational leaders must demonstrate their commitment to SHRM and champion it.

Exhibit 2.1 presents an example of a strategic human resources plan.

Problems and Implications of Strategic Human Resources Management

If strategic human resources management makes such intuitive sense, why aren't more organizations engaging in it? Researchers have suggested that organizational leaders claim they want a greater integration of the human resources management function

Exhibit 2.1. A Strategic Human Resources Plan.

U.S. Department of Labor

E-Government Strategic Plan

• Addresses the need to conduct workforce planning within the context of e-government.

Organizations face three critical questions:

What effect will the implementation of e-government have on my workforce?

Does the existing workforce have the capability to become an e-government workforce?

What strategies and resources are needed to ensure that our future workforce competency and capability requirements are met?

To answer these questions, the Department of Labor (DOL) established an e-government workforce planning program in FY 2002 to systematically address future human capital requirements. For each workforce analysis, the DOL uses the following methodology.

1. Strategic Business Definition. During this step, the DOL identifies and validates the organization's critical functions to create an accurate description of the work being performed. The department then identifies the influences affecting workforce capabilities, including workload and competencies, and assesses internal and external factors. Based on this assessment, anticipated changes to work and requisite competencies are outlined, generating a future vision of the organization. The results of the strategic business definition provide the empirical foundation for subsequent supply and demand analyses.

2. Workload Assessment. During this step, the DOL evaluates the organization's current workload distribution among work activities. Backlog workload and future workload requirements are also quantified on the basis of identified workload drivers and subject matter expertise.

3. Competency Assessment. Competencies are defined as the knowledge, skills, abilities, attributes, and behaviors required to perform a given job. This step identifies and defines key competencies required for successful performance within the organization.

4. Workforce Composition Assessment. This step entails development of workforce profiles to evaluate the current workforce's composition, assessment of the distribution of the organization's current workforce across

Exhibit 2.1. A Strategic Human Resources Plan, Cont'd.

---

various elements, and calculation of attrition and recruitment trends. Together these activities enable the DOL to project the workforce through the planning period.

5. Gap Analysis. A comprehensive gap analysis is performed after the completion of the workload, competency, and workforce analyses. This analysis identifies gaps between current workforce capabilities and future workload requirements, as well as gaps in requisite competencies between the current and target proficiency levels. To better focus the subsequent solutions analysis, these workload-to-workforce and competency gaps are then prioritized.

6. Solution and Recommendation Development. Finally, the DOL develops a set of specific strategies to address all high-priority gaps between workforce capabilities and workload requirements.

Source: Adapted from U.S. Department of Labor, 2003a.

with organizational strategy but often do not understand what this entails. They are reluctant to give HRM professionals the flexibility to initiate new programs or to suggest new organizational structures. This is especially true when organizational change issues conflict with established operating procedures and the organizational culture.

Another reason why SHRM is neglected is that very often HRM professionals lack the capabilities and skills necessary to move human resources management to a more proactive role. HRM professionals may need to be trained in the skills that are necessary to align the organization's strategy with its core competencies. These professionals may need training in organizational redesign, job and service redesign, and performance measurement. Kansas is piloting what it calls the Human Resources Training Academy for state human resources managers. The program is designed to enhance their effectiveness as strategic planners and organizational leaders. Senior human resources managers from a variety of state agencies are participating in the project and are joined by subject matter experts from the public and private sectors. The intent of the program is to challenge the participants to "go beyond the daily nuts and bolts of personnel management and to recognize the pivotal role they play in carrying out their agency's mission" (Andrews & Molzhon, 1999, p. 5). However, not all public organizations are willing to invest the time and money in training, nor are they willing to support the efforts of their HRM professionals in the change process.

Organizational change also requires higher levels of coordination across functions and departments, and employees and management must be committed to continuous improvement. There must be greater interdepartmental cooperation. Trust and open communication throughout the organization will have to be developed. Organizations must encourage creativity and recognize such creativity through their reward systems. Change requires fairness, openness, and empowerment. Fairness, openness, and empowerment may be contrary to an organization's culture and may require several incremental steps.

Some employees may be reluctant to change. Over the years, they may have acquired a certain degree of proficiency in the performance of their jobs. Changing their routines and standards of performance, requiring them to learn new skills, or obliging them to work with unfamiliar persons may be unsettling. Employees unwilling or unable to make the transition may choose to resign or may even in some cases attempt to sabotage new initiatives.

There are also financial costs associated with SHRM. As you can see from Exhibit 2.2, which presents the city of Clearwater, Florida's, human resources initiatives for FY 2003–2004, many of them require that some monies be spent. Clearwater contracted with outside consultants in developing its human resources communication plan, employee wellness program, diversity plan, and performance management system. Consultants were also hired to conduct a job evaluation and pay study and an employee benefits analysis and review. Some public organizations may be reluctant to spend additional resources on employees, fearing a backlash from its elected officials and citizens.

Sometimes the political realities of public organizations undermine change. Very often elected and appointed officials have a short-term perspective toward the operation of their agencies. Changes in policies and procedures take time to implement and are often not immediately apparent. Officials may want a quick fix and not be patient enough for systemic changes to occur. Elected

**Exhibit 2.2. Strategic Human Resources Management
in the City of Clearwater, Florida.**

The city of Clearwater is located on the west coast of Florida. Its population has remained relatively constant between 101,000 and 108,000 residents for the past ten years. Clearwater's market consists of a large tourism-based economy, but it has been able to attract some high-technology companies. The city has no open land, so its strategy has been to improve its infrastructure and aesthetics and try to attract companies to redevelop existing properties.

Clearwater provides a full range of municipal services: police and fire protection; city-operated marina; a business airpark; convention center and exhibition hall; planning, zoning, subdivision and building code regulation and enforcement; park and recreation programs; a public library system with four branch locations; solid waste collection and recycling; water supply and distribution, wastewater treatment and disposal, and reclaimed water treatment and distribution; and a citywide parking system.

The members of the city commission decided that a formal strategic vision would articulate their motivating beliefs and intent for the city, serving as a framework for the city's future and for the everyday operations of city government. With the help of the city manager, and after a series of consensus-building steps, new mission and vision statements were drafted. These are geared toward helping achieve a high quality of life today and in the next twenty years. The ultimate goal is to shape a livable city that eliminates barriers and provides opportunities for all citizens to succeed. Though Clearwater will change over the years, the vision must stay the same to ensure that policy decisions of future commissions, and the resulting progress the city makes, remain consistent and beneficial to all.

Eleven goals were identified in five priority areas. The goals were as follows:

A safe, clean, green environment

Diverse, high-paying jobs

High-quality education

A variety of cultural and recreational offerings

Efficient, responsive city services

Safe, comfortable, walkable neighborhoods

Well-maintained housing stock in all markets

A vibrant downtown that is mindful of its heritage

Well-maintained infrastructure

Exhibit 2.2. Strategic Human Resources Management in the City of Clearwater, Florida, Cont'd.

Efficient transportation systems

A quality beach environment

The city integrated these goals into five strategic priorities:

Public Safety. All public safety services must concentrate on continual personnel training to be prepared for any emergency on a moment's notice, including large-scale calamities such as terrorist threats or natural disasters.

Economic Development. Strategic public investment in the downtown area and partnerships with private investors and nonprofit entities will spur redevelopment. Preservation of local history and character will be mirrored in all new projects. With public support of local businesses, property values will increase and aesthetics will improve. Clearwater's beaches will continue to remain open to the public. They will be redeveloped through city and county incentives that will address residential, commercial, and transportation issues.

Infrastructure Maintenance. Assessment of the current infrastructure will determine needs for the future. Existing infrastructure assets will be maintained through the repair and replacement of worn parts, and future projects will implement new technologies that improve function and durability and reduce operating costs.

Quality of Life. The high quality of life we enjoy here is why we live, learn, work, and play in Clearwater. It can be reinforced by encouraging diversity in cultural and recreational programs and by supporting neighborhoods. Beautification programs and expansion of our nationally known brownfield program will promote a safe, clean, green environment. We must also continue to provide and improve on the excellent customer service our residents and visitors have come to expect.

Human Resources Issues. None of the vision can become reality without the people to achieve it. Therefore, the city must provide and support a healthy working environment and a competent workforce and must plan for future employment trends.

Human Resources Strategic Plan

As one of the five defined priority levels, the city's Human Resources Management Department developed its own strategic business plan consistent with the city's strategic plan.

**Exhibit 2.2. Strategic Human Resources Management
in the City of Clearwater, Florida, Cont'd.**

The mission of the HRM Department is as follows:

To help the city of Clearwater provide premier service to our customers by recruiting, selecting, training, developing, and retaining a diverse, highly qualified, satisfied, motivated, and productive workforce.

Its core HR values are to be *strategic, responsive, professional, flexible,* and *caring,* and its HR vision is *to deliver results that add value and help our customers achieve their goals.*

Included in the strategic business plan are five specific goals that are linked with the city's mission statement, key intended outcomes, and measurable objectives, as follows.

Goal 1

Create a high-performance-organizational climate that encourages superior customer service and continuous quality improvement through effective recruitment, selection, and retention programs, training, and development initiatives and reward and recognition programs.

Key Intended Outcomes

Improve customer satisfaction

Increase customer trust and confidence in government

Develop employees who have the skill and commitment to deliver
quality service

HR Initiatives for FY 2003–2004

Strategic Planning and Management System

Performance Management System

HRIS Strategic Implementation System

New Employee Mentoring Program

Employee and Team Reward and Recognition Program

Long-Range Training Assessment Plan

SAMP[a] Incentive Pay System

SAMP Paid Time-Off System

Labor-Management Partnerships

Leadership Development and Succession Planning Program

Exhibit 2.2. Strategic Human Resources Management in the City of Clearwater, Florida, Cont'd.

Measurable Objectives

- Increase the percentage of employees who agree with the statement "HR staff help recruit and retain high-quality employees."
- Increase the percentage of employees who agree with the statement "HR staff provide quality and timely service."
- Increase the percentage of employees who agree with the statement "I am able to apply the skills and knowledge learned through city-sponsored educational, training, and development programs to improve my personal and organizational effectiveness."
- Increase the percentage of employees who agree with the statement "I am motivated by the city's reward and recognition programs."

Goal 2

Improve communication, interaction, and cooperation between HR and its customers.

Key Intended Outcomes

Improve customer satisfaction

Increase customer trust and confidence in government

Strive for overall effective communication

Initiate capital projects needed to improve the levels of service

HR Initiatives for FY 2003–2004

HR Liaison Program

Supervisory Leadership Certification Program

HR Customer Communication Plan (newsletter, Internet, intranet)

Revised SAMP Manuals

HR Policy Handbook

Measurable Objectives

- Increase the percentage of employees who agree with the statement "HR seeks and listens to employee input on issues and policies affecting employees."
- Increase the percentage of employees who agree with the statement "I am satisfied with HR communication and liaison services."

**Exhibit 2.2. Strategic Human Resources Management
in the City of Clearwater, Florida, Cont'd.**

Goal 3

Help foster an organizational climate that makes the city of Clearwater a
"premier place to work."

Key Intended Outcome

Recognition of Clearwater as a preferred place to live, work, and play

HR Initiatives for FY 2003–2004

Employee Salary and Benefits Survey

Revised and Modified Light-Duty Program

Employee Benefit Analysis

Employee Wellness Program

Job Evaluation System

Measurable Objectives

- Increase the percentage of employees who agree with the statement
  "I enjoy working for the city of Clearwater."
- Increase the percentage of employees who agree with the statement
  "I am proud to be a city employee and would recommend city em-
  ployment to a friend."
- Increase the percentage of employees who agree with the statement
  "The city cares about my well-being."
- Increase the percentage of employees who agree with the statement
  "I am satisfied with my salary or wage range."
- Increase the percentage of employees who agree with the statement
  "I am satisfied with my benefits package."

Goal 4

Promote programs and activities that expose the city's workforce to community organizations.

Key Intended Outcome

Proactive promotion of community well-being

Exhibit 2.2. Strategic Human Resources Management in the City of Clearwater, Florida, Cont'd.

HR Initiatives for FY 2003–2004

City-Community Education, Training, and Development Partnership Programs

City Student Internship Program

Measurable Objectives

- Increase the percentage of employees who participate in city-sponsored community programs and activities.
- Increase the percentage of employees who agree with the statement "The city and community benefit from employees who participate in city-sponsored community programs and activities."

Goal 5

Promote an organizational workforce that reflects the city's demographics.

Key Intended Outcome

A city that values diversity

HR Initiatives for FY 2003–2004

Support City Diversity Plan

ESL and Bilingual Language Training Programs

Business Case for Diversity

Measurable Objectives

- Increase the percentage of minorities and protected-class members in the workforce to more closely reflect city demographics.
- Increase the percentage of bilingual employees.
- Increase the percentage of employees who agree with the statement "The city promotes a work environment in which diversity is valued."

[a]SAMP refers to supervisory, administrative, managerial and professional. employees who are exempt from belonging to a union under Florida law or are in middle or upper management positions.

Source: Adapted from Pynes, 2003.

officials may also be predisposed to favor short-term budget considerations over long-term planning. In the public sector, support for top administrators may change quickly and often capriciously. To transform an organization requires chief executive and top administrative support, managerial accountability, fundamental changes in HRM practices, employee involvement, and changes in corporate culture (Gilbert & Ivancevich, 2000).

The Changing Role of Human Resources Management

Human resources management is changing. Public, nonprofit, and for-profit organizations are facing some daunting challenges. For HRM departments to play a strategic role, they must focus on the long-term implications of HRM issues. For example, how will changing workforce demographics and workforce shortages affect the organization, and what strategies will be used to address them? The downsizing and reorganization of public and nonprofit agencies, along with a strong focus on results, are forcing agencies to validate their business processes, reassess the role of the HR function, and evaluate the adequacy of the work performed by HR employees.

To be strategic partners, HRM departments must possess high levels of professional and business knowledge. HRM must establish links to enhance organizational performance and be able to demonstrate on a continual basis how HRM activities contribute to the success and effectiveness of the organization. Unfortunately, many HRM departments have spent so much of their time ensuring compliance with rules and regulations that they lack the skills and competencies needed to act as a strategic partner. A number of books and articles addressing the need for new HRM skills and competencies have appeared in recent years. Some of the books addressing this topic include *Tomorrow's HR Management,* edited by Dave Ulrich, Michael R. Losey, and Gerry Lake (1997); *Human Resource Champions,* by Dave Ulrich (1997); *The ROI of Human Capital,* by Jac Fitz-enz (2000); *The HR Scorecard,* by Brian E. Becker, Mark A. Huselid, and Dave Ulrich (2001); and *Measuring ROI in the Public Sector,* edited by Patricia Pulliam Phillips (2002). The consistent themes in all the books and articles are as follows:

HRM practices must create value by increasing the intellectual capital within the agency.

HRM professionals must focus more on the outcomes of the HRM systems and policies.

The impact of HRM practices on business results can and must be measured.

HRM professionals must learn how to translate their work into financial performance.

The reality, however, is that there is a gap between the competencies that HRM professionals are currently using on the job and those that are viewed as important to the HR function. Most organizations do not have a formal plan in place to close the competency gaps that have been identified, and closing the gaps and developing new expertise and experience will take commitment, planning, money, and time.

In *Human Resource Champions,* Dave Ulrich (1997) asks, "How can HR create value and deliver results?" He states that managers and HR professionals should constantly seek the capabilities necessary for success. They should routinely ask themselves and each other the following questions (p. 11):

What capabilities currently exist within the firm?

What capabilities will be required for the future success of the firm?

How can we align capabilities with business strategies?

How can we design HR practices to create the needed capabilities?

How can we measure the accomplishment of the needed capabilities?

To answer these questions, HRM professionals need to move beyond their administrative roles of providing clerical and administrative support, pension administration, benefits administration, and reference checks. Instead, a new focus needs to address how quickly the organization can adapt to change. Does it have the human capital and knowledge management capabilities of learning, responsiveness, and agility? What employee competencies exist in the workforce?

The Office of Personnel Management (OPM; 1999a, 1999b, 2000) conducted a special study titled "HR: An Occupation in Transition." As a result of its research, it developed a list of HR competency roles drawn from the work of the National Academy of Public Administration (NAPA), the International Personnel Management Association for Human Resources (IPMA-HR), and OPM's Personnel Resources and Development Center. The HR competency roles include the following:

Strategic partner. Serves as a partner with management, sharing accountability with line management for organizational results. The HR professional works with management to analyze and devise solutions to organizational problems and is involved in strategic planning and aligning HR with the organization's mission and strategic goals.

Leader. Ensures that merit system principles are adhered to, along with other issues of ethics and integrity, while serving as a champion for diversity. In addition, balances the need for employee satisfaction with organizational goals.

Employee champion. Serves as a voice for employee concerns and deals with employee problems. Ensures fair and equitable treatment for employees; represents employee concerns and issues to management.

Technical expert. Possesses a high level of HR knowledge and ability to strengthen HR programs to better meet organizational goals.

Change consultant. Serves as a catalyst for change in the organization (helps the organization see the need for change, helps by providing training, installing new information systems, adjusting compensation strategies to meet changing job requirements, and so on).

The IPMA-HR competency model is presented in Exhibit 2.3.

SHRM Audit

One method used to assess SHRM effectiveness is through an HRM audit. An HRM audit is an in-depth analysis that evaluates the current state of SHRM in an organization. The audit identifies areas

Exhibit 2.3. The IPMA-HR Competency Model.

Knows the Mission

Understands the purpose of the organization, including its statutory mandate; its customers, products, and services; and its measure of mission effectiveness. Is able to articulate the relationship between human resources activities and successful mission accomplishment. Keeps current with factors that may have a future impact on mission.

Understands the Business Process and How to Change to Improve Efficiency and Effectiveness

Approaches assigned HR program responsibilities with a broad perspective of the way business is done with the organization. Is able to recognize and implement changes to improve efficiency and effectiveness.

Understands Clients and the Organizational Culture

Researches unique characteristics of client organizations to ensure that assistance and consultations are appropriate to the situation. Maintains awareness of differing cultures and provides service that is tailored to the requirements of the culture.

Understands the Public Service Environment

Keeps current on political and legislative activities that may affect the organization or the HR community. Seeks to understand the intent as well as the letter of laws, orders, and regulations that result from the political process so that implementation is consistent with intended outcomes of legal and policy changes.

Understands Team Behavior

Applies knowledge of team behavior to help achieve organizational goals and objectives. Maintains currency with new approaches to human motivation and teamwork that may apply to the organization.

Communicates Well

Expresses ideas and exchanges information clearly and persuasively. Speaks in terms of business results and goals rather than using HRM technical terms. Communicates effectively with all levels of the organization.

Possesses the Ability to Be Innovative and Create a Risk-Taking Environment

Thinks outside the box. Creates and presents new approaches that are outside the current policies when warranted by mission needs. Understands and applies techniques that are designed to encourage creativity and innovation. Creates an environment in which risk taking is valued.

Exhibit 2.3. The IPMA-HR Competency Model, Cont'd.

Assesses and Balances Competing Values

Manages competing priorities and work assignments by continuously evaluating the organization's mission against pending work. Maintains contact with senior management to ensure a clear understanding of mission priorities. Explains priorities to key customers to ensure that they understand the rationale for decisions regarding work priorities.

Applies Organizational Development Principles

Maintains knowledge of social science and human behavior strategies, which can be used to improve organizational performance. Establishes strategies to promote greater learning within the organization. Provides advice that supports the creation of opportunities for employees to grow.

Knows Business System Thinking

Applies whole systems thinking to HR work processes by ensuring consideration of all external and internal environmental factors in providing advice and solutions to customers.

Applies Information Technology to Human Resources Management

Maintains awareness of current and emerging technologies that have the potential to improve efficiency or effectiveness of HRM within the organization. Develops proposals to implement new HR-based technology within the organization when justified.

Possesses Good Analytical Skills Including the Ability to Think Strategically and Creatively

Analyzes a multiplicity of data and information from several sources and arrives at logical conclusions. Recognizes the gaps in available data and suggests other ways to obtain the needed information.

Designs and Implements Change Processes

Is able to recognize the potential benefits of change and to create an infrastructure that supports change. Is flexible and open to new ideas and encourages others to value change.

Uses Consultation and Negotiation Skills Including Dispute Resolution

Takes the initiative in solving or resolving problems. Knows a variety of problem-solving techniques and uses them or recommends them to involved parties.

Exhibit 2.3. The IPMA-HR Competency Model, Cont'd.

Possesses the Ability to Build Trust Relationships

Has integrity and demonstrates professional behavior to gain the trust and confidence of the customer. Follows up on commitments on a timely, accurate, and complete basis. Can keep confidences and does not abuse the privilege of accessibility to confidential information.

Possesses Marketing and Representational Skills

Persuades internal and external customers of the needs and beneficial outcomes of programs or actions. Develops the pros and cons of an issue and persuades interested parties of the best course of action. Ensures that customers are aware of the importance of the role.

Uses Consensus-Building and Coalition-Building Skills

Enhances collaboration among individuals and groups by using consensus-building skills. Objectively summarizes opposing points of view. Incorporates all points of view and assists in arriving at consensus positions or agreements. Reconciles disagreements with officials through reasoning and presentation of the facts. Uses differences of opinions to build solutions to problems or concerns. Understands when and how to elevate issues to higher-level line officials when actions being taken are inconsistent with legal or higher-level requirements. Has the courage to take a stand when an issue is considered important to the well-being of the organization's mission or reputation.

Knows Human Resources Laws and Policies

Keeps current and understands statutory and regulatory requirements affecting HR. Recognizes and uses the intent of requirements as an HR tool to assist in managing resources.

Links Human Resources to the Organization's Mission and Service Outcomes

Understands mission needs and context in terms of people needs. Understands the HR roles within the organization and adapts behaviors and approaches that are consistent with these roles.

Demonstrates a Customer Service Orientation

Keeps abreast of organizational climate and mission changes and is keenly sensitive to customer needs and concerns. Responds to client needs, questions, and concerns in an accurate and timely manner.

Exhibit 2.3. The IPMA-HR Competency Model, Cont'd.

Understands, Values, and Promotes Diversity

Understand the potential contributions that a diverse workforce can make to the success of the organization. Is aware of the potential impact of HR processes and ensures that diversity needs are considered.

Practices and Promotes Integrity and Ethical Behavior

Behaves in ways that demonstrate trust and gain confidence. Treats customers fairly and courteously, and effectively responds to their needs regardless of organizational location or grade level. Provides and maintains a high level of integrity.

Source: International Public Management Association for Human Resources. Printed with permission.

of strengths and weaknesses and areas where improvements are needed. During the audit, current practices, policies, and procedures are reviewed. Many audits also include benchmarking against organizations of similar size or in the same industry. Some areas that are typically included in an audit are legal compliance (Equal Employment Opportunity, Occupational Safety and Health Administration, Fair Labor Standards Act, Family and Medical Leave Act, Employment Retirement Income Security Act, privacy), current job descriptions and specifications, valid recruiting and selection procedures, compensation and pay equity and benefits, employee relations, absenteeism and turnover control measures, training and development activities, performance management systems, policies and procedures as set forth in the employee handbook, terminations, and health, safety, and security issues.

Human Resources Information Systems

Information technology enables organizations to maintain and retrieve information and records with greater accuracy and ease than older methods. An HRIS provides current and accurate data for decision making and broader applications such as producing reports, forecasting HR needs, strategic planning, career and promotion planning, and evaluating HR policies and practices. Having accessible data enables HR planning and managerial decision making to be based to a greater degree on information rather than on perceptions. Common applications of human resources information systems include maintaining employee records, overseeing payroll and benefits activities, handling absence and vacation records, and administering recruitment and training programs, employee communications, and affirmative action tracking.

Many agencies use networks as part of their HRIS. Many agencies allow employees to read current job openings and apply for positions online; they also provide information on employee benefits, training opportunities, and occupational safety and health information.

Developing an HRIS can be expensive; therefore, it is important that department managers and users, HRM professionals, and technology experts jointly develop it and plan for its implementation. Some factors that should be considered when developing an HRIS include the anticipated initial costs and annual maintenance costs, the ability to upgrade the system, the availability of relevant software packages for users, compatibility with current IT systems in place, the availability of technical support to maintain the system, the ability to customize the system for different types of information, the time required to implement the system, and the amount of training required for users to become proficient.

HR Benchmarking and Return on Investment

HRM departments, like other units, are being asked to demonstrate their value to public and nonprofit organizations. HR audits and HRIS are being used with greater frequency to obtain information on HR performance. Once information on HR performance has been gathered, it must be compared to a standard. One method of assessing HR effectiveness is comparing specific measures of performance against data on those measures in other organizations known for their "best practices."

Employee costs in public and nonprofit organizations can be anywhere from 50 to 80 percent of expenses; therefore, measuring the return on investment (ROI) in human capital is necessary to show the impact and value of SHRM. According to Jac Fitz-enz (2000, p. 3), "Management needs a system of metrics that describe and predict the cost and productivity curves of its workforce." Quantitative measures focus on cost, capacity, and time, whereas qualitative measures focus on more intangible values such as human reactions. ROI calculations are used to show the value of expenditures for HR activities. HR activities and programs that have been subject to measurement include training programs, diversity programs, wellness and fitness initiatives, safety and health programs, skill-based and knowledge-based compensation, performance improvement programs, education programs, organizational development initiatives, change initiatives, career development programs, recruiting systems, and technology implementation (Phillips & Phillips, 2002).

Despite the belief that only for-profit organizations can evaluate ROI programs, public and nonprofit agencies can use measures of performance such as productivity, quality, time improvements, and cost savings through efficiency enhancements as well as qualitative measures.

Summary

The future viability of an organization and its human resources capabilities are interrelated and must be considered together. HRM must be vertically integrated with strategic planning and horizontally integrated with other human resources functions such as training and development, compensation and benefits, recruitment and selection, labor relations, and the evaluation of the human resources planning process, to allow for adjustments to be made to confront rapidly changing environmental conditions. SHRM guides management in identifying and implementing the appropriate human resources learning activities for resolving organizational problems or adapting to meet new opportunities.

SHRM determines the human resources needs of the agency and ensures that qualified personnel are recruited and developed to meet organizational needs. Should there be a shift in demand for services, agencies must know whether there are potential employees with the requisite skills available to provide these services and whether the agency's finances can afford the costs associated with additional compensation and benefits. Forecasting an agency's human resources supply reveals the characteristics of its internal supply of labor; it also helps assess the productivity of incumbent employees, implement succession planning and salary planning, and identify areas where external recruitment or training and development are necessary.

Training and development are essential to the effective use of an organization's human resources and are an integral part of its human resources planning. Training is used to remedy immediate needs, while development is concerned with long-term objectives and the ability to cope with change. Training and development should be viewed as continuous processes. There will always be new employees, new positions, new problems, changes in technology, and changes in the external and internal environments that require a planned approach to training and development and their integration with other HRM functions. Training and development influence recruitment, selection, career planning, and the compatibility between agency goals and employee aspirations. Training and development programs must be integrated to complement the organization's mission and operations. Organizations should use employees wisely with respect to the strategic needs of the organization.

Turnover, including retirements, must be anticipated and planned for. HRM departments must track the skills of incumbent employees and keep skill inventories. Recruitment and training must be tied to the organization's mission. The availability and stability of financial support; the advancement of technological changes, legal regulations, and social and cultural changes; and the evolution of human resources requirements must be considered when developing strategic plans.

Organizations once hired employees to fit the characteristics of a particular job. Now it is important for organizations to select employees who fit the characteristics not only of the position but also of the organization. HRM professionals must serve as internal consultants working with managers to assess human resources needs. Together they must project the demand for services, develop new resources, and determine the appropriate reallocation of services. The SHRM process, once established, can anticipate and prepare for major changes affecting the workplace.

Effective strategic human capital management approaches serve as the foundation of any serious HRM initiative. They must be at the center of efforts to transform the cultures of agencies so that they become results-oriented and externally focused. To facilitate these changes, HRM personnel and department managers must acquire new competencies to be able to deliver HRM services and shift toward a more consultative role for HR staff.

Like service industries and new-economy companies, public and nonprofit organizations are driven by the knowledge and skills their employees possess. It is shortsighted for elected officials, board members, funders, executives, and other agency leaders to dismiss or downplay SHRM. Equally important, organizations must reinforce the value of human capital and the contribution knowledge management makes to the effective delivery of services. HRM departments must have the knowledge, skills, and authority to identify and facilitate changes that may be necessary.

Questions and Exercises

1. What are the main barriers that prevent an organization from taking a more strategic approach to HR? Why do they exist, and how can they be overcome?
2. What is the role of HR in your organization? Why does it assume that role?
3. What can HRM do to make senior and line managers take more of an investment approach to human assets?
4. Why must HR planning be seen as a process flowing from the organization's strategic plan?
5. In groups of four or five, compare and contrast similarities and differences among the organizations you work for. What factors appear to influence how an organization perceives the value of its employees?
6. Assume that as a result of HR planning, you discover a shortage of direct service workers but a surplus of administrative workers. Discuss the actions that might be taken to address the imbalance, and explain why these actions must be approached carefully.
7. Go to the General Accounting Office (GAO) Web site (http://www.gao.gov), and review its reports on human capital. What strategies and recommendations do you think should be used by your agency?
8. Go to the Office of Personnel Management (OPM) Web site on federal human capital (http://www.fhcs.opm.gov), and review its reports on federal human capital. What strategies and recommendations do you think should be used by your agency?

Chapter Three

Strategic Human Resources Management and Technology

The changing dynamics noted in the first two chapters have brought about changes in the way public and nonprofit agencies are organized and managed. In June 2003, the journal *Public Performance and Management Review* published a symposium on electronic government (e-government). According to Stowers and Melitski (2003), the editors of the symposium, public organizations are using the Internet in innovative ways to deliver services, engage citizens, and improve performance. They note that e-government is enabling public organizations to achieve their strategic objectives and improve public administration. But to do that, public organizations need employees with particular skills, creativity, and knowledge.

Computers and automation now play a major role in the design of traditionally routine jobs and are expected to be a major contributor to productivity in the future. For example, the introduction of computers into offices has changed the nature of even clerical jobs, including the management of information. Stenographic talents such as speed and accuracy in typing and note taking have become less relevant than problem solving, decision making, and critical thinking (McIntosh, 1990).

Saidel and Cour (2003), investigating how technology affected human services nonprofits in New York State, found that the introduction of new technology often results in task compression, tasks expansion, and task migration. Tasks such as writing, printing, and distributing correspondence and reports, once performed separately and in sequence first by a manager with follow-up by administrative support staff, are now compressed into a single function and performed by a manager. Not only have the tasks been compressed, but they have migrated upward as well. Lateral task migration occurs when tasks that were typically executed by middle managers in a central office are now tracked and scheduled by the direct care staff often while in the field. Tasks often expand or become differentiated. For example, in one human services nonprofit, professionals are responsible for preparing and disseminating their own reports and correspondence; as a result, support staff have the opportunity to perform different tasks that are not clerical. A professional supervisor commented (p. 12):

> Their roles have totally changed over time. I mean, they are not just sitting at their PCs typing memos every day. . . . They're freed up to do more direct service. They are able to sometimes attend field trips in the community with the consumers. . . . They have different things to do. We're putting different levels of importance on what their roles are. . . . We can use them in ways that are valuable to us as directors. And what is valuable to us has changed over time because we aren't so reliant on them to do all the typing and that kind of thing.

When we think of public organizations and large nonprofits, we think of a hierarchical, centralized structure of specialists that typically rely on a fixed set of standard operating procedures. Today, agencies are flatter and decentralized. These new organizational structures rely on networks of teams and individuals to establish goals and to ensure the effective delivery of services. Advances in information technology have assisted in making this possible. In a knowledge- and information-based economy, information technology and systems take on greater importance. Computers and information technology are also being used to design and manage public sector programs. Pennsylvania created the Commonwealth of Pennsylvania Application for Social Services (COMPASS) to serve as a single access point for all of the state's social services programs by enabling residents to apply at any time from any location with Internet access. The Department of Public Welfare discovered that many residents just wanted to know if they were eligible for aid. Rather than requiring them to spend twenty to thirty minutes filling out an application, the department added a screening component. Using COMPASS, Pennsylvania residents can see if they are eligible and can apply for health care coverage, cash assistance, food stamp benefits, long-term care, home- and community-based services, and free and reduced-cost lunch and breakfast programs (Brown, 2003a). This technology follows the successful development of a food stamp program that issues ATM cards to its food stamp recipients for purchasing groceries. No paper changes hands; instead, all accounting information is kept online, eliminating the need for the merchants, the banks, and the agency to reconcile separate paper transactions each month (Andersen, Belardo, & Dawes, 1994). New York State has established an interactive Web site that will provide parents with instant access to information concerning their child support payments, as well as allow them to submit updated information about themselves and their children online. In the past, applicants applying for teaching positions in Florida had to wait two to three months for a fingerprint check. Applicants were required to visit a local sheriff's department for fingerprinting. Fingerprints were placed on a paper card. The applicant would take the card to the school district, and the district would send it to the Florida Department of Law Enforcement for a check against the state database. Assuming no match at the state level, the card was mailed to the FBI. The FBI would send the card to its card-scanning service so that the print could be digitized. The FBI would then scan for matches against its database, generate a printed response, and mail it back to the school. Because of the delay, schools hired applicants on a contingent basis before receiving the results. Today, there is an automated fingerprint identification system in place. Applicants' fingerprints are scanned the same day they fill out their application and are electronically forwarded to the Florida Department of Law Enforcement and the FBI. Within forty-eight hours, the school district knows whether the selection process can continue (Brown, 2003b).

Not only is information technology being used to automate routine tasks, but it is also increasingly being used to restructure and integrate service delivery procedures and programs. The Stanislaus County Superior Court developed a Web-based information system to coordinate efforts of court personnel by collecting case information from the time a case is opened until the case is settled by interfacing with the district attorney's office and the department of motor vehicles. When a 911 call comes in, a dispatcher writes up a report on that call, and if a police officer is involved, he or she also writes up a report. Those reports go to the sheriff's office and then to the district attorney's office; it is then up to the district attorney to file a complaint or sit on the reports until more evidence is collected. The district attorney may hold on to the reports for up to one year until prosecutors have sufficient evidence to file. If the district attorney's office determines that there is sufficient evidence to file a complaint, it files the necessary paperwork, which is integrated with the superior court system. Each case is given a number by which it can be tracked for the remainder of its life. The system can handle cases from any division in the court, be it traffic, probate, or small claims. The system also permits cross-referencing between courts, allowing personnel to access any information on an individual in the system regardless of which court possesses the information (McKay, 2003b).

Information systems optimize the flow of information and knowledge within the organization and help management maximize knowledge resources. Because the productivity of employees will depend on the quality of systems serving them, management decisions about information technology are important to the effectiveness of public and nonprofit organizations.

Information Systems Technology

To understand information systems, one must understand the problems they are designed to solve, their architectural and design elements, and the organizational processes that are needed to accomplish the required tasks. To be able to use an information system, a manager must understand the organization, the management, and the technology dimensions of the systems and how they can be used to provide information leading to effective solutions. Computer-based information systems rely on computer hardware and software technology to process and disseminate information. Computers are only part of an information system.

Information systems (IS) technology uses computer hardware, software, storage, and telecommunications technologies. Computer hardware is the physical equipment used for input, processing, and output activities in an information system. Computer software consists of the detailed preprogrammed instructions that control and coordinate the computer hardware in an information system. Storage technology includes media for storing data, such as magnetic or optical disk or magnetic tape. Telecommunications technology consists of physical devices and software that links the various pieces of hardware and transfers data from one physical location to another. Computers and communications equipment can be connected in networks for sharing voice, data, images, sound, and video. A network links two or more computers to shared data and resources such as a printer.

The capabilities of information technology can affect organizations in a variety of ways (Davenport & Short, 1990, p. 17):

Transactional capability. IT can transform unstructured processes into routine transactions.

Geographical capability. IT can transfer information with rapidity and ease across large distances, making processes independent of geography.

Automational capability. IT can replace or reduce human labor in a process.

Analytical capability. IT can bring complex analytical methods to bear on a process.

Informational capability. IT can bring vast amounts of detailed information into a process.

Sequential capability. IT can enable changes in the sequence of tasks in a process, often allowing multiple tasks to be worked on simultaneously.

Knowledge management capability. IT allows the capture and dissemination of knowledge and expertise to improve the process.

Tracking capability. IT allows the detailed tracking of task status, inputs, and outputs.

Disintermediation capability. IT can be used to connect two parties within a process that would otherwise communicate through an intermediary (internal or external).

Organizational Change

Information technology can promote various degrees of organizational change. The most common change is the automation or mechanization of routine tasks. However, information technology can also be used for higher levels of sophistication, such as reengineering and redesigning business processes, whereby business and work processes are analyzed, simplified, and reconstructed. Processes have two important characteristics: they have defined business outcomes, and the outcomes have recipients, the customers. Customers can be internal or external to the organization. Processes also occur across or between organizational subunits. Davenport and Short (1990) provide the following examples of processes: investigating and paying an insurance claim, writing a proposal for a contract, creating a marketing plan, developing a new product or service, and ordering goods from a supplier. There are typically five steps in process redesign:

1. Develop a business vision and process objectives to prioritize objectives and set targets.
2. Identify the processes to be redesigned so as to identify critical or bottleneck processes.
3. Understand and measure existing processes to identify current problems and set baseline performance expectations.
4. Identify IT levers to brainstorm new process approaches.
5. Design and build a prototype of the process to implement organizational and technical aspects.

The most likely objectives related to process redesign are reducing costs, reducing the time it takes for tasks to be completed, increasing or improving the quality of output, and empowering individuals and providing them with more control over their output (Davenport & Short, 1990).

Improved workflow management has enabled many agencies to reduce costs and improve customer service at the same time. Information systems can make organizations more efficient. Information technology can be used to redesign and reshape organizations, transforming their structure, scope of operation, reporting and control mechanisms, work practices, workflows, products, and services. Flatter organizations have fewer levels of management; lower-level employees are given greater decision-making authority, and employees may work away from a manager. Information systems make information available to line workers so that they can make decisions that were previously made by managers. Networks of computers have made it possible for employees to work together as a team. Information technologies like e-mail, the Internet, and videoconferencing allow employees to work from different locations. For example, employees can work remotely from their homes or cars and can collaborate while miles away from the office or other particular structures, thus vastly expanding organizational boundaries.

Types of Information Systems

There are four main types of information systems, each serving a different organizational level: operational-level systems, knowledge-level systems, management-level systems, and strategic-level systems.

Operational-Level Systems

Operational-level systems support operational managers by keeping track of the elementary activities and transactions of the organization, such as sales, receipts, cash deposits, payroll, and the flow of materials in a hospital. The principal purpose of systems at this level is to answer routine questions and to track the flow of transactions through the organization.

Workflow systems support agency operations. The Southwest Florida Water Management District (SWFWMD) is developing a new workflow management system to streamline its environmental permit approval process by using workflow and document management software. Using software to store and process documents electronically, organizations can redesign their workflow so that documents can be worked on simultaneously or moved more efficiently from one person or location to another. Workflow and document management software automates processes such as routing documents to different locations, securing approvals, scheduling, and generating reports. Two or more people can work simultaneously on the same document, allowing much quicker completion. Work need not be delayed because a file is out or a document is in transit. For example, in the permit approval processes, SWFWMD engineers, attorneys, and planners can simultaneously review the documents.

Knowledge-Level Systems

Knowledge-level systems support knowledge and data workers in an organization. The purpose of knowledge-level systems is to help the organization integrate new knowledge into the agency and control the flow of paperwork. *Reporting systems* support knowledge-level systems. Generating reports is a basic function of most information systems. For example, demographic data can be used to complete required government forms, or a time and attendance system could be used to generate reports on sick time used by different departments to identify those with high absenteeism. Or in the case of a direct service nonprofit receiving public funds, the hours of services delivered can be reported to receive reimbursements.

Management-Level Systems

Management-level systems are designed to serve the monitoring, controlling, decision-making, and administrative activities of middle managers. *Decision support systems* support management-level systems. They go beyond simply reporting information; they typically incorporate rules, formulas, or specialized displays that are designed to help end users make decisions. Scheduling and staffing are areas where decision support can be useful. In scheduling, a routine question is how many people should be scheduled for a given time period or a particular event. If there are changes in workload or seasonal variations due to increasing or decreasing need for services or attendance at events, it may be helpful to have a model that recommends the number of people in each job category that should be scheduled. The same kinds of questions emerge over the longer term with respect to recruitment and staffing. If increased retirements are expected, what are the KSAOCs of people that need to be hired, and how many hires should there be? Other HRM topics such as benefits planning and analysis are good candidates for decision support.

Strategic-Level Systems

Strategic-level systems help senior management address strategic issues and long-term trends, both in the agency and in the external environment. *Executive support systems* support strategic-level systems. Whereas traditional decision support systems are directed at well-defined, narrowly focused problems, executive support systems bring together data from diverse sources to help assess broader strategic questions. SHRM figures into these decisions. When considering the privatization of services, in the case of public sector agencies, or when considering a merger, in the case of nonprofit agencies, labor costs, including pensions and benefits, are usually significant concerns. Having access to timely and accurate information can provide a broader perspective.

All organizations and departments need to be aware of their revenue and expenditures. All organizations have an accounting function that is responsible for maintaining and managing the agency's financial records, its receipts, disbursements, and payroll expenditures. An *accounting information system* enables a manager to keep track of the financial assets and flow of funds. It provides a record of transactions for disbursements, receipts, and other expenditures. Most nonprofits, regardless of size, have an accounts receivable system to keep track of its money.

For example, nonprofits must keep track of the grants they receive from public and private sources. They must track their donations, gifts, and contributions, which may be cash or noncash. They need to monitor their fees for services and have a system in place for billing and collections. Some nonprofits may have income from investments, membership dues, and special events that need to be accounted for. The information system keeps track of all the outstanding bills and can produce a variety of reports. The system supplies information to the general ledger system, which tracks the cash flow of the agency. The financial reports that can be gleaned from the accounting information system can be used to make immediate and strategic decisions.

Information Systems Design

The design of information systems often becomes entangled in the politics of the organization. Because information systems can potentially change an organization's structure, culture, politics, and work, they are often resisted when first introduced. Consequently, to ensure a successful introduction of information technology, the process must be planned. Factors to consider in your systems plans include the following:

The environment in which the organization functions

The structure of the organization—its hierarchy, specialization, and standard operating procedures

The culture and politics of the organization

The type of organization

The nature and style of leadership

The extent and support of top management

The principal interest groups affected by the system

The kinds of tasks and decisions that the information system is designed to assist

Information Technology Resource Policies

In July 2003, Governor Bill Richardson issued an executive order creating New Mexico's first uniform information technology resources policy for state agencies. The policy covers Internet and intranet use by state employees, e-mail, and use of the state's digital network. The executive order permits the state to install software to "monitor and record all IT resources usage, including e-mail and Web site visits." "Staff shall have no expectation of privacy while on the state's Internet or intranet." The directive also prohibits employees from using IT resources for anything other than official state business. Any staff members who violate the policy will be subject to immediate suspension and termination of access to IT resources, as well as disciplinary action up to and including termination of employment.

Under what condition should the employer invade the privacy rights of employees? Many employees are subject to electronic and other forms of high-tech surveillance. Information technology and systems make the invasion of privacy inexpensive and widely available. Organizations should have policies and procedures in place that govern the use and dissemination of information that may be considered private. This is especially important for employees working in HRM departments who have access to insurance information and medical records.

Adams (1992) identifies some procedures that organizations can implement to secure privacy and maintain confidential information. Employers should train users to handle equipment, data, and software securely; train employees to "sign off" personal computers after use; not allow passwords to be shared and change them frequently; ensure that backup copies, data files, software, and printouts are used only by authorized staff; and ensure that software and mainframe applications include a record of all changes and transactions that occur in the system, including when and who performed the changes. In addition, there should be no personal record system whose existence is secret; employees should have the right to access, inspect, review, and amend information about themselves; there must be no use of personal information for purposes other than those for which it was gathered without prior consent of the employees; and the managers of systems should be held accountable and liable for any damage done by systems, as well as their reliability and security.

Human Resources Information Systems

The HRM function is responsible for attracting, developing, and maintaining the agency's workforce. Human resources identifies potential employees, maintains complete records on existing employees, and creates programs to develop employees' talents and skills. Strategic-level human resources information systems identify manpower requirements—such as the skills, educational level, types of positions, number of positions, and cost—for meeting the agency's strategic plans. At the management level, an HRIS helps managers monitor and analyze the recruitment, allocation, and compensation of employees. HR knowledge systems support analysis activities related to job design, training, and the modeling of employee career paths and reporting relationships. HR operational systems track the recruitment and placement of the agency's employees (see Figure 3.1).

Technological advances have not only changed how organizations are structured and work is performed but have also begun to change the tasks of HRM specialists. Computers are being used to perform many of the functions for which employees were once responsible.

A typical HRIS for employee record keeping maintains basic data, such as the employee's name, age, sex, marital status, address, educational background, salary, job title, date of hire, and date of termination. The system can produce a variety of reports, such as lists of newly hired employees, terminated employees, leaves of absence, employees classified by job type or educational level, or employee job performance levels. Such systems are typically designed

Figure 3.1. Uses of Human Resources Information Systems.

HR Planning and Analysis

Organization charts
Staffing projections
Skills inventories
Turnover analysis
Absenteeism analysis
Restructuring costing
Internal job matching

Compensation and Benefits

Pay structures
Wage and salary costing
Flexible benefits
  administration
Vacation usage
Benefits usage analysis
401(k) statements
COBRA notification

Equal Employment

Affirmative action plan
Applicant tracking
Workforce utilization
Availability analysis

Health, Safety, and Security

Safety training
Accident records
OSHA reports
Material data records

HRIS

HR Development

Employee training profiles
Training needs assessments
Succession planning
Career interests and
  experience

Employee and Labor Relations

Union negotiation cost
Auditing records
Attitude survey results
Exit interview analysis
Employee work history

Staffing

Recruiting sources
Applicant tracking
Job offer refusal analysis

to provide data necessary for federal and state record-keeping requirements.

Compensation and Benefits

At a higher level of HRIS is the integration of payroll operations with the HRIS and benefits unit in HR. Government regulations and the complexity of benefits in many organizations warrant HRM expertise. Efficiency can be enhanced when payroll and HR systems are interfaced or integrated, as data entry and maintenance can be reduced.

When payroll operations are moved to the HR department, the benefits and compensation expertise of the human resources department makes certain that benefits plans remain qualified under government regulations, ensures the accuracy of payroll deductions for HR-managed plans, and provides the opportunity to answer employees' questions about pay and benefits, either in person or through interactive HRIS technology.

When organizations offer flexible benefits plans to employees, HRIS can be used to communicate benefits information to the employees that can have an impact on the costs of benefits and their administration. Employees can obtain information about the benefits available and make changes in their plans, enrolling in new benefits, adding or changing dependents, changing the amount of monthly savings deducted from paychecks, or making a cash withdrawal or taking out a loan or withdrawing from a plan altogether. In some systems, these decisions are supported by a simple "what if?" analysis that shows the employee available choices, pension projections, how much would be saved after five years at a certain rate of deduction, and so on.

Direct access to benefits plans and employees' ability to self-enroll or change benefits reduce staffing requirements in the benefits department, eliminate paperwork, and otherwise improve the administration of benefits. New employees who want to know when they are eligible to enroll in a certain plan can find this out without going to the benefits department, a change in dependents covered by health insurance can be made without paperwork, and retirement benefits at different ages can be projected.

Career Planning and Management Staffing Systems

Extending the reach of the HRIS to employees can generally be used for career planning and staffing systems. At the simplest level, electronic bulletin boards list basic job posting information and at a more complex level include online position descriptions, job advertisements when openings arise, résumés of all covered employees, knowledge-based assessment modules, and systematic procedures that link qualified candidates and open positions, providing managers with the backgrounds and résumés of employees and applicants that meet the position requirements.

Career planning and staffing systems that are accessible to employees permit their direct involvement in their own career development or movement in the organization. A career development system able to be accessed by employees can provide information about positions at the next level, job descriptions, information about steps in career paths leading to certain positions, training and development activities that may be required, and information about trends in workforce movement, surpluses and shortages, and other career-relevant information. In some systems, the employee can select a training class or another development activity or can create an entirely new career plan, subject to authorization, which can also be handled electronically. Most career development is essentially self-development and requires individual motivation, commitment, and clear linkages between individual effort and career results. Extending information through HRIS involves the employees being managed.

Communicating Policies and Procedures

The distribution of agency policies and procedures through technology is less expensive than printing hard copies and distributing them to employees. Changes can be made and communicated in an expedited manner. Information systems permit automatic communication that provides uniformity and consistency of some policies and procedures yet is flexible for audience-specific variations in others.

For example, regional pay levels may influence hourly rates, different labor contracts may be in effect in different locations, and paid holidays may vary. However, other policies with respect to nondiscrimination, privacy, and federal legislation such as the Fair Labor Standards Act (FLSA) may apply to all employees, requiring overtime pay and record keeping.

Organizations are using technology to offer quicker access to company policies online. Entering the systems, managers and employees can examine the company policy with respect to treatment for time off, vacations, holiday pay, or infractions leading to discipline. Such things as merit pay guidelines, performance appraisal instructions, access to training programs, and instructions on how to transfer or hire an individual can be provided online.

Employee Participation

Systems access to employees also permit employees to make their views and ideas known to management in a timely, cost-efficient manner. When employee attitudes are important to the organization, the timeliness, accuracy, and identification of different attitudes and perceptions among different types or categories of employees are important. Online employee surveys can eliminate the administration of paper-and-pencil surveys and can automatically summarize data and trends such as changes in attitudes that may deserve prompt management intervention. Linked to HRIS data, an automated attitude survey can produce summaries of responses by such groupings as management level, job function, location, or demographic characteristics without manual analysis.

Training and Performance Support

In a complex HRIS, job analysis data, productivity data, skills and competencies information, performance ratings, applicant qualifications, test results, and other types of information relevant to training can be integrated.

- HRIS demographic data can be analyzed to develop audience-specific curricula and training formats that are most effective for different groups.
- Job requirements can be linked to training. This could include competency-based training and assessment.
- HRIS can provide online training courses or provide links to approved vendor-supplied training courses.
- HRIS can analyze the relationships between training and performance ratings, turnover, compensation, and other variables to establish cost-benefit data on specific types of training.
- HRIS can develop new recruitment practices, preemployment tests, and other employment process tools based on analysis of training data and the requirements of positions.

Restructuring Work and Technology Transfer

The introduction of e-mail, computer-based training and testing, voice-activated systems, and the range of telecommunications technologies do not necessarily lead to improvements in performance or gains in productivity. Integrating employees and technology can be a complex, multifaceted function. For information systems to work, many factors need to be considered and implemented. Job and workflow analyses should be conducted, qualified people must be recruited and selected, and training and retraining must be provided.

HRIS can also lead to the outsourcing of the HRM function. Many small nonprofits lack the organizational capacity to develop and administer HRM programs and find it less expensive to outsource HRM functions than to hire new employees with expertise and to invest in technology. Even large public employers like the state of Florida may choose to outsource the HRM function. Florida entered a seven-year deal with an information management firm to handle some of the state's HRM responsibilities. The Florida Department of Management Services decided that replacing and continually updating its present HRIS was too expensive. It felt that it would be more cost-effective to outsource some of its HR functions. State employees will use a self-service Web portal to manage changes of address, dependents, emergency contacts, marital status, and other personal information. The portal will also be used to enroll in benefits programs and access benefits information. As a result of the outsourcing, some state employees will be displaced, and others have expressed concerns about the security of records (McKay, 2003a).

Strategic Human Resources Management

HRIS applications must go beyond payroll and benefits administration and tracking employee records such as attendance and absences. They must connect to the strategic objectives of the agency. Human resources information systems should be used to facilitate more effective recruitment and selection, training and development, communication, manpower planning, and other core HR processes. Data assembled and gleaned from an HRIS can be used by managers and workers to analyze problems and make informed decisions.

Ashbaugh and Miranda (2002) identify the following strategic applications of HRIS:

- *Align HRM systems to organizational performance issues.* Use technology to evaluate organizational performance.
- *Improve core business processes.*
- *Develop a human capital inventory.* Organizations can combine information for education and skills tracking and matching, career planning, succession planning, and performance evaluations.

- *Link position control to budgeting.* By integrating HR with the financial planning process, organizations can develop a compensation management program that includes automated position control to serve as a check that a department will not exceed its salary budget and the ability to develop projections or forecasts based on hours, actual expenditures, or staff totals. Link HR, benefits, and payroll data to the budget planning process that includes the ability to develop "what if?" analyses.
- *Facilitate labor-management relations.* Providing accurate information and tracking seniority, disciplinary actions, and grievances filed. Data can also be provided for labor negotiations such as pension changes, trend analysis for employee absences and use of sick time, analysis of the costs for overtime, and comprehensive employee benefits costs.

Other strategic applications include having employees update address changes, enroll in training courses, change benefits plans, and disseminate policies. Business intelligence can also be increased by using new technology. Advanced analytical tools, such as online analytical processing, data mining, and executive information systems, provide insight into trends and patterns and can be used to improve the decision-making capability of the organization. In an SHRM context, those tools can be used to support HRM decisions.

Managers must deal with new employee issues because the changes brought about by information technology require a new kind of employee. Employees need to be more highly trained than in the past as tasks become more automated. Employees need the skills and ability to work in an electronic environment, the ability to digest new information and knowledge and act on that information, and the ability and willingness to learn new software and workflow procedures.

Summary

Computers are used to advertise job vacancies in public places and on computer bulletin boards. Citizens can dial in or push appropriate buttons to see what agencies are recruiting and for what types of positions. Computers have also been used to replace interpersonal screening and interviewing. In computer-assisted screening, applicants are screened automatically over the telephone. A digitized voice asks applicants to respond to a variety of job-related questions, inquiring about work experience, attitudes, interests, and skills.

Many civil service systems have adopted computerized testing. Applicants read questions at a computer screen and use the keypad or mouse to select the correct answer. Tests that require the ability to read, write, and follow oral and visual instructions have been developed that use interactive video and multimedia. The computer scores exams as soon as the candidates complete them, immediately notifying the candidates of the results.

Tasks that used to require many human hours spent retrieving data from archival files can now easily be performed by computers. Administrative responsibilities such as tracking applicants and employees for equal opportunity and affirmative action goals and timetables is being done by computers. Computer programs are also being used for salary administration and performance evaluations. Benefits administration is increasingly being done through computer technology. Interactive voice response systems are providing twenty-four-hour access to retirement plan enrollment, savings plan inquiries and enrollment, and medical plan inquiries. With more and more information being compiled into agency databases, it is imperative that security measures be developed that protect sensitive or confidential information such as medical records and employee personnel files.

Increases in the uses of information technology require different combinations of skills and other resources. As public and nonprofit organizations confront these challenges, strategic human resources management will become even more important. Innovative human resources strategies will be imperative and necessary to assist organizations to prepare for changing missions, priorities, and programs.

Questions and Exercises

1. Describe the advantages and disadvantages of employees using a Web-based HRIS.

2. Has technology transformed your job? If so, in what ways?
3. In small groups, identify and discuss significant current trends related to information technology.
4. What initiatives have been established to meet technology challenges?
5. Go to the online version of *Governing Magazine* (http://www. governing.com), and look under "Technology." What are some of the topics being discussed, and how might they affect your organization?
6. Go to *Government Technology Executive News* (http://www.govtech. net/news). What are some important topics that government executives need to be aware of?
7. Go to the online version of the *Chronicle of Philanthropy* (http:// philanthropy.com). What are some of the technology topics being discussed, and how might your organization be affected?
8. Go to the Center for Technology in Government (http:// www.ctg.albany.edu) and the Center for Digital Government (http://www.centerdigital.gov.com). What are some of technology topics being discussed, and how might your organization be affected?

Chapter Four

Equal Employment
Opportunity

Public and nonprofit human resources management (HRM) is influenced by a variety of laws governing equal employment opportunity. Equal employment opportunity has implications for all aspects of HRM, from human resources planning, recruitment and selection, training and career development, compensation and benefits, and performance evaluation to labor-management relations. This chapter explains the federal legal environment that governs equal employment opportunity. Administrators must understand the federal, state, and local laws that affect HRM. These laws are designed to eradicate discrimination in the workplace for non-job-related or non-performance-related reasons. However, many employers do not understand the laws, misapply them, or choose to ignore them. Employers must consider these laws when developing employment policies and practices.

Federal Equal Employment Opportunity Laws

This section explains the federal laws governing equal employment opportunity. It is recommended, however, that you check with your state and local governments' fair employment practice agencies for additional laws and regulations that may affect the equal employment opportunity practices of your agency.

Civil Rights Acts of 1866 and 1871

The Civil Rights Act of 1866 was based on the Thirteenth Amendment to the United States Constitution; it prohibits racial discrimination in the making and enforcement of contracts, which could include hiring and promotion decisions. Nonprofit and private employers, unions, and employment agencies fall under its coverage. The Civil Rights Act of 1871 covers state and local governments. It is based on the Fourteenth Amendment and prohibits the deprivation of equal employment rights under state laws.

Title VII of the Civil Rights Act of 1964

The Civil Rights Act was signed by President Lyndon Johnson in 1964. It covers all employers having more than fifteen employees except private clubs, religious organizations, and places of employment connected to an Indian reservation.

Title VII of the act deals specifically with discrimination in employment and prohibits discrimination based on race, color, religion, sex, or national origin. The passage of this law was not without controversy. Many politicians (mostly in the South) thought that a federal law forbidding discrimination would usurp states' rights. Congressman Howard Smith of Virginia tried to defeat the bill by including sex as one of the protected classifications. He hoped that the insertion of sex would render the bill foolish and lead to its defeat. The act passed with the inclusion of sex, and today litigation concerning sex discrimination is very common.

The Civil Rights Act of 1964 created the U.S. Equal Employment Opportunity Commission (EEOC) to investigate complaints and to try to resolve disputes through conciliation. The act was amended in 1972 by the Equal Employment Opportunity Act, which extended its coverage to state and local governments and to educational institutions. At this time, the EEOC was granted enforcement powers to bring action against organizations in the courts if necessary to force compliance with Title VII.

The EEOC requires that most organizations submit annual EEO forms. Data from these forms are used to identify possible patterns of discrimination in particular organizations or segments of the workforce. The EEOC may then take legal action against an organization on the basis of these data.

Title VII does not prohibit discrimination based on seniority systems, veterans' preference rights, national security reasons, or job qualifications based on test scores, background, or experience, even when the use of such practices may correlate with discrimination based on race, sex, color, religion, or national origin. Section 703(e)(1) of Title VII permits an employer to discriminate using religion, sex, or national origin in instances where religion, sex, or national origin is a "bona fide occupational qualification" (BFOQ) reasonably necessary to the normal operation of that particular business or enterprise. For example, a BFOQ that excludes one group (for example, males or females) from an employment opportunity is permissible if the employer can argue that the "essence of the business" requires the exclusion, that is, if the business would be significantly affected by not employing members of one group exclusively. One case dealing with this issue was *International Union, United Automobile Workers* v. *Johnson Controls* (499 U.S. 187, 1991). Johnson Controls, Inc., is a car battery manufacturer that excluded fertile women from jobs where there was high exposure to lead. Fertile men, however, were not automatically excluded and were given a choice as to whether they wanted to risk their reproductive health. The company argued that this policy falls within the BFOQ exception to Title VII. In its 1991 decision, the U.S. Supreme Court disagreed. The Court found that the policy was discriminatory since only women employees were affected by the policy. "Respondent's fetal protection policy explicitly discriminates against women on the basis of their sex. The policy excludes women with childbearing capacity from lead-exposed jobs and so creates a facial classification based on gender. Despite evidence in the record about the debilitating effect of lead exposure on the male reproductive system, Johnson Controls is concerned only with the harms that may befall the unborn offspring of its female employees." The Court stated that women who are as capable of doing their jobs as their male counterparts may not be forced to choose between having a child and having a job. In general, the position of the courts regarding BFOQs clearly favors judgments about the performance, abilities, or potential of specific individuals rather than discrimination by class or categories. The Supreme Court has said that the BFOQ exception to Title VII is a narrow one, limited to policies that are directly related to a worker's ability to do the job. The burden of proof is on the employer to justify any BFOQ claim.

For most public sector jobs, it is very difficult to substantiate the necessity of gender, race, religion, national origin, age, or disability as a BFOQ. However, there are some instances where a

BFOQ case can be made. In *Dothard* v. *Rawlinson* (433 U.S. 321, 1977), the state of Alabama was permitted to exclude females from being guards in an all-male maximum-security prison where 20 percent of the prisoners were sex offenders. In 1996, the U.S. Court of Appeals at Philadelphia ruled that gender can be considered a BFOQ for the purposes of staffing a psychiatrist hospital unit that treats emotionally disturbed and sexually abused children. A female child care worker was assigned to work the night shift because the hospital needed a balance of men and women to provide therapeutic care to female and male patients who might want to talk with a staff member of their own sex. The court held that Title VII excuses discrimination that is justified as a BFOQ when it is reasonably necessary to the normal operation of the business. The essence of the hospital's business requires consideration of gender in staffing decisions because if there are not members of both sexes on a shift, the hospital's ability to provide care to its patients is impeded (*Healey* v. *Southwood Psychiatric Hospital*, Calif. 3, 70 FEP 439, 1996).

The question of whether race, religion, national origin, color, and sex constitute a BFOQ does arise often in the nonprofit sector. Is gender a legitimate BFOQ for an executive director position at a rape and sexual abuse center? Can a qualified male perform the administrative and leadership tasks, or must the executive director be a female? Would race be a BFOQ for a leadership position in a community-based nonprofit that provides services to racial minorities? If a BFOQ is challenged, the burden is on the employer to justify any claim.

Laws That Address Religious Discrimination

Under Section 701(j) of Title VII, employers are obligated to accommodate their employees' or prospective employees' religious practices. Failure to make accommodation is unlawful unless an employer can demonstrate that it cannot reasonably accommodate the employee because of undue hardship in the conduct of its business. In *Trans World Airlines, Inc.,* v. *Hardison* (432 U.S. 63, 1977), the Supreme Court ruled that the employer and union need not violate a seniority provision of a valid collective bargaining agreement, the employer has no obligation to impose undesirable shifts on nonreligious employees, and the employer has no obligation to call in substitute workers if such accommodation would require more than de minimis cost.

Nonprofit organizations that provide secular services but are affiliated with and governed by religious institutions are exempt from the law under Section 702 of the Civil Rights Act of 1964, which states: "This title shall not apply to an employer with respect to the employment of aliens outside any State, or to a religious corporation, association, educational institution, or society with respect to the employment of individuals of a particular religion to perform work connected with the carrying on by such corporation, association, educational institution, or society of its activities" (as amended by P.L. 92-261, eff. Mar. 24, 1972).

Educational institutions such as universities, schools, or other institutions of learning are also exempt from the law. Section 703(e)(2) of the Civil Rights Act of 1964 states that "it shall not be an unlawful employment practice for a school, college, university, or other educational institution or institution of learning to hire and employ employees of a particular religion if such school, college, university, or other educational institution or institution of learning is, in whole or in substantial part, owned, supported, controlled, or managed by a particular religion or by a particular religious corporation, association, or society, or if the curriculum of such school, college, university, or other educational institution of learning is directed toward the propagation of a particular religion."

In *Corporation of the Bishop of the Church of Jesus Christ of Latter-Day Saints* v. *Amos* (483 U.S. 327, 1987), the Supreme Court upheld the right of the Mormon Church to terminate a building engineer who had worked at its nonprofit gymnasium for sixteen years because he failed to maintain his qualification for church membership. The Court claimed that the decision to terminate was based on religion by a religious organization and was thus exempted from the Title VII prohibition against religious discrimination. The Section 703(e)(2) exemption is broad and is not limited to the religious activities of the institution.

Pregnancy Discrimination Act of 1978

The Pregnancy Discrimination Act prohibits employment practices that discriminate on the basis of pregnancy, childbirth, or related medical conditions. A woman is protected from being fired or refused a job or promotion simply because she is pregnant. She also cannot be forced to take a leave of absence as long as she is able to work.

Under the law, employers are obligated to treat pregnancy like any other disability. For example, if other employees on disability leave are entitled to return to their jobs when they are able to work again, so should women who have been unable to work due to pregnancy.

The Pregnancy Discrimination Act also requires that employers provide full benefits coverage for pregnancy. A woman unable to work for pregnancy-related reasons is entitled to disability benefits or sick leave on the same basis as other employees unable to work for other medical reasons.

States may pass their own laws requiring additional benefits for pregnant employees beyond the scope of the federal law. The Supreme Court upheld a California law that required employers to provide up to four months' unpaid pregnancy disability leave with guaranteed reinstatement, even though disabled males were not entitled to the same benefit (*California Federal Savings and Loan Association* v. *Guerra*, 479 U.S. 272, 1987).

Age Discrimination in Employment Act of 1967

The Age Discrimination in Employment Act (ADEA) was enacted by Congress in 1967 to prohibit discrimination in employment because of age in matters pertaining to selection, job retention, compensation, and other terms and conditions of employment. Congress intended to promote the employment of older persons based on their ability rather than age and to prohibit arbitrary age discrimination in employment. In 1974, the ADEA was amended to extend coverage to state and local government employees as well as most federal employees. The ADEA protected workers between the ages of forty and sixty-five. Employers were granted four exemptions to the act: (1) where age is a bona fide occupational qualification reasonably necessary to normal operation of a particular business; (2) where differentiation is based on reasonable factors other than age; (3) to observe the terms of a bona fide seniority system or a bona fide insurance plan, with the qualification that no seniority system or benefit plan may require or permit the involuntary retirement of who is covered by the ADEA;

and (4) where an employee is discharged or disciplined for good cause.

The ADEA was amended in 1978 by raising the upper limit to seventy years of age; that limit was removed in 1987, meaning that compulsory retirement for most jobs is now illegal. The ADEA now applies to employers with twenty or more employees, unions of twenty-five or more members, employment agencies, and federal, state, and local governments.

On April 1, 1996, the Supreme Court ruled that an individual claiming age discrimination must show a logical connection between his or her age and his or her discharge, but there is no requirement to show that the replacement was under forty. Justice Antonin Scalia wrote that "the fact that one person in the protected class lost out to another person in the protected class is thus irrelevant, so long as he has lost out because of age" (*O'Connor* v. *Consolidated Coin Caters Corporation*, 517 U.S. 308, 1996).

In 2000, the Supreme Court ruled in *Kimmel* v. *Florida Board of Regents* (528 U.S. 62) that the Eleventh Amendment to the U.S. Constitution bars state employees from suing a state employer in federal court for violation of the ADEA. This ruling does not apply to local government employees or employees working for nonprofit agencies.

American with Disabilities Act of 1990

In 1990, Congress passed the Americans with Disabilities Act (ADA). Title I of the ADA provides that qualified individuals with disabilities may not be discriminated against on the basis of disability in all aspects of the employment relationship, from the application stage through retirement. The law took effect on July 26, 1992, for organizations with twenty-five or more employees and on July 26, 1994, for organizations with fifteen to twenty-four employees. Employment practices covered by the ADA include job application procedures, hiring, firing, advancement, compensation, training, and other terms and conditions and privileges of employment.

The ADA recognized the following categories of disabilities:

1. Individuals with a physical or mental impairment that substantially limits one or more major life activities. This could include walking, seeing, hearing, or speaking. Examples of other physical

or mental impairments that might be considered disabilities include speech impediments, learning disabilities, AIDS, mental retardation, chronic mental illness, and epilepsy. To qualify as disabled and be protected by the ADA, a person must have substantial limitations on abilities that are "central to daily life" and not only to life in the workplace (*Toyota Motor Manufacturing, Inc.*, v. *Williams,* 534 U.S. 184, 2002).

2. Having a record of such an impairment. This could include people who have recovered from a heart attack, cancer, back injuries, or mental illness.

3. Being regarded as having an impairment. This would include individuals who are perceived as having a disability, such as individuals suspected of having the HIV virus.

Under the ADA, to be considered qualified, an individual must be able to perform the "essential functions of the position," meaning that the individual must satisfy the prerequisites for the position and be able to perform the essential functions of the job with or without reasonable accommodation.

Employers must provide the disabled with "reasonable accommodations" that do not place an undue hardship on the organization. Undue hardship is defined as an adjustment related to an employer's operation, financial resources, or facilities that require significant difficulty or expense. Undue hardship and reasonable accommodation are to be determined on a case-by-case basis, taking into account things such as the size of the employer, the number of employees responsible for a particular job or task, and the employer's ability to afford the accommodation. Accommodations may include interventions such as reassignment, part-time work, and flexible schedules, as well as modifications in equipment and the work environment, such as acquiring a special telephone headset or a larger computer screen or moving a training workshop to a location accessible to wheelchairs.

In 2001, the U.S. Supreme Court, using similar reasoning to that in *Kimmel,* ruled that the Eleventh Amendment to the U.S. Constitution bars state employees from suing their state employer for alleged violations of the ADA (*Board of Trustees of the University of Alabama* v. *Garrett,* 531 U.S. 356, 2001). This case, like the *Kimmel* decision, limits state employer liability and also limits congressional authority to impose antidiscrimination regulations on state governments.

Civil Rights Act of 1991

The Civil Rights Act of 1991 (CRA) was passed by Congress on November 7, 1991, and signed into law by President George H. W. Bush on November 21, 1991. The CRA provides additional remedies to protect against and to deter unlawful discrimination and harassment in employment and to restore the strength of federal antidiscrimination laws that many people felt had been weakened by several Supreme Court decisions. The CRA amends five civil rights statutes: Title VII of the Civil Rights Act of 1964, the Americans with Disabilities Act of 1990, the Age Discrimination Act of 1967, the Civil Rights Act of 1866, and the Civil Rights Attorney's Fee Awards Act of 1976. In addition, three new laws were created: Section 1981A of Title 42 of the U.S. Code, the Glass Ceiling Act of 1991, and the Government Employee Rights Act of 1991. Compensatory and punitive damages were made available to the victims of private and nonprofit employers. Public employees are now entitled to only compensatory damages. There is now a cap on damages permitted under the law that is determined by the number of workers employed by an organization.

Family and Medical Leave Act of 1993

The Family and Medical Leave Act (FMLA) was signed by President Bill Clinton shortly after his inauguration in January 1993 and took effect on August 5 of that year. The FMLA applies to all public agencies, including state, local, and federal employers; educational institutions; business entities engaged in commerce or in an industry affecting commerce; and private sector employers who employ fifty or more employees during twenty or more workweeks in the current or preceding calendar year, including joint employers and successors of covered employers.

Family and medical leave is available as the result of the birth or adoption of a child or the placement of a child for foster care; to care for a spouse, child, or parent with a serious health condition; or to accommodate the disabling illness of the employee. To be eligible for the leave, an employee must have worked for at least twelve months and for at least 1,250 hours during the year preceding the start of the leave.

The law requires employers to maintain coverage under any group health plan under the condition that coverage would have been provided if no leave had been taken. When the leave ends, employees are entitled to return to the same jobs they held before going on leave or to equivalent positions. An equivalent position is defined as a position that has the same pay, benefits, and working conditions and that involves the same or substantially similar duties and responsibilities. Employees must be restored to the same or a geographically proximate worksite.

Not all employees are eligible for leave under the FMLA. An employee who qualifies as a key employee may be denied restoration to employment. A key employee is salaried and is among the highest-paid 10 percent of the employees at the worksite. Employees must be notified by the employer of their status as a key employee if there is any possibility that the employer may deny reinstatement. Employees are required to give thirty days' advanced notice of the need to take family and medical leave when it is foreseeable for the birth of a child or the placement of a child for adoption or foster care or for planned medical treatment. When it is not possible to provide such notice, employees must give notice within one or two business days of the time when the employee learns of the need for leave.

Employers can require a medical certification from a health care provider to support leave requests. Employees who are denied leave or who are denied reinstatement at the end of leave in violation of the law may file a complaint with the Department of Labor. Employees may also file a private lawsuit against the employer to obtain damages and other relief. The FMLA does not supersede any state or local law that provides greater family or medical leave rights. Employers covered by both federal and state laws must comply with both. In a recent decision, *Nevada Department of Human Resources v. Hibbs* (538 U.S. 721, 2003), the Supreme Court upheld the right of state employees to sue their employers (state governments) in federal court for alleged violations of the FMLA.

Proving Employment Discrimination

Cases of alleged discrimination in violation of federal or state statutes can be made under one of two theories: disparate impact and disparate treatment.

Disparate Treatment

Disparate treatment occurs when an employer treats a protected-class employee differently from a non-protected-class employee in a similar situation. For example, deliberately using different criteria for selection depending on the candidate's sex or race would constitute disparate treatment, as when an employer asks female applicants but not male applicants questions about their marital status or child care arrangements or requires African American applicants to take preemployment tests that other equally qualified applicants for the same position are not required to take.

The following test, set forth in *McDonnell Douglas* v. *Green* (401 U.S. 424, 1973), permits plaintiffs to establish that an employer treats one or more members of a protected group differently than the employer treats members of another group:

1. The applicant or employee is a member of a class protected by the statute alleged to be violated (sex, race, age, national origin).
2. The applicant or employee applied for the vacancy and is qualified to perform the job.
3. Although qualified, the applicant or employee was rejected.
4. After rejection, the vacancy remained, and the employer continued to seek applications from persons with the same qualifications.

The Supreme Court established that in disparate treatment cases, the burden is on the plaintiff to prove that the employer *intended* to discriminate because of race, sex, color, religion, or national origin. In *St. Mary's Honor Center* v. *Hicks* (509 U.S. 502, 1993), the Supreme Court ruled that in addition to showing that all of the employer's legal reasons are false, an employee must prove that the employer was motivated by bias. The plaintiff must show direct evidence of discrimination.

Disparate Impact

Disparate impact occurs when an employer's policy or practice, neutral on its face and in its application, has a negative effect on the employment opportunities of protected-class individuals. "Neutral" means that the employer requires all applicants or employees to take the same examination or to possess the same qualifications for a given position. Unlike the examples provided under disparate treatment, in which the employer deliberately treated males and females or black and white applicants and employees differently, under disparate impact all applicants and employees are treated the same but protected-class members are not hired or promoted. Such impact is illegal if the employment practice is not job-related or is unrelated to the employment in question. For example, if an agency hired fifty whites and no Hispanics from one hundred white and one hundred Hispanic applicants, disparate impact has occurred. Whether or not the employer had good intentions or did not mean to discriminate is irrelevant to the courts in this type of lawsuit. After the plaintiff shows evidence of disparate impact, the employer must carry the burden of producing evidence of business necessity or job-relatedness for the employment practice. Finally, the burden shifts back to the plaintiff, who must show that an alternative procedure is available that is equal to or better than the employer's practice and has a less discriminatory effect.

The Uniform Guidelines on Employee Selection Procedures (1978) were jointly adopted by the EEOC, the Civil Service Commission, the Department of Labor, and the Department of Justice. Though not administrative regulations, the guidelines are granted deference by the courts. The purpose of the guidelines is to provide a framework for determining the proper use of tests and other selection procedures. They are applicable to all employers: federal, state, local, nonprofit, and private.

The Uniform Guidelines and many courts have adopted the "four-fifths rule" as a yardstick for determining disparate impact. This rule states that a selection rate (determined by the number of applicants selected divided by the number who applied) for a protected group should not be less than four-fifths, or 80 percent, of the rate for the group with the highest selection rate.

Disparate impact theory has been used in many cases involving neutral employment practices such as tests, entrance requirements, and physical requirements. In 1988, the Supreme Court extended use of the disparate impact theory in cases involving "subjective" employment practices such as interviews, performance appraisals, and job recommendations (*Watson v. Fort Worth Bank and Trust*, 487 U.S. 977, 1988). Statistical data based on the four-fifths rule can be used in a disparate impact case to establish prima facie evidence

of discrimination when decisions are based on subjective employment practices.

Affirmative Action: Executive Orders and Other Federal Laws

This section explains affirmative action and the requirements imposed on employers through Executive Orders 11246 and 11375,
the Rehabilitation Act of 1973, and the Vietnam Era Veterans
Readjustment Act of 1974. Chapter Five briefly discusses equal employment opportunity and the executive orders and federal laws
that require employers to engage in affirmative action.

Executive Orders 11246 and 11375

In 1965, President Johnson signed Executive Order 11246, which
prohibited discrimination in federal employment or by federal
contractors on the basis of race, creed, color, or national origin. In
1967, it was amended by Executive Order 11375 to change the
word *creed* to *religion* and to add sex discrimination to the prohibited types. The executive order applies to all federal agencies, contractors, and subcontractors, including all the facilities of the
agency holding the contract regardless of where the work is conducted. Contractors and subcontractors with more than $50,000
in government business and fifty or more employees are not only
prohibited from discriminating but must also take affirmative action
to ensure that applicants and employees are not treated differently
as a function of their sex, religion, race, color, or national origin.
The order also authorizes the cancellation of federal contracts for
failure to meet the order's guidelines. It requires a contractor to
post notices of equal employment opportunity and to document its
compliance to the Department of Labor (DOL).

Executive Order 11246 is enforced by the Department of Labor
through the Office of Federal Contract Compliance Programs
(OFCCP). The OFCCP is a branch of the DOL's Employment Standards Administration. It promulgates guidelines and conducts audits of federal contractors to ensure compliance with the executive
orders. The OFCCP is charged with processing complaints as well
as compliance review. The OFCCP reviews complaints; it can visit
an employer's worksite and review the affirmative action plans for

compliance with the law. Minority availability is measured by the proportion of qualified applicants (actual or potential) who are minorities. OFCCP defines "underutilization" as fewer minorities or women in a particular job group than would reasonably be expected by their availability. When a job group is identified as underutilized, the contractor must set goals to correct the underutilization. The goals for each underutilized group, together with the utilization analysis, becomes part of the written affirmative action plan. A federal contractor must monitor information about the status of employees when creating and using an affirmative action plan. The employer must demonstrate that its employment practices comply with Executive Order 11246 and the OFCCP's guidelines by documenting employment decisions on hiring, termination, promotion, demotion, and transfer.

If noncompliance is found, the OFCCP generally first tries to reach a conciliation agreement with the employer. Special hiring or recruitment programs, seniority credit, or back pay may be some of the provisions included in the agreement. If an agreement cannot be reached, the employer is scheduled to have a hearing with a judge. If an agreement is still not reached during this time, employers may lose their government contracts or have their payments withheld. They may also lose the right to bid on future government contracts or be barred from all subsequent contract work.

While equal employment opportunity is a legal duty, affirmative action can be voluntary or involuntary. Although Executive Order 11246 applies only to organizations receiving federal funds, many public and nonprofit organizations have decided to implement voluntary affirmative action programs to redress previous discriminatory employment practices or to make their workforce more representative. Involuntary affirmative action is permitted under the Civil Rights Act of 1964, Section 706(g), which states that if a court finds that an employer has intentionally engaged in an unlawful employment practice, it may order appropriate affirmative action. Affirmative action is not required unless the employer has adopted the plan as a remedy for past discrimination or if the employer must comply with an executive order required by a federal or state agency requiring affirmative action as a condition of doing business with the government. Employers who are not the recipients of government contracts may be forced to develop affirmative action plans if an investigation by a state or federal compliance agency finds that an employer's personnel practices discriminate against protected-class members.

There are three types of involuntary affirmative action plans. They are presented here in order from least to most restrictive.

Conciliation agreement. After an investigation by a compliance agency, the employer may acknowledge that there is merit to the allegation of discriminatory employment practices and agree to change its practices to comply with the recommendations of the compliance agency.

Consent decree. A consent decree is an agreement between an employer and a compliance agency negotiated with the approval of a court and is subject to court enforcement.

Court order. Court orders result if a compliance agency must take an employer to court because neither a conciliation agreement nor a consent decree can be agreed on. If the court finds the employer guilty of discrimination, the judge may impose court-ordered remedies. These can include hiring or promotion quotas, changes in personnel practices, and financial compensation for the victims of discrimination.

A summary of Supreme Court decisions pertaining to affirmative action programs is presented in Exhibit 4.1.

Exhibit 4.1. Supreme Court Affirmative Action Decisions Regarding Employment.

United Steelworkers of America v. *Weber* (443 U.S. 193, 1979)

In the first important private sector decision, the justices ruled 5–2 that private companies and unions could voluntarily adopt quotas to eliminate "manifest racial imbalance." Affirmative action plans that meet four conditions are permissible: (1) the plan is temporary, (2) it is undertaken to eliminate manifest racial imbalance, (3) it is for nontraditional or traditionally segregated job categories, and (4) the plan does not require the discharge of white workers or create an absolute bar to their advancement.

Exhibit 4.1. Supreme Court Affirmative Action Decisions Regarding Employment, Cont'd.

Firefighters of Local Union 1784 v. *Stotts* (467 U.S. 561, 1984)

The justices held that seniority systems may not be abrogated to benefit individuals who were not proven victims of discrimination.

Wygant v. *Jackson Board of Education*
(476 U.S. 267, 1986; 478 U.S. 1014, 1986)

The court again upheld seniority, ruling that laying off more experienced white teachers violates the constitutional guarantee of equal protection. The court said that governments might be allowed to use race for hiring preferences to redress past discrimination but not layoffs.

Local 93 of the International Association of Firefighters v.
City of Cleveland (478 U.S. 501, 1986)

The court held that trial judges may approve voluntary pacts between employee associations and public employers to give minorities hiring preferences. Because Local 93 was not a party to the consent decree, it could not protest its terms.

Local 28 of Sheet Metal Workers v. *EEOC* (478 U.S. 421, 1986)

Two important rules emerged. First, a court may order a union to use quotas to overcome a history of "egregious discrimination." Second, black and Hispanic applicants can benefit even if they themselves were not victims of past union bias.

United States v. *Paradise* (480 U.S. 149, 1987)

District federal judges may impose strict racial quotas where there is a history of "egregious" racial bias to remedy the effects of past discrimination.

Johnson v. *Transportation Agency, Santa Clara County* (480 U.S. 616, 1987)

Organizations may adopt voluntary affirmative action programs to hire and promote qualified minorities and women to correct a "conspicuous imbalance in job categories traditionally segregated by race and sex." Gender can be considered in promotional decisions even when there is no evidence of past discrimination.

Martin v. *Wilks* (490 U.S. 755, 1989)

A consent decree between one group of employees and its employer cannot possibly settle, voluntarily or otherwise, the connecting claims of another group of employees who do not join in the agreement. Consent decrees may be challenged by parties who were not originally involved in reaching the settlement.

The Rehabilitation Act of 1973

The Rehabilitation Act prohibits discrimination on the basis of physical or mental disability. A disabled person is defined as one who has an impairment that affects a major life activity, has a history of such an impairment, or is considered as having one. Major life activities refer to functions such as seeing, speaking, walking, and caring for oneself. Disabled individuals would also include those with mental handicaps and may include those with illnesses making them unfit for employment such as diseases (tuberculosis, heart disease, cancer, diabetes, drug dependency, or alcoholism, for example). The Supreme Court ruled in *Arline* v. *School Board of Nassau County* (479 U.S. 8937, 1987) that individuals with contagious diseases who are able to perform their jobs are protected by the Rehabilitation Act of 1973. The Court stated that the assessment of risks cannot be based on "society's accumulated myths and fears about disability and disease." Most states have similar laws protecting disabled workers from discrimination.

Section 501 of the Rehabilitation Act requires the federal government, as an employer, to develop and implement affirmative action plans on behalf of disabled employees. Congress enacted this provision with the expectation that the federal government would serve as a model for other employers.

Section 503 requires all federal contractors or subcontractors receiving funds in excess of $2,500 to take affirmative action for the employment of qualified disabled persons. Enforcement is carried out by the Department of Labor's Employment Standards Administration. Under the Rehabilitation Act, as under the Americans with Disabilities Act of 1990, a disabled person is considered qualified for a job if an individual analysis determines that he or she can, with reasonable accommodation, perform the essential functions of the job. Employers must make such accommodations unless it can be shown that the accommodation would impose an undue hardship on the firm.

Section 504 prohibits federally funded programs and government agencies from excluding from employment an "otherwise qualified handicapped individual . . . solely by reason of handicap." The enforcement of Section 504 rests with each federal agency providing financial assistance. The attorney general of the United States has responsibility for the coordination of the enforcement efforts of the agencies.

In 1993, the United States Court of Appeals for the First Circuit ruled that an individual who suffered from morbid obesity was denied a job in violation of Section 504 of the Rehabilitation Act of 1973 (*Cook* v. *State of Rhode Island, Department of Mental Health, Retardation, and Hospitals,* 10 F.3d 17, 1st Cir. 1993). Cook had worked as an institutional attendant for the mentally retarded from 1978 to 1980 and from 1981 to 1986. She reapplied for the position in 1988 and was rejected since she was found to be morbidly obese. She was 5 feet 2 inches tall and weighed over 320 pounds. The state claimed that her obesity limited her ability to evacuate patients in case of an emergency and put her at greater risk of developing serious ailments. She filed a lawsuit claiming that her rejection violated Section 504 of the Rehabilitation Act of 1973, which prohibits an otherwise qualified disabled individual from being discriminated against by a program or activity that receives federal financial assistance. The Court stated that to prevail in her claim, it would be necessary to show that (1) she applied for a job in a federally funded program, (2) she suffered from a disability, (3) she was qualified for the position, and (4) she was not hired due to her disability. The state argued that obesity was a condition that could be changed, that it was voluntary, and that it therefore did not constitute a disability. The Court found that even if people who are morbidly obese lose weight, they still suffer from metabolic dysfunction. The Court said that the Rehabilitation Act "contains no language suggesting that its protection is linked to how an individual became impaired, or whether an individual contributed to his or her impairment. The law applies to conditions such as alcoholism, AIDS, diabetes, cancer and heart disease that can be made worse by voluntary conduct." Concern over excess absenteeism and increased workers' compensation costs were prohibited reasons for rejecting Cook.

Vietnam Era Veterans Readjustment Act of 1974

The Vietnam Era Veterans Readjustment Act of 1974 applies to employers with government contracts of $10,000 or more. Contractors are required to take affirmative action to employ and advance disabled veterans and qualified veterans of the Vietnam era. Enforcement of the act is by complaint to the Veterans' Employment Service of the Department of Labor.

Summary

Equal employment opportunity has continued to evolve over the years so that it now prohibits not only race discrimination but also discrimination on the basis of sex, religion, color, national origin, disability, and age. The equal employment opportunity and affirmative action laws create legal responsibilities for employers and affect all aspects of the employment relationship. Recruitment, selection, training, compensation and benefits, promotions, and terminations must all be conducted in a nondiscriminatory manner.

Whereas equal employment opportunity is a policy of nondiscrimination, affirmative action requires employers to analyze their workforces and develop plans of action to recruit, select, train, and promote members of protected classes and to develop plans of action to correct areas in which past discrimination may have occurred.

Affirmative action is used by the federal government to promote a more diverse workforce. Recipients of federal funds are required to develop affirmative action plans that encourage the recruitment, selection, training, and promotion of qualified disabled individuals, Vietnam War veterans, and individuals who may have been discriminated against because of their race, sex, color, or national origin. Affirmative action plans can be either involuntary or voluntary. Involuntary action plans have increasingly come under intense scrutiny, and affirmative action itself is presently being challenged. On April 1, 2003, the Supreme Court heard arguments challenging the use of race in the admissions policies at the University of Michigan and its law school (*Gratz* v. *Bollinger,* 539 U.S. 244, and *Grutter* v. *Bollinger,* 539 U.S. 306, respectively). Major corporations including Microsoft, Bank One, General Motors, Shell, and American Express, and the Army, Navy, and Air Force academies filed briefs supporting the University of Michigan's race-conscious admissions policies. Supporters of using race as one of many factors in the admission process believe that diversity creates stronger organizations. On June 23, 2003, the Supreme Court upheld the affirmative action plan of the law school. Justice Sandra Day O'Connor, writing for the majority, which included Justices Stephen G. Breyer, John Paul Stevens, Ruth Bader Ginsburg, and David H. Souter, stated the following:

The hallmark of the law school's policy is its focus on academic ability coupled with a flexible assessment of applicant's talents, experiences and potential "to contribute to the learning of those around them.". . . . The policy aspires to "achieve that diversity which has the potential to enrich everyone's education and thus make a law school class stronger than the sum of its parts.". . . . We have held that all racial classifications imposed by the government "must be analyzed by a reviewing court under strict scrutiny." This means that such classifications are constitutional only if they are narrowly tailored to further compelling governmental interests. To be narrowly tailored, a race-conscious admissions program cannot use a quota system. . . . Instead a university may consider race or ethnicity more flexibly as a "plus" factor in the context of individualized consideration of each and every applicant.". . . . The Law School engages in a highly individualized, holistic review of each applicant's file, giving serious consideration to all the ways an applicant might contribute to a diverse educational environment. . . . In order to cultivate a set of leaders with legitimacy in the eyes of the citizenry, it is necessary that the path to leadership be visibly open to talented and qualified individuals of every race and ethnicity.

In *Gratz* v. *Bollinger,* however, the Court found the University of Michigan's undergraduate affirmative action admission program unconstitutional. Justice William Rehnquist, writing for the majority, stated, "The university's policy which automatically distributes 20 points, or one-fifth of the points needed to guarantee admission, to every single underrepresented minority applicant solely because of race, is not narrowly tailored to achieve the interest in the educational diversity." In essence, the Supreme Court ruled that race and ethnicity may be taken into account as a "plus factor" when making admission decisions but limited how much a factor race can play in the selection of students.

Several other federal court decisions concerning affirmative action have been especially important. One case addressed affirmative action and the granting of federal contracts, and the second case dealt with affirmative action and law school admission policies. In *Adarand Constructors* v. *Pena* (515 U.S. 200, 1995), the Supreme Court ruled that federal programs that use race or ethnicity as a basis for decision making must be strictly scrutinized to ensure that they promote compelling government interests and that they are narrowly tailored to serve those interests. Federal affirmative action programs giving preferences to minorities are subject to the same strict scrutiny applied to state and local programs. In *Hopwood et al.* v. *State of Texas et al.* (84 F.3d 720, 1996), the Fifth Circuit Court of Appeals struck down the affirmative action program at the University of Texas Law School. The law school set up an admission system that viewed minorities and whites separately, resulting in an unconstitutional quota system. The court ruled that racial diversity can never be a compelling government interest, that racial diversity "may promote improper racial stereotypes, thus fueling racial hostility."

At this time, the Supreme Court has upheld the use of court-ordered affirmative action programs designed to eliminate egregious past discrimination (*United States* v. *Paradise*, 480 U.S. 149, 1986) and voluntary affirmative action plans designed to increase the representation of women and minorities in nontraditional jobs or in traditionally segregated positions (*Johnson* v. *Transportation Agency, Santa Clara County*, 480 U.S. 616, 1987; *United Steelworkers of America* v. *Weber*, 443 U.S. 193, 1979). Voluntary affirmative action plans are permitted as long as they meet four conditions: (1) the affirmative action plan is temporary, (2) it is undertaken to eliminate manifest racial imbalance, (3) it is for nontraditional jobs or traditionally segregated job categories, and (4) the plan does not require the discharge of white workers or create an absolute bar to their advancement.

The Supreme Court has not upheld the use of racial quotas when race serves as the only criterion for admission to universities and advanced graduate programs (*Regents of the University of California* v. *Bakke*, 483 U.S. 265, 17 FEP 1000, 1978) or when race is used to abrogate seniority systems in layoffs. Hiring and promotional preferences may be permissible to redress past discrimination but not layoffs (*Firefighters Local 1784* v. *Stotts*, 467 U.S. 561, 1984; *Wygant* v. *Jackson Board of Education*, 476 U.S. 267, 1986).

The focus on equal employment opportunity and affirmative action programs has increased the importance of strategic human resources management and planning. Compliance with equal employment opportunity laws and affirmative action regulations are essential components of human resources planning and the effective utilization of all employees. One day, affirmative action programs may be eliminated, and many of the paperwork requirements for compliance audits will no longer be necessary. However, organizations will still need to develop and implement progressive HRM strategies if they wish to successfully manage a diverse workforce.

Questions and Exercises

1. If you were asked by an employer to review an employment decision to determine if discrimination had occurred, what factors would you consider, and how would you evaluate them?
2. In small groups, determine what kinds of policies and training programs exist in your organizations that address equal employment opportunity.
3. Visit the Equal Employment Opportunity Commission Web site (http://www.eeoc.gov). What kind of discrimination (race, sex, disability, national origin, religion) is most prevalent in the region where you live? Why do you think that is so?
4. What is your opinion of the EEOC Web site from an employer's perspective and from an employee's perspective? Are there any changes you would make? If so, what are they?

| **Valuing a Diverse Workforce**

The demographics of American society have changed. Hispanics (who can be of any race) are now the largest minority in the United States, at approximately 37 million. The number of Americans who declared themselves black in combination with one or more other races is now 37.7 million, slightly higher than the overall figures for Latinos, indicating a growing multiculturalism in America. There are approximately 32.5 million foreign-born residents in the country, about 11 percent of the total U.S. population of 282.1 million (U.S. Census Bureau, 2003b). Nontraditional families are now prevalent. Divorce, death, domestic partnerships, and different generations of the same family living together have become commonplace. The number of children being raised by grandparents has increased 30 percent since 1990. Nationally, 43 percent of unmarried couples living together are raising children, nearly matching the 46 percent figure for married couples. According to the 2000 census, one-third of female couples and one-fifth of male couples have children at home (Cohn, 2003; U.S. Census Bureau, 2003a). Same-sex couples accounted for one of every nine unmarried live-in households; however, this number may be understated because of fear of prejudice or confusion over the "unmarried partner" category on the census form (Marquis, 2003).

As the demographics of American society have changed, so has the composition of the workforce. Women, persons of color, persons of different ethnic and religious backgrounds, persons with physical and mental disabilities, and homosexuals are more visible in the workplace. To be successful, employers need to manage a diverse workforce. They need to ensure that agency rewards such as promotional opportunities and compensation are determined by job performance, initiative, or special skills.

Although members of protected classes and homosexuals have received the most attention in the literature, diversity can also include differences in underlying attributes or nonobservable differences, such as working styles, values, and personality types, as well as differences in culture, socioeconomic background, educational background, spirituality, occupational background or professional orientation, industry experience, organizational membership, group tenure, and spirituality (Denhardt & Leland, 2003; Milliken & Martins, 1996). Loden (1996, p. 14) defines diversity as the important human characteristics that affect individuals' values, opportunities, and perceptions of self and other others at work. She identifies age, ethnicity, gender, mental and physical abilities and characteristics, race, and sexual orientation as the core dimensions of diversity. Secondary dimensions of diversity include communication style, education, family status, military experience, organizational role and level, religion, first language, geographical location, income, work experience, and work style. This chapter emphasizes management challenges such as valuing organizational diversity as a vital organizational resource.

Employers must learn how to manage diversity and capitalize on each member's contributions to enhance the organization's effectiveness. Fairness in recruitment, selection, promotion, performance evaluation, training and development, compensation, and benefits are just some of the challenges that strategic human resources management must face. Consider the following examples:

- In June 2002, President George W. Bush signed a bill allowing death benefits to be paid to domestic partners of firefighters and police officers who die in the line of duty, permanently extending a federal death benefit for the first time ("Same-Sex Couples Earn Death Benefit," 2002).
- In an attempt to bridge the language and cultural gap between Fort Lauderdale police and the city's growing Haitian population, the city, following a nationwide search, hired the first and only Haitian-born, Creole-speaking officer on its 480-member force (Bennett, 2001).

- The CIA has placed advertisements in *Newsweek* and other popular magazines in an attempt to recruit Arabic-speaking applicants.
- Former Maryland state trooper Kevin Nussman was awarded $375,000 in 1999 for the first-ever sex discrimination verdict in conjunction with the Family and Medical Leave Act. When Nussman requested paternity leave, his supervisors told him that "God made women to breast-feed babies, and men can't fulfill that role" ("Unspoken Rule," 2000).
- Four Pakistan-born men will share $1.1 million from settling an employment discrimination lawsuit in which they said they were abused by coworkers who ridiculed their turbans, mocked their daily Muslim prayers, and called them derogatory names. According to the EEOC, there has been an increase in complaints of discrimination by Muslim Americans since the September 11, 2001, terrorist attacks (Downey, 2003).

The first three examples reflect proactive attempts to managing a diverse workforce and to recognize that a diverse workforce can assist an organization in the delivery of its services. However, the fourth and fifth examples demonstrate that individuals and employers have much to learn in regard to diversity. For organizations to remain viable in today's multicultural workplaces, they must comply with the laws governing equal employment opportunity and also understand the role that cultural differences can play in an organization.

Glass Ceilings

The term *glass ceiling* refers to the artificial barriers that block the advancement of women and minorities to upper-level managerial and executive positions within organizations. Such obstacles must be eliminated.

Studies have shown that African Americans, Asian Americans, Hispanics, and women are underrepresented in upper-level supervisory, management, and senior executive positions of federal employment (Cornwell & Kellough, 1994; General Accounting Office,

2003; Guy, 1993; Kim, 1993; Kim & Lewis, 1994; Lewis, 1988, 1994; Naff & Kellough, 2002; Page, 1994, Riccucci, 2002; Sisneros, 1992; Swift, 1992–1993; U.S. Merit Systems Protection Board, 1992). A recent study found that the diversity of the Senior Executive Service is not going to change much over the next few years unless agencies step up their efforts to recruit and promote minorities. White women will essentially replace white men leaving the government (General Accounting Office, 2003). Other studies confirm the existence of a glass ceiling at the state and local levels (Bullard & Wright, 1993; Guy, 1993; McCabe & Stream, 2000; Rehfuss, 1986; Slack, 1987).

The New Nonprofit Almanac (Weitzman, Jalandoni, Lampkin, and Pollak, 2002) reports that in 1998, some 71 percent of employees in the nonprofit sector were female. But Michael O'Neill (1994) questions whether the influence of women in and through the nonprofit sector is as great as their statistical predominance. Steinberg and Jacobs (1994) and Odendahl and Youmans (1994) suggest that the nonprofit sector is in reality controlled by an elite male power structure and that within the sector, occupations are distributed according to gender. For example, men are financial officers and doctors, while women are teachers and nurses. Women may constitute the majority of the nonprofit workforce, but they are typically prevented from reaching top executive and policy-making positions.

A study by Gibelman (2000) confirms the existence of a glass ceiling in nonprofit human services organizations. Men are disproportionately represented in management, particularly upper-level management, whereas women are disproportionately represented in the direct-service and lower management levels. Men earn higher salaries than women at all hierarchical levels of the organization, and women of minority status earn the lowest salaries. The implications of this are important for all organizations but especially for nonprofits, where there is a higher proportion of females (71 percent) and African Americans (14 percent) employed in the independent sector than in either the government or the private sector. Female employees are especially predominant in the health services and social and legal services subsectors (Weitzman et al., 2002). This was confirmed by recent research that found that while female nonprofit leaders continue to be paid less than their male counterparts, the compensation gap is shrinking except at the smallest charities (Kerkman, 2003).

Other research indicates that female executives and fundraisers make less than males in similar jobs at comparable organizations and that women, while heading the majority of all charities, are less likely to lead the largest ones. One reason that has been suggested for the disparity is the fact that most trustees, especially at big organizations, are men, and often men from traditional backgrounds, who may feel a greater kinship with male executives (Joslyn, 2003).

The commitment of women and minorities to their jobs is typically questioned because of their family responsibilities, perceived inability to relocate, or doubts about their leadership styles. The assumption that they are less committed often results in their being bypassed for important assignments and developmental opportunities. However, recent research indicates that the personal multiple life roles that women play provide them with opportunities to practice multitasking and enrich their interpersonal skills and leadership effectiveness, which in turn actually increase their effectiveness in management positions (Ruderman, Ohlott, Panzer, & King, 2002).

Regardless of the employment sector, subtle assumptions, attitudes, and stereotypes exist in the workplace, manifesting as organizational cultures that affect the mobility patterns of women and minorities. The rest of this chapter discusses why managing a diverse workforce is important, the difference between equal employment opportunity and affirmative action, and the implications for managing a diverse workforce. Strategies that employers can implement to accommodate multicultural differences are reviewed.

Why Diversity Is Important

Evidence is growing that managing diversity leads to greater service effectiveness, efficiency, and productivity. Diversity can lead to more creative alternatives and higher-quality ideas, primarily from the introduction of different and opposing concepts and viewpoints. Employers who respect their employees are better able to use their talents; diversity helps increase one's understanding of the community and the marketplace and also increases the quality of team problem solving (Cox, 2001; Naff & Kellough, 2002; Sidberry, 2002).

The Diversity Initiative is a collaborative of Boston-area funders that evolved from observations and research that documented that a lack of diversity within nonprofit organizations had an impact on the effectiveness of their services and program delivery. The Diversity Initiative supported seventy organizations that were committed to creating greater racial, ethnic, and cultural diversity on their staff and boards. The participating agencies reviewed their missions, programs, and constituents and typically uncovered problems. Sometimes the agencies were not financially viable because they were no longer relevant to their market; sometimes they lacked credibility and were thus no longer effective within their communities. Whatever the reason, the organizations realized they risked extinction if they did not become more inclusive (Sidberry, 2002).

One nonprofit that recognizes the importance of a diverse workforce is Planned Parenthood of Rhode Island (PPRI). The Hispanic population in Rhode Island doubled in the 1990s. Today, 51 percent of the residents of Providence, the capital, belong to one of several minority groups and account for half the state's minority population. The Hispanic population is made up primarily of people from the Dominican Republic, as well as Central and South American countries. There are also significant numbers of people from Liberia, Sierra Leone, Nigeria, Cape Verde, Portugal, Laos, Cambodia, and Vietnam. Many of them do not speak English or have limited English language skills.

The staff at PPRI were not accustomed to serving people who did not speak English and whose cultural understanding of health care was very different from their own. Service delivery was complicated because reproductive health care service providers must also be skilled in understanding cultural differences regarding sexuality, gender roles, family dynamics, and general views about health. The PPRI staff and board were white, middle-class, and English-speaking. As a result, PPRI was culturally inaccessible to many potential customers in its neighborhood. To facilitate change so that the agency could remain relevant and accomplish its mission, PPRI hired Miriam Inocencio, a black Cuban American, as president and CEO. Over a six-year period, the board and staff have begun to reflect more closely the diversity of the community. To reach out to the diverse communities and establish collaborations with other community social service organizations, two bilingual and bicultural health educators were hired. When the health educators go out into the community, they communicate in the language that the community speaks, paying respect to its cultures and traditions. As a result, PPRI has been able to develop working relationships with more organizations serving the minority community (Inocencio & Gravon, 2002).

In Florida, the city of Clearwater, the YWCA of Tampa Bay, the U.S. attorney's office, the Regional Community Policing Institute, the Mexican government, and the local community have collaborated to manage diversity in the community and in its public and nonprofit agencies. In the late 1990s, the non-English-speaking Hispanic community in Clearwater grew to about 15 percent of the city's population. There were only five bilingual police officers on its 250-officer force. The city discovered that young Hispanic males seemed to fear the police. They would not cooperate with investigations, and other crime problems were not being reported within the Mexican community. In 1999, the city set up the Hispanic Task Force, made up of representatives from city departments that deal directly with the public. In 2000, a police officer was appointed to the new position of Hispanic outreach officer to act as a liaison among the police department, the community, and the city government. Members of the Hispanic Task Force traveled to Hidalgo, Mexico, to study the cultural differences between the two places. The city held public forums and asked the Hispanic community to tell how the city and its respective departments and the police department could improve their service and communicate with the Hispanic community. A new program was developed, called Joining Hands: Operation Apoyo Hispano. The program consists of ten parts:

Communicators. Fifteen bilingual interpreters were trained by the police department and the YWCA to assist police officers. The communicators are trained in police procedures and taught how to translate verbatim, to take notes in the event that a case goes to court, and to notify the officers if anything was said to put the officers at risk.

Victim advocacy. The YWCA program has two full-time, bilingual victim advocates to help victims of crime by explaining the criminal justice system and even accompanying the crime victim to court.

Mobile outreach program. To overcome the residents' fear of the police and their reluctance to come to the police, the police go to the community. Using a mobile command post vehicle, the police department goes where the Hispanic community gathers, whether it be soccer fields or church. Information about government services and cultural programs are presented.

Officer recruitment. The police department is recruiting bilingual officers. The department offers bilingual incentive pay for new officers.

Television and radio. The program uses Spanish radio and television stations to reach the community. *Blueline CPD* is a local, live interactive television show in which Clearwater officers answer questions called in by viewers.

Community education and crime prevention. The Clearwater Police Department and the YWCA conduct programs in both English and Spanish. Topics include immigration, landlord-tenant issues, employment, child abuse, domestic violence, and education.

English for speakers of other languages. English classes are held to help residents become familiar with English and in the long run make them more employable and eligible for higher-paying positions. GED instruction and job training are also offered.

Basic Spanish for officers. Clearwater police officers and other employees are taught Spanish by the local school board so that they will not have to rely on the YWCA interpreters. Because there are no bilingual employees in the 911 Communications Center, the center uses an AT&T "language line" to connect employees with a bilingual interpreter who translates via a three-way call. Having staff who can speak Spanish is important because under the present system, time is lost in an emergency, and the cost of the service is expensive.

Training. Job skills training are offered at the police facility.

Partnership with the regional community policing institute. As a result of this partnership, a video and printed material to assist other law enforcement agencies have been developed.

In both examples, the demographics of the community, as well as the clients of public and nonprofit agencies, have changed. PPRI and the city of Clearwater recognized the advantages and importance of recruiting and managing diversity within their organizations.

Equal Employment Opportunity and Affirmative Action

Many statutes, executive orders, court decisions, and administrative regulations exist that prohibit employment discrimination due to race, color, sex, national origin, religion, or disability. Employment decisions are to be based on merit and job-related qualifications, not on a person's membership in a demographic classification. Equal employment opportunity requires employers not to discriminate in the administration and execution of all human resources management practices such as recruitment, selection, promotions, training, compensation, career development, discipline, and labor-management relations. An overview of these laws is provided in Chapter Four. In passing the laws, Congress assumed that outlawing deliberate discrimination and punishing employers found guilty of unfair practices would eradicate the vestiges of years of discrimination.

Although the passing of these laws meant that overt discrimination was no longer tolerated, women and minorities were still underrepresented in the workforce. A more assertive strategy was needed to correct for past and present discrimination. That strategy was affirmative action; Executive Order 11246 states, "An affirmative action program is a set of specific and results-oriented procedures to which the contractor commits itself to apply in a good faith effort." The objective of those procedures and efforts is equal employment opportunity.

In 1965, President Lyndon Johnson signed Executive Order 11246, which prohibits discrimination in federal employment on the basis of race, creed, color, or national origin. In 1968, this order was amended by Executive Order 11375, in which the word *creed* was changed to *religion* and sex discrimination was added to the list of prohibited types. The executive order applied to all federal agencies, contractors, and subcontractors, including all of the facilities of the agency holding the contract, regardless of where the work is conducted. Contractors and subcontractors with more than $50,000 in government business and fifty or more employees are not only prohibited from discriminating but must also take affirmative action to ensure that applicants and employees are not treated differently because of their sex, religion, race, color, or national origin. The Rehabilitation Act of 1973 and the Vietnam Era Veterans Readjustment Act of 1974 also require federal contractors or subcontractors to take affirmative action for the employment and advancement of qualified disabled persons and veterans and qualified veterans of the Vietnam era.

Affirmative action has often been interpreted and criticized as requiring the implementation of quotas regardless of individuals' qualifications and ability to perform a job. In reality, affirmative action may refer to several strategies, including active recruitment of groups underrepresented in an organization, eliminating irrelevant employment practices that bar protected groups from employment, and the most controversial one, granting preferential treatment to protected groups. The effectiveness of affirmative action is represented by the extent to which employers make an effort through their SHRM practices to attract, retain, and upgrade members of protected classes as a condition of doing business with the government.

Critics of affirmative action claim that it results in reverse discrimination and that the costs of complying with its guidelines are too expensive. Claims of reverse discrimination suggest that special advantages or preferential treatment given to women and minorities promote unfair treatment against white males and are thus still discriminatory. A second argument against affirmative action is that the costs associated with complying with the regulations are high and that compliance results in lower productivity because of a less qualified workforce. However, there is little evidence to validate these arguments (Pincus, 2003).

Although Executive Order 11246, the Rehabilitation Act of 1973, and the Vietnam Era Veterans Readjustment Act apply only to the recipients of federal funds, many organizations have decided to implement voluntary affirmative action programs to redress previous discriminatory employment practices or to make their workforce more representative of the constituents or clients they serve.

The Difference Between Compliance with Laws and Managing Diversity

Equal employment opportunity and affirmative action are legal requirements designed to bring women and minorities into the workforce. Managing diversity requires more than just compliance with laws. The management of diversity consists of "management processes to create a supportive work environment for employees already on board, and to develop and fully include all of them in order to make the organization more productive" (U.S. Merit Systems Protections Board, 1993, p. xiii).

To manage diversity, employers must first understand and then manage their organizational cultures. The organizational culture is the values, beliefs, assumptions, expectations, attitudes, and norms shared by a majority of the organization's members. James Q. Wilson (1989) believes that "every organization has a culture, that is, a persistent, patterned way of thinking about the central tasks of and human relationships within an organization. Culture is to an organization what personality is to an individual. Like human culture generally, it is passed from one generation to the next. It changes slowly, if at all" (p. 91).

Not only do organizations possess a dominant culture, but subcultures can emerge as well. Subcultures often develop to reflect common problems, situations, or experiences that employees face. Wilson (1989) notes that in the U.S. Navy, different subcultures exist for personnel assigned to submarines, aircraft carriers, or battleships.

Organizational culture is perceived to be valuable when it helps orient new employees to expected job-related behaviors and performance levels. A strong culture can minimize the need for formal rules and regulations because values, traditions and rituals, heroes and heroines, and the informal communication network that provides information and interprets messages sent through the organization serve to reduce ambiguity (Deal & Kennedy, 1982). Employers must be aware that an entrenched organizational culture can be a liability when the shared culture will not react to change or will not change to enhance the organization's effectiveness. In the aftermath of September 11, 2001, the culture of the FBI has come under scrutiny. Intelligence collection and analysis have been undervalued in a culture that has celebrated the myth of the FBI agent "crime fighter." Counterintelligence agents had been deemed second-class citizens compared to those in criminal investigation units. Whether or not the FBI will become more open to ideas and criticism from both within the agency and outside remains to be seen. The culture of the FBI has been to discourage dissent. If the FBI is going to be effective in its new focus on fighting terrorism, the insular culture of the agency must change (Bromwich, 2002; Ragavan, 2003). Other federal agencies whose culture has been criticized are the Secret Service, the Bureau of Alcohol, Tobacco and Firearms (ATF), and the U.S. Customs Service. Black agents from the Secret Service and the ATF and Hispanic agents from the Customs Service are joining forces to file a consolidated discrimination suit against the Department of the Treasury. The plaintiffs say they were subjected to pervasive discrimination in a variety of employment practices, including hiring, training, and performance evaluations, and were blocked from special assignments, promotions, and awards. The combined case lodges a broader charge of systematic discrimination and a "good old boy" network that permeates the Treasury Department (Clemetson, 2002). The case involving the Hispanic customs agents asserts that there has been a pattern of discrimination dating back to the 1970s. The ATF case was settled in 1996 when the agency agreed to overhaul its personnel policies and paid $4.7 million in compensatory damages and back pay to black agents and $1.2 million in lawyer's fees. However, lawyers for the plaintiffs say the agency has yet to make good on the terms of the agreement. If the allegations are found to be accurate, more than seven hundred Secret Service and customs agents would be entitled to $300,000 each in compensatory damages, in addition to back pay and lawyers' fees. The total damages could top $200 million (Clemetson, 2002).

The increase of women, minorities, and persons with disabilities in the workforce is going to continue. The attitudes, beliefs, values, and customs of people in society are an integral part of their culture and affect their behavior on the job. Research has found that men, women, and minorities do not have a common culture or organizational life; rather, each group identifies, defines, and organizes its experience in the organization in unique ways that influence group members' reactions to work assignments, leadership styles, and reward systems (Fine, Johnson, & Ryan,

1990). These differences create the potential for communication problems, which lead to increased organizational conflict.

Management must balance two conflicting goals: getting employees to accept the dominant values and encouraging acceptance of differences. Robbins (1994) calls this the "paradox of diversity" (p. 259). It is important for new employees to accept the organization's culture; otherwise, they are not likely to be accepted. But at the same time, management must acknowledge and demonstrate support for the differences that these employees bring to the workplace. Valuing diversity means recognizing and appreciating that individuals are different, that diversity can be an advantage if it is well managed, and that diversity should be encouraged. Accepting diverse ideas encourages employees to be more creative, which leads to greater flexibility and problem-solving capabilities (Fine et al., 1990; Ospina & O'Sullivan, 2003).

Human Resources Implications for Managing Diversity

Employers must understand that compliance with equal employment opportunity and affirmative action policies does not necessarily mean that incumbent employees will respect or accept new entrants. Employers need to value diversity. Diversity is often addressed in terms of visible differences, such as race, gender, age, or disability. But an employee's sexual orientation, religion, inconspicuous disability, education, work style, lifestyle, and culture are not as readily visible, and various combinations of differences in these less visible differences can exist in one person. Even differences such as parenthood or responsibility for elderly relatives are components of employee diversity, needing accommodation through parental leaves, flexible work schedules, or child care or elder care assistance. Employers and employees must understand that there are many dimensions to diversity.

Training management and employees to welcome diversity is essential but not sufficient for success. Gilbert and Ivancevich (2000) note that even when organizations have implemented policy or training initiatives to focus on diversity, the initiatives often do not translate into changes in the quality of work life for employees. Simply responding to laws, executive orders, or guidelines does not automatically result in greater inclusion. If blatant discrimination does not occur, often more subtle forms of discrimination, such as exclusion from informal work groups, conversations, and social gatherings outside of work, happen. These exclusionary tactics lead to reduced opportunities and isolation for minorities ← and a loss of valuable human capital for the organization.

Cox (2001) suggests that employers conduct cultural and systems audits. The audits should provide comprehensive analyses of the agency's organizational culture and HRM systems such as recruitment, performance appraisals, career patterns, and compensation. The objective of the audits is to uncover whether there are sources of potential bias that may inadvertently put some employees at a disadvantage. If changes are made in the system, they should be monitored and evaluated. Continued training and modifications in rewards and sanctions may need to be institutionalized.

Cox (2001) provides three reasons why diversity efforts often fail. Often the problem is misdiagnosed, often the wrong solution is implemented or the agency failed to use a systematic approach, and often there is a failure to understand the shape of the learning curve for leveraging diversity work. Cox's Change Model on Diversity is presented in Figure 5.1. The model is comprised of leadership, research and measurement, education, the alignment of management systems, and follow-up.

Leadership establishes a direction or goal for change (vision), facilitates the motivations of others, and cultivates necessary conditions for achievement of the vision. For any organization to use managing diversity as an approach to achieve its mission and goals, it needs to start by establishing a clear vision of how a more diverse workforce contributes to the bottom line. Leaders must believe that to integrate a diverse workforce, a company must go beyond what is required by regulation. There must be both a business imperative and a moral obligation. Mission statements can be modified to incorporate diversity related goals (Cox, 2001; Gilbert & Ivancevich, 2000).

Research and measurement are important because successful organizational change work must be informed by relevant data, with results systematically measured at appropriate intervals during the process.

Education imparts new information and skills that can be used to facilitate change.

Figure 5.1. Change Model for Work on Diversity.

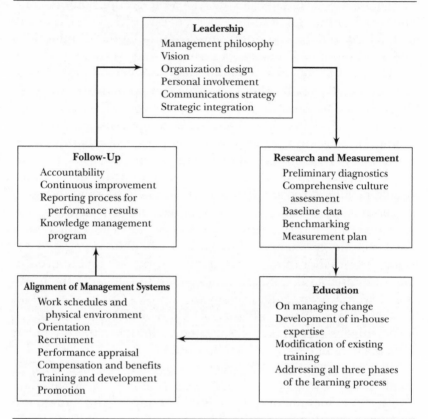

Source: Cox, 2001, p. 19. Copyright © 2001. This material is used by permission of John Wiley & Sons, Inc.

Alignment of management systems broadly includes any organizational policy, practice, rule, or procedure. This covers such major HRM activities as recruitment, promotion, performance appraisals, training and development, compensation, work schedules, employment security, benefits, and the design of the physical environment.

Follow-up involves implementing action, establishing managerial and employee accountability, fundamental changes in HRM practices, employee involvement and buy-in, overreaching corporate philosophy regarding diversity, ongoing monitoring and improvement of diversity climate, and using multiple measures to evaluate success.

In addition to the traditional topics of race, gender, disability, religion, and national origin that are typically included in diversity training programs, sexual harassment and discrimination against gays and lesbians are topics that should also be included. Allegations of sexual harassment and unfair treatment toward homosexuals continue to increase.

Sexual Harassment

If women are going to contribute to an organization's effectiveness, their daily routines must be free from intimidation and the distraction brought about by sexual harassment. Employers have become more sensitive to the growing need for policies and procedures to eliminate sexual harassment in the workplace. Today, most organizations have sexual harassment policies in place and are demanding that managers and supervisors enforce them.

The Supreme Court ruled in *Meritor Savings Bank* v. *Vinson* (477 U.S. 57, 1986) that sexual harassment is a form of sexual discrimination, illegal under Title VII of the Civil Rights Act of 1964. Any workplace conduct that is "sufficiently severe or pervasive to alter the conditions of employment and create an abusive working environment" constitutes illegal sexual harassment. Sexual harassment is illegal because it constitutes discrimination with respect to a person's conditions of employment. The Equal Employment Opportunity Commission (1989, p. 197) has defined sexual harassment as follows:

Unwelcome sexual advances, requests for sexual favors, and other verbal or physical conduct of a sexual nature when (1) submission to such conduct is made either explicitly or implicitly a term or condition of an individual's employment, (2) submission to or rejection of such conduct by an individual is used as the basis for employment decisions affecting such individual, or (3) such conduct has the purpose or effect of unreasonably interfering with an individual's work performance or creating an intimidating, hostile, or offensive working environment.

There are two forms of sexual harassment: *quid pro quo harassment* (*quid pro quo* is a Latin term meaning "this for that," or one thing in return for another) and *hostile environment harassment.* Quid pro quo harassment exists when the employer places sexual demands on the employee as a condition of that person's receiving employment benefits—for example, when a supervisor requires that a subordinate go out on a date as a condition of receiving a promotion or a pay increase. The reverse is also considered quid pro quo harassment. For example, because a subordinate will not date a supervisor, the supervisor retaliates by assigning work of a less desirable nature to the employee or lowers the employee's performance evaluation rating.

Hostile environment sexual harassment does not require the loss of a tangible employment benefit. Instead, the focus is on unwelcome contact that is sufficiently severe or pervasive to alter the conditions of the employee's employment and create an abusive working environment. In *Ellison* v. *Brady* (924 F.2nd 872, 1991), the Ninth Circuit Federal Appeals Court created a "reasonable women" standard that it applied to the issue of whether sexually oriented conduct constituted a hostile or offensive environment. The court believed that it was important to examine the behavior from the perspective of a reasonable woman since "a sex-blind reasonable person standard tends to be male-biased and tends to systematically ignore the experiences of women." Since research demonstrates that women and men differ in their responses to sexually oriented behavior, the court believed that it was inappropriate to use the viewpoint of a man (or men in general) to determine whether a reasonable woman would have found the conduct to be unwelcome, a requirement that the woman must meet in order to prevail. The standard moved from the "reasonable person" perspective to the "reasonable victim" perspective.

In *Harris* v. *Forklift Systems, Inc.* (510 U.S. 17, 1993), the Supreme Court ruled that victims need not show they suffered serious psychological injury as a result of the harassment in order to prevail in court. In this case, the Supreme Court reversed the decision of the U.S. Court of Appeals at Cincinnati, which held that Theresa Harris was not the victim of sexual harassment because she did not prove that she suffered any psychological harm. The Supreme Court said that "Title VII comes into play before the harassing conduct leads to a nervous breakdown. . . . The conduct's effect on the employee's psychological well-being is just one factor that may be considered along with all other circumstances to be considered in determining hostile environment harassment, including the frequency of the discriminatory conduct, its severity, whether it is physically threatening or humiliating or a mere offensive utterance, and whether it unreasonably interferes with an employee's work performance."

In 1998, the Supreme Court heard three cases dealing with sexual harassment. *Oncale* v. *Sundowner Offshore Services, Inc.* (523 U.S. 75), *Faragher* v. *City of Boca Raton* (524 U.S. 75), and *Burlington Industries* v. *Ellerth* (524 U.S. 742). The *Oncale* case addressed sexual harassment involving persons of the same sex. Joseph Oncale worked aboard an oil platform in the Gulf of Mexico. According to Oncale, his male supervisors and coworkers abused and sexually abused him, pushing a bar of soap into his anus and threatening homosexual rape. Although he complained to his employer, the company did not respond, so he quit. The Supreme Court held that "nothing in Title VII necessarily bars a claim of discrimination . . . merely because the plaintiff and the defendants . . . are of the same sex." Title VII of the 1964 Civil Rights Act prohibits sexual harassment between members of the same sex, and the legal standards governing same-sex claims are the same as those applied to claims of sexual harassment by a member of the opposite sex. The court's ruling resolved a conflict among the federal appeals courts, which had disagreed on whether alleged sexual harassment by a person of the same gender could be considered discrimination in violation of Title VII.

The court noted that the inquiry to same-sex harassment, as in all harassment cases, "requires careful consideration of the social context in which particular behavior occurs and is experienced by its target." For example, the court pointed out, a coach's smacking of a professional football player's buttocks as he runs to the field would not be evidence of an abusive environment, even if it would be considered abusive by the coach's male or female secretary in the office. By using "common sense" and "appropriate sensitivity to social context," courts and juries will be able to distinguish between "simple teasing and roughhousing among members of the same sex, and conduct which a reasonable person in the plaintiff's position would find severely hostile or abusive." This decision provides employees previously overlooked protection against sexual harassment under Title VII.

In *Faragher*, the Court held that public employers can be held liable for harassment under Title VII even if the employee has not explicitly alerted the employer about the sexual harassment. Employers may defend against a suit by showing that they took reasonable steps to prevent and correct the harassment and the employee failed to take advantage of the employer's procedures.

Beth Ann Faragher worked for the city of Boca Raton, Florida, as a lifeguard while attending college. During her five-year employment, her immediate supervisors subjected her and other women lifeguards to uninvited touching and lewd remarks and spoke of women using offensive terms. One of Faragher's supervisors told her to "date me or clean toilets for a year." The city of Boca Raton asserted that because the harassment was not reported to management and occurred in a remote location, the city should not be held liable. Boca Raton had drawn up a sexual harassment policy but did not disseminate it throughout city departments. The Court held that this failure to distribute the policy negated an affirmative defense to liability.

In *Burlington Industries* v. *Ellerth*, Kimberly Ellerth's second-level supervisor repeatedly threatened her job unless she succumbed to his advances. She never registered a formal complaint, nor was her job ever jeopardized, but after fifteen months as a salesperson for Burlington Industries, she resigned because of the constant harassment. Burlington Industries argued that it should not be held liable because Ellerth had suffered no job consequence, was promoted, and failed to use the company's sexual harassment complaint procedure. The Supreme Court held that an employer may be held liable in situations where a supervisor causes a hostile work environment, even when the employee suffers no tangible job consequences and the employer was unaware of the offensive conduct.

As a result of these rulings, employers will be held presumptively liable for sexually hostile environments created by supervisors. If an employee is sexually harassed by a supervisor and loses his or her job, is demoted, or is given an undesirable reassignment, the employer will be held legally responsible for the harassment even if company officials did not know about it or had strong anti-harassment policies in place. If the employee is sexually harassed by a supervisor but suffers no tangible job loss, the employer will be held legally responsible for the harassment unless the employer can prove that it used "reasonable care" to prevent harassment through effective policies and complaint procedures; that the employee "unreasonably failed" to make use of the complaint procedures; and that if the employee had complained, the behavior would have been stopped.

Sexual Orientation

No federal laws presently prohibit discrimination on the basis of sexual orientation. Senators Edward M. Kennedy, Joseph E. Lieberman, Arlen Specter, and James Jeffords have sponsored the Employer Non-Discrimination Act (ENDA). The act would prohibit discrimination on the basis of sexual orientation. It defines sexual orientation as "lesbian, gay, bisexual, or heterosexual orientation, real or perceived, as manifested by identity, acts, statements, or association." If the act were to be passed, it would apply to private employers with fifteen or more employees, as well as employment agencies and labor organizations; civilian federal employees, including Congress, the White House, and the Executive Office of the President, would be generally covered. The act would exempt tax-exempt "bona fide private membership" clubs and all religious organizations, including religious educational institutions.

Although no federal protection presently exists, many state and local governments have enacted their own laws that prohibit discrimination against gays and lesbians.

As of January 6, 2003, thirteen states prohibited discrimination on account of sexual orientation. Some states have amended their state human rights acts specifically to prohibit discrimination in employment on the basis of actual or perceived sexual orientation. In other states, governors have issued executive orders. Approximately two hundred counties and municipalities prohibit such discrimination. There are a number of support groups for public employees across the federal, state, and local governments. In California, the Golden State Peace Officers Association has a support group call PRIDE Behind the Badge. Other support groups include FireFLAG/EMS in New York City, GOAL-DC: Gay Officers

Action League, and the Gay Officers Action Leagues of New York and New England. There are groups for state employees such as Pride in Wisconsin Government, StatePride: Gay, Lesbian, Bisexual, Transgendered and Allied Employee of the State of Texas, and State Pride for Connecticut public employees.

Federal employees are protected by the Civil Service Reform Act of 1978. It prohibits job discrimination for any non-job-related issue. In 1980, the Carter administration issued a policy statement specifically including sexual orientation bias. The statute covered executive branch offices and the Government Printing Office but not the General Accounting Office or intelligence agencies.

On August 4, 1995, President Bill Clinton issued Executive Order 12968, which forbade federal agencies from using sexual orientation as a reason for denying security clearances to lesbians and gays. The executive order extended coverage to private citizens working for defense contractors, engineering firms, and high-tech industries involved with the government. This order created the first uniform standard for U.S. agencies in granting security clearances and required federal agencies to recognize one another's security clearances. The Defense, Energy, and State departments, the Office of Personnel Management, the U.S. Information Agency, the Federal Bureau of Investigation, the Secret Service, and the U.S. Customs Service had already stopped using homosexuality as a reason for denying security clearances for civilian workers. In 1998, President Clinton signed an amendment to Executive Order 11478 ensuring that *all* federal agencies banned employment discrimination based on sexual orientation.

A general support group called Federal GLOBE exists for gay, lesbian, or bisexual employees working for the federal government. Other federal departments such as the Federal Aviation Association, the departments of Energy and Labor, and the National Institute of Standards of Technology have their own GLOBE groups for their employees.

Many nonprofit and private employers were at the forefront of prohibiting discrimination against gays and lesbians. They willingly promulgated their own personnel policies that protected the rights of gay and lesbian employees. Not fearing reprisals, many gay, lesbian, and bisexual support groups were first founded in those organizations. In addition to nondiscrimination policies, many nonprofit and private employers initiated the extension of domestic partnership benefits to homosexual couples. A survey taken in 2000 indicates that one out of ten foundations offers domestic partnership benefits to their employees (Billitteri, 2000).

However, there have been changes in the nonprofit landscape. The complex environment in which nonprofit administrators must operate was made even more complicated when the U.S. Supreme Court, in a 5–4 decision, held that the application of New Jersey's public accommodation law to the Boy Scouts of America (BSA) violated the organization's First Amendment right of expressive association (*Boy Scouts of America and Monmouth Council et al.* v. *James Dale,* 530 U.S. 640, 2000). The Boy Scouts argued successfully that as a private organization, it has the right to determine criteria for membership. The Supreme Court heard this case on appeal from the BSA in response to the New Jersey Supreme Court's decision against its position.

The New Jersey Supreme Court held that the Boy Scouts of America is a place of "public accommodation" that "emphasizes open membership" and therefore must follow New Jersey's antidiscrimination law. The court further held that the state's law did not infringe on the group's freedom of expressive association (*Dale* v. *Boy Scouts of America and Monmouth Council Boy Scouts,* A-2427-9573, N.J. Sup.Ct., 1998; A-195/196-97, N.J. Sup.Ct., 1999). The court reasoned that the New Jersey legislature, when it enacted the antidiscrimination law, declared that discrimination is a matter of concern to the government and that infringements on that right may be justified by regulations adopted to serve compelling state interests.

The New Jersey Supreme Court noted the BSA's historic partnership with various public entities and public service organizations. Local BSA units are chartered by public schools, parent-teacher associations, firehouses, local civic associations, and the U.S. Army, Navy, Air Force, and National Guard. The BSA's "learning for life" program has been installed in many public school classrooms throughout the country. Many troops meet in public facilities. The BSA in turn provides essential services through its scouts to the public and quasi-public organizations. This close relationship underscores the BSA's fundamental public character.

Nonprofit administrators must stay current with the changing and sometimes contradictory community norms and legal requirements across a diverse set of local communities and reconcile them with mandates from the national or parent organization. This is especially true for sexual orientation discrimination. When confronted with sexual orientation discrimination, nonprofit managers find themselves in a complex legal environment. No federal legislation has been passed defining a national standard; nonprofit managers therefore face a patchwork of state and local laws, executive orders, and judicial and commission decisions barring such discrimination. The organizations that have withdrawn their support from the Boy Scouts have clearly stated that they cannot fund or support organizations that have policies that conflict with their own antidiscrimination policies. Despite the U.S. Supreme Court's ruling supporting the BSA's exclusionary policy, the stand of the Boy Scouts' National Council to refuse local councils to determine local policy has jeopardized funding and support from their local communities.

The New Jersey Supreme Court's analysis of the public nature of the Boy Scouts is shared by many. The BSA's decision to exclude homosexuals has become controversial. The state of Connecticut has banned contributions to the Boy Scouts of America by state employees through a state-run charity. The state is also considering whether to block the BSA from using public campgrounds or buildings. In addition to Connecticut, local governments and school districts in Chicago, San Diego, and San Francisco told scout troops they can no longer use parks, schools, or other municipal sites. Chase Manhattan Bank and Textron, Inc., have withdrawn hundreds of thousands of dollars in support, and many United Ways have cut off money (Zernike, 2000). The California Supreme Court is considering a proposal that would forbid the sixteen hundred judges in the state to belong to the Boy Scouts because of its refusal to accept gays. California judges are prohibited from joining groups that discriminate on the basis of sexual orientation, but nonprofit youth organizations are exempt. The California Supreme Court took up the proposal to consider changing the rule at the request of the San Francisco and Los Angeles bar associations. Superior court judges in San Francisco announced they would cut all ties to the Boy Scouts except for local branches that disavowed the national policy on gays (Liptak, 2002).

In July 2001, the Boston Minuteman Council approved a bylaw that extends membership to gays who don't reveal their sexual orientation. In May 2003, the Cradle of Liberty Boy Scout Council, which has 87,000 members in Philadelphia and two neighboring counties, voted to expand its nondiscrimination policy to include sexual orientation. Shortly after the decision was publicized, it was withdrawn, having come under fire from the BSA and from religious conservatives. But now there is a movement endorsed by the city's two major newspapers to end the local council's rent-free use of the prime city land for its headquarters (Rimer, 2003). For example, in 2002, Big Brothers Big Sisters of America told its affiliates to give openly gay and lesbian volunteers an equal chance to serve as mentors, while the Girl Scouts of the USA have deferred to the norms of each local community and let each troop decide how to handle this potentially divisive issue.

Another change that may affect how one manages religious diversity is the introduction of "faith-based initiatives." President George W. Bush signed Executive Orders 13198 and 13199 in January 2001, and in December 2002, Executive Orders 13279 and 13280, requiring executive branch agencies to identify and remove internal bureaucratic barriers that have impeded greater participation in federal programs by faith-based organizations. The executive orders permit religious or faith-based organizations to receive federal funds for use in providing social services. Under the executive orders, faith-based organizations have a right to use religious criteria in the selection, termination, and discipline of employees. Faith-based service providers are permitted to require applicants to be a member of a particular denomination in hiring personnel, though they are still prohibited from discriminating on the basis of race, gender, disability, or national origin.

Employer Liability

Employers are generally held liable for the acts of their supervisors and managers, regardless of whether the employer is aware of these people's acts. If an employer knew or should have known about a supervisor's or manager's harassment of a coworker and did nothing to stop it, the employer will be liable. The employer may also be liable for behaviors committed in the workplace by nonemployees, clients, or outside contractors if the employer knew or should have known about the harassment and did not take appropriate action. The courts have made it clear that an organization is liable for sexual harassment when management is aware of the activity yet does not take immediate and appropriate corrective action.

An employer is likely to minimize its sexual harassment liability under the following circumstances: (1) if it has issued a specific policy against sexual harassment; (2) if it established a sexual harassment complaint procedure with multiple avenues for redress (an employee who is harassed by his supervisor must be able to go elsewhere in the organization to file a complaint rather than to his supervisor); (3) if the employer educates supervisors and employees as to the actions and behaviors that constitute sexual harassment and alerts the supervisors and employees that the organization will not tolerate such behavior; (4) if charges of sexual harassment are investigated promptly and thoroughly; and (5) if the employer takes immediate and appropriate corrective action.

The Civil Rights Act of 1991 provides for compensatory damages in addition to back pay for intentional discrimination and unlawful harassment. Private and nonprofit employers may also be liable for punitive damages.

Summary

Changes in society and the workplace have resulted in diversity's becoming an important issue for strategic human resources management. Current personnel systems must be reviewed and interrelated to produce and retain a diverse workforce. The organization's culture must be evaluated. This can be done through the review of formal documents, HRM policies and procedures, rewards systems, recruitment and selection procedures, and succession planning. These components should all be interrelated, and attention should be paid to the provision of flexible benefits and alternative work schedules or flextime as they relate to work and family life.

When diversity is well managed, all workers are valued and included. As a result, productivity is improved because the work environment is supportive and nurturing, and all contributions are appreciated. The successful management of diversity leads to enhanced interpersonal communication among employees, responsiveness to social and demographic changes, a reduction in equal employment litigation, and a climate of fairness and equity. Diverse groups offer a wider range of ideas because different individuals are likely to perceive problems in a different light and thus develop alternative solutions.

Employers who are mistreated tend to be less productive. Energy is spent feeling anxious, angry, frustrated, or fearful instead of concentrating on job-related tasks. Mistreated employees tend to have greater rates of absenteeism and are more likely to seek other employment opportunities.

Organizations also suffer when the work environment is hostile. Higher turnover rates result in increased recruitment and selection expenses, as well as an "us versus them" atmosphere, which manifests as decreased cooperation and teamwork and increased distrust among employees. Organizations that promote diversity will be able to attract and retain the best employees. Workforces that are representative of the constituents they serve will also be more successful in expanding their constituent and customer base and will be poised to capture new markets.

A supportive environment in which employees can contribute and achieve their fullest potential is necessary. All managers and supervisors should be held accountable for making the workplace supportive. Diversity programs will not be successful unless top managers provide leadership and exemplify the commitment to diversity. Agency and department mission statements should acknowledge respect for individuals and appreciation for the contributions each can make; they should state that diversity is accepted and valued and that equal opportunities will be provided for each employee to achieve his or her potential.

Questions and Exercises

1. In small groups, identify and discuss the significant trends related to diversity. What initiatives have been established in your agencies to meet these challenges?
2. Visit the U.S. Census Bureau Web site (http://www.census.gov). Select a state, and identify the demographic trends in that state.

What do the trends indicate? How can employers prepare for the future?

3. Visit the American Association of Retired Persons (AARP) Web site (http://www.aarp.org). What are the most pressing issues facing senior citizens?

4. Visit the 9 to 5 National Association of Working Women Web site (http://www.9to5.org). What issues are of concern to working women?

5. Visit the Department of Justice Pride Web site (http://www.DOJ Pride.org) and the FederalGLOBE Web site (http://www.fed globe.org). What issues are of concern to gay and lesbian federal employees?

Chapter Six

Volunteers in the Public and Nonprofit Sectors

There is a tradition of volunteerism in this country that began with religious-affiliated organizations and local government councils. Today a wide range of nonprofit and public sector organizations provide a variety of volunteer opportunities, ranging from serving as board members of nonprofit organizations to serving on local government boards and commissions. Parents volunteer as coaches of nonprofit and municipality-sponsored sports and recreation activities, and volunteers provide myriad services in public and nonprofit cultural, educational, social service, and health care agencies. Volunteers assist employees in meeting their agency's mission and thus become an important part of strategic human resources management and planning. When one thinks of volunteers and civic participation, nonprofit agencies typically come to mind. However, the public sector has also come to rely on volunteers for an assortment of purposes and in a variety of environments.

While the use of volunteers in the public sector has grown, volunteer participation has become even more pervasive in the nonprofit sector. *The New Nonprofit Almanac* (Weitzman et al., 2002, pp. 18–19) reports that in 1998, about 5.7 million individuals, or 62 percent of all volunteers, worked in the independent sector. The public sector benefited from the services of more than 2.4 million volunteers, or 26 percent of total volunteer employment. The rise in volunteer activities has necessitated the increasing professionalism of volunteer administration. Organizations such as the National Volunteers Center, the National Information Center on Voluntarism, the National Center for Voluntary Action, and the

Minnesota Office on Volunteer Services provide books, pamphlets, training materials, and videos targeting the recruitment and management of volunteers. These agencies also provide training related to the recruitment and use of volunteers. The Association for Volunteer Administration has a certificate program for managers of volunteers (Brudney, 2001).

In both public and nonprofit agencies, attention needs to be paid to the recruitment, selection, training, evaluation, and management of volunteers. Though volunteers can be tremendous assets to any organization, they also present new human resources management challenges. Administrative responsibilities are increased as agencies must keep records and extend their liability insurance and workers' compensation policies to volunteers. Managing volunteer programs requires the development of personnel policies and procedures to assist with the integration of volunteers into the everyday operations of the agency. Paid staff, unions, and board members need to support the use of volunteers, oversight needs to be provided so that volunteers are properly utilized, and strategies need to be developed to motivate and retain volunteers. This chapter addresses these issues. At the end of the chapter, special attention will be given to volunteers who serve on governing boards.

Use of Volunteers

As funding has tightened, government agencies have come to rely on volunteers as a way to deliver services and foster community involvement (National Association of Counties, 2003; Sanecki, 2000; Scott, 2003). Volunteers are an attractive resource for agencies because they cost little, they can give detailed attention to people for whom paid employees do not always have the time, they often provide specialized skills, they provide an expansion of staff in emergencies and peak load periods, they enable agencies to expand levels of service despite budgetary limitations, and they are good for public relations. Public agencies use volunteers to serve on task forces, to oversee and instruct in recreation programs, to staff libraries, to serve as advocates for community causes, and as firefighters, police auxiliary officers, senior citizens center assistants, park maintenance workers, file clerks and office workers, fingerprint takers, hospital and nursing home attendants, teaching assistants in school and correctional facilities, activity assistants for the developmentally and physically disabled, and museum guides. Volunteers also participate in community programs such as public safety, services for the homeless, and AIDS prevention and in programs addressing the health and well-being of children (Brudney, 1999; Lane, 1995; National Association of Counties, 2003; Sanecki, 2000). At least 60 percent of state parks use volunteers, and at least 39 percent of state agencies use volunteers to assist in delivering services (Brudney & Kellough, 2000). In Alaska, volunteer opportunities exist for archaeological assistants, backcountry rangers, museum assistants, park caretakers, and natural history interpreters. In FY 2002, the National Park Service's Volunteers-In-Parks (VIP) program used 125,000 volunteers, who contributed 4.5 million hours of service, equivalent to the work of 2,156 full-time employees. The dollar value of their services, based on $16.05 an hour, was $72,225,000 (National Park Service, 2003). Examples of other federal agencies that use volunteers include the Cooperative Extension Service of the U.S. Department of Agriculture, Head Start Programs, the Department of Health and Human Services' Older Americans Programs, the Department of Veterans Affairs, the U.S. Forest Service, the Bureau of Prisons, the Department of the Interior, the U.S. Geological Survey, and the Bureau of Indian Affairs (Brudney, 1999).

Promising though the use of volunteers may be, agencies must also be aware that there are costs associated with volunteer programs. Ellis (1995, p. 3) notes that "because volunteers are agents of the organizations, their work poses potential risk management questions and insurance needs. Anyone acting on behalf of an organization can put others at risk or can be at risk. Volunteers are not inherently more or less likely to have accidents or make mistakes. However, the board should make sure that the organization has taken all the necessary steps to protect the client, the volunteer and the paid staff." This means that volunteers need to be screened for possessing the appropriate qualifications, and they need to be trained. For example, volunteers who would not be hired as police officers because of antisocial or aberrant personalities should not be selected as police auxiliary volunteers. Individuals who exhibit short tempers or low frustration levels should not work with children, senior citizens, or the disabled in capacities that require patience or in situations that, despite planning, often become unstructured. To minimize the frequency and severity of mistakes, volunteers need to receive general training concerning the agency's mission, policies, and regulations, as well as training that is tailored to the specialized tasks or responsibilities they will perform.

Agencies must anticipate the reactions to paid staff and unions if they plan to use volunteers as replacements for paid employees. If volunteer programs are going to be effective, agencies must work with employees to establish the parameters of volunteer programs. The volunteers with the Massachusetts Commission Against Discrimination were helpful in reducing the workload of the paid staff, but in other situations, such as in Michigan, where layoffs had occurred, volunteers being used to replace paid staff were resented. In most instances, volunteers are used to enhance the effectiveness of paid staff, not to eliminate paid positions or to compensate for deliberately understaffed programs. According to Brudney (1993, p. 130), "The literature leaves no question, however, that volunteer scholars and managers endorse labor's stance that the substitution of nonpaid workers for paid is unethical. No evidence exists that volunteers feel any differently. Hence, if agency administration intend to use volunteers to reallocate funds away from designated positions, they can anticipate resistance not only from employees but also from volunteers."

Volunteer Motivation

Why do individuals volunteer? When surveyed, volunteers expressed a variety of reasons. It appears that both intrinsic and extrinsic rewards motivate volunteers. *Intrinsic rewards* are such things as satisfaction, a sense of accomplishment, and being challenged, which result from the work itself. *Extrinsic rewards* are benefits granted to the volunteers by the organization.

For example, many individuals use volunteering as a means for career exploration and development, as when individuals volunteer at a community nonprofit for developmentally disabled adults, thus experiencing what it is like to work with that population. By volunteering as a reserve police officer, individuals can receive enough exposure to determine whether law enforcement is a suitable career choice for them. Some people volunteer to develop skills that might enhance their paid positions. For example, volunteering to make presentations in front of large groups, write grants, or prepare budgets develop essential skills needed by employers.

Some people volunteer because it provides them with the opportunity to meet new and different people. Some volunteer as a way to contribute or give back to the community in which they live. Some professionals such as nurses and social workers who are taking time off to raise children keep active professionally through volunteer work. Others volunteer as a way to interact with community leaders or because they value the goals of the agency. Still others volunteer because they are concerned about people or desire personal growth or external recognition (Cnaan & Goldberg-Glenn, 1991; Dailey, 1986; Fisher & Cole, 1993; Pearce, 1993).

The Family Nurturing Camp is an example of a partnership between two North Carolina agencies that uses a volunteer staff for a program offered during a complete weekend. The Family Nurturing Camp is funded by the Pamlico Partnership for Children (Smart Start) and coordinated by Neuse Center for Mental Health, Developmental Disabilities, and Substance Abuse Services to provide a weekend experience for parents with young children to develop and enhance their parenting skills. All family members attend. The "campers" range in age from birth through seniors as parents, children, and extended family members are encouraged to attend. The camp strives for a 1-to-2 ratio of volunteers to participants. Given the commitment required and the nature of the interactions with the campers, the key requisite is that the volunteer be a nurturing person. The volunteers typically receive two days of "nurturing facilitator" training and are recruited by word of mouth and through referrals. Volunteers come from a variety of occupations, and diversity in terms of age, gender, race, and ethnicity is emphasized. The coordinators of the camp, Pat Goldstein and Donna Smart, strive to recruit volunteer staff that resemble the diversity of the families attending. One of the volunteers is a Department of Social Services social worker who refers families to the camp. Other volunteers include persons with disabilities, Sunday school teachers, college students, a retired teacher, an employee of the local utility company, and an administrative supervisor at the regional hospital. Volunteers consistently relate that they gain more than they give, and some have used their Nurturing Camp experience to enhance their careers and educational opportunities. At the conclusion of each camp, the volunteer staff complete evaluations that address what they got out of participating at the camp along with recommendation for changes and improvements. The volunteers are recognized at a celebration before leaving camp.

As a result of the recent recession and the many professionals who found themselves out of work, nonprofits are finding that more professional people are donating their skills to charity as a way to stay sharp. Some unemployed software developers are developing Web sites, graphic designers are creating ads for nonprofits, and lawyers are doing pro bono work. According to Pamela Kinney, volunteer manager for Family Eldercare in Austin, Texas, "It seems to be a trend. . . . A lot of people tell me up front that they're out of work and they want to keep their skills up by volunteering in an administrative capacity" (Ball, 2003).

There is no one reason that individuals volunteer. What motivates one volunteer may not motivate others. Therefore, the volunteer experience should attempt to provide both intrinsic and extrinsic rewards by promoting satisfying and interesting opportunities and some form of external recognition.

Recruitment

Volunteers are individuals who donate their time, efforts, and experience to an organization without receiving money or in-kind payment (Brudney, 1990). Consequently, there is a lot of competition among public and nonprofit agencies for these quality people. Unlike paid staff, who typically initiate the employment process themselves, volunteers need to be actively recruited. Communication is the key to finding volunteers. People need to know that the agency is looking for and receptive to volunteers. Word-of-mouth referrals from other volunteers or paid staff, newspaper articles and advertisements, radio and television spots, presentations before community or professional groups, and tapping the relatives and friends of clients have proved to be successful methods for recruiting volunteers.

Recruiting volunteers can be difficult. Brudney (1993) found that there has been an increase in competition among public and nonprofit agencies for volunteer talent. Contributing to the difficulty in recruiting volunteers is the nature of today's society. The United States ranks among the highest on a global scale in the percentage of employees working fifty hours per week or more. Many workers are finding it difficult to balance job and family demands (Jacobs & Gerson, 1998), leaving little time for volunteer work. Many Americans believe that the time pressures on working families are getting worse (National Partnership for Women and Families, 1998). The increased pressure on working adults with families has forced many nonprofits like the Girl Scouts to target new audiences for recruiting volunteers. One poster to recruit Girl Scout troop leaders shows a girl with green hair and fingernails, and another poster shows a girl sporting a tattoo of the Girl Scout trefoil on her back. The message: "Sure we wear green. But a lot else has changed." The posters are designed to attract young single volunteers in their twenties and thirties, not the stay-at-home moms who anchored the volunteer corps since its inception (Wyatt, 2000). As a result of the many economic and demographic changes affecting communities, some Girl Scout councils wanting to provide services in rural and urban communities and unable to recruit volunteers have begun to pay "program specialists." The job of paid specialists is different from being a traditional volunteer. Most paid specialists oversee more than one troop of girls from ages five to seventeen. They must meet the standard Girl Scout leader qualifications and go through the same training as volunteer leaders. They can work up to nineteen hours a week, the starting pay is $10 an hour, and they are paid for mileage but do not receive fringe benefits. Without their paid leaders, many girls would never become Girl Scouts. According to the Suncoast Council's director of outreach services, "The key thing is that the girl can say in 20 years that she had a Girl Scout leader. She is not going to know she was in an outreach group" (Davis, 2001, p. 7B).

Other nonprofits are rethinking the assignments they give to volunteers in terms of time, location, and length of commitment. Many communities have established volunteer banks where volunteers can be assigned to projects that do not require a long-term commitment to the agency or require volunteers to work scheduled hours each week.

Ellis (2002) discusses the possibilities of using the agency's Web site to recruit volunteers. Visitors to an agency's Web site should be able to find out about volunteer opportunities and be given the name, telephone number, or e-mail address of a person to contact about volunteering. Other nonprofits are using online or Internet volunteering as a way to fit volunteering into their busy and sometimes unpredictable schedules. iMentor is a nonprofit that encourages volunteers to exchange e-mails with New York high school students. Volunteers and students exchange e-mail messages several times a week on such topics as career development and college applications. Best Buddies is a Miami nonprofit that matches online volunteers with people with mental retardation. Volunteers make a one-year commitment to exchange e-mail messages at least once a week with their "e-buddies." The e-mail exchanges encourage participants to develop computer skills and help ease some of the social isolation they might be experiencing (Wallace, 2001).

The Prerecruitment Process

Before recruitment begins, it is important to identify what type of volunteer is needed or the specific skills that are required. Some agencies might need volunteers to perform clerical or receptionist duties, which require generic skills, while others may need volunteers capable of coaching an athletic team or writing grant proposals, which require specific skills. Some agencies may need a combination of specialized volunteers and volunteers who can be trained to provide support services to paid staff. Still others can be expected to want volunteers who are qualified to serve by specific education or experience, such as city planning commissions that want to use volunteers to develop and administer zoning laws. Some agencies need volunteers for a finite amount of time to focus on one project or program, while other agencies need volunteer support on a continuing basis, such as for a GED or tutoring program.

During the prerecruitment process, it is also important to note whether certain days of the week or set hours are required or whether volunteers may select the days and hours that are most convenient for them. This is important because more women are entering the paid labor force, leaving fewer volunteers available to work traditional daytime hours. Individuals who hold full-time jobs may be reluctant to volunteer on an ongoing basis. Agencies may need to identify or develop projects that do not require long-term commitments. Many local communities and United Way agencies sponsor "paint your heart out" days or "Christmas in July" events that allow a team of volunteers to paint houses or nonprofit buildings, perform landscaping, build fences, patch roofs, and perform other tasks. These projects typically last one day or are completed in one weekend. If one-day programs are not possible, agencies should try to create positions where the volunteer does not have to be in the office for long periods or can work independently at home, like the Internet volunteer programs discussed earlier.

For programs that require consistent hours and long-term commitments, agencies may target retired citizens or students, both of whom are likely to be more flexible than working adults.

The agency must be able to communicate what a volunteer position requires, both verbally and with written job descriptions. Each volunteer position should have a description that outlines the job's duties and responsibilities, as well as the knowledge, skills, abilities, and other characteristics (KSAOCs) required to perform it. For example, a volunteer bus or van driver might need a chauffeur's license or be required to take a driving test. Volunteers wanting to work with children will be subject to a background investigation. Work hours should also be included in the description. Prospective volunteers need to be told whether the working hours for a position are flexible or will require a commitment to meet a specific number of hours per week or specific days. In this way, they can understand what is expected of them before they make a firm commitment (Alexander, 1991; Anderson & Baroody, 1992).

Volunteers should be asked to complete applications identifying their interests, special skills, and preferred working days and hours. This information enables the organization to match the interests and skills of the volunteers with the positions available. For example, someone who volunteers for the opportunity of social interaction would be unhappy working in isolation. Exhibit 6.1 presents the application form used by a local government, and Exhibit 6.2 gives the descriptions of volunteer citizen boards and commissions in that community. Notice the variety of skills the different

Exhibit 6.1. Application for
Appointment to a Citizen Board or Commission.

1. Name in full _____

2. Address _____
           (Number)   (Street)   (Ward)

3. Phone _____ (Home) _____ (Business)

4. Occupation _____ How long? _____

5. Business address _____
               (Number)   (Street)   (City)

6. How many years have you lived in this city? _____

7. Are you a registered voter in this city? _____ (Yes) _____ (No)

8. Have you ever served on a city board or commission? If so, state the name of the board or commission _____
(Years) _____

9. Comment on your professional background, specialties, training, or abilities.

10. List civic, social, and professional organizations to which you belong.

11. Are you interested in appointment to any particular board or commission? If so, indicate which.

                         (Signature) _____

                         (Date) _____

Please return to the City Clerk.

Exhibit 6.2. Descriptions of Volunteer Boards and Commissions.

Park Commission

The Park Commission is an advisory body whose duties are to survey and plan for an adequate system of parks and recreational facilities, to approve Park Department rules and regulations, and to advise and investigate problems in administration of the parks. There are nine members on the commission, all of whom must have been residents for two years prior to appointment. The Park Commission meets at 7:30 P.M. on the fourth Tuesday of the month (except in December). The term of office is three years.

Board of Appeals

The Board of Appeals (Board of Building Code Appeals) has jurisdiction to hear and decide appeals when it is alleged that there is an error in any order, requirement, or decision made by the building commissioner. The board has five citizen members and meets on call. At least three of the members must have ten years of experience as a licensed architect, builder, superintendent of building construction, or licensed professional engineer with structural, civil, or architectural engineering experience. The term of office is five years.

City Planning Commission

The City Planning Commission is responsible for preparing and submitting to the council a master plan for the physical development of the city and for recommending changes to the plan in the city's interest. The commission also acts as the zoning commission and recommends such changes or amendments as may seem desirable. The commission has seven members, each of whom must have lived in the city for at least two years and be qualified by knowledge and experience to act on questions pertaining to the development of the city and the administration of the zoning laws. The term of office is three years. Ex officio, nonvoting members include a member of the city council, the city manager, the director of planning, and the zoning administrator. The commission meets on the fourth Wednesday of the month at 7:30 P.M.

Civil Service Board

The Civil Service Board advises the council and director of personnel on problems concerning personnel administration, hears appeals for disciplinary action, makes investigations that it considers necessary into the administration of personnel in the municipal service, and approves civil services rules. The board consists of five members, each of whom must have resided in the city for at least two years prior to his or her appointment. The term of office is three years. Members of political party committees are not eligible to serve. The board meets quarterly, with additional meetings called by the chair, if necessary.

boards and commissions are seeking. Included are the term lengths and how often meetings are held.

The key for motivating and retaining volunteers is finding the best employee-position match. Research by Dailey (1986) found that job satisfaction plays a critical role in understanding the commitment to volunteer. Because volunteers often fill higher-order needs through their volunteer activities, it is necessary to design volunteer tasks to be enriched. Dailey found that work autonomy, job involvement, and feedback from the work itself were strong predictors of organizational commitment. Research by Jamison (2003) found that volunteer turnover is reduced when volunteers receive preservice and in-service training and are assigned challenging tasks.

An organization that wants to make itself more attractive to potential volunteers might consider reimbursing clients for out-of-pocket expenses such as meals and transportation, providing flexibility in scheduling volunteer hours, increasing position responsibilities, and working with private sector agencies that encourage employee volunteerism. To be competitive in attracting volunteers, agencies must be creative. For example, for certain positions in Alaska's state park system, volunteers are provided with housing and an expense allotment (Brudney, 1990, 2001; Mergenbagen, 1991; Watts & Edwards, 1983).

Managing Volunteers

In organizations that use volunteers, there are two or even three hierarchies: volunteers, paid staff, and professionals (Anderson & Baroody, 1992; Fisher & Cole, 1993; Selby, 1978). Volunteers must understand their roles relative to the paid and professional staff. Farr (1983, p. 18) states, "There are two aspects of the staffing issue—who will oversee and coordinate the volunteer effort and how other staff will be involved in working with volunteers." The effectiveness of volunteers will depend on how they are integrated into the organization.

Fisher and Cole (1993) recommend that volunteer programs and positions be developed that directly relate to the organization's mission, and the organization's mission should reflect a commitment to volunteers. Those authors provide the following example of a program mission statement (p. 28):

The agency's volunteer program promotes quality involvement in the delivery of agency services to families based on the following beliefs:

1. Volunteers bring unique contributions to the delivery of services to families; areas such as prevention, education, and support are best served by their involvement.
2. Volunteers allow the agency to expand its resources and reach more families than it could with paid staff alone.
3. Volunteers bring a useful community perspective to program planning, implementation, and evaluation.
4. Volunteers are strong representatives of the agency throughout the community.

Employee relationships with volunteers are critical. Often there is tension between employees and volunteers. To eliminate this tension, the plans for volunteer staffing should be developed in two distinct phases. First, the organization should examine the tasks that might best be performed by volunteer staff in light of the organization's mission, structure, and personnel policies. Second, specific volunteer positions and position guides need to be developed. This step should involve the participation of board members, union leaders, paid staff, direct service volunteers, and clients. It serves to encourage broad support for the volunteer program, as well as to ensure that the creation of volunteer jobs balances the needs of clients, paid staff, and volunteers (Fisher & Cole, 1993).

Questions to be considered in the development of volunteer positions and position guides include the following (Fisher & Cole, 1993, pp. 30–31):

What are the characteristics, strengths, and needs of the target population?

What qualifications will volunteers need in order to serve this population effectively through the program?

What are the preferences of the target population regarding service delivery by paid staff or volunteers?

How do the possible volunteer positions relate to the overall mission of the agency?

Ellis (1995) recommends that boards should play key roles in supporting volunteer programs. She suggests that they should expect reports on volunteer involvement, that they should schedule time to discuss volunteers, that board members should refer volunteer candidates to the agency and carry recruitment materials to distribute, and that they should take part in volunteer recognition events. Ellis also advises agencies to remember that board members themselves are volunteers despite their legal and fiduciary responsibilities, and attempts should be made to occasionally link board members and direct-service volunteers.

As important as it is for board members to understand the benefits of volunteers, it is more important for paid staff to support volunteer programs. Employees must not feel that volunteers are clients who need attention. Volunteers and staff must be trained to work with each other. Volunteers need to know their scope of authority and when to retreat from interfering with employees or clients.

Organizations that have volunteer programs must also decide whether they need to add a position such as a volunteer coordinator to administer the volunteer program or if existing employees can assume the responsibilities. According to Farr (1983, p. 18), major program management responsibilities include the following:

Obtaining and maintaining support for the volunteer program

Developing, monitoring, and evaluating the volunteer program budget

Keeping key officials informed about the scope of volunteer services

Establishing and monitoring program goals

Assigning volunteer responsibilities and monitoring results

Recommending policy changes or action steps to top management to maintain, improve, or expand the volunteer effort

A variety of administrative tasks need to be taken care of as well. Someone needs to recruit volunteers, provide training and orientation, keep records of their attendance and any expenses for which they might need to be reimbursed, secure liability insurance for volunteers or verify that they are covered, work with departments to establish the need for volunteers and develop job descriptions, work with agency supervisors to integrate volunteers into their departments or programs, decide how incentives and rewards will be used to motivate volunteers, and keep the volunteers informed about issues that will affect them (Farr, 1983; Fisher & Cole, 1993). Pearce (1993) notes that organizations have less control over the time of volunteers than employees; thus there needs to be a large pool of volunteers to accommodate different preferences, talents, and time constraints (Montjoy & Brudney, 1991). For these reasons, more and more organizations that rely on volunteer assistance for executing their missions are hiring volunteer coordinators to assume the management and administrative responsibilities.

Orientation and Training

Volunteers should be made familiar with the agency's mission, history, accomplishments, financial goals, and strategic plans (Alexander, 1991), as well as what the agency expects from them. It has been suggested that an agency's mission statement be translated into operational objectives, making it easy for volunteers to see how their contributions reinforce the mission (Muson, 1989). Understanding what the agency is about should increase commitment to its programs.

Volunteers need to be trained. Often employees expect them to be clairvoyant and know what to do, how to do it, or what the standard operating procedures are. This is a mistake; volunteers do not necessarily have the same expertise or experience that employees have. On-the-job training time should be devoted to providing instructions, answering questions, and allowing volunteers to witness and absorb how the agency operates. This experience will reduce their insecurity about performing new tasks. Volunteers working for social service or public organizations may need to receive training in appropriate laws or policies, such as client confidentiality, what to do in case of an emergency, or how to handle citizens' questions or complaints.

Alexander (1991) found that the organizations with the most formalized training and orientation programs had the least turnover. These programs not only teach volunteers necessary skills but also clarify expectations and integrate volunteers socially into the organization. Orientation and training programs reinforce agency expectations.

Volunteer Recognition

Volunteers and the paid staff who supervise them should be recognized for their efforts. Recognition impresses on volunteers and the paid staff that their contributions are appreciated by the organization. Research by Cnaan and Goldberg-Glenn (1991) indicates that volunteers not only give to the organization but also get back some type of reward or satisfaction from volunteering. As discussed earlier, some of these rewards and satisfactions are intrinsic, an inherent part of doing the job—such as the satisfaction of task accomplishment, self-development and learning opportunities, self-fulfillment, opportunities for social interaction, and the opportunity to help other people. Other rewards and satisfaction are extrinsic, external to the work. Extrinsic rewards are reinforcers that are controlled by the agency—tokens of recognition that compliment volunteers for jobs performed well, including letters of appreciation, awards, and pictures or articles about the volunteers published in the local newspaper or the agency newsletter. Praise from supervisors and the paid staff, the opportunity to train other volunteers, and expanding the volunteer's area of responsibility are some intangible rewards that agencies often bestow on volunteers. Because individuals volunteer for different reasons, organizations must be prepared to recognize volunteers in a variety of ways.

Evaluation

Performance evaluations inform volunteers about whether they are meeting the supervisor's and agency's expectations. The evaluation must be job-related. Volunteers should be assessed on the tasks they perform as well as their contributions to the agency. Supervisors and volunteers need to understand each other's expectations and establish specific goals and objectives to use as evaluation standards. A schedule should be developed so that the performance evaluation takes place at regular intervals.

The primary purposes of evaluation should be to provide feedback and to develop volunteers. Sometimes, however, a volunteer does not meet the agency's expectations. Should this occur, McCurley (1993) recommends that the following steps be taken:

1. *Resupervise.* You may have volunteers who do not understand the policies of the organization, or they may be testing the rules to see what can be expected.
2. *Reassign.* Move volunteers to different positions. The volunteer coordinator may have misread the volunteer's skills, or the volunteer may not be getting along with paid staff or fellow volunteers.
3. *Retrain.* Send the volunteers back for a second training program. Some people take longer to learn new techniques. Do not let the lack of knowledge lead you to believe that new volunteers are not motivated.
4. *Revitalize.* Longtime volunteers may need a rest. They may not be aware that they are burned out.
5. *Refer.* Refer volunteers to other agencies more appropriate to their needs.
6. *Retire.* Allow longtime volunteers the dignity to resign.

If these steps do not work, you will have to terminate the volunteer. It is important to have policies in place to ensure consistent termination procedures. Supervisors should be trained in these steps and familiar with the documentation that may be required before terminating a volunteer.

Governing Boards

Governing boards in the public and nonprofit sectors bear the ultimate accountability for organizational activity and accomplishment; they make policy and provide oversight (Carver, 1990). The duties and authority of public governing boards are regulated by ordinances or statutes, while nonprofit governing boards are regulated by the organization's bylaws. Public boards, whether they are elected or appointed, are typically more bound by legal requirements than nonprofit boards are. Public governing boards are also subject to a greater variety of statutes (Carver, 1990).

Public sector governing boards deal primarily with particular aspects of policymaking, such as planning, personnel or civil service, parks and recreation, zoning and building, and probation and corrections (Baker, 1994). What differentiates most public sector governing boards from those in the nonprofit sector is that they typically serve in only an advisory capacity; final approvals or decisions are the responsibility of the legislative body. Governmental board members may be appointed by elected officials or may be elected directly by citizens. The provisions that govern local government boards and commissions are typically found in the community's ordinances or are required by state statute. Members of both types of boards, however, play important policymaking roles and serve as volunteers.

In nonprofit organizations, directors or trustees typically develop policies relating to the organizations' management. It is the responsibility of the directors to make sure that the public purpose of the nonprofit organization is carried out. Ingram (1988) identifies the basic responsibilities of nonprofit boards:

- Determining the organization's mission and purposes and setting policies for its operation
- Selecting the executive director and evaluate executive performance
- Ensuring effective organizational planning by engaging in long-range planning to establish its future course
- Ensuring adequate resources by establishing financial policy and boundaries and seeing that resources are managed effectively
- Determining and monitoring the organization's programs and services
- Enhancing the organization's public image by promoting the work of the organization
- Serving as a court of appeals for employees with grievances
- Assessing its own performance in relation to its responsibilities

The oversight responsibilities of nonprofit governing boards have come under closer scrutiny following the well-publicized controversies of prominent nonprofit organizations such as the American Red Cross and the United Way of the National Capital Area (UWNCA). The American Red Cross came under fire for its misleading fundraising practices after the September 11, 2001, terrorist attacks. Many donors believed that their contributions would be used to help people affected by the attacks, but the Red Cross initially was planning to use some of the money to deal with future disasters. Attention became focused on the UWNCA for extending a twelve-month consulting contract to the outgoing executive vice president for $6,000 a month. He was also to be provided with up to $5,000 in monthly expenses. The contract was approved by a board committee, but some trustees said they were unaware of it and thought it was too generous. Allegations also arose that the chief executive used United Way funds to pay for trips that were not related to agency business. The board also approved $85,000 to make restrooms accessible to disabled people but instead spent the money on refurbishing executive offices (Lipman, 2002).

Houle (1989, p. 6) defines a governing board as "an organized group of people with the authority collectively to control and foster an institution that is usually administered by a qualified executive and staff." Board members are volunteers, and like other volunteers, they join boards for a variety of reasons. Research on the motivations of citizens who serve on public sector boards indicates that they expect to receive certain benefits, and there are a number of selective incentives. Baker (1994) identifies five types of incentives: material, solidarity, purposive, developmental, and service (see also Clark & Wilson, 1961; Widmer, 1985). *Material incentives* are tangible rewards such as the opportunity to advance politically or the opportunity to make professional contacts. *Solidarity incentives* are intangible rewards such as socializing, a sense of group membership, status, and a sense of involvement. *Purposive incentives* are also intangible and relate to the satisfaction or gratification of working toward the stated goals of the organization. *Developmental incentives* are intangible rewards such as the ability to assume civic responsibility or using one's capabilities. Finally, *service incentives* include fulfilling or reducing a sense of civic responsibility; they are focused on relieving or fulfilling one's sense of obligation. Different board members are motivated by different incentives. Personal enrichment, substantive interest, social and business contacts, and feelings of accomplishment are just some of the reasons why individuals become board members.

But what should an organization look for in board members? Characteristics identified by O'Connell (1988) and Houle (1989) include distributions in age, sex, location of residence, representatives of the constituency work being served by the organization, political contacts, clientele, expertise, and training in personnel, finance, law, fundraising, and public relations. Each board member should have KSAOCs that enhance the policymaking and oversight responsibilities of the board as a whole.

To select new board members, the existing board or nominating committee should identify the characteristics needed in new board members. The KSAOCs should relate to the organization's mission and objectives. To determine what KSAOCs are needed, the incumbent board members should be evaluated (Houle, 1989). Table 6.1 presents a grid identifying the match among the relevant criteria and the incumbent board members. Notice that space is provided to add prospective board members to the grid. The grid identifies five criteria for determining the composition of the board:

1. There should be a greater spread in the ages of the members of the board.
2. The board should be representative of the whole community.
3. The board should be evenly divided between men and women.
4. Major ethnic groups should be represented in roughly the same proportion as is found in the population served.
5. Board members should have expertise or substantive knowledge about the programs provided by the agency or skills in personnel, finance, public relations, law, and building maintenance or acquisition.

This particular board has ten members serving three-year terms. Look at the grid and decide if this is a well-balanced board of directors.

After reviewing the KSAOCs needed by new board members, the names of possible new members should be identified. These names might be retrieved from a list of people previously considered as board members, professional people whose names are given to the agency by a board bank sponsored by the United Way or Junior League, other volunteers, and individuals providing professional services to the agency. People associated with the agency, such as clients, employees, or present board members, often recommend prospective board members.

Nonprofits need to be vigilant about recruiting board members committed to serving the organization's best interest. For example,

	Present Board Members										Potential Board Members				
Criteria	A	B	C	D	E	F	G	H	I	J	V	W	X	Y	Z
Age															
Under 35	X														
From 35 to 50		X			X		X								
From 51 to 65				X		X		X		X					
Over 65			X						X						
Gender															
Women	X	X		X	X	X		X	X						
Men			X				X			X					
Residence															
Central city	X	X	X					X		X					
North side		X				X		X							
West side					X				X						
South side															
Suburbs				X			X								
Background															
Black	X								X						
White		X	X	X		X		X		X					
Hispanic					X										
Asian															
Responsibilities															
Program	X	X		X		X		X		X					
Personnel	X		X												
Finance		X					X	X	X	X					
Public relations						X		X	X						
Legal							X	X							
Building						X									

Source: Houle, 1989, p. 40. Copyright © 1989. This material is used by permission of John Wiley & Sons, Inc.

for many years before John Ott became the executive director of the Atlanta Historical Society, the board functioned more as a social group than as a policymaking body. Since Ott became executive director, the board's focus has changed. One board member stated, "Now it's much more serious. We discuss puzzlements and long-range planning" (Knauft, Berger, & Gray, 1991, p. 10).

Agencies need to seek members who have special skills they can bring to the board. For example, Seattle Emergency Housing made a point of recruiting a former budget analyst at the United Way to review its financial statements, as well as a city employee with expertise and knowledge about public funding (Knauft et al., 1991). The Spring of Tampa Bay, Inc., provides programs and services to victims of domestic violence. Its board of directors has individuals from the fields of law enforcement, medicine, law (judges and attorneys), accounting, public relations, human resources management, finance, financial planning, and business administration.

The expertise and competency of board members needed by a nonprofit often change over time. For example, the Tampa Theatre is a movie palace that was built in 1926. After it began to deteriorate in the 1970s, a nonprofit group, the Tampa Theatre, Inc., was established to preserve and revitalize the theater. In 1978, the theater was added to the National Register of Historic Places. At first, since the mission of the nonprofit emphasized restoration and preservation, most of the board members were individuals with real estate, architecture, finance, and construction expertise. Now the emphasis is on programming and community outreach, so board members with different skills are being sought.

Bylaws or statutes usually specify the procedures that should be followed to formally nominate candidates, as well as the selection procedures. Refer to the relevant policies and procedures for your organization.

After new board members have been selected, they should be provided with an orientation outlining their responsibilities as board members. They should also be informed regarding the organization's mission, objectives, and administrative and management structures. Morrison (1994, p. 43) recommends that the following information be provided to board members:

Constitution and bylaws

Mission or purpose statement

Goals and current plans, both strategic and long-range

Annual report

Budget and financial report

Program description along with goals and objectives

Organization chart (staff names and numbers)

Committees and their goals and plans, such as fundraising expectations and commitments and public relations strategies

Personnel policies and expectations

Board list with names, addresses, and phone numbers

Meeting information and attendance and time requirements

Minutes from meetings for the previous fiscal year

Any appropriate procedures governing the conduct of meetings

Any evaluations conducted during the past year

Training and orientation are important for all board members regardless of their professional expertise and experience. Bowen (1994) acknowledges that when people from the for-profit sector join a nonprofit board, they often lack an appropriate frame of reference as to the nature of the missions served by nonprofits. Bowen cites the following example: "A businessman on the board of directors for a church kept pushing for 'double-digit' growth no matter what the implications were for the church's capacity to fulfill its mission" (p. 41). Herzlinger (1994) notes that board members may be perplexed about their appropriate roles. Because some board members are intimidated about the talent and professional expertise of the organization's employees, they abandon their oversight role. "How can I tell a symphony orchestra how to play Beethoven? How can I tell a doctor how to operate?" (p. 53). Other board members become overly involved in the organization's work. They feel free to give unsolicited and unwanted counsel on orchestra programs, museum exhibitions, educational curricula, or social service intervention strategies. Some board members pour themselves into fundraising, while others use their appointment for status seeking and social climbing. According to Herzlinger, the role of a board's director is to ensure that the organization's mission is appropriate to its charitable orientation and that it accomplishes its mission efficiently.

Board members must be prepared to assume responsibility for guiding the agency. Bowen (1994) notes that often hard-nosed businesspeople become permissive when serving on a board of directors. He provides an example of the board at a private school with severe financial difficulties that approved a request for new equipment the school could not afford because the board could not say no to such dedicated teachers (p. 39). In another case, a board of directors felt guilty about the low salary given to the director of a small arts organization, so it granted her permission to take the summer off (p. 39).

Board members, like other volunteers, should be evaluated on their performance and the contributions they make to the agency. Board members who miss meetings or who are unprepared when they do attend should be held accountable. The fiduciary and oversight responsibilities of governing boards necessitate individuals who are committed to the agency for the length of their terms. Organizations cannot afford to retain board members who dismiss their responsibilities.

Summary

Volunteers have become an integral part of public and nonprofit organizations. Despite the belief of some people that volunteers take paid positions away from employees, volunteers typically perform tasks that otherwise would not get done or would have to be handled by already overextended employees.

The guidance and support provided to volunteers and incumbent staff are essential to the successful integration of volunteers into the agency, to their performance, and to the achievement of agency goals. To minimize any conflicts, staff-development programs should be provided that communicate the differences in authority and responsibilities between paid staff and volunteers.

Agencies should develop volunteer recruitment strategies to reach individuals whose interests and skills are likely to match the needs of the organization. To facilitate good staffing decisions, key staff should be involved in the development of job descriptions for the volunteers they will supervise or work beside. Volunteers should receive training on how to perform their tasks and on the performance standards of the agency.

Agencies alone should not benefit from the use of volunteers. The volunteer experience should provide individuals with opportunities for personal and professional growth.

Questions and Exercises

1. What are some of the organizational benefits associated with having volunteer programs?
2. What are some of the organizational disadvantages associated with having volunteer programs?
3. In small groups, discuss the types of volunteer programs offered by your organizations.
4. Visit the city of Virginia Beach's Web site on volunteer opportunities (http://www.vbgov.com/dept/vcc). What types of volunteer positions are available?
5. Visit the Girl Scouts of the USA Web site (http://www.girl scouts.org). What types of volunteers are needed?
6. Visit the Minnesota Council of Nonprofits Web site (http://www.mncn.org). What resources are available for volunteer programs?

Part Two

Methods and Functions of Human Resources Management

Strategic human resources management (SHRM) depends on the successful integration and execution of human resources management (HRM) methods and functions. The chapters in this part of the book explain the importance of job analysis, recruitment and selection, performance evaluation, compensation, benefits, training and career development, and collective bargaining.

Chapter Seven discusses the importance of job analysis. A job analysis is a systematic process of collecting data for determining the knowledge, skills, abilities, and other characteristics (KSAOCs) required to successfully perform a job and to make judgments about the nature of a specific job. Information collected through a job analysis is applied to most HRM activities, such as recruitment and selection, development of compensation systems, human resources planning, career development and training, performance evaluation, risk management, and job design. The nature of work—how tasks, behaviors, and responsibilities are assigned to different jobs and how different jobs relate to one another—are explained.

Recruitment and selection are discussed in Chapter Eight. SHRM depends on the successful recruitment and selection of qualified individuals. Recruitment is the process of attracting qualified candidates to apply for vacant positions within an organization. Selection is the final stage of the recruitment process, when decisions are made as to who will fill those positions. In public and nonprofit organizations, the recruitment and selection of competent employees are critical responsibilities because people are central to delivering the programs and services that constitute these organizations' reason for existence.

Selection techniques used to hire applicants must comply with federal laws and guidelines and be job-related; that is, they must not unfairly screen out protected group members for reasons unrelated to the job.

The importance of performance management is addressed in Chapter Nine. Performance evaluations provide management with essential information for making strategic decisions on employee advancement, retention, or separation. Evaluation links training and development with career planning and an agency's long-term human resource needs. Used to support job analysis and recruitment efforts, performance evaluations are an important component for forecasting the KSAOCs available within the organization.

Chapter Ten explains the development and maintenance of compensation systems. Compensation is the largest expense that public and nonprofit organizations face. Some 60 to 80 percent of the operating budget goes to employees' salaries and benefits. The design, implementation, and maintenance of compensation are therefore important parts of SHRM. Decisions about salaries, incentives, benefits, and quality-of-life issues are important in attracting, retaining, and motivating employees. Strategic decisions about pay levels, pay structures, job evaluation, and incentive pay systems influence the ability of an organization to compete in the marketplace, to attract the most qualified and most competent applications, and to retain its most talented and productive employees. Compensation systems are influenced by federal laws and by external, internal, and employee equity considerations.

Benefits are part of the compensation system and are commonly referred to as indirect compensation. Benefits are an important part of the compensation package. An attractive benefit package can assist in the recruitment and retention of qualified employees. Chapter Eleven discusses some of the more traditional benefits offered by employers, such as health insurance, retirement pensions, and paid time away from work, in addition to less traditional benefits such as child and elder care, flexible scheduling, and educational assistance. Changing demographics, family needs, and employee priorities require a greater range of employer-provided benefits than what was offered in the past.

The demands placed on organizations keep changing, and technology has eliminated many of the mentally and physically repetitive tasks once performed by employees. Positions today require employees to possess greater skills as they assume more challenging responsibilities. Jobs have become less specialized, forcing employees to work in teams to deliver services. New equipment and technology, the enactment of new laws and regulations, fluctuations in the economy, and the actions of competitors are just some of the variables that influence change. As organizations keep changing, they must implement training and development programs to ensure that their staff have the necessary KSAOCs to confront these new challenges. Chapter Twelve discusses training and career development. Developing a comprehensive, long-range training program requires an SHRM plan and a recognition that employees are a most valuable resource. Training and development must become integrated into the core HRM functions.

Labor-management relations is an important component of SHRM. To remain competitive, management and unions have had to rethink their adversarial relationship and work together to creatively resolve problems and develop solutions that benefit both labor and management. Chapter Thirteen explains the legal framework governing collective bargaining in the public and nonprofit sectors and provides some examples of the different types of benefits unions have negotiated for their members consistent with the workforce and workplace changes. Mental health and substance abuse benefits, child care benefits, incentive awards, employee individual development plans, and flexible work schedules are just some examples of nontraditional benefits that have been negotiated.

| Job Analysis

For organizations to remain competitive, they must accurately identify and forecast their human resources needs. Organizations must assess past trends, evaluate their present situation, and project what human resources will be needed to meet the requirements of their strategic plans. Before informed decisions can be made about recruitment and development needs, compensation plans, training and career development objectives, performance management systems, and job design, data must first be collected and analyzed. The technique used to acquire the data needed to make informed decisions is called job analysis.

A job analysis is a systematic process of collecting data for determining the knowledge, skills, abilities, and other characteristics (KSAOCs) required to successfully perform a job and to make judgments about the nature of a specific job. A job analysis identifies a job's activities, behaviors, tasks, and performance standards; the context in which the job is performed; and the personal requirements necessary to perform the job, such as personality, interests, physical characteristics, aptitudes, and job-related knowledge and skills. Each position is also analyzed in terms of its relationship to other positions in the organization.

Chapter Two emphasized the need for human resources management (HRM) departments to assist their organizations in improving organizational effectiveness. Strategic job analyses are integral to SHRM planning. Strategic job analyses recognize that most jobs will not remain stable but will change to meet future demands.

Job analyses provide the foundation for most HRM activities. Following is a brief introduction to each area of activity:

Recruitment and selection. Job analysis identifies the knowledge, skills, abilities, and other characteristics required for each position. It identifies the minimum education, certification, or licensing requirements. A job analysis also identifies the tasks and responsibilities that are essential functions of the job. This information distinguishes the skills that will be needed by the people the agency recruits and hires. A job analysis is critical when an organization uses preemployment examinations for selection and promotion. Tests must be job-related; the knowledge, skills, abilities, personality variables, and constructs to be tested need to be identified through an up-to-date job analysis. An organization does not know what knowledge, skills, and abilities to test for unless it knows what competencies are required for successful performance.

Developing compensation systems. Compensation is typically related to a job's requirements, such as education, the skills and experience needed to perform the job, and whether or not the employee is working in hazardous circumstances. A job analysis provides a standardized procedure for systematically determining pay and other benefits across the organization. It provides all employees with a basis for gaining a common understanding of the values of each job, of its relationship to other jobs, and of the requirements necessary to perform it.

Human resources planning, career development, and training. Job analysis information can help employers design training and career development programs by identifying what skills are required for different jobs. Identifying the knowledge, skill, and responsibility requirements of each job makes it possible to train and develop employees for promotional opportunities. Available information helps all employees understand promotion and transfer requirements and recognize career opportunities.

Performance evaluation. Performance standards should be derived from what employees actually do on the job. A job analysis identifies the tasks and responsibilities that employees perform in the course of their jobs. Areas of accountability can be identified, and evaluation standards can be developed.

Risk management. A job analysis can be used to identify job hazards such as exposure to flammable materials or complicated machinery. Employers should use this information to develop training programs to alert employees to possible dangers.

Job design. Jobs are arranged around a set of work activities that enable the organization to carry out its mission. External and internal changes, however, often force organizations to rearrange or restructure work activities. The traditional tasks associated with a particular job may change over time; a job analysis is necessary to identify and accommodate these changes.

This chapter discusses the legal significance of job analysis, the types of information obtained through a job analysis, the factors to consider when designing a job analysis program, and some of the advantages of strategic job analysis and generic job descriptions. The chapter concludes with a look at some of the job analysis techniques commonly used in the public and nonprofit sectors.

Legal Significance of Job Analysis Data

To demonstrate the validity and job-relatedness of an employment test, the Uniform Guidelines on Employee Selection Procedures (1978) require that a job analysis be conducted. The test's content, criterion, and construct validation strategies must be based on a thorough and up-to-date job analysis. Employers must show that the requirements established for selecting workers are related to the job. When used as the basis for personnel decisions such as promotions or pay increases, performance evaluations are also considered to be examinations and fall under the same rigorous scrutiny as employment tests. Furthermore, the Americans with Disabilities Act (ADA) defines a qualified applicant as one who can perform the essential functions of the job. Essential functions are the primary job duties intrinsic to the position; they do not include marginal or peripheral tasks that are not critical to the performance of the primary job functions. It is important that positions be analyzed to identify these functions. The applicant must then satisfy the prerequisites for the position and be able to perform the essential functions of the job with or without reasonable accommodation.

The most common reasons for conducting a job analysis are to gather information so that a job description can be written, so that job specifications can be identified, and so that the job can be placed within a job family classification. A job description is a summary of the most important features of a job. It states the nature of the work involved and provides information about tasks, responsibilities, and context. Information typically found in job descriptions includes job title, job family, job summary, task statements, reporting relationships, and job context indicators.

The ADA does not require employers to develop written job descriptions. However, a written job description that is prepared before advertising or interviewing applicants for the job should be reviewed to make sure that it accurately reflects the actual functions of the job. The Equal Employment Opportunity Commission and the Civil Rights Division of the Department of Justice recommend that job descriptions focus on the results or outcomes of a job function, not solely on the way it is customarily performed. This is because a person with a disability may be able to accomplish a job function, either with or without a reasonable accommodation, in a manner that is different from the way an employee who is not disabled may accomplish the same function.

Job specifications contain information about the KSAOCs of the position. Whereas each job description is specific to a particular job, job specifications may be more general. They contain the minimum qualifications that a person should possess in order to perform the job. A job family is a collection of jobs that require common skills, occupational qualifications, technology, licensing, and working conditions.

Job Analysis Information and Methods

As noted earlier, job analysis is used as the basis for many HRM activities. However, different types of job analysis information, instruments, and procedures lend themselves more easily to different purposes. The first steps in conducting a job analysis are to define the purpose behind the analysis and then to determine what information is required.

Job Analysis Information

Different types of information are collected during a job analysis, and a variety of methods can be used. The information most commonly collected are data on job activities, educational requirements, types of equipment or tools, working conditions, supervisory or management responsibilities, interpersonal or communication skills, agency contacts, external contacts, and the KSAOCs. *Knowl-*

edge is the information required for the position. It can be factual, procedural, or conceptual and is related to the performance of tasks, such as a general knowledge of accounting principles or of fund accounting as used in nonprofit organizations. *Skills* are the specific observable competencies required to perform the particular tasks of the position, such as the ability to input data accurately at one hundred characters per minute or to diagnose and repair personal computers. *Abilities* are the applicant's aptitudes for performing particular tasks—what the applicant is able to do and how well—such as the ability to prepare and make presentations or to read city maps. *Other characteristics* include attitudes, personality factors, or physical or mental traits needed to perform the job.

Methods of Collecting Job Data

Job analysis information can be obtained through a variety of methods. Data collection depends on the nature of the positions, the number of incumbents in and supervisors of the positions being analyzed, the geographical dispersion of jobs, and the time available, as well as the type of information needed and the purpose of the analysis. The job analyst and the agency supervisors must work together to determine what will be the most effective method for collecting information. The job analyst can be an employee from the HRM department, an employee working for a consulting firm hired to perform job analysis studies, or—in a small organization—a support staff employee such as the administrative assistant to the city administrator or executive director of a nonprofit agency. The next few paragraphs describe the most common methods used for data collection; specific job analysis techniques are discussed later in the chapter.

Interview. The analyst interviews the incumbent performing the job, the immediate supervisor, another subject matter expert (SME), or a combination of all three, about the essential functions of the position.

Questionnaire. SMEs are asked to complete an open-ended questionnaire. The job incumbent is usually asked to complete the questionnaire first and then the supervisor is asked to review it to add anything that may have been neglected or to clarify statements made by the incumbent. Exhibit 7.1 provides an example of a job analysis questionnaire.

Exhibit 7.1. Job Analysis Questionnaire.

Name: _____ Date Completed: _____

Job Title: _____

1. Please specify the percentage of your total time spent in performing each task.

   Work that is performed daily:

Essential Activities	Tasks	Percentage of Time

2. Indicate by "X" the organizational level of people in the agency and in other organizations with whom you come in contact. Also indicate the primary means by which you contact these individuals.

   Within Agency (Employees of Agency)

   a. _____ Contact mainly within own department or office

   b. _____ Regular contact with other departments or offices furnishing and obtaining information

   c. _____ Regular contact with other departments or offices, requiring tact and the development of utmost cooperation

   d. _____ Regular contacts with major executives on matters requiring explanations and discussions

   Means of Contact

   _____ Personal conversation _____ Telephone _____ Letter

   _____ Other (specify) _____

   Outside Agency (Nonemployees)

   e. _____ Regular contact with persons outside the organization, involving effort that necessitates a great deal of tact and diplomacy

   f. _____ Regular contact with others by presenting data that may influence important decisions

Exhibit 7.1. Job Analysis Questionnaire, Cont'd.

g. _____ Regular contact with persons of high rank, requiring
tact and judgment to deal with and influence these people

Means of Contact

_____ Personal conversation _____ Telephone _____ Letter

_____ Other (specify) _____

3. What types of errors are possible on your job, and what would be
the consequences of such errors in terms of additional expense to
the organization, rework, or loss of goodwill?

Structured checklist. This is another form of questionnaire. The
SMEs are asked to respond to information presented on the checklist. The SMEs check the responses most appropriate for their positions. Exhibit 7.2 presents an example of a structured checklist.

Observation. In this method, the analyst actually observes the incumbent performing the job and records what he or she sees. This
method works primarily for jobs in which activities or behaviors are
readily observable. This method would not work well for intellectual or cognitive processes.

Diary or log. In this procedure, employees are asked to keep
track of and record their daily activities and the time spent on
each.

Combination of all methods. Depending on the purpose of the job
analysis and the targeted job, it may be necessary to use a combination of all of the methods introduced here. Not all jobs lend
themselves to observation. Many public and nonprofit incumbents
sit behind desks, use personal computers, and talk on the telephone. An analyst can observe those behaviors but will not understand the cognitive processes that accompany them or the requisite
educational requirements and knowledge that may be specific to
each position.

Exhibit 7.2.   Structured Task Checklist.

For each question, three responses are required:

A. Indicate the *frequency* with which this function is performed in this position.

B. Indicate the *importance* of this function to the position.

C. Indicate whether *knowledge* of this function is essential for a newly hired employee in this position.

A	B	C
Frequency	Importance	Knowledge
0 = Never	0 = Not applicable	0 = Not required for job
1 = Rarely	1 = Not important	1 = Essential for newly
2 = Sometimes	2 = Somewhat important	hired employee
3 = Often	3 = Important	2 = Not essential at hire,
4 = Very often	4 = Very important	can be learned on
		the job

Typing

1. Type or keyboard letters from handwritten rough drafts
   A _____   B _____   C _____

2. Type or keyboard letters to students, faculty, staff, applicants, or outside individuals or companies A _____   B _____   C _____

3. Type or keyboard inventory reports or budget reports
   A _____   B _____   C _____

4. Type or keyboard monthly status reports A _____   B _____   C _____

5. Type or keyboard general office forms (such as purchase requisitions, work orders, travel vouchers, or printing requisitions)
   A _____   B _____   C _____

6. Type or keyboard course materials, transparencies, syllabi, or tests for faculty A _____   B _____   C _____

7. Compose various letters and memos without written or verbal instructions A _____   B _____   C _____

8. Compose letters and memos from a simple written outline of verbal instructions A _____   B _____   C _____

9. Proofread for spelling, grammar, and punctuation in correspondence and reports A _____   B _____   C _____

Exhibit 7.2. Structured Task Checklist, Cont'd.

10. Type or keyboard or edit manuscripts or drafts for supervisor
    A _____   B _____   C _____

11. Prepare manuscripts for publication, including correction
    of errors and consultation on other editing matters
    A _____   B _____   C _____

12. Lay out format and spacing for tables, charts, or other illustrations
    in preparation for typing A _____   B _____   C _____

Many organizations have a variety of positions, from very skilled to nonskilled. For example, a local government may have city planners, experts in computer applications, budgeting and finance personnel, clerk-typist positions, and groundskeeper and laborer positions. The analyst may use different methods of data collection for different positions. For example, the groundskeeper and laborer positions may not require reading and writing skills. To ask incumbents who may lack those skills to complete an open-ended written questionnaire may not provide the analyst with the information he or she is seeking. Instead, interviews and observation might be more appropriate data collection techniques. The city planner, however, might be asked to complete a questionnaire, followed by an interview to clarify any jargon or statements that the analyst does not understand. A follow-up interview also allows the incumbent to add information that he or she may have omitted when completing the questionnaire.

In large organizations composed of many incumbents in the same position or in state or federal organizations with geographically dispersed locations, the analyst may first want to meet with a small number of incumbents and supervisors and ask them questions or have them fill out an unstructured questionnaire. The analyst may then develop a structured questionnaire based on the information provided and distribute it to all of the incumbents who hold that position and then analyze the data for common work activities and responsibilities.

Designing a Job Analysis Program

Why are you collecting job information? For what purpose will the data be used? The answer to these questions is important because different purposes require different information. For example, if the job analysis is to serve as the basis for determining compensation, the analyst would need to obtain information about educational requirements and level of experience and training. However, if the analysis is to serve as the basis for developing performance appraisal instruments, the job analyst will need to identify levels of task proficiency.

Another consideration is that employees may be sensitive to some of the purposes behind the job analysis. For example, employees are more likely to be more concerned about a job analysis when it will be used to develop a compensation system than when the information will be used to develop training and orientation material for new hires. Employees are thus likely to emphasize different information depending on the purpose of the analysis.

The analyst should work with representatives of the organization to determine the most effective method and procedures for collecting information. It is important for the analyst to understand how the organization operates and when would be the best time to obtain information from incumbents and supervisors because not all jobs or tasks require the same intensity at the same times or for forty hours a week. Different tasks are likely to be performed on different days or at different times of the month or year. Also, some jobs have busy cycles during which the incumbents cannot be interrupted to visit with an analyst or to take the time to complete an extensive questionnaire.

The following factors should be taken into consideration when deciding on the most effective way to collect information:

Location and number of incumbents. Will a particular method or procedure enhance or restrict data collection because of a job's location? Will it be hazardous or too costly for an analyst to observe the job being performed? In the public sector, many jobs are geographically dispersed throughout the city, state, or country. It might be too expensive and time-consuming for an analyst to visit and interview, for example, all of the child-protective investigators across a state. Asking the investigators to complete a questionnaire would be more feasible.

Work conditions and environment. Would work need to shut down during interviews because of a dangerous working environment? Would the incumbent or analyst be at risk if work were disrupted? Are there distractions in the work environment such as noise, heat, hazardous materials, or risk management requirements that would impair the data collection?

Knowledge, technology, and personal factors. Do the knowledge, technology, or personal characteristics of the incumbents lend themselves to a particular method or procedure? As stated earlier, not all jobs or aspects of jobs are conducive to observation. A teacher's classroom performance can be observed. But what about the preparation? What would an analyst see? Can the thought processes be observed or the knowledge required to prepare a lesson? Other factors to consider are whether the job consists of routine or unpredictable tasks and whether the complexity of the job favors a particular method. Will the SME prefer a particular method? Are there peer or organizational factors that may influence whether a procedure may be effective? For example, will a group interview inhibit employees from speaking up because they are intimidated by the presence of others? If supervisors and incumbents are asked to collaborate, will the supervisor dominate the conversation with the analyst?

After considering the factors just presented, the jobs to be studied need to be identified and the types of instruments that will be used to obtain relevant data and information need to be chosen. Management should notify the incumbents and supervisors in advance that a job analysis will be undertaken and explain to them the purpose or purposes behind the endeavor. The quality of the data collected depends on assistance from SMEs.

Strategic Job Analysis

Advances in information technology have changed many public and nonprofit organizations. Positions are being redefined to mesh more congruently with new missions and services. Organizations have become less hierarchical as many managerial responsibilities have been transferred to employees and work teams. Positions have become more flexible in the attempt to capitalize on improved information management capabilities and the changing characteristics of employees. Today many employees are expected to plan and organize their own work. One result of these changes is that employees are now expected to perform a variety of complex tasks that go beyond formal job descriptions. Positions today are more flexible and contingent on changing organizational and job conditions.

Traditional job analysis tends to focus on the KSAOCs required for performance of a position as it currently exists or as it has existed in the past. However, if agencies want to prepare for future changes, they must integrate into the job analysis strategic issues that may affect jobs in the future. To adopt a future-oriented approach to job analysis, agencies should convene a panel of SMEs to discuss the types of issues that are likely to challenge specific positions and the organization as a whole in the future. Recommended SMEs include job incumbents, managers, supervisors, strategic planners, human resources staff, and experts in a technical field related to the job to be analyzed. After potential future issues have been identified, tasks and KSAOCs need to be revised in anticipation of changes. Implementation of this strategic job analysis process can assist HRM practitioners by anticipating and forecasting future organizational needs.

Sanchez and Levine (1999) use the term *work analysis* rather than *job analysis*. They believe that the analysis of *work* should serve to propel the change process, whereas the word *job* serves to define and make rigid job boundaries. They note that the circumstances and situations that once influenced traditional job analysis are changing. For example, at one time, many jobs were defined by a division of labor. Tasks were routine and broken down into distinct elements. Today most public and nonprofit employees are professionals, and tasks have been replaced by cross-functional responsibilities. Changing responsibilities require employee flexibility. Employees are more involved in planning and controlling their own work. For organizations adapting to change, job descriptions are likely to be short-lived, and there needs to be a system of continuous work analysis. The shift to teamwork and self-managed groups requires that greater emphasis be placed on interactive activities. Organizational citizenship behaviors and contextual performance have become more important as employees interact with a greater variety of people. Managing the emotional aspects of work, such as displaying sensitivity to culturally different individuals, is important. Emotional stability and other personality attributes have received little attention in conventional job analysis when compared with cognitive and technical aspects of the job. However, interpersonal, team, and customer-oriented attributes can be decisive in many of today's work assignments and should in such cases be acknowledged.

Not only may organizations want to review the way they analyze work, but they may also want to focus on the level of general characteristics important for success in the organization's culture and in dealing with change. For example, the focus could be on general categories important for success, such as adaptability, self-motivation, and trainability, in addition to job context and specific technical skills. The job description could be on a broader set of KSAOCs instead of on specific tasks or behaviors.

Job Analysis Techniques

A variety of job analysis approaches have been developed over the years. These approaches gather information on job content and worker characteristics that are common to jobs across a wide spectrum. They might describe how the incumbent does the job, the behaviors that are required to perform the job, or the activities that are performed. Let's look at some of the common approaches used.

Position Analysis Questionnaire (PAQ)

The PAQ was developed by researchers at Purdue University. It is a structured job analysis questionnaire consisting of 187 worker-oriented job activities and work situation variables divided into the following six categories:

1. *Information input.* Where and how does the worker get the information that is used in performing the job?
2. *Mental processes.* What reasoning, decision-making, planning, and information-processing activities are involved in performing the job?

3. *Work output.* What physical activities does the worker perform, and what tools or devices are used?
4. *Relationships with other people.* What relationships are required in performing the job?
5. *Job context.* In what physical and social contexts is the work performed?
6. *Other job characteristics.* What activities, conditions, or characteristics other than those already described are relevant to the job?

The PAQ items are rated using different scales, including importance, amount of time required, extent of use, possibility of occurrence, applicability, and difficulty. The PAQ is scored by computer, and a profile for the job is compared with standard profiles of known job families, enabling the comparison of one job to another. The quantitative nature of the PAQ enables it to be used for evaluating job worth and for identifying applicable exams for screening applicants.

Department of Labor Procedure (DOL) and Functional Job Analysis (FJA)

The DOL and FJA are comprehensive approaches that concentrate on the interactions among what an employee does with respect to data, people, and things (see Table 7.1). In addition, the FJA considers the goals of the organization, what workers do to achieve those goals in their jobs, level and orientation of what workers do, performance standards, and training content.

Comprehensive Occupation Data Analysis Program (CODAP)

The CODAP is a task inventory developed for Air Force specialties by the Air Training Command of the United States Air Force. Detailed task statements are written to describe the work. Each statement consists of an action, an object of the action, and essential modifiers. Job incumbents are asked to indicate the relative amount of time they spend on each task. Responses are then clustered by computer analysis into occupational groupings so that jobs having similar tasks and the same relative time-spent values are listed together.

Table 7.1. Department of Labor Worker Functions.

Data	People	Things
0 Synthesizing	0 Mentoring	0 Setting up
1 Coordinating	1 Negotiating	1 Precision working
2 Analyzing	2 Instructing	2 Operating, controlling
3 Compiling	3 Supervising	3 Driving, operating
4 Computing	4 Diverting	4 Manipulating
5 Copying	5 Persuading	5 Tending
6 Comparing	6 Speaking, signaling	6 Feeding, offbearing
	7 Serving	7 Handling
	8 Taking instruction and helping	

Job Element Method (JEM)

The JEM was developed by Ernest Primoff of the Office of Personnel Management in Washington, D.C. The purpose of the JEM is to identify the behaviors and accompanying achievements that are significant for job success. A combination of behavior and achievements is referred to as an element. Elements may include job behaviors, intellectual behaviors, motor behaviors, and work habits.

A panel of SMEs identifies tasks significant to the job. Next the panel identifies the KSAOCs necessary to perform the job. At this stage, the job tasks are turned into job elements. For example, the task described as "writes computer programs to perform statistical analyses, interprets the data, and writes reports" is transformed into the element "ability to write computer programs to perform statistical analyses, interpret data, and write reports."

The SMEs then rate the elements on four dimensions or factors (Primoff, 1975, p. 3):

1. *Barely acceptable.* What relative portion of even barely acceptable workers are good at the element?
2. *Superior.* How important is the element in picking out the superior worker?

3. *Troublesome.* How much trouble is likely if the element is ignored when choosing among applicants?
4. *Practical.* Is the element practical? To what extent can we fill our job openings if we demand it?

The ratings on these four factors are analyzed to identify the elements that have the greatest potential for selecting superior applicants. The premise behind the JEM is that the same elements may traverse different tasks and different jobs. The JEM is used by the federal government to establish selection standards and to validate selection examinations.

The Occupational Information Network (O*NET)

O*NET is a database compiled by the U.S. Department of Labor to provide basic occupational data. The O*NET framework is organized around six sets of descriptors: worker requirements, experience requirements, worker characteristics, occupational requirements, occupation-specific requirements, and occupation characteristics. The information is available online and can be used to develop job descriptions, job specifications, and career opportunity information. It can be accessed at http://www.onetcenter.org/rd/index.html.

For a comprehensive compilation of different types of job analysis techniques and job analysis studies across a variety of occupations, refer to the two-volume *Job Analysis Handbook for Business, Industry, and Government,* by Sidney Gael (1988).

Summary

Forecasting human resources needs is a critical component of SHRM. Organizations must assess past trends, evaluate their present situation, and project their human resources needs. Before decisions can be made on recruitment and selection or training and development objectives, organizations need to audit the skills and positions of their incumbent employees. This audit will provide information on the inventory of KSAOCs and positions available within the agency and will call attention to any KSAOCs or positions that may be missing. Jobs change, and the KSAOCs required to perform them also change. To remain competitive, agencies must keep abreast of changing skill and position requirements.

Not only is a job analysis required for the planning and development of recruitment and selection strategies and for planning training and development programs, but it also provides the foundation for other HRM functions. A job analysis is essential for the development of compensation systems, for identifying job-related competencies that can objectively evaluate employees' performance, for restructuring work activities, and for assessing risks in the workplace. An up-to-date job analysis is required to validate the job-relatedness of other human resources functions.

Questions and Exercises

1. Discuss the various methods by which a job analysis can be completed. Compare and contrast these methods, noting the pros or cons of each.
2. Discuss why the American with Disabilities Act (ADA) has heightened the importance of job analysis activities.
3. Explain how you would conduct a job analysis for an agency that had never conducted one and that did not have job descriptions.
4. Do you agree with the reasons Sanchez and Levine (1999) use the term *work analysis* instead of *job analysis*? Explain your thinking.
5. Why are strategic job analyses important for organizations that want to be competitive in the next ten or twenty years?
6. Visit the O*NET Web site (http://online.onetcenter.org). Conduct a skills search for your position. Are the skills identified by O*NET similar to the skills you possess?
7. Identify five job titles and their job descriptions in your agency. Visit the Dictionary of Occupational Titles Web site (http://www.theodora.com/dot_index.html). Are the job descriptions for the positions you identified consistent with the position descriptions in your agency?

| Recruitment and Selection

The need to adapt to rapidly changing situations requires agencies to recruit and select qualified individuals. Strategic human resources management (SHRM) provides agencies with the opportunity to use recruitment and selection to influence the operational strategy of public and nonprofit organizations. Recruitment is the process of attracting qualified candidates to apply for vacant positions within an organization. Selection is the final stage of the recruitment process, when decisions are made as to who will be selected for the vacant positions. Both recruitment and selection require effective planning to determine the human resources needs of the organization. The organization must determine its immediate objectives and future direction, and it must forecast its employment needs so that those needs are aligned with the organization's strategies.

To fill positions, agencies have a variety of options. They can recruit new employees, promote or transfer incumbent employees who possess the skills necessary for the vacant positions, or provide training or educational support to lower-level or paraprofessional employees in anticipation of future needs.

The recruitment and selection of qualified and competent employees is critical for public and nonprofit agencies because mission-driven agencies are dependent on their staff. It is people who deliver the programs and services that public and nonprofit stakeholders expect; therefore, planning for and selecting qualified and competent employees must be done with a strategic purpose.

Vacancies arise when employees are promoted or transferred to different positions within the agency or when people retire or leave to seek employment elsewhere. Some departments or agencies may expand into new service or program areas, requiring additional staff. Recruitment is an ongoing process in most organizations; however, often it is not planned and is therefore less successful than it could be. For recruitment to be successful, planning is essential. Recruitment efforts must be consistent with the agency's mission. Employers must understand how to determine the job requirements—where to seek and how to screen applicants so that qualified and competent individuals are selected.

This chapter discusses internal and external recruitment, applicant screening, selection methods, preemployment testing under the Americans with Disabilities Act (ADA), and executive and managerial recruitment and selection. An explanation of employment-test-related psychometric concepts is also provided.

Recruitment

As noted in Chapter Two, recruitment must be tied to the organization's mission, and attempts should be made to anticipate the agency's future personnel needs. An SHRM plan should exist that will facilitate the agency's ability to accomplish its objectives. This may mean hiring individuals who possess KSAOCs that are different from those of incumbent employees. This makes it possible for an agency to implement a wide range of strategies within a short time frame in response to external demands.

Before recruitment for candidates begins, the human resources management (HRM) recruiter and the unit manager should review the qualifications needed for the vacant position or positions. This review enables them to identify the knowledge, skills, abilities, and other characteristics (KSAOCs) they will be looking for in the applicants, and it will guide them in developing an accurate job bulletin or advertisement.

Internal Recruitment
Public sector agencies often look at current staff first to fill vacancies in the workforce. In fact, many public agencies give extra credit or points to employees already working for the organization; the city of Saint Louis, Missouri, for example, gives additional

points to candidates who are already part of the workforce. In some cases, there may be collective bargaining agreements in place that stipulate that incumbent employees should receive preferential consideration. Preference for incumbent employees may also exist in many nonprofit agencies in which program stability and connections to the community and funding sources are important. In these cases, employers would first consider the internal labor market.

For internal recruitment to work, agencies need to be proactive and incorporate strategic planning into their human resources practices. Organizations need to track the KSAOCs needed for the various jobs within the organization. Employees who possess those needed skills, whether they be administrative, managerial, or technological, should be identified. HRM departments and department managers should work together and make workforce projections based on the present level of employee skills. They should review transfers, retirements, promotions, and termination patterns. They should do succession planning, whereby individuals are identified who might fill positions when an incumbent leaves. This requires keeping track of and updating the records of each employee's KSAOCs and the demands required of each position.

Internal recruitment is favored by many organizations because administrators have the opportunity to review and evaluate the KSAOCs of internal applicants prior to selection. It also enables agencies to recoup the investment they have made in recruiting, selecting, training, and developing their current employees. Promoting qualified incumbent employees rewards them for their past performance and signals to other employees that the agency is committed to their development and advancement.

Before organizations limit recruitment efforts to internal recruitment, however, other factors should be considered. Some positions in public and nonprofit organizations require specialized skills that may not be found within the agency, and for such positions, it may be necessary to recruit and hire from outside. Organizations with homogeneous workforces—that is, agencies composed of all women, all men, or all Caucasians, for example—should also consider outside recruitment to increase the demographic diversity of their staff. Another important reason for the organization to consider external recruitment is to change the existing internal culture.

Applicants hired from outside are not hampered by "sacred cows," relationships with colleagues, or the agency's history.

External Recruitment

External recruitment is the seeking of qualified applicants from outside the organization. Typically, the agency would seek qualified applicants from the *relevant labor market*. A relevant labor market is defined by the skills required for the position and the geographical location where those skills can be found. The nature of specific occupations or jobs often demarcates the labor market. Local labor markets, for example, are small areas, cities, or metropolitan statistical areas. Laborer, office and clerical, technical, and direct service provider positions are often filled from the local labor market. It is common for federal, state, and local governments and nonprofits to recruit clerical and trade employees, such as maintenance or custodial personnel, from the local labor market. Applicants for these positions are typically abundant, and the salaries that accompany the positions preclude relocating new employees.

Regional labor markets are larger. They usually comprise a particular county or even several areas of a state. Depending on the skill supply in the region, technical, managerial, and professional workers, as well as scientists and engineers, may be recruited from a regional labor market. Agencies in New England, for example, can use the regional labor market to recruit applicants for all kinds of positions because of the number and variety of colleges, universities, and industries located there.

State, local, and nonprofit agencies use the national labor market when critical skills are in short supply locally. Scientists, engineers, managers, professionals, and executives are most likely to be sought at the national level. The federal government, for example, recruits nationally through regional offices for all of its professional positions.

Public and nonprofit organizations need to develop a recruitment strategy. Decisions need to be made about when and where to look for qualified applicants, and action needs to be taken. In some organizations, vacancies are posted but there is no recruitment plan, which is necessary in a competitive job environment. Agencies need to anticipate their future needs and actively and creatively promote the opportunities available in their organizations. Techniques such as internships, co-ops, and on-the-job training should be integrated into the recruitment and selection process (Ban & Riccucci, 1993; U.S. Merit Systems Protection Board, 2003b).

Recruitment planning and strategies at the federal and state levels are typically directed by central personnel offices and for large local governments by centralized civil service offices. It would be remiss to generalize any more than that because many changes are currently taking place at all levels of government in regard to recruitment and selection. For example, the Office of Personnel Management (OPM) has delegated responsibility for recruiting and examining new employees to the agencies. Giving agency managers more direct control of federal hiring was meant to eliminate red tape and delays. States such as Wisconsin and South Carolina have also made changes in the way applicants are recruited and selected.

Despite the well-deserved criticism of centralized personnel offices, they have begun to change with the times. Technology has made information more accessible to job seekers. The federal government has developed personal-computer-based kiosks that provide job seekers with current job information at the touch of a finger. Job seekers can access USAJobs, which is an automated employment information system in which all federal jobs are announced via telephone, fax, personal computer, and touch screen kiosks. This system includes vacancy announcements and application forms and is available around the clock. Federal agencies can access USACareers, an automated package that they can use to help employees affected by downsizing to determine training needs, plot career paths, and find new jobs.

Recruiting for Local Governments and Nonprofits

Recruitment efforts for local governments and nonprofit organizations should begin with a review of the competencies and skill levels of the positions that need to be filled. After these elements have been identified, the government or agency needs to develop a recruitment plan and target the local, regional, or national labor market. Clerical, trade, and technical positions can typically be filled by the local or regional labor market. Executive, scientific, and medical positions such as executive directors of nonprofits, directors of development, city managers, police chiefs, and directors of large departments such as personnel, community development, public health, and finance may be recruited nationally. Some national recruitment sources used by the public and nonprofit sectors are general professional journals and newsletters such as the *PA Times,* the *International City/County Management Association Newsletter,* the *Public Personnel Management Newsletter, Community Jobs,* the *Nonprofit Times,* and the *Chronicle of Philanthropy.* There are also a variety of newsletters or job services targeted directly at special occupations. For example, positions in the arts and entertainment are targeted by such publications as the *National Arts Placement Affirmative Action Arts Newsletter, National Arts Placement, Entertainment Employment Journal,* and *Community Arts News.* An organization looking for social workers could advertise in *Social Service Jobs,* the National Association of Social Workers' newsletter *NASW News,* or *Professional Opportunities Bulletin Finder.* The Foundation Center has an e-mail listserv called *Job Corner Alert* (http://fdcenter.org/pnd/jobs) that posts jobs in nonprofit organizations, and for individuals looking for social justice positions, there is *idealist.org: Action Without Borders* (http://www.idealist.org).

Local governments and nonprofits have also begun to use online recruiting methods. Today most local governments post positions and applications on their Web sites, and more and more nonprofits are doing so as well. Santa Barbara County, California, not only recruits applicants online but also tests them online. County departments developed customized supplemental questionnaires that automatically score applications as they are submitted and immediately notifies applicants if they fail to meet the standards for a job (Duer, 2002). The city of Medford, Oregon, also uses Web-based employment applications. Each job posted to the site requires an applicant to submit an application, an affirmative action questionnaire, and a questionnaire asking where the applicant heard about the job. Applicants may also be required to submit answers to a supplemental questionnaire if the position requires it. The information is submitted through a security-protected process that allows for the transmittal of private information such as Social Security number, driver's license number, and home and e-mail addresses. The applicant with an e-mail address also receives an automatic response from the recipient computer that the application has been received and has been automatically forwarded to the city's human resources staff. Online recruiting has expanded the number of qualified individuals who find out about position openings in the city of Medford (Detling, 2002).

When advertising is part of the recruitment process, it should be written in a manner that will attract responses from qualified individuals and deter responses from those who are not qualified. It is important for the advertisement to focus on the job qualifications that are required for the position so that only candidates with qualifications matching the requirements of the position are attracted to apply. To comply with the ADA, employers should inform applicants on an application form or a job advertisement that the hiring process includes specific selection procedures (for example, a written test; demonstration of job skills such as typing, making a presentation, or editing a report; or an interview). Applicants should be asked to inform the employer within a reasonable time period prior to the administration of the selection procedure of any reasonable accommodation needed to take a preemployment examination, accommodate an interview, or demonstrate a job skill. Employers may request from the applicant documentation verifying the need for an accommodation.

To ensure compliance with equal opportunity requirements, it is important for agencies to scrutinize their recruitment procedures for practices that may result in discrimination. For instance, the recruitment strategies used should not exclude certain groups.

The Equal Employment Opportunity Commission (EEOC) bans the use in recruitment of preferences based on age, race, national origin, religion, or sex. Some organizations, however, will undertake targeted recruitment. Targeted recruitment means that deliberate attempts are made to recruit protected-class members who have been identified as absent from or underrepresented in an agency. For example, the federal government has introduced a recruiting program designed to increase the representation and advancement of Hispanics in the federal workplace and also makes a concerted effort to recruit students at historically black colleges and universities and provide them with better access to federal employment information. This targeting may be done to comply with an affirmative action plan or a conciliation agreement. Nonprofits that provide services to particular constituency groups, such as persons with AIDS, unwed mothers, or senior citizens, may deliberately target applicants from those groups during recruitment.

Screening Applicants

Once the organization has communicated its need to fill positions and applicants have responded, it needs to screen the applicants to identify those with the requisite KSAOCs.

Employment applications are often the first step in the screening process. Applicants fill out a form asking them to answer a variety of questions. The questions must not violate local, state, or federal employment discrimination laws. The rule followed by the EEOC, state agencies, and most courts is that if the employer asks a question on an employment application form, it is assumed that the answer is used in the hiring process. If the question does not pertain to the job applicant's qualification for the job in question, the question maybe held illegal if it has a disparate impact on a covered group. When developing an application, an organization should refer to the state's fair employment laws to eliminate any potential discriminatory questions. Questions about age, race, gender, and disability are permitted only when responding is voluntary and the information is required for record-keeping purposes. Equal employment opportunity data should be collected by the personnel office and not used to screen out applicants.

Most applications are generic and not tailored for any one position. They usually provide limited space for applicants to provide detailed information about relevant work or educational experience. A supplemental questionnaire should be developed that asks questions related to the specific job to facilitate the screening process.

After individuals apply for a position, the applications need to be screened to identify qualified applicants and eliminate applicants who are not qualified. This process will be different for each position. It is not uncommon for a large urban government that is recruiting for police or fire personnel to have hundreds or even thousands of applicants. Positions typically inundated by applicants use multiple screening procedures to pare down the number of candidates. The first screen is to weed out applicants who do not meet the minimum requirements, such as age (for example, law enforcement positions require applicants to be at least twenty-one years old), level of education, or required certification. The second screen might include the elimination of applicants who lack the requisite experience.

For administrative or professional positions, which usually have more stringent education and experience requirements, there are likely to be fewer applicants. However, in today's competitive market, it is still possible to have many applicants for such positions. To reduce the number of applicants to the most qualified, it is important to have preestablished criteria to facilitate the screening. Requiring previous experience as a city planner or community development specialist might be one standard. Previous financial management experience with a budget of $2 million might be another. To screen résumés, an instrument such as a checklist might be developed to keep track of the relevant experience and education required. Anybody who has spent time reading many résumés knows that after the first ten or so, fatigue sets in. You become less attentive as the review progresses. A checklist keeps you focused on the salient KSAOCs.

Employment screening techniques and tests must comply with the general principles and technical requirements of the *Uniform Guidelines on Employee Selection Procedures* (1978).

Pre-employment testing is used to measure the KSAOCs of applicants and predict their ability to perform a job. It is an attempt to standardize the screening process and determine whether applicants possess the characteristics necessary to be successful on the job. Along with the Uniform Guidelines, the *Principles for the Validation and Use of Personnel Selection Procedures* developed by the American Psychological Association's Division of Industrial and Organizational Psychology (1987) broadly define tests as a variety of instruments or procedures used in the selection or promotion process. I next examine some of the selection techniques commonly used in employment settings, as well as some alternative approaches.

Cognitive ability and aptitude tests are designed to reflect both the general and the specific capabilities and potentials of the individual applicant by measuring verbal, quantitative, nonverbal, and oral skills or motor functions such as mechanical ability, numerical aptitude, finger dexterity, or perceptual accuracy. They are used to determine whether applicants possess the aptitude to learn the KSAOCs required in the position.

Achievement tests are designed to measure the degree of mastery of specific material, to assess whether an individual has profited from prior experience and learned specific materials. Most of the items on achievement tests assess whether the individual possesses specific knowledge of concepts considered critical for a job. Trade tests are examples of this type.

Personality inventories are designed to assess a person's typical behavioral traits and characteristics by measuring such traits as dominance, sociability, self-control, or introversion-extroversion. Some of the more common personality tests used in the public sector are the Minnesota Multiphasic Personality Inventory, the California Psychological Inventory, and the Edwards Personal Preference Schedule. They are used when interpersonal skills are key to successful performance.

Interest inventories are designed to predict job choice behavior rather than job performance by ascertaining the occupational likes and dislikes of the individual and indicating the occupational areas that are most likely to be satisfying to that person. They are used to make a compatible person-job match.

Experience and training (E&T) rating is a procedure that quantifies the education, experience, training, achievements, and other relevant data that applicants provide on job applications and questionnaires. Points are assigned to applicants based on the number of years of experience, education, and training relevant to the position. E&T exams are often referred to as unassembled examinations.

Structured oral exams are used to evaluate job requirements that are not easily assessed by paper-and-pencil measures, such as interpersonal communication, verbal ability, and supervisory skills. Although the specifics of the exams may differ, all structured oral exams share similar components. They are based on a job analysis that captures the critical KSAOCs necessary for the position. The questions are job-related, and all applicants are asked the same questions. Rating scales are used to evaluate the responses, and the raters receive training prior to conducting the examination. Structured oral exams are used a great deal in the public sector. The Office of Personnel Management uses structured oral exams for a variety of positions from entry-level to senior, such as those in the Presidential Management Fellows Program, and in the administrative law judge selection process. Many local governments use oral exams to determine promotions to supervisory positions in police and fire departments.

Work sample or performance tests require applicants to demonstrate that they possess the necessary skills needed for successful job performance. Applicants are asked to perform tasks that are representative of actual job activities. For example, applicants applying for the position of editor of a nonprofit newsletter may be asked to actually edit and write copy, or applicants applying for a training position could be required to prepare and present a training module.

Liberty Resources, Inc., a nonprofit human services agency located in New York State, screens applicants for Multisystemic Therapy (MST) positions by requiring a master of social work (M.S.W.) degree and several years of experience working with families. The MST treatment model has been proved to be effective in reducing the frequency and severity of criminal activity in delinquent youth and helping youth succeed in the community independently rather than be placed in supervised residential facilities. The therapist's responsibility is to facilitate long-term change in the "ecology of the child." Therapists work primarily with parents or caregivers, as well as the youth, and their network of extended family, peers, school, and community toward positive behavioral outcomes. The position requires the ability to apply analytical and systemic principles and processes to clinical skills with families and to collaborate as a team member with families, a clinical team, and other community care providers.

After résumés have been screened, eligible applicants interested in the position must demonstrate their clinical and interpersonal skills by answering behaviorally based questions to assess the applicants' personal character, ability to think systematically, conceptualization skills, and counseling skills. The applicants are interviewed by a team of therapists and a supervisor and are provided with scenarios of family situations that they will encounter on the job; for example:

> This family consists of a single mother and her two sons, aged eleven and twelve. The boys have had chronic problems in school, which resulted in their being placed out of the home in the past. Mom has a poor relationship with the school personnel and is fearful of talking with them. Since their return home, the boys have begun acting out again in the school (arguing with teacher, not following rules, refusing to complete schoolwork, and so on). What would be your focus with the mother?

Anne Goldych Dailey, current program supervisor, uses this screening procedure because she found that possession of an M.S.W. degree did not guarantee strong interpersonal and clinical skills. She believes that to be successful in this position, therapists also need to engage people and establish effective relationships. Such skills are not always obvious in a traditional interview situation. Although the scenario simulations may be stressful for some candidates, the ability to function in stressful situations is key to effective performance. The client population is families raising challenging, high-maintenance youth who have not been successful in multiple areas of their lives and are heading to or returning from residential placement. Therapists are highly autonomous, spending most of their time out in the field and not under direct supervision.

In-baskets are written tests designed to simulate administrative tasks. The in-basket exercise consists of correspondence designed to be representative of the job's actual tasks. A set of instructions usually states that applicants should imagine that they have been placed in the position and must deal with the memos and other items that have accumulated in their in-basket. The test is used to measure such skills as task prioritization, written communication, and judgment.

Leaderless group discussions assess attributes such as oral communication, leadership, persuasiveness, adaptability, and tolerance for stress. Applicants are assembled to work on solving a problem that requires cooperation. For example, they may be asked to compose a statement in response to charges that the agency's employees are treating clients unfairly, or they may be asked to work on a problem involving competition, such as deciding how to allocate a limited amount of money among a number of community projects. Nobody is designated as the group leader. Assessors evaluate the individual applicant's participation in the group's discussion.

Assessment centers are special selection programs that rely on performance tests. The purpose of an assessment center is to obtain multiple measurements of key job dimensions by using a variety of instruments such as role-playing exercises, in-baskets, leaderless group discussions, paper-and-pencil tests, and other written exercises. Judgments about each applicant's behavior are made by assessors who are trained in the scoring of each exercise. Assessment centers are frequently used to select administrators and supervisors, who need skills in such areas as leadership, planning, and decision making. In the public sector, assessment centers are commonly used for the selection of city managers and the promotion of public safety managers.

Biodata selection procedures require that applicants complete a questionnaire that asks for biographical information. Questions may include topics such as level of education, demographic profile, work experience, interests and social activities, habits, hobbies, family history, attitudes, values, achievements, and personal characteristics. Individuals are selected based on whether their answers to the questions are related to job success. Schmidt and Hunter (1998) reported mean biodata validity coefficients of .35 and .30 against job and training success, respectively. As a result of the high predictability, the ease of administration of biodata instruments, and diminished adverse impact, the use of biodata has increased in both the public and private sectors.

Drug testing has become commonplace for reasons of on-the-job safety. Drug-dependent employees are more likely than nondependent employees to be involved in workplace accidents, and decreased productivity, increased absenteeism, and threats to fellow employees' or clients' safety are some of the other problems manifested by substance abusers (Office of National Drug Control Policy, 2001). Consequently, many organizations have instituted drug testing as part of preemployment screening. It is important to note that applicants do not have the same rights as employees. Although applicants for a position may be tested for substance abuse at the organization's request, organizations do not necessarily have the right to test employees who are already on the payroll.

Lie-detector exams are permitted in certain circumstances. The Employee Polygraph Protection Act of 1988 prevents employers involved in or affecting interstate commerce from using lie detectors. The law makes it unlawful for employers to require prospective employees to take lie detector tests or for employers to use test results or a worker's refusal or failure to take a test as grounds for failure to promote, discharge, or discipline. The law does not, however, apply to the federal government, to state or local governments, or to any political subdivision of a state or local government. Other exemptions include individuals or consultants working under contract for federal intelligence agencies; makers and distributors of controlled substances; and security companies whose business involves the protection of currency, financial instruments, or vital facilities or materials.

The right of a public employer to require a lie detector test may be limited by state statute. The federal law and most state laws prohibit questions about religion; political, racial, and union activities; and sexual and marital matters. Subjects must be informed of their rights, and written consent must be obtained before administering the test. The test results must remain confidential, and only licensed, bonded examiners may be used. Polygraph exams are used primarily for law enforcement and public safety positions.

Honesty and integrity tests are lawful under the Employee Polygraph Protection Act of 1988 and most state polygraph laws. There are two kinds of honesty and integrity tests: overt and personality. Overt tests deal with attitudes toward theft or admission of theft or other illegal activities. Personality tests do not look at honesty per se but at a variety of counterproductive work behaviors such as impulsiveness, nonconformance, and dislike of authority. A review of the literature on selection indicates that integrity tests produce a 27 percent increase in predictive validity over general intelligence alone (Schmidt & Hunter, 1998).

Physical ability tests are used when a significant level of physical activity is involved in performing the job. In the public sector, physical ability tests are used most often in the selection of law enforcement and public safety officers, such as police officers, firefighters, corrections officers, and park and conservation safety officials. Physical ability testing has replaced height and weight requirements, which were often used to screen applicants, resulting in adverse impacts on women and Hispanics, and were difficult to defend as being job-related. Agencies have turned instead to physical ability tests that were developed to replicate the physical tasks necessary to perform specific jobs (Arvey, Nutting, & Landon, 1992; Hughes, Ratliff, Purswell, & Hadwiger, 1989).

Preemployment Testing Under the ADA

Congress intended the ADA to prevent discrimination against individuals with "hidden" disabilities such as cancer, heart disease, mental illness, diabetes, epilepsy, and HIV infection or AIDS. Employers are permitted to ask applicants about their ability to perform job functions, but they may not ask about disabilities before a job offer has been made. Once a conditional job offer has been made, however, the employer may require a medical examination and make disability-related inquiries. Employers may ask applicants to describe or demonstrate how they would perform job-related tasks with or without reasonable accommodation. If the examination screens out an individual with a disability as a result of the disability, the employer must demonstrate that the exclusionary criterion is job-related and consistent with business necessity. The employer must also show that the criterion cannot be satisfied and the essential job functions cannot be performed with reasonable accommodation.

Medical examinations are procedures or tests that seek information about the existence, nature, or severity of an individual's physical or mental impairment or that seek information regarding an individual's physical or psychological health. The following are some of the guidelines established by the EEOC to determine whether a procedure or test is a medical examination:

The procedure or test must be administered by either a health care professional or someone trained by a health care professional. The results of the procedure or test must be interpreted by either a health care professional or someone trained by a health care professional.

The employer must administer the procedure or test for the purpose of revealing the existence, nature, or severity of an impairment or to determine the subject's general physical or psychological health.

The procedure or test may be invasive (for example, drawing blood, testing urine, or analyzing breath).

The procedure or test may measure physiological or psychological responses of an individual only if the results determine the individual's ability to perform a task.

The procedure or test must be one that is normally administered in a medical setting (a health care professional's office, a hospital).

Medical diagnostic equipment or devices may be used for administering the procedure or test.

Physical agility and physical fitness tests, in which applicants demonstrate their ability to perform actual or simulated job-related tasks, are not medical examinations. These tests measure applicants' ability to perform a particular task; they do not seek information concerning the existence, nature, or severity of a physical or mental impairment or information regarding applicants' health. They may be administered at the preoffer stage.

Psychological examinations such as aptitude tests, personality tests, honesty tests, and IQ tests are all intended to measure applicants' capacity and propensity to successfully perform a job and are not considered to be medical examinations. Psychological tests that result in a clinical diagnosis and require interpretation by health care profession are considered to be medical examinations and are prohibited at the preoffer stage.

Interviews

Interviews are often the deciding factor in who gets hired for a position. This is unfortunate because interviews are a subjective selection tool. It is easy for interviewers to inject their own prejudices into the selection decision. Another problem with interviews is that job-related questions that can differentiate between successful and unsuccessful employees often are not asked.

Successful interviewing requires planning and structure. The components of a structured oral exam should be incorporated into the interview process. Questions related to the dimensions of the job should be asked. The interviewers should agree in advance what competencies the position requires. The focus should be on the KSAOCs that interviews can assess most effectively, such as interpersonal or verbal communication skills and job knowledge.

To minimize subjectivity, the interview process should be structured. The U.S. Merit Systems Protection Board (2003a) and Dixon, Wang, Calvin, Dineen, and Tomlinson (2002) propose the following steps:

1. Develop questions based on a job analysis.
2. Ask effective questions.
3. Ask each candidate the same questions.
4. Use detailed rating scales. Anchor the rating scales for scoring answers with examples and illustrations.

5. Train interviewers.
6. Use interview panels so that more than one person conducts the interview.
7. Take notes during the interview.
8. Assess candidates' responses objectively, use the rating scales, and use the ratings to score candidates.
9. Evaluate selection decisions based on subsequent employee performance.

Research indicates that team interviews reduce individual interviewer biases about the applicant (Campion, Pursell, & Brown, 1988) and that mixed-race interview panels serve as a check and balance on the evaluation process (Dobbins, Lin, & Farh, 1992).

Interviewers should be trained to accurately receive and evaluate information. Even if a structured interview format is not used, interviewers should still document the candidates' responses to the questions.

Interviewers must also comply with the EEOC guidelines concerning preemployment disability-related inquiries. They may not ask about the existence, nature, or severity of a disability, but they may inquire about the ability of an applicant to perform specific job-related functions.

Here are some examples of questions prohibited under the ADA:

Do you have a disability that would interfere with your ability to perform the job?

How many days were you sick last year?

Have you ever been treated for mental health problems?

Have you ever filed for workers' compensation?

Here are examples of questions permitted under the ADA:

Can you perform the essential functions of this job with or without reasonable accommodation?

Please describe how you would perform these functions.

Can you meet the attendance requirements of this job?

Do you have the required licenses to perform this job?

The interview should be just one of many factors considered when selecting applicants. Not all competent people interview well, and not all jobs require superior interpersonal and communication skills. Many positions use a combination of the screening techniques. For example, it is common for applicants for public safety positions to have to pass a written cognitive ability test, a medical examination and drug screen, a polygraph examination, a background investigation, a physical ability test, and an oral interview before the decision to hire is made. Positions that encompass a lot of responsibility, that require time-consuming and expensive training, or in which risk to the organization or public is great typically have more demanding screening procedures.

Testing Issues

Employment tests that measure cognitive skills and abilities are controversial because they often have an adverse impact on protected-class members. Arvey and Faley (1988) report that African Americans score 1.0 to 1.5 standard deviations lower than whites. Not only have state, local, and private sector employers found themselves facing litigation, but so has the federal government. In 1979 the Department of Justice signed a consent decree in which it agreed that the Professional and Administrative Career Examination for entry into federal employment would be eliminated. African Americans and Hispanics as groups did not score as high on the exam as white candidates. A class action suit asking for an injunction and a declaratory judgment was filed against the director of the Office of Personnel Management. The plaintiffs alleged that the exam violated Title VII of the Civil Rights Act of 1964 because the test had a disproportionately adverse effect on African Americans and Hispanics and was not validated in accordance with the Uniform Guidelines on Employee Selection (Nelson, 1982). An outcome of the consent decree was the establishment of a variety of selection avenues, such as the outstanding-scholar and cooperative education programs used to hire entry-level federal employees.

State and local governments have found themselves mired in controversy over tests and adverse impact. Most large urban police and fire departments have found themselves in federal court or having to negotiate consent decrees with the Department of Justice in efforts to remedy the effects of either intentional discriminatory practices or neutral employment practices such as paper-and-pencil tests, which resulted in adverse impact against protected-class members.

Why are tests used? Organizations needing to distinguish among a large pool of applicants must develop formal, objective methods of screening, grouping, and selecting applicants. Testing is a way to do that. Research on testing has established that cognitive ability tests are equally valid for virtually all jobs and that failure to use them in selection would typically result in substantial economic loss to individual organizations (Schmidt, 1988). Hunter (1986, pp. 342, 346) found the following evidence in regard to cognitive ability tests:

- General cognitive ability predicts performance ratings in all lines of work, though validity is higher for complex jobs than for simple jobs.
- General cognitive ability predicts training success at a uniformly high level for all jobs.
- Data on job knowledge shows that cognitive ability determines how much and how quickly a person learns.
- Cognitive ability predicts the ability to react in innovative ways to situations in which knowledge does not specify exactly what to do.

Psychometric Terms and Concepts

Employers need to be familiar with a number of psychometric concepts as they pertain to employment testing.

Reliability

The concept of *reliability* is concerned with the consistency of measurement. An exam's reliability can be determined through a number of different procedures. *Test-retest* reliability occurs when individuals taking the test score about the same on the test in each administration. If a test is reliable, there should be consistency between two sets of scores for the test taken by the same person at different times. *Split-half* reliability is derived by correlating one part of the exam with another part of the exam. If the exam is measuring an aptitude reliably, it should do so throughout the exam. *Odd-even* reliability is when a score is computed for all the even-numbered exam items and then correlated with a score derived from the odd-numbered items. *Internal consistency measure* reliability is when each exam item is correlated with every other exam item. *Equivalent-forms* reliability is when different forms of an exam have been constructed. Each version of the exam is administered to the participants, and the two sets of exam scores are correlated.

Validity

Is the test or selection instrument measuring what it is intended to measure? *Validity* is the most important characteristic of measures used in personnel selection. Why use a particular test or procedure if it is not correctly predicting or evaluating the most qualified candidates? Validity and reliability are often confused. Reliability is necessary for a test to be considered valid, but it cannot stand alone; just because a test gives consistent results does not mean that it is measuring what it is intended to measure.

Three types of validity are recognized by the Uniform Guidelines on Employee Selection: content, criterion, and construct.

Content validity. Selection instruments and procedures are considered to be content-valid if they reflect the KSAOCs considered essential for job performance. If you want to see if, at the time of hire, an applicant possesses the skills or knowledge necessary to perform a job, content validity is an appropriate validation strategy. The most common example cited is the typing test. How does an employer know if applicants can type eighty words per minute? By requiring applicants to demonstrate their skills in a test.

The procedures that need to be followed to develop a content-valid test are as follows. First a job analysis must be conducted. The KSAOCs and responsibilities required for the position must be discovered. Once they have been identified, they need to be rated for their relevance, frequency, and importance to the job. It must then be determined whether it is essential for candidates to possess those KSAOCs at the time of hire or whether they can be learned once the person is on the job. Test items must be written or performance measures must be developed to capture the KSAOCs that are essential at the time of hire. Then incumbents and supervisors who are familiar with the job (subject matter experts, or SMEs) must evaluate the test items or performance samples to determine whether the test accurately reflects the competencies required by the job. A majority of SMEs must agree that the items are representative of the types of skills, knowledge, and behaviors required for the job.

Content validity is used very often in the public and nonprofit sectors. Personnel specialists and managers often possess the skills needed to develop content-valid exams. One can be trained how to conduct job analyses and how to work with SMEs to develop selection instruments. Large applicant or incumbent populations are not required, and content validation studies do not necessarily require consultants or an extensive background in psychometrics. Content-valid exams have "face validity": candidates easily understand how the exam relates to the position. Studies have shown that exams with face validity lead to litigation less often than other types of tests.

Criterion validity. Criterion validity measures whether the test scores (called predictors) are related to performance on some measure (called a criterion), such as supervisory evaluations or success in a training program. Does the test predict subsequent job performance? The most common example is the correlation of test scores with supervisory ratings of job performance.

There are two types of criterion-related validity, *predictive* and *concurrent.* Both methods demonstrate a statistical relationship between the test scores and performance measures. What differs is the sample of test takers and the amount of time between taking the exam and obtaining job performance measures. The meaning of this will become clearer as the procedures are explained.

Predictive validity. The procedure for predictive validity studies is as follows. First, a job analysis is conducted to determine the relevant KSAOCs for the position. Based on the KSAOCs, an exam is developed. Candidates are then tested for the job using the selection instrument developed. Next, candidates are selected using some other standard. For example, decisions may be based on letters of reference, the interview, or previous experience.

After the new employees have been working for the organization for six to twelve months, job performance measures are obtained. These could be supervisory ratings or performance in a training program. After these measures have been collected, a statistical analysis is conducted to evaluate the relationship between the test and the job performance measure. If the test is to be considered useful for selection, the high scorers on the test should have higher performance ratings and the low scorers on the test should have lower performance ratings. You are probably wondering why the test is not used to select employees. Why develop an instrument and then ignore it? Good question. The test was not originally used to select candidates because to determine whether the test could predict performance, both high and low test scores are needed. If only people who scored high on the test were selected, it would not be clear whether individuals with low scores on the test could be good employees. If indeed individuals with low test scores turn out to be the best performers, then the test is not measuring what it was intended to measure in order to predict which applicants would be most successful on the job. If it is not yet known whether the test is valid, making selection decisions on its results would be premature.

Concurrent validity. Concurrent validity also statistically demonstrates a relationship between the predictor and criterion measures. However, the procedures are different from those used in a predictive validity study. Instead of applicants, incumbents take the examination. Because incumbents are already working for the agency, job performance data can be collected immediately. Then the predictor and criterion data can be correlated and a relationship between the selection instrument and job performance can be determined.

There are some factors to consider when doing a concurrent validity study. Because job incumbents are being used, it must be recognized that over time they may have become more proficient in performing the jobs, and hence they might perform better on the exam than applicants. Or they may perform worse: because they are already employed, they may not care about performing well, or they may even resent having to spend the time taking the test.

Concurrent validity studies are conducted more frequently than predictive validity studies because they take less time to administer and are less costly to develop. Also, research shows that their results tend to be comparable to predictive validity studies (Barrett, Phillips, & Alexander, 1981).

Criterion validity studies are used more frequently at the federal or state levels, where large samples can be obtained. At the local level, they are conducted for public safety positions (police and fire), for which hundreds or thousands of applicants are available. They may also be used for positions for which large numbers of people are hired and then sent for specific training, such as to the police or fire academy, or to receive specialized training to become Internal Revenue Service agents. The employer is relying on the test to screen in applicants with the cognitive skills likely to be successful in training.

Construct validity. Construct validity is the most theoretical type of validity. Selection instruments are developed or used that measure hypothesized constructs or traits related to successful job performance. Constructs are intangible or abstract characteristics that vary in individuals—for example, intelligence, motivation, aggressiveness, anxiety, honesty, initiative, and creativity. To validate exams designed to measure constructs requires expertise in psychometrics. The existence of personality or character traits that are often abstract and intangible is difficult to establish through a job analysis. The burden is on the employer to prove empirically that the test is valid for the job for which it is being used. Organizations that are considering adopting a test to measure constructs should seek advice from a qualified person (not the test vendor).

New Directions

Historically, most of the research on testing and selection has focused on the ability of cognitive ability tests to predict success on a particular job. Recent scholarship has recognized that performance in an organization is influenced by more than cognitive ability. People differ in terms of personality, interpersonal relations, vocational interests, values, orientations, motivations, and perceptions. Each of those individual difference variables affects behavior in organizations (Zedeck, 1996).

Murphy (1996), the editor of *Individual Differences and Behavior in Organizations,* noted that research in industrial and organizational psychology from the mid-1960s to the mid-1980s can be roughly categorized as research on the relationship between scores on written ability tests and job performance and other research (p. 5). What has been omitted from scholarship was the relationship between individual employees' behavior in the organization and how their behavior affected the organizations' outcomes. Variables, such as whether employees work to advance the goals of the organization, the organizational experience, the climate and culture of the organization, the quality of interpersonal relations within the organization, the amount of conflict within the organization, and whether employees identify with the organization, are important characteristics that affect job performance.

Murphy (1996) further stated that current theories of job performance suggest that the performance domain is multifaceted and that it is likely to include dimensions that are not highly or even positively correlated. Individual difference domains that contribute to effective job performance include cognitive ability, personality, orientation (values and interests), and affective disposition (mood, affect, temperament). Given today's team-oriented environment, there are a variety of individual behaviors that bear directly on accomplishing the goals of the organization. These include not only individual task performance but also nontask behaviors such as teamwork, customer service, organizational citizenship, and prosocial organizational behaviors. These behaviors may not be included in an individual's job description, yet they are crucial to the effective function of the organization. Individual differences in ability, personality orientation, and affective states might affect any or all of these variables. I next look at some of the other variables that often affect performance and are becoming important in HRM selection research.

Practical Intelligence

Two decades ago, Sternberg (1985) recognized the importance of practical intelligence, defining it as how people deal practically with different kinds of contexts—how they know and use what is needed to behave intelligently at school, at work, or on the streets. He suggested that practical intelligence and tacit knowledge play a role in job success. Practical intelligence is often described as the ability to effectively respond to practical problems or demands in situations that people commonly encounter in their jobs. Practical intelligence is important for success in our society and yet is rarely taught explicitly or tested systematically. The efficacy of using tests that measure practical intelligence or common sense to predict job performance has started to be discussed in the personnel literature. McDaniel, Finnegan, Morgenson, Campion, and Braverman (1997, 2001) found that measures of common sense or practical intelligence are correlated with job performance and cognitive ability. Smith and McDaniel (1997) found that situational judgment measures also correlate with job performance and are influenced by experience, personality, and cognitive factors. Their study provided an observed validity coefficient of .31 across aggregated occupations in the service, engineering, and business sectors.

Adaptability

Adaptive job performance is characterized by the ability and willingness to cope with uncertain, new, and rapidly changing conditions on the job. Personnel must adjust to new equipment and procedures, function in changing environments, and continuously learn new skills. Technological change requires the organization of work around projects rather than well-defined and stable jobs, and this requires workers who are sufficiently flexible to be effective in poorly defined roles. Pulakos, Arad, Donovan, and Plamondon (2000) identified eight dimensions of adaptive performance: (1) handling emergencies or crisis situations, (2) handling work stress, (3) solving problems creatively, (4) dealing with uncertain and unpredictable work situations, (5) learning work tasks, technologies, and procedures, (6) demonstrating interpersonal adaptability, (7) demonstrating cultural adaptability, and (8) demonstrating physically oriented adaptability.

Multiple Intelligences

The theory of multiple intelligences (MI) maintains that there are many kinds of intelligence that are not measured through standardized paper-and-pencil tests. Howard Gardner has identified eight and one-half intelligences. The eight intelligences are logical-mathematical, linguistic, musical, spatial, bodily-kinesthetic, interpersonal, intrapersonal, and naturalist. Gardner considers spiritual-existential intelligence as half an intelligence because of its perplexing nature (Gardner, 1993, 1999; Gardner & Hatch, 1989).

Emotional Intelligence

Daniel Goleman (1995, 1998) defines emotional intelligence as being able to motivate oneself and persist in the face of frustrations, to control impulses and delay gratification, to regulate one's moods, and to keep distress from swamping the ability to think, empathize, and hope. He suggests that the focus on logical-mathematical intelligence has neglected an important set of skills and abilities, such as how an individual deals with people and emotions.

Personality Measures

A meta-analysis investigating the relationship of the "big five" personality dimensions (extroversion, emotional stability, agreeableness, conscientiousness, and openness to experience) found personality measures to be predictors for some occupations (Barrick & Mount, 1991; Barrick, Mount, & Judge, 2001).

Citizenship Performance and Organizational Citizenship Behavior

Employees may engage in activities that are not directly related to their main task functions but are nonetheless important for organizational effectiveness because they support the organizational, social, and psychological context for task activities and processes (Borman & Motowidlo, 1993; Borman, Penner, Allen, & Motowidlo, 2001; Organ, 1988; Podsakoff, Mackenzie, Paine, & Bachrach, 2000; Smith, Organ, & Near, 1983).

Executive and Managerial Recruitment and Selection

At the federal and state levels, executives are typically appointed to their positions by the chief elected officials or their designees and are referred to as political executives. They lack permanent status and retain their positions only for as long as the president or governor desires or until the next election. Often these executives have been referred to the respective executive branches by someone they know, such as a legislator, a professional associate, a campaign worker, a university classmate, or a corporate executive.

At the local level and in nonprofit agencies, the recruitment and selection of city managers or executive directors is usually conducted by search committees. Ordinarily, the personnel committee of the city council or board of directors will be responsible for the search. The committee will identify what qualifications are needed and determine the recruitment strategies that will be used. Often citizens or clients and representative staff persons will be asked to participate in the effort.

Search committees that lack the time or expertise to recruit executives may choose to delegate responsibility for the recruitment and screening efforts to professional recruitment firms or consultants. An advantage of using professional recruitment firms is that they can devote complete attention to the search process. Unlike council or board members, professional recruiters are not part-time volunteers committed to other jobs. Developing recruitment strategies, placing advertisements, screening résumés and applications, responding to correspondence, verifying references, and conducting preliminary interviews are time-consuming. Professional recruitment firms are knowledgeable about fair employment laws and practices and will document the procedures used should allegations of discrimination arise. Their livelihoods and reputations depend on conducting professional and legal searches.

Another advantage in using recruitment firms is that they can provide an objective viewpoint if internal candidates apply for the position. Board or council members may place loyalty, politics, or familiarity above proficiency. Lawrence Davenport was selected to rebuild Hale House after the daughter of the founder was charged with stealing $1 million from the Hale House Foundation and from donations. Hale House is a nonprofit in the Harlem neighborhood of New York City that takes care of HIV-infected infants and children born to drug-addicted or jailed mothers. Having outsiders direct the process should mitigate much of the subjectivity that is a natural part of the process (Anft, 2002; Bernstein, 2001a, 2001b; Pristin, 2001).

An additional reason to consider a professional firm is that sometimes organizations wish to remain anonymous in the early stages of the recruiting process. Screening applicants through a professional firm retains that anonymity (Ammons & Glass, 1989; Snelling & Kuhnle, 1986).

Even if a professional firm is hired to direct the recruitment and selection process, council and board members should not abrogate their oversight responsibility. They need to work with the firm to identify the professional and personal qualifications that are needed to guide the organization and that are consistent with the organization's mission. They must determine the strategic challenges the organization faces—where it is and where it is going (Albert, 2000; Axelrod, 2002; Gilmore, 1993; Stene, 1980). For example, a county health department in financial distress might look for an executive with strong financial management skills, or a nonprofit agency having to contend with declining donations due to a former director's scandalous behavior might need to recruit someone who is known to have integrity and who also possesses successful fundraising experience.

The recruitment and selection process for executive and managerial positions is more complex than for other positions because it is difficult to describe the components of effective job behavior. Taxonomies commonly used to describe executive effectiveness include good planning, organization, communication, leadership, and decision-making skills, as well as industry technical knowledge and management techniques. Competencies more specific to the public sector could include skill in fiscal management and budgeting, council communication, citizen relations, media relations, intergovernmental relations, program development, and the execution of policies and programs (Wheeland, 1994).

Herman and Heimovics (1989) identified twelve other categories of competencies needed to deal with critical events occurring in nonprofit organizations: developing new programs, establishing program decline, collaborating, managing mergers, fundraising, lobbying, relating with government officials, responding to personnel actions, developing human resources, leading accreditation efforts, reorganizing, and interacting with the board. Proficiency in one competency does not necessarily mean proficiency in the others. An individual may have excellent communication skills but lack technical knowledge. Someone may have wonderful fiscal management skills but lack the skills necessary for effective council or board relations. Because of the vast array of skills that are needed for executive positions, organizations should employ a combination of selection methods. Some of the screening techniques commonly used for executive and managerial selection are in-baskets, leaderless group discussion, assessment centers, performance tests, and structured oral exams.

For executive selection to be successful, organizations must invest the time and effort to recognize the interrelationships among individual behaviors, managerial effectiveness, and organizational success, and they must plan the search process accordingly (Cascio, 1991).

Summary

Organizations periodically need to attract applicants for their present or future staffing needs. Recruitment is the process of locating qualified candidates. Recruitment strategies should be planned in advance of the agency's needs. Strategic job analyses and audits of positions and employee skills should be updated on a regular basis to determine whether incumbent employees are qualified for promotions or newly created positions. For some positions, depending on the qualifications or experience needed, agencies may prefer to seek applicants from the external labor market.

After applicants submit résumés or employment applications, the organization must use job-related criteria to screen the applicants' qualifications for the positions. Applicants who do not meet the initial criteria are eliminated from consideration. A variety of selection techniques are available for organizations to use to help assess the applicants' present skill levels or potential for success. Cognitive ability tests, personality or interest inventories, performance tests, ratings of experience and training, assessment centers, and structured interviews are examples of some of the techniques that can be used to evaluate applicants. Organizations must be vigilant that their recruitment and selection procedures do not violate federal or state equal employment opportunity laws.

The recruitment and selection process should not end with the hiring or promotion of employees. Agencies should record their recruitment and selection procedures so that they can be evaluated later. The evaluation should identify the successes and failures at each step of the recruitment process so that modifications can be made if necessary. Future recruitment and selection strategies should be based on the procedures that attracted the most qualified applicants and the screening techniques that best predicted successful on-the-job performance.

Questions and Exercises

1. What are some of the risks associated with not staffing an organization correctly?
2. Discuss what strategic recruiting considerations should be addressed by your organization and why.
3. Does your organization use Internet recruiting? If so, what are the advantages and disadvantages? If your organization does not use Internet recruiting, go online and find an organization that does employ Web-based recruitment. What is your opinion of the Web site?
4. Devise a recruitment and selection system for the following positions: (a) executive director of a human services nonprofit, (b) budget analyst for a local government, (c) city manager, (d) police officer, (e) social worker. What considerations need to be taken into account for each?
5. Visit the Web sites for the *Chronicle of Philanthropy* (http://phil anthropy.com), idealist.org: Action Without Borders (http:// www.idealist.org), and the Foundation Center's Job Corner Alert (http://fdncenter.org/pnd/jobs). Do you notice any patterns with respect to the types of positions that are advertised?

| Performance Management

The increasing demands for accountability made by the stake-holders of public and nonprofit organizations have focused greater attention on performance management. As a result, agencies have begun to reevaluate their performance management systems. Because employees are essential to the delivery of quality services, performance evaluation is a critical component of strategic human resources management (SHRM) in public and nonprofit agencies. The information gleaned from an effective evaluation system can be used to assist agencies in accomplishing their missions. The performance evaluation process also provides feedback to the agency about whether the other human resources management (HRM) functions are working in concert to execute the agency's mission.

Performance evaluations provide management with essential information for making strategic decisions about employee advancement, retention, or separation. Evaluation links training and development with career planning and the agency's long-term human resources needs. Used to support job analysis and recruitment efforts, performance evaluations are an important component of evaluating the knowledge, skills, abilities, and other characteristics (KSAOCs) available among the agency's internal supply of labor. Evaluations can be used to assess career advancement opportunities, to assist in succession planning, and to develop compensation and reward systems, as well as to identify deficiencies in existing KSAOCs.

Accurate evaluations provide information and feedback to employees. Employees must be informed about the goals and objectives of the agency and the role the employees play in the agency's success. They must know what standards will be used to judge their effectiveness. Supervisors must communicate to employees the employees' strengths as well as their deficiencies, thus providing the opportunity for employees to correct their weaknesses before serious problems emerge. Through the evaluation process, training and development needs can be identified and addressed.

Performance evaluation systems are indispensable for planning and research. A review of existing competencies and KSAOCs may indicate that certain skills needed by the agency are lacking, thus necessitating that external recruitment efforts be undertaken or, if time permits, that incumbents be trained and developed. Performance evaluations are also used to validate selection instruments or techniques. There should be a positive relationship between the methods and criteria used to screen employees and successful performance. If there is not, the recruitment and selection system should be reevaluated and changed.

When used in the context of SHRM, performance evaluation should provide feedback to employees, facilitate personnel decisions, and provide information essential for planning and research. Feedback about the effectiveness of other HRM functions can also be obtained through the evaluation process.

Reflecting widespread disappointment in the efficacy of performance evaluation systems, performance appraisal is one of the most researched and written-about topics in both the academic and the professional HRM literature. Employee ("ratee") dissatisfaction with performance evaluation systems has been based on a number of factors. For example, objective performance measures have been lacking; employees have believed that supervisors are often biased in their ratings, and because of this perceived bias, unions have tended to distrust management and to prefer that promotions and pay increases be based on seniority; and employees have recognized that many of their performance outcomes are dependent on the efforts of other individuals or groups, which are typically ignored in traditional performance evaluation systems.

Rater dissatisfaction with evaluation systems is also common. Supervisors complain that agencies often promote the use of evaluation systems without devoting the necessary time, supervision, and financial resources to make the system work. Raters are expected to evaluate employees and provide feedback without first receiving training, which leaves them ill-prepared to coach and counsel their subordinates. Raters are also not held accountable for the accuracy and quality of their ratings, which signals to them that their efforts are better spent elsewhere because upper management is not committed to the process.

Another reason that performance evaluation systems have been heavily researched is that they play an important role in court cases involving promotions, discharges, layoffs, and merit pay increases. Employees who find themselves the victims of adverse personnel decisions, such as terminations or layoffs, seek redress through human rights agencies and the courts. Employers are likely to defuse potential lawsuits or investigations if they can show that performance appraisals are job-related and reflect fair and accurate evaluations of performance.

This chapter discusses how to develop an appraisal program, train raters, prepare documentation, and review evaluations, as well as ethical issues in performance appraisal. It also provides examples of performance appraisal techniques and instruments and concludes with a discussion of alternative evaluation practices.

Developing an Evaluation Program

There is little consistency in performance evaluation systems used by federal, state, and local governments and nonprofit organizations. At the federal level, the evaluation system used to assess federal employees was developed to link performance with pay. Yearly evaluations determine pay increases or bonuses (or both). The approach is different at the state and local levels, where formal performance evaluation systems often do not exist. In many states and local governments, collective bargaining agreements or civil service systems determine promotions and pay increases. In this environment, if evaluations are performed, they are used strictly as communication vehicles.

The performance evaluation systems of nonprofit organizations also vary widely. In many nonprofits, formal appraisal systems do not exist. Health care facilities are known for evaluating direct service providers such as nurses, social workers, and medical assistants on the basis of their individual behaviors and performance, and executive directors receive bonuses or pay increases that are tied to the organization's financial performance.

The only commonality found in the performance evaluation systems of public and nonprofit organizations is that both raters and ratees typically dislike having to participate in the process. Yet despite the reservations expressed about performance evaluation systems, most organizations do undertake some form of appraisal. Because performance evaluations are used for different and sometimes multiple purposes, it is important for both employees and supervisors to understand why evaluations are being conducted.

The integrity of a performance appraisal system depends on the raters' and ratees' understanding its objective. The following statement is taken from a state agency evaluation instrument for civil service employees:

> The Employee Performance Evaluation is designed to encourage all civil staff members to grow professionally and to reach full potential in their work. Using actual job performance as a basis for discussion, this review provides supervisors and employees with an opportunity to identify developmental needs on a mutual basis. In addition, it supplies a means of defining goals and objectives and the most appropriate course of action to pursue in order to increase competency and accelerate career progression. Supervisors are urged, in the strongest possible terms, to discuss the completion of this form during, as well as after, the evaluation process. This review is a tool of that process, not just the result of it.

In this agency, evaluation serves one purpose: employee training and development.

Rater Training

Training is essential for both ratees and raters if performance evaluation systems are to be used in the strategic human resources planning process. Ratees who receive training and understand the evaluation system tend to be more committed to its goals. They should understand why the evaluation is being conducted, how it will be used, and what their role is in the evaluation process. Through training, they become aware of the difficulty that raters face in evaluating performance. Training also informs ratees of the levels of performance expected of them.

For evaluations to be as accurate as possible, raters should receive training in the development of performance standards and objectives, goal setting, observation, and recall and documentation skills; they should also learn how to complete the evaluation instruments, how to give performance feedback, and how to avoid rating errors. Because performance appraisals rely on human judgment, which is subject to error, personal biases need to be removed from the rating process. Employees must be rated on the basis of job-related, nondiscriminatory criteria. The appraisals must accurately reflect job performance. Exhibit 9.1 lists some of the most common rating errors.

Because different organizations evaluate employees for different purposes and use different types of instruments, organizations must provide raters with training relevant to the organization's instruments and objectives. Raters must understand how to use the instruments with which they are provided. In agencies where evaluations are used for training and development purposes, supervisors also need to be taught how to develop performance objectives and standards, how to motivate employees to achieve the agreed objectives, and how to counsel employees whose performance is unsatisfactory. In agencies where evaluations are used to substantiate personnel decisions such as promotions, terminations, or pay increases, supervisors must understand how the relationship between the evaluation process and the agency's policies and personnel regulations govern those decisions. They must be able to document that their decisions are based on job-related behaviors or performance. Supervisors may not use the evaluation process as a subterfuge for unjust discrimination.

Because of the sensitive nature of performance evaluations, agencies have a responsibility to train their raters. Training can improve raters' documentation and counseling skills, thereby not only reducing their discomfort but also enabling them to help employees understand and acknowledge their own strengths and areas that need improvement. Training can teach raters how to describe job-related behaviors and develop performance standards, how to emphasize the importance of accuracy and consistency in the appraisal process, and how to provide constructive feedback. Training can be provided through a variety of methods: in workshops conducted in-house by the HRM department or off-site by

Exhibit 9.1. Common Rating Errors.

Halo Effect

Rating an employee excellent in one quality, which in turn influences the rater to give that employee a similar rating or a higher-than-deserved rating on other qualities. A subset of the halo effect is the "logic error." In this situation, a rater confuses one performance dimension with another and then incorrectly rates the dimension because of the misunderstanding. For example, an employee demonstrates a high degree of dependability (is never absent or late), and from this behavior, a comparable high degree of integrity is inferred (such as "would never use organization property for personal use").

Central Tendency

Providing a rating of average or around the midpoint for all qualities. This is the most common and most serious kind of error. Since many employees do perform somewhere around the average, it is an easily rationalized escape from making a valid appraisal.

Strict Rating

Rating consistently lower than the normal or average; being overly harsh in rating performance qualities.

Lenient Rating

Rating consistently higher than the expected norm or average; being overly loose in rating performance qualities.

Latest Behavior

Rating influenced by the most recent behavior; failing to recognize the most commonly demonstrated behaviors during the entire appraisal period.

Initial Impression

Rating based on first impressions; failing to recognize most consistently demonstrated behaviors during the entire appraisal period.

Spillover Effect

Allowing past performance appraisal ratings to unjustly influence current ratings. Past performance ratings, good or bad, result in a similar rating for the current period, even though demonstrated behavior does not deserve the rating, good or bad.

Exhibit 9.1. Common Rating Errors, Cont'd.

Same as Me

Giving the ratee a rating higher than deserved because the person has qualities or characteristics similar to those of the rater (or similar to those held in high esteem).

Different from Me

Giving the ratee a rating lower than deserved because the person has qualities or characteristics dissimilar to the rater (or similar to those held in low esteem).

---

trainers from universities or consulting firms or using video packages tailored to the performance evaluation process.

Who Should Rate?

In most organizations, the employee's immediate supervisor evaluates the employee's performance. This is because the supervisor is responsible for the employee's performance, providing oversight, disseminating assignments, and developing the employee. A problem, however, is that supervisors often work apart from their employees and therefore are not able to observe their subordinates' performance. Should supervisors rate employees on performance dimensions they cannot observe? To eliminate this dilemma, more and more organizations are implementing appraisals referred to as 360-degree evaluations. Employees are rated not only by their supervisors but also by coworkers, clients or citizens, professionals in other agencies with which they work, and subordinates. The reason for this approach is that often coworkers and clients or citizens have a greater opportunity to observe an employee's performance and are in a better position to evaluate many performance dimensions. Clients or citizens, for example, are a more appropriate source for evaluating such dimensions as the employee's manner of performance, how the employee treated them, or whether the employee answered their questions in an understandable way.

Performance dimensions such as leadership, training and developing employees, communicating agency policies, and delegating and assigning work are common responsibilities in supervisory or management positions. Competency in these dimensions can best be assessed by subordinates who have frequent contact with the supervisor or manager and can observe different aspects of their performance. The South Carolina Department of Archives and History developed a subordinate appraisal process as a tool for improved communication and feedback between managers and staff. Employees were asked to rate their immediate supervisors on thirty-seven items under five dimensions: communication, managerial support of employees, management skills, leadership, and support of quality improvement (Coggburn, 1998).

Bernardin (1986) notes, however, that some caveats do exist with subordinate evaluations. Like supervisors, subordinates often lack the training necessary to evaluate their managers; ratings may be based on political considerations; subordinates may not tell the truth, fearing retaliation from their boss; employees pushed hard may be strict in their ratings; and subordinates may not have a chance to gain an awareness of the larger picture by observing the manager in diverse situations. Despite these difficulties, Bernardin still believes that subordinate appraisals result in useful feedback to managers, reinforce good management behavior, encourage greater attention to subordinate needs, and facilitate needed group changes.

Research conducted by McEvoy (1990) in five different public sector organizations suggests that managers would accept the use of subordinate appraisals if the following conditions were met: subordinates were made aware of the requirements of the manager's job, subordinates were asked to rate only the people-oriented dimensions of their boss's performance, the accuracy and fairness of subordinate evaluations were monitored, morale issues were discussed in advance, and the ratings were used primarily for developmental purposes.

Aspects of performance such as providing timely and accurate information to other departments or agencies can often best be assessed by asking the individuals who interact with the employees to evaluate their performance. The absence of complaints does not mean that employees are satisfactorily performing their tasks, so supervisors should not depend on such unreliable indicators. Instead, information should come from the sources who are in the best position to evaluate an employee's performance on specific dimensions. The Army Management Engineering College and the U.S. Department of Energy, for example, have successfully adopted automated 360-degree evaluations (Office of Personnel Management, 1994).

Many organizations require employees to evaluate their own performance independent of other evaluations. This is referred to as self-appraisal. Supervisors and employees complete appraisal instruments and then meet to compare their evaluations. Differences in their perceptions and expectations are clarified, and strategies for improving future performance or developing career goals are discussed. This process is helpful because employees are often aware of performance constraints or have received commendations for their performance that their supervisor does not know about.

Executive Evaluation

The evaluation of city managers and executive directors of nonprofits is typically performed by city councils, board directors, or council or board subcommittees. Again, there is little consistency in evaluation procedures. The International City/County Management Association (ICMA) recommends that as part of the employment contract, the council should attach a statement of performance standards and evaluation procedures. The simplest approach is to specify an annual review and the evaluation of the manager's performance based on standards agreed on by the manager and the council. Another recommended approach is to use evaluation forms that are completed by members of the council. Each council member rates the manager on performance dimensions, targeting their critical responsibilities, such as budget management, supervision, personnel management, leadership, execution of policy, and community reputation. The evaluations are sent to the mayor, who compiles the data and determines an overall rating. Other recommendations include having the council and manager meet in executive session to evaluate the manager's performance or having the manager, council, and mayor set annual work objectives and goals and evaluate the manager's progress toward the goals. The ICMA recommends that councils provide yearly evaluations but leaves the details to be developed by the council and manager in each city (Page, 1994).

In a study seeking information about the methods used to evaluate city managers in Pennsylvania, Wheeland (1994) found that the majority of councils used an "informal, unstructured, haphazard evaluation method" (p. 155). Evaluation forms were used by only 15 percent of the councils, and only 10 percent of the councils received any training on how to evaluate their city manager. Wheeland also found that the evaluations lacked comprehensiveness. Managers were often evaluated on less than a majority of their responsibilities.

Like the ICMA, the National Center for Nonprofit Boards recognizes that there is no one best technique that can be used to evaluate chief executives. Instead, each board must decide which procedures will serve the agency best. Four general methods of assessment have been identified by Nason (1993):

- *Intermittent or continuous observation of the chief executive by board members, especially the chairperson.* This method is used mostly in small organizations in which the board works closely with the chief executive. If problems arise, it is easy to identify the cause and provide remedies; Nason (1993) notes, however, that as organizations expand and board members become less involved in the agency's operations, this method may no longer be effective. Should this become the case, the board will have to reanalyze its oversight role and restructure its own performance.

- *Periodic assessment of the chief executive by the board's chairperson or other board members.* This assessment should reflect the chief executive's performance over the previous year. The evaluation should consider the assessments of other board members, especially those of the chairs of standing committees.

Nason (1993) believes that the board members should not discuss the chief executive's performance with the staff. He claims that "to do so is to risk good morale within the organization and to distort proper lines of responsibility" (p. 5). That statement needs further consideration. Some aspects of the chief executive's performance—such as communicating agency policies, informing employees about changes, delegating tasks and responsibilities, and leadership traits—are best evaluated by subordinates. Should subordinate evaluations be used, it is important that employees first receive training and be asked to evaluate only relevant dimensions.

Information from proximate sources is important because council and board members spend most of their time away from the organization. For evaluating responsibilities such as council and board relations and communication, board members are the most appropriate source. But for other dimensions, such as financial management, they may need to rely on an audit prepared by an outside accounting firm or government regulators to verify that the chief executive's money management performance was satisfactory. One case where accountability was missing was the Tampa Bay Make-a-Wish Foundation. Delores Crooks (her real name) was sentenced to jail for six months and four months' probation along with restitution of $6,567 for stealing that amount from the foundation. She maintained a bank account at the foundation without the board's knowledge and used a foundation credit card to charge personal expenses.

• *Annual board committee review designed to assess the state of the agency and the chief executive's performance.* This is a formal review of the chief executive's goals and accomplishments and is conducted by the executive committee, the personnel committee, or an ad hoc committee. The standard procedure is for the chief executive to review the accomplishments of the previous year in relation to the goals originally set and to propose goals for the next year. During the evaluation, the chief executive's strengths and weaknesses are identified and discussed, and the evaluation concludes with an agreement about the next year's goals.

• *Full-dress public assessment of the chief executive, including formal hearings and survey data from an extensive variety of interested parties.* Only a few nonprofit organizations use this approach because it is time-consuming, often requires an outside consultant to administer the process, and can be an emotionally charged procedure.

Regardless of the type of assessment used, chief executives must have advance notice of the board's expectations and of the criteria used for the evaluation. Self-assessments by chief executives are recommended because they permit them to review how they have met the responsibilities, expectations, and objectives of the position. Opportunities are provided for chief executives and boards to resolve any differences they might have in their perspectives about the requirements of the chief executive's position and the role of the board in its governance and management functions.

The strategic purpose of the chief executive's evaluation is to strengthen the agency by improving its management. The board's evaluation of the chief executive should assist in improving his or her performance by identifying the executive's strengths and the areas in which improvement is needed. Boards should also support and encourage executives' participation in professional development activities (Nason, 1993; Pierson & Mintz, 1995).

Documentation

During the evaluation period, raters should document both positive and negative aspects of job performance. One way to do this is by maintaining employee performance logs. Raters note in the logs any critical behaviors (positive as well as negative) exhibited by employees. Information such as when an employee volunteered for difficult assignments or received letters of commendation are examples of positive aspects of performance. Noting that an employee failed to submit an assignment at its deadline or submitted reports that were inaccurate and incomplete are examples of unacceptable performance that should be recorded. By documenting performance throughout the evaluation cycle, raters are able to provide specific feedback and to minimize their susceptibility to committing rating errors.

It is important that employees receive feedback throughout the evaluation cycle, not only when it is time to review the formal evaluation. Employees who receive feedback from their raters on a regular basis know how well they are performing their jobs and what improvements might be needed. Poor performers should be receiving feedback on what they can do to improve their performance, and excellent employees should receive positive recognition for performing well. For many employees, positive reinforcement is a powerful motivator that encourages them to sustain excellent performance.

Prior to completing the formal evaluation instrument, raters should retrieve the employee performance logs for inclusion in the evaluation. Raters should be required to justify each rating they give with explicit examples. This corroborates the job-relatedness of the evaluation and diffuses allegations of unfairness, prejudice, favoritism, and so on. For employees whose performance must be improved, supervisors should recommend some potential strategies for employee development. Raters should provide feedback that is clear, descriptive, job-related, constructive, frequent, timely, and realistic.

Evaluation Review

It is not enough for raters to complete performance appraisal instruments; they must also review the evaluation with their employees. Employees should play a critical role in the process. They should be given advance notice when the review is scheduled so that they too can prepare. Employees should be encouraged to bring to the review any documentation they feel is relevant, such as letters of commendation or records of accomplished objectives of which their raters are not aware. Some raters ask their employees to complete a self-evaluation (complete with relevant documentation) prior to the scheduled review. This puts employees at ease, making them feel that they are part of the process, not just its victim. By asking employees to complete self-evaluations, raters are able to elicit input from employees about how they rated themselves and why, what accomplishments they are most proud of, and in what areas they believe performance improvement is needed.

In many public and nonprofit organizations, supervisors lack the authority to determine the purpose of evaluation. As noted earlier, promotions may be based on competitive examinations and seniority, and pay-for-performance systems may not exist. In such cases, supervisors can nevertheless use the evaluation process to develop their employees. The evaluation process should open up communication between supervisors and employees. The process should be used to discuss with employees areas for development and the best ways to achieve their goals. A systematic approach to performance appraisal will help employers make sure that they and their employees have the same understanding of the expectations for satisfactory performance.

Ethical Issues in Performance Appraisal

Requiring documentation by raters is crucial if employees and supervisors are to believe in the integrity of the process. Longenecker and Ludwig (1990) report that supervisors often inflate or deflate performance appraisals. More than 70 percent of supervisors surveyed admitted that they intentionally inflated or deflated subordinates' ratings for a variety of reasons, such as because they believed that accurate ratings would have a damaging effect on the subordinate's motivation and performance, because they wanted to avoid airing the department's dirty laundry, because they wanted to improve an employee's eligibility for merit raises, because they wanted to reward employees for displaying great effort even when results were relatively low, or because they needed to avoid confrontation with certain hard-to-manage employees. Reasons provided by supervisors as to why they often deflate employee ratings included wanting to scare better performance out of an employee, wanting to punish a difficult or rebellious employee, or wanting to encourage a problem employee to leave the organization.

The deliberate distortion of performance evaluations can be discouraged by the organization by not only requiring documentation to substantiate ratings but also by holding supervisors accountable for their ratings. Supervisors should be evaluated on the accuracy and comprehensiveness of the performance appraisals they complete. Although inflating performance ratings may be benevolent or may discourage conflicts in the short term, the long-term consequences may prove to be deleterious for the agency. Poorly performing employees may not improve, or an unforeseen reduction in force might necessitate the layoff of staff. The courts require documentation for dismissals or layoffs to prove that they were based on performance. And guess what? Inflated evaluations do not demonstrate cause, nor do they differentiate the levels of performance of different employees, thus discrediting the supervisor's and agency's credibility.

Recent findings by Reinke (2003) indicate that variables such as the relevance of the rating instrument, the length and complexity of the instrument, and the amount of training received on the appraisal system are less important than the level of trust between the employee and supervisor as the most important predictor of acceptance of the performance evaluation system.

Another problem with disingenuous evaluations is that when they are used for SHRM, the data they provide are inaccurate. Any decisions based on the evaluations could prove to be harmful to the future growth and success of the organization by not recognizing liabilities or identifying where the agency needs to acquire talent. Inaccurate evaluations also do not develop individuals (Longenecker & Ludwig, 1990).

Performance Appraisal Techniques

Before I discuss specific types of rating instruments, it should be understood that there are three general approaches to performance appraisals: absolute, comparative, and goal setting.

Absolute methods evaluate the employee without referring directly to other employees. Instead, employees are evaluated against their own standards. For example, John Doe is evaluated in March and then again in September of the same year. John's September evaluation is compared to his March evaluation. The strengths identified in March should have been maintained, and any deficiencies or problems identified in March should have been corrected by the September evaluation. Absolute evaluations are used most frequently for developmental purposes.

Comparative methods evaluate the employees in one unit relative to everyone else in the group. In March, all of the juvenile probation officers were evaluated on the same performance dimensions and then compared to one another. For example, probation officer A received the highest ratings in accuracy and timeliness of presentencing investigation reports, and probation officer C received the lowest rating for that dimension. Probation officer C, however, received the highest rating for number of clients supervised and number of collateral contacts, and probation officer B received the lowest rating on that dimension. Comparative evaluations are used to differentiate levels of performance across employees.

Goal setting evaluates whether the ratee attained predetermined goals. For example, the supervisor and employee agree that the employee will prepare seven more grant applications in the next five months to secure a greater percentage of external funding. After five months have passed, the supervisor will evaluate whether or not the employee met the preagreed goal.

There are differences not only in the format of evaluation but also in the types of data that are collected and evaluated. Some evaluations rely on *direct indices* or objective data. Direct indices can be quantified, such as the number of errors, the number of clients on caseloads, the number of grants that received funding, the number of arrests made, or the number of proposals written. Direct indices are referred to as objective measures because they do not depend on someone's opinion to be verified. Another type of data commonly used are *subjective measures,* which depend on human judgment and should be based on a careful analysis of the behaviors viewed as necessary for effective job performance. Decision-making skills, the ability to solve problems, and oral communication skills are examples of subjective measures.

The types of data and the performance standards used should be based on a current job analysis. Performance standards should be developed based on the critical tasks and responsibilities of each position. The standards should be measurable through quantifiable or observable methods. I next provide an overview of some of the most common types of evaluation instruments used in the public and nonprofit sectors.

Trait Rating

Raters are provided with a list of personality characteristics, such as cooperation, creativity, attitude, and initiative. Raters then assign a rating number or an adjective, such as "average," "above average," or "superior," to indicate the degree to which employees possess those traits. Trait ratings are difficult to defend in court if challenged. They tend to be subjective, and raters often disagree on their definitions and how they should be measured. Trait ratings are also often not related to job performance or relevant behaviors. Someone may have a poor attitude but still be technically proficient. The scales also do not define what is meant by "average" or "superior." Different raters may apply different standards in evaluating the same behaviors.

An example of a trait-rating scale is presented in Exhibit 9.2.

Exhibit 9.2.   Trait-Rating Scale.

Name _____ Section _____ Unit _____

Use the following scale to rate each trait:

Outstanding = 1   Very good = 2   Average = 3   Improvement needed = 4
Unsatisfactory = 5

Judgment _____	Cooperation _____
Dependability _____	Knowledge of work _____
Work initiative _____	Public contacts _____
Quality of work _____	Supervisory ability _____
Appearance _____	Overall job performance _____

Behavioral-Anchored Rating Scales (BARS)

Raters evaluate employees using a set of behavioral descriptions. The descriptions list various degrees of behavior with respect to a specific performance dimension. They identify a range of behaviors, from unacceptable performance to outstanding performance. Ratees do not have to actually exhibit the behaviors on the scale; rather, the behaviors serve a guide to help the rater and ratee understand the level of performance that is required for an assigned rating. Unlike some of the other instruments, BARS rely on employee behaviors—what employees actually do and what is under their direct control.

A problem for many public and nonprofit service providers is that often, despite their best efforts, unacceptable outcomes result. For example, a psychiatric client may have a relapse that requires hospitalization, despite the social worker's best efforts to help the client remain in the community. BARS would evaluate the social worker on his or her behaviors, not on the number of patients needing hospitalization. An advantage to using BARS is that they reduce ambiguity because employees are provided with descriptions of desired levels of performance. They are also accepted by both raters and ratees because both employees and supervisors participate in their development. A disadvantage to BARS is that their development is time-consuming and complex because each dimension requires its own behavioral anchors.

An example of a behavioral-anchored rating scale is presented in Exhibit 9.3.

Essay

The rater writes a narrative essay describing the employee's performance. The weakness in this method is that the evaluation may depend on the writing skills of the supervisor or on the amount of time the supervisor takes to complete the evaluation. Another problem is that raters and employees do not necessarily use common criteria.

Productivity Data or Work Standards

Raters evaluate employees on expected levels of output and on the quality of output. If employees are to believe that the standards are fair, they should understand how the standards were set.

Management by Objectives (MBO)

Raters and employees together determine goals or objectives and a plan of action for achieving them that the employee is to achieve during the upcoming evaluation cycle. At a scheduled time, the two participants reconvene and determine whether the goals have been met. The effectiveness of MBO depends on the skills of supervisors and subordinates in defining appropriate goals and objectives. Often easy objectives are set. Sometimes there is an overemphasis on objectives at the expense of specifying how these objectives are to be obtained. For example, Internal Revenue Service collection agents need to retrieve revenue from delinquent taxpayers but not through illegal or intimidating tactics. Nonprofits must be successful in raising money but not through dishonest fundraising activities.

A typical MBO rating scale is presented in Exhibit 9.4.

Critical Incidents

Raters record actual incidents of successful or unsuccessful performance or work actions and then use these observations to evaluate employee performance. An example of a critical incidents report is presented in Exhibit 9.5.

Exhibit 9.3. Behavioral-Anchored Rating Scale.

Job: Lieutenant Investigator

Dimension: Assign and review cases to investigators

Check the rating that describes this person's job performance most accurately.

___ *Superior:* Reviews all cases sent to investigations from records section on a daily basis. Assigns cases to investigators on a daily basis, giving clear verbal instructions about what is expected of them by the supervisor in reference to a particular case. Attaches case assignment log sheet with handwritten scheduled time once a week. Keeps a case management log of all cases assigned.

___ *Very Good:* Reviews all cases sent to investigations. Assigns cases to investigators. Attaches a case assignment log sheet with written instructions. Reviews cases with investigators when necessary.

___ *Good:* Reviews all cases refereed to investigations from patrol division and records division. Assigns cases to investigators.

___ *Needs improvement:* Takes several days before cases are reviewed. Rarely reviews investigators' work. Assignment of cases to investigators takes several days to a week.

___ *Unsatisfactory:* Allows investigators to review all reports given to investigations by records section and to pick their own assignments. Does not review investigators' work.

Comments:

_____

_____

_____

Rater's signature: _____

_____

Exhibit 9.4. Management by Objectives Rating Scale.

Position evaluated:	Lieutenant Investigator
Dimension:	Maintaining and updating standard operating procedures (SOP) manual for the investigations section
Objective:	Create a documented review procedure for investigations personnel to review SOP manual
Type of measure:	Timeliness
Present level:	Manual is reviewed with investigations personnel on a yearly basis but with no formal documented procedure
Desired level:	Manual to be reviewed with investigations personnel once a year, on a scheduled date, with captain present. A review form is signed and initialed by each individual investigator, the supervising lieutenant, and the captain. Review forms are kept on file with the SOP manual.
Time frame:	One month

Method used to achieve objective:

1. Create SOP review form and submit it to the captain for approval.

2. Check with captain and establish a yearly review date in the month of January.

3. Update manual to include file for review forms.

4. Immediately file completed review forms.

Employee signature:

_____

Supervisor signature:

_____

Date completed: _____   Date of review: _____

_____

Exhibit 9.5. Critical Incidents Report.

Positive:

(Date)   Employee volunteered for four extra assignments.

(Date)   Phone call received from professional X commending the assistance given by employee A.

(Date)   Employee submitted progress report B two weeks ahead of deadline. The report was complete and accurate. Employee exercised independent judgment.

Negative:

(Date)   Employee failed to submit accurate and complete verification reports. Auditors found deficiencies that warranted a payback.

(Date)   Employee refused to return phone calls to client, resulting in loss of client.

(Date)   Employee missed the deadline for a grant proposal submission. This resulted in the agency not receiving X amount of funds. Program X had to be eliminated.

Personnel Data

Raters tabulate information such as the number of absences or the number of times employees report to work late. The data are used to regulate employees' conformance to organizational policies.

Each of the evaluation instruments has advantages and disadvantages and may be appropriate when used in the correct context. It is important that a chosen appraisal instrument be congruent with the objective for the evaluation and suitable for the positions being evaluated. For example, personnel data such as tardiness or absenteeism do not address task proficiency or job-related behaviors. BARS or critical incidents would be more appropriate for capturing such behaviors. Personnel data tend to enforce rules and regulations.

Many agencies also make the mistake of believing that evaluation instruments should be uniform across the organization, regardless of the position being evaluated. That is not the case. The evaluation process is valuable only if it is relevant to the particular position. There must be a direct link between the requirements of the job and the instrument used to evaluate performance in that job. The KSAOCs that some jobs require incumbents to possess will be different from the KSAOCs required in other jobs. For example, nonprofit executive directors or public agency managers need to be evaluated more comprehensively than individuals who perform limited and routine tasks. Performance dimensions such as decision making and oral communication might be very relevant for management positions but less so for trade positions. Because the responsibilities of different jobs in public and nonprofit agencies vary, different instruments or even different evaluation procedures might be needed. The National Performance Review (1993) has recognized that agencies need the flexibility to develop their own performance management and reward systems that improve the performance of both their employees and the agency. Policymakers, executives, managers, and employees need to understand that to accomplish this, systems must be updated, revised, and redesigned as job responsibilities and employee abilities change to reflect current organizational performance standards.

Alternative Performance Management Techniques

As agencies move to team-based environments that focus on continuous improvement such as total quality management (TQM), traditional performance appraisal techniques are being reexamined, and there is a movement away from individual appraisals. The National Commission on the State and Local Public Service (1993), the National Performance Review (1993), and the literature on team building and gainsharing have all suggested that the public sector should move toward team-based pay-for-performance systems in which team members share the savings from higher productivity.

Total Quality Management

TQM is the name given to a variety of management systems designed to improve organizational quality. W. Edwards Deming, an American statistician, is often credited with its invention, and his version is influential and widespread (Swiss, 1992). He believed that to improve quality, the following steps are necessary:

1. Create constancy of purpose for the continuous improvement of product and service.
2. Break down barriers between departments to build teamwork.
3. Drive fear out of the workplace.
4. Eliminate quotas on the shop floor.
5. Create conditions that allow employees to have pride in their workmanship, including abolishing annual performance reviews and merit ratings.
6. Institute programs of education and self-improvement.

Common practices that he deemed harmful to quality improvements include a lack of constancy of purpose, an emphasis on short-term projects, and individual performance evaluations.

Noting some important differences between private sector organizations and public and nonprofit organizations, Cohen and Eimicke (2002) developed a government-oriented adaptation of TQM that they call *project-oriented TQM*. They note that in the public and nonprofit sectors, organizations often have independent power bases such as middle managers who cannot be forced to comply with quality initiatives. If they do not support TQM, they will simply wait out the transitory elected and appointed officials who are championing the initiative. Another difference these authors note is the difficulty of reconciling the claims of competing or contradictory customer demands. The people who supply the resources for a service such as taxpayers or donors are often not the recipients of the service. The result is one set of individuals paying for a particular service and a different set of individuals receiving that service. This makes performance management problematic because often agency and employee performance measures are not linked to the goals of the agency. For example, Riccucci and Lurie (2001) found that the performance evaluation systems of welfare offices used to evaluate the performance of frontline staff charged with implementing the goals of the 1996 Federal Personnel Responsibility and Work Opportunity Reconciliation Act (PRWORA) were not linked to the new goals of the program and agency. Workers were not evaluated under the new goals of finding people jobs and helping them become self-sufficient. Instead they were evaluated on criteria such as the accurate processing of food stamp applications and completing Temporary Assistance for Needy Families applications in a timely fashion.

Cohen and Eimicke (2002) emphasize that the analysis and suggested improvements in work processes should come from the workers who perform the tasks and that continuous improvement requires constant training and the modification of standard operating procedures.

TQM promotes the continuous improvement of procedures in an agency from the top to the bottom so that clients are satisfied with the agency's performance. The organization's culture is changed to focus on establishing and maintaining high performance standards. Unlike traditional management techniques that emphasize control, in TQM quality is achieved by improving the process, not by blaming employees.

Gainsharing

Gainsharing is a group incentive plan that distributes gains from improved performance to employees in a department or an organization, based on an established sharing formula. Participative management and teamwork are used to develop performance techniques and standards that control costs or units of output. All members of the team, department, or agency benefit from the increased cost savings. Lawler (2000) refers to gainsharing as a management style, a technology for organizational development, and an incentive system. A gainsharing program was used by the federal government in its Pacer Share demonstration project at McClellan Air Force Base in California. An evaluation of the program found improvements in attitudes toward the work environment, satisfaction with supervisors and coworkers, trust in management's control of the work, and increased training opportunities and organizational involvement (Siegel, 1994). Gainsharing and increases in compensation will be discussed in greater detail in Chapter Ten.

Goalsharing

Goalsharing plans, like gainsharing plans, pay bonuses when performance is above a standard. The difference is that goalsharing plans seek to leverage an organization's operational strategy by measuring performance on key strategic objectives. Goalsharing plans can reward things that do not have an immediate or direct dollar payoff for an organization, such as quality or customer satisfaction. A specific bonus amount is tied to achieving performance on the goals that were set. At the end of the year, a different set of measures and standards may be established as part of a new plan, or the old plan may continue. Goalsharing plans are typically used when the external environment is rapidly changing and the organization wants to target a particular kind of performance improvement for a limited time period (Lawler, 2000).

Another strategy that goes beyond financial indicators to evaluate performance and is related to goalsharing is the balanced scorecard (Kaplan & Norton, 1996). Though no one would dispute the importance of financial measures and of operating in the black, financial measures are not always the best indicators of effectiveness in the public and nonprofit sectors. Public and nonprofit agencies often provide services that are not profitable and provide such services to citizens and clients that need special and often expensive assistance. The balanced-scorecard approach to evaluating performance includes measures such as customer satisfaction, employee satisfaction, and quality, in addition to relevant financial measures.

Can Performance Appraisals and Quality Improvement Processes Coexist?

Many of you reading this probably think, as I do, that gainsharing, goalsharing, a balanced-scorecard approach, TQM, and other quality improvement processes rely on many of the same principles as performance evaluation and are not antithetical to the performance evaluation process. If done correctly, quality improvement processes require the development of performance standards and of measures to determine whether the standards have been achieved; they require feedback from multiple sources and also the development of an action plan for reaching future goals. What is key to the success of any of these quality improvement and performance assessment systems is not the name of the process used but the personnel policies and rules that support and enhance the total-quality environment of the entire organization. Exhibit 9.6 identifies key questions that management should consider prior to developing a performance evaluation system.

Exhibit 9.6. Questions to Consider When Developing a Performance Evaluation System.

1. How can your agency effectively involve employees and their representatives in redesigning performance management to promote the credibility and acceptance of the system? Have you identified your mutual interests?

2. Does your performance management system include effective performance planning, goal setting, and communications processes that link to your strategic objectives?

3. Should you be developing measures of customer service and group or team performance outcomes that can be used for planning performance and for distributing rewards based on improved performance?

4. Have you given enough attention to planning, measuring, and rewarding internal customer service for your various staff operations and administrative functions?

5. Have you developed collateral processes for establishing performance goals and monitoring performance and established how these might be integrated into the formal appraisal and reward process?

6. Do you provide ongoing performance monitoring and feedback to employees about their individual and group performance?

7. Are the people who have the best knowledge of the quality and effectiveness of employee performance providing feedback, either for developmental purposes or as input to a performance appraisal? Should you explore using 360-degree assessment where it is appropriate?

8. Do the elements and standards of your employee performance plans capture the results and accomplishments you expect, or do they merely describe the same tasks and process inputs year after year?

9. Are the distinctions you make among levels of performance credible to internal and external stakeholders? How many distinctions can be made credibly, given your culture and the nature of your work?

Source: Office of Personnel Management, 1994, p. 51.

To facilitate change, HRM departments must expand their awareness to ensure that all work focuses on the agency's mission and its customers. Continuous improvement must be integrated into its culture. Mutual respect and teamwork between all levels of the organization are necessary. Quality improvement requires that supervisors give workers more autonomy and allow their participation in decision making. Employee training must therefore extend beyond job or technical skills. Since all workers will be expected to function in a group setting, quality improvement and performance evaluation programs must provide training in group dynamics, problem-solving techniques, and the use of quality improvement tools. Quality improvement processes and performance evaluation systems do not have to be at odds with each other. Evaluation systems can be developed that focus on developing individual job skills that support the group's efforts for quality and productivity improvements. The competitive nature of evaluation can be eliminated by comparing employees to standards instead of to one another.

Changing to a quality improvement culture may require the modification of many HRM policies that have become institutionalized throughout the years. Organizations need to analyze their selection, training, development, compensation, and evaluation systems to ensure that they reify the values necessary for quality improvement efforts.

Summary

Performance management is the process that reviews and measures employee performance. Performance evaluations should be objective, job-related, and consistent with the organization's mission. When correctly developed and executed, they should enhance the organization's effectiveness. The performance management process provides management with important information for making strategic decisions on employee promotions, training and development activities, compensation decisions, and retention or separation. Employees who are performing at high levels in their present positions should be informed as to what career progression paths exist within their organization so that career development activities can be planned. Likewise, employees who fail to meet performance standards should be provided with training or, if necessary, be dismissed. In today's competitive environment, nonproductive employees can no longer be tolerated.

Performance evaluations are used to support many HRM functions, but because the appraisal process and instruments cannot serve all purposes simultaneously, the organization must first decide on the specific objectives it wishes to achieve and then develop the appropriate instruments and performance management system. Regardless of the type of instrument used or the purpose of the evaluation, all raters must be trained.

Many researchers have suggested that traditional performance evaluation systems that focus on individual performance should be eliminated and replaced with team approaches. Other researchers believe that individual assessments complement team approaches because they foster individual accountability and identify individual developmental needs, which in turn benefit the work team (Masterson & Taylor, 1996).

Questions and Exercises

1. Identify the major strategic issues an employer, department, or supervisor faces in designing a performance management system.
2. What are the advantages and disadvantages of 360-degree feedback systems?
3. Select five different positions in your organization, and decide what sources would be appropriate for performance feedback.
4. In small groups, select a particular job in a specific industry, and design a performance management system for this position.
5. Visit the Web site of the Office of Personnel Management (http://www.opm.gov/perform). What performance management strategies does the OPM recommend?
6. Assuming that you are a performance evaluation consultant, visit the University of California at San Diego's Guide to Performance Management Web site (http://www-hr.ucsd.edu/~staff education/guide). How comprehensive is the guide? Is there any information that needs to be added? Deleted?
7. Visit the U.S. Department of the Interior's Office of Planning and Performance Management Web site (htpp://www.doi.gov/ppp). Do you find information there that would be useful to your organization? Explain.

| **Compensation**

The design, implementation, and maintenance of compensation systems are important parts of strategic human resources management (SHRM). Decisions about salaries, incentives, benefits, and quality-of-life issues are important in attracting, retaining, and motivating employees.

Strategic decisions about pay levels, pay structures, job evaluation, and incentive pay systems influence the ability of an organization to compete in the marketplace to attract the most qualified and competent applicants and to retain its most talented and productive employees. Compensation is a topic that most employees are concerned with, yet most of us do not understand the underlying premises that drive compensation systems. What factors, for example, explain the difference in compensation between an administrative specialist working for the federal government in a general salary classification GS-6, step 3, at an annual salary of $19,386 and a fellow GS-6, step 8, making $22,416? They perform the same tasks, but the step 3 administrative specialist is more proficient. Or why are the starting salaries for police officers in adjacent municipalities different? Police officers in municipality A start at $32,230 per year, while the starting salary for police officers in municipality B is $27,567 per year. Or what explains the differences in the salaries of executive directors of Boys and Girls Clubs of America at different clubs? The advertised salary range for the executive director of the Boys and Girls Club of Central Maryland, located in Baltimore, is $70,000 to $85,000, while the advertised salary range for executive director of the Boys and Girls Club of Syracuse, New York, is $66,000 to $106,000.

From an SHRM perspective, employers use compensation to attract, retain, and motivate employees to achieve organizational goals. Employees expect fair remuneration for the services they perform. However, what is often lacking is the understanding that compensation is affected by many factors: the expectations and perception of fairness by employees, competitive labor market wages, the extent of other benefits provided to employees, the organization's ability to pay, and federal and state laws. This chapter introduces the concepts of equity, competitive labor markets, and comparable worth, as well as job evaluation methods, the design of pay structures, and federal laws that influence compensation. Indirect financial compensation, more commonly referred to as employee benefits, are discussed in Chapter Eleven.

Equity

Individuals have expectations about what they will be paid. They expect fair compensation. The standards that individuals use to determine whether the compensation they receive is fair are based on perceptions of equity. According to equity theory, employees compare their job inputs and outputs to the inputs and outputs of other employees performing similar tasks. If they perceive that their ratio of inputs to outputs is on a par with those of the others to whom they compare themselves, a state of equity is said to exist. If the ratios are unequal, inequity exists, and employees who feel that they are outperforming their colleagues will believe that they are underrewarded. To develop compensation systems, employers rely on three types of equity: external, internal, and employee.

External Equity

External equity is the standard that compares an employer's wages with the rates prevailing in external markets for the employee's position. What do other organizations pay employees who perform similar jobs and have similar responsibilities? For example, what do other counties pay entry-level budget analysts? What do program directors at nonprofits that provide services to the victims of domestic violence get paid? The federal government and state governments would be interested in the salary range for chemists with Ph.D. degrees working in industry or universities.

To determine external equity, the competitive labor market is surveyed. Labor markets are identified and defined by some combination of the following factors: education and technical background requirements, licensing or certification requirements, experience required by the job, occupational membership, and geographical location, such as local, regional, or national labor markets (Wallace & Fay, 1988). The labor market reflects the forces of supply and demand for qualified labor within an area. These forces influence the wages required to recruit or retain qualified employees. If employees do not see their pay as equitable compared to what other organizations pay for similar work, they are likely, if provided with an opportunity, to leave.

Criteria that are typically used by local governments to determine relevant employers for wage comparisons include the size of the government's population, the size of its workforce, its urban-rural mix, and its equalized assessed value (EAV). EAV is the assessed value of real property multiplied by the state equalization factor. (The state equalization factor is a device to provide equity across the state in property tax by equalizing or balancing the property value between jurisdictions.) The EAV is divided by the population to reveal per capita wealth. Each state has its own ratio. It is the base against which tax rates are calculated and translates into the government's ability to pay salaries. Using these criteria, small local governments would seek other small local governments with similar features as their reference points, rather than large industrial cities.

Nonprofit agencies should also look for comparable organizations. That may be more difficult because nonprofit services and structures evolve in response to a variety of forces. Often programs and services have been developed by the professional staff and board of directors to be consistent with the agency's mission. Programs also evolve in response to local, state, and federal funding opportunities. Nonprofit staffing patterns and the ability to pay employees are subject to a greater variety of influences than in the public sector. When looking for comparable employers, agencies must seek organizations that provide similar services and that are similarly situated in terms of size and structure (including number of employees), revenue sources (size of operating budget, types of grants and contributions received for nonprofit agencies), cash compensation (base and merit pay, increase schedules, cost-of-living adjustments) and benefits (number of paid holidays, personal days, and sick days; nature and extent of health care coverage; contributions made to retirement), and position titles and benchmark equivalents (scope of responsibilities, education requirements, years in position, salaries paid to incumbents). For example, a small community-based social service nonprofit that provides services to the developmentally disabled should compare itself with other organizations of the same size and with similar characteristics that provide comparable services. An agency staffed by fifteen employees should not compare itself with a large metropolitan nonprofit hospital. These same characteristics (except for grants and contributions as sources of revenue) can be used by local governments to determine comparable employers.

If conducting a survey or hiring consultants to do so is not feasible, various government agencies such as the state or federal department of labor or commercial firms such as the Bureau of Labor Statistics, the Bureau of National Affairs, and the Commerce Clearing House publish area wage surveys and industry wage surveys as well as professional, administrative, technical, and clerical surveys. Professional associations and consulting firms also publish salary data. For example, the Child Welfare League of America and the National Association of Homes and Services for Children publish the salaries of youth service workers. The *Nonprofit Times* and the *Chronicle of Philanthropy* also publish studies of management salaries in nonprofit organizations. A recent salary study conducted by the *Nonprofit Times* (Jones, 2003) found that the mean projected salaries for 2003 were as follows:

Executive director, CEO, or president: $88,749

Chief financial officer: $60,675

Program director: $52,253

Planned giving officer: $62,019

Development director: $55,807

Major gifts officer: $56,850

Chief of direct marketing: $52,812

Director of volunteers: $35,498

Webmaster: $38,498

Chief of technology: $58,595

The nonprofits with the largest budgets paid executive directors the most. Table 10.1 presents the results of the survey.

Internal Equity

Internal equity is the standard that requires employers to set wages for jobs in their organizations that correspond to the relative internal value of each job. Positions that are determined to be more valuable to the organization receive higher wages. Typically, high-level employees receive greater compensation than low-level employees.

The internal value of each position to the organization is determined by a procedure known as job evaluation. Job evaluation determines the worth of one job relative to another. To institute internal equity in its compensation structure, Congress passed the Classification Act of 1923. Prior to the establishment of the classification system, federal employees were paid according to the agency they worked for, and wages were at the discretion of agency management. The lack of procedures and standardization permitted disparities among employees performing the same type of work. Different positions were often given the same title, and similar positions were often given different titles. Pay was not necessarily related to the work performed. The act created the Personnel Classification Board, which mandated that positions be grouped according to similar responsibilities and duties and be compensated accordingly. Employees would be paid according to the value of their work, which would be determined according to the job's compensable factors, such as level of education and amount of experience required, the amount of responsibility, the job hazards, and so on. Exhibit 10.1 lists some of the most common compensable factors.

A variety of factor comparison systems are used to determine job value. Compensable factors are identified, weighed, and assigned point values that reflect their weight. Jobs are broken down into their compensable factors and rated along a continuum of points or placed in rank order. After the compensable factors have been rated or ranked, they are summed to derive a total point value for the job. Positions with higher point values are considered more valuable to the agency.

In 1949, Congress passed the Classification Act of 1949, which established the General Schedule (GS) system. The GS system defines the basic compensation system used by nonmanagerial white-collar positions. There are eighteen grade levels, with ranges of pay

Table 10.1. *Nonprofit Times* Salary Survey: National Average Salaries for 2002 and 2003, by Budget Size.

	Overall Average	$500,000–$999,999	$1–$9.9 Million	$10–$24.9 Million	$25–$49.9 Million	$50 Million or More
Chief Executive Officer	89,001/88,749	66,155/66,816	88,876/91,390	122,848/127,303	111,024/82,286	214,619/167,540
Chief Financial Officer	59,842/60,675	40,104/41,828	55,773/56,894	80,537/84,566	92,500/85,000	116,607/116,799
Program Director	51,210/52,253	39,819/39,972	51,320/52,428	66,398/68,772	40,000/40,000	105,241/103,716
Planned Gifts Officer	66,166/62,019	42,000/50,000	60,902/53,167	87,000/90,000	N.A./N.A.	88,333/83,254
Development Director	55,279/55,807	42,077/42,607	54,678/55,795	62,300/63,313	69,000/55,000	101,714/98,408
Major Gifts Officer	57,265/56,850	55,000/58,000	47,930/48,830	62,500/64,750	53,000/N.A.	100,000/80,000
Chief of Direct Marketing	52,675/52,812	45,000/44,188	47,443/48,354	66,200/68,390	75,000/N.A.	80,911/79,845
Director of Volunteers	33,352/35,267	28,656/30599	33,511/35,411	30,875/34,986	28,000/29,000	52,734/51,953
Webmaster	38,571/38,498	34,125/39,398	38,349/38,106	47,500/41,500	29,000/30,000	42,510/48,854
Chief of Technology	56,501/58,595	36,625/38,125	47,096/49,499	69,841/76,236	56,000/47,000	122,435/123,720

Note: First figure given is the actual average for 2002; second figure is the projected average for 2003.

N.A. = not available.

Source: Jones, 2003, pp. 22–23. Used by permission of *The Nonprofit Times.*

Exhibit 10.1. Typical Compensable Factors.

Compensable Factors	Definitions and Questions Addressed in Job Specifications
Experience	Experience is the training and development acquired from previous work that is necessary to qualify for a position, plus the training and development on the job that is necessary for proficiency. The requirement for this factor is usually expressed in terms of the time necessary to acquire the experience. *How long should the incumbent have worked in this job or in a closely related job?*
Education	Education refers to the basic ability, skill, and intellectual requirements the position demands, normally assumed to have been acquired by attending high school, business school, trade school, college, or graduate school. Referring to periods of formal schooling is convenient when comparing positions; however, the expression "or its equivalent" should ordinarily form a part of the educational specifications when such reference is made. *What does the job require in terms of formal schooling, training, or knowledge of a specialized field?*
Complexity of duties	This factor is a measure of the variety and difficulty of the work performed and the degree of skill and judgment necessary in performing it. Complexity is found to some extent in all positions. *Does the job require the incumbent to show judgment and initiative and to make independent decisions?*
Supervision received	This refers to the degree to which the work is supervised and is guided by practice or precedent and the requirements of the position for problem solving and decision making.

Exhibit 10.1. Typical Compensable Factors, Cont'd.

Compensable Factors	Definitions and Questions Addressed in Job Specifications
	How closely does the incumbent's supervisor check his or her work and outline specific methods or work procedures?
Supervision exercised	This factor measures the responsibility for directing the work of others. Its value is determined by the nature and complexity of the work supervised, the degree of responsibility for attaining desired results, and the number of persons supervised.
	How many people does the incumbent supervise directly or indirectly?
Mental demands	This factor appraises the amount and continuity of mental demand required to perform the job. It is a value factor in positions requiring a degree of concentrated mental effort or constant attention to detail.
	What degree of concentration is required by the job?
Physical demands	This factor appraises the amount and continuity of physical effort required to perform the job. It is a value factor in jobs that require the employee to stand, lift, carry, bend, or walk for extended periods.
	Are there special physical demands on this job?
Working conditions	This factor has value in positions where excessive heat, noise, use of chemicals, poor ventilation, and so forth are elements in the job environment.
	Is there anything in the work environment that is unusually hazardous or uncomfortable? If so, what percentage of the time is the incumbent exposed to this?

within each grade. There are approximately 450 categories in the GS, sorted into specialized groups such as finance and accounting, social science, psychology and welfare, engineering and architecture, and physical science. Each grade contains examples of the kind of work performed in jobs that would be assigned to that grade. These examples are referred to as *benchmark positions*. Benchmark positions are jobs with characteristics similar enough to jobs performed in other organizations that can serve as market anchor points using a comparison system called the Factor Evaluation System. Jobs are described and placed in grades on the basis of their duties and responsibilities and the qualifications required to perform them. Nine factors with different levels and different point values are used to evaluate jobs: knowledge required by the position, supervisory controls, guidelines, complexity, scope and effect, personal contacts, purpose of contacts, physical demands, and work environment. After all nine factors have been evaluated and levels have been established for the position, the points are summed across each factor until an aggregate total is derived. The total points are then compared to a chart, and the position is assigned to a grade.

A problem with this job evaluation system is that the duties and responsibilities of a specific job do not always fit neatly into one grade or job class. The GS has been criticized for its lack of flexibility in supporting individual agency missions, structures, and cultures and for its inability to respond to rapidly changing external conditions. The National Performance Review (1993) has recommended modifying the GS by reducing the number of occupational categories and permitting agencies to establish broadbanding systems. (Broadbanding will be described later in this chapter.)

Employee Equity

Employee equity is the comparison of pay across employees performing the same or similar work. It focuses on the contributions of an individual worker within a job classification. At issue is what coworkers performing the same job get paid. Are differences in levels of proficiency or contribution reflected in compensation?

Most compensation structures include pay ranges. A pay range exists when one or more rates are paid to employees in the same job. The range permits organizations to pay different wages for differences in experience or in performance. A pay range reflects the minimum and maximum that the employer will pay for the position.

Table 10.2 presents the General Schedule Pay Scale for federal employees. Each grade has ten pay-level increments. New college graduates usually begin at the base pay for the grade, but the Office of Personnel Management may authorize recruitment at rates above the minimum for jobs in which there are shortages, such as engineers, chemists, and architects.

Pay grades and pay ranges for a city-county library district are presented in Table 10.3. Each of the thirteen pay grades in this salary schedule has six pay-level increments. Employees move up to the next higher level on the anniversary of their employment. After six years, they have reached the top of the salary grade, or "maxed out." Employees at the top of the salary grade can expect to receive only cost-of-living increases.

To determine pay ranges, the employer needs to establish what the current market rates are for benchmark jobs. After the data have been compiled, organizations develop salary ranges to fit their structure. Each salary range should have a midpoint, a minimum, and a maximum. The distance separating a grade's minimum and maximum salaries is called the grade's range. The midpoint for each range is usually set to correspond to the external labor market. It specifies the pay objectives for employees performing at satisfactory levels. The minimums and maximums are usually based on a combination of the size of the range identified in survey data and judgments about how the ranges fit the organization. These judgments are based on a variety of factors, including salaries paid by the organization's competition, the organization's culture, and standard pay across an occupational classification. For example, production and maintenance positions typically have ranges of 20 to 25 percent, whereas professional, administrative, and managerial positions might have ranges of 40 to 50 percent under certain circumstances. Wider ranges are designed to reflect greater discretion, responsibility, and variations in performance. Pay ranges are useful because they allow an organization to provide a competitive salary and recognize individual differences among employees. Table 10.4 illustrates current market rates and their minimums, maximums, and midpoints for selected benchmark positions in local government.

Table 10.2. Salary Table 2003-GS: General Schedule Pay Scale, Annual Rates by Grade and Step.

GS Grade	Step									
	1	2	3	4	5	6	7	8	9	10
1	15,214	15,722	16,228	16,731	17,238	17,536	18,034	18,538	18,559	19,031
2	17,106	17,512	18,079	18,559	18,767	19,319	19,871	20,423	20,975	21,527
3	18,664	19,286	19,908	20,530	21,152	21,774	22,396	23,018	23,640	24,262
4	20,952	21,650	22,348	23,046	23,744	24,442	25,140	25,838	26,536	27,234
5	23,442	24,223	25,004	25,785	26,566	27,347	28,128	28,909	29,690	30,471
6	26,130	27,001	27,872	28,743	29,614	30,485	31,356	32,227	33,098	33,969
7	29,037	30,005	30,973	31,941	32,909	33,877	34,845	35,813	36,781	37,749
8	32,158	33,230	34,302	35,374	36,446	37,518	38,590	39,662	40,734	41,806
9	35,519	36,703	37,887	39,071	40,255	41,439	42,623	43,807	44,991	46,175
10	39,115	40,419	41,723	43,027	44,331	45,635	46,939	48,243	49,547	50,851
11	42,976	44,409	45,842	47,275	48,708	50,141	51,574	53,007	54,440	55,873
12	51,508	53,225	54,942	56,659	58,376	60,093	61,810	63,527	65,244	66,961
13	61,251	63,293	65,335	67,377	69,419	71,461	73,503	75,545	77,587	79,629
14	72,381	74,794	77,207	79,620	82,033	84,446	86,859	89,272	91,685	94,098
15	85,140	87,978	90,816	93,654	96,492	99,330	102,168	105,006	107,844	110,682

Source: Office of Personnel Management, 2003.

When establishing pay ranges, employers must look at the degree of overlap in adjacent pay ranges. Overlap is the amount of comparability of pay between pay grades. The amount of overlap between pay grades signifies the similarities in the responsibilities, duties, and KSAOCs of the job whose pay ranges overlap. Overlap between pay ranges permits more valuable senior employees in lower-paying jobs to be paid more than new employees in higher-level jobs who have not yet begun to make significant contributions to the organization (Henderson, 1989). In Tables 10.2 and 10.3, GS-1 or Grade A employees at steps 5 and above receive higher compensation than GS-2 or Grade B employees at step 1.

When developing a salary structure, you may find that certain jobs in the organization have been underpaid or overpaid. Underpaid positions are referred to as green-circled and overpaid positions are referred to as red-circled. To bring these wages in line with market rates and internal equity standards, underpaid employees should be given pay increases that raise their rates to at least the minimum of the range for their pay grade. The salaries of overpaid employees may need to be frozen until other jobs are brought into line with them. Other options include cutting the wages to the maximum in the pay range for the pay grade, increasing the employees' responsibilities, or transferring or promoting them to positions in which they can be paid their current rate.

Compression

Compression results when the salaries for jobs filled from outside the organization are increasing faster than incumbent wages (that is, when new employees are paid salaries that are comparable to those of more experienced employees) or the salaries of jobs filled from within the organization. Compression occurs in most public and nonprofit organizations. For example, ten years ago, the starting salary for county probation officers might have been $20,500. Today, probation officers hired ten years ago might be making $32,000 while new probation officers might start at salaries around $27,500. The pay differential between an employee with ten years of experience and a new employee is compressed because of market wages.

Table 10.3. City-County Library District Salary and Wage Schedule.

Grade	Annual Pay-Level Increments						
A	1,707	1,775	1,846	1,920	1,996	2,076	Monthly
	20,484	21,300	22,152	23,040	23,952	24,912	Yearly
	9.81	10.20	10.61	11.03	11.47	11.93	Hourly
B	1,920	1,996	2,076	2,159	2,246	2,335	Monthly
	23,040	23,952	24,912	25,908	26,952	28,020	Yearly
	11.03	11.47	11.93	12.41	12.91	13.42	Hourly
C	2,159	2,246	2,335	2,429	2,525	2,625	Monthly
	25,908	26,952	28,020	29,148	30,300	31,500	Yearly
	12.41	12.91	13.42	13.96	14.51	15.09	Hourly
D	2,429	2,525	2,625	2,731	2,840	2,954	Monthly
	29,148	30,300	31,500	32,772	34,080	35,448	Yearly
	13.96	14.51	15.09	15.70	16.32	16.98	Hourly
E	2,731	2,840	2,954	3,071	3,194	3,322	Monthly
	32,772	34,080	35,448	36,852	38,328	39,864	Yearly
	15.70	16.32	16.98	17.65	18.36	19.09	Hourly
F	3,071	3,194	3,322	3,456	3,594	3,738	Monthly
	36,852	38,328	39,864	41,472	43,128	44,856	Yearly
	17.65	18.36	19.09	19.86	20.66	21.48	Hourly

Grade		Step 1	Step 2	Step 3	Step 4	Step 5	Step 6
G	Monthly	3,456	3,594	3,738	3,887	4,042	4,203
	Yearly	41,472	43,128	44,856	46,644	48,504	50,436
	Hourly	19.86	20.66	21.48	22.34	23.23	24.16
H	Monthly	3,887	4,042	4,203	4,372	4,547	4,729
	Yearly	46,644	48,504	50,436	52,464	54,564	56,748
	Hourly	22.34	23.23	24.16	25.13	26.13	27.18
I	Monthly	4,372	4,547	4,729	4,917	5,114	5,318
	Yearly	52,464	54,564	56,748	59,004	61,368	63,816
	Hourly	25.13	26.13	27.18	28.26	29.39	30.56
J	Monthly	4,917	5,114	5,318	5,531	5,753	5,982
	Yearly	59,004	61,368	63,816	66,372	69,036	71,784
	Hourly	28.26	29.39	30.56	31.79	33.06	34.38
K	Monthly	5,531	5,753	5,982	6,222	6,471	6,730
	Yearly	66,372	69,036	71,784	74,664	77,652	80,760
	Hourly	31.79	33.06	34.38	35.76	37.19	38.68
L	Monthly	6,222	6,471	6,730	6,999	7,279	7,569
	Yearly	74,664	77,652	80,760	83,988	87,348	90,828
	Hourly	35.76	37.19	38.68	40.22	41.83	43.50
M	Monthly	6,999	7,279	7,569	7,872	8,187	8,515
	Yearly	83,988	87,348	90,828	94,464	98,244	102,180
	Hourly	40.22	41.83	43.50	45.24	47.05	48.94

Table 10.4. Municipal Market Study for Comparable Local Government Positions.

Administrative Classifications	City A	City B	City C	City D	City E	Lowest Minimum	Highest Minimum	Midpoint
Personal Property Auditor	26,022	41,112	—	30,611	—	26,022	41,112	30,611
Department Secretary Assessor's Office	33,100	23,303	15,148	—	—	15,148	33,100	23,303
Finance Director	66,780	42,210	55,770	61,797	68,948	42,210	68,948	61,797
Administrative Assistant	56,603	39,060	37,670	29,597	48,673	29,597	56,603	39,060
Treasurer	42,719	43,872	40,963	33,994	65,620	33,994	65,620	42,719
City Clerk	39,333	41,474	30,846	46,178	62,812	30,846	62812	41,474
City Librarian	50,503	—	—	39,930	55,188	39,930	55,188	50,503
Director of Community Development and Planning	66,780	42,210	39,128	33,994	50,231	33,994	66,780	42,210

to move slowly and secretively

Grade Creep

Grade creep is a form of classification inflation. Supervisors and incumbents request that positions be reclassified to the next higher grade so that the incumbent receives higher compensation despite no change in job tasks or responsibilities. Grade creep typically results when incumbents are at the top of their pay level and no other mechanism exists to increase their pay.

Pay Differentials

Employee equity addresses pay differentials within the same position. It recognizes that employees who possess the same job title and responsibilities often perform at different levels of productivity or proficiency, making different contributions to the agency's mission.

In the public sector, seniority is frequently used to differentiate pay. More senior employees receive higher wages regardless of their performance. For each year of service, employees' salaries are automatically increased to the next grade step to reward their years of service to the organization. This is why the administrative specialist in step 3 receives a lower salary than a coworker at step 8. The problem with seniority-based differentials is that longer tenure does not *Permanent position* necessarily translate into more effective performance. If seniority is the only system in place to differentiate pay, organizations may find it hard to attract and retain competent employees. Employees who believe that their pay is low after comparing their inputs and level of pay to other employees in similar positions will become less motivated over time. Dissatisfied employees are prone to file more grievances, to be absent more frequently, and to search for higher-paying positions elsewhere. Employers must have in place different strategies to address employee equity concerns. The following paragraphs provide brief descriptions of alternative pay systems that are used to enhance traditional pay systems.

Broadbanding

There has been a movement away from using a system of many pay grades. Instead, salary grades are being collapsed into broader bands with wider ranges. The use of broadbands eliminates having to maintain many narrow salary grades. Broadbanding was introduced by the federal government out of frustration with the inflexible federal classification and pay system and to increase flexibility, managerial control, and accountability (Risher & Schay, 1994). Two naval research and development laboratories found it difficult to recruit and retain scientists and engineers. The laboratories designed a new classification and compensation system that would give their managers the flexibility needed to compete with the private sector. The states of California, Michigan, Minnesota, and Wisconsin are undertaking the legislative and regulatory changes necessary to replace their current classification systems with broadbanding, and the governments of Charlotte, North Carolina; Virginia Beach, Virginia; and Loudoun County, Virginia, have already implemented broadbanding (Smith, 1999). Broadbanding grants managers the discretion to offer a variety of starting salaries and to reward employees with pay increases or different job assignments as needed to fulfill the agency's mission. Advocates of broadbanding claim that it simplifies pay administration, facilitates career development, and links compensation with SHRM.

Skill-Based Pay or Pay for Knowledge

In skill-based or pay-for-knowledge plans, pay is determined by the number of tasks or jobs or the amount of knowledge an employee masters. It is a compensation system based on paying for what employees can do, for the knowledge or skills they possess. Under skill-based pay, employees can be expected to perform a broad range of duties. Benefits attributed to skill-based pay from an organizational standpoint include developing a cross-trained and more flexible workforce, improving the flow of information throughout the organization, placing an emphasis on the work to be done rather than on the job itself, encouraging the acquisition of skills needed to perform a variety of jobs, and increasing employees' interest in and commitment to their work. Benefits from the employees' perspective include higher motivation, increased job satisfaction, and greater opportunities for increased pay (Feuer, 1987; Gupta, Jenkins, & Curington, 1986; Shareef, 1994, 1998; Thompson & Le Hew, 2000; Towers Perrin, 1992). The implementation of skill-based pay is not without problems. Changing a compensation system in the public sector typically requires obtaining the approval of multiple external stakeholders such as legislative bodies and union representatives, as well as the managers, supervisors, and employees who will be affected. Employees may be reluctant to give up annual step or cost-of-living increases while developing new competencies (Gupta, 1997; Shareef, 1998, 2002; Thompson & Le Hew, 2000).

Thompson and Le Hew (2000) provide a comprehensive and critical review of skill-based pay for public organizations. They developed a theoretical model that suggests broadening the framework to include a discussion of environmental contingencies such as threats and crises; competition and performance pressures; the proximate environment, including the various stakeholders, unions, and elected officials; the design features of the plan, such as how radical it is; training opportunities available for employees and the certification process that is involved; and the relevance of those components to organizational contingencies such as workforce characteristics, managerial practices and attitudes, and congruence with skill-based pay.

Organizations that implement skill-based pay need to be aware that wages and salaries will increase as employees learn new skills. And despite the strategic focus of skill-based training, all other HRM systems must be aligned. Performance evaluation systems, training and development systems, communication systems, and record-keeping systems all must change to reinforce the implementation of skill-based pay systems, or the implementation will not be successful (Shareef, 2002).

Merit Pay or Pay for Performance

Merit pay or pay-for-performance systems are grounded in the belief that individuals should be paid according to their contributions. Increases are rewarded on the basis of performance rather than seniority, equality, or need (Heneman, 1992). As logical as that may sound, research over the years has indicated that merit pay systems have not achieved the expected and desired results (Heneman, 1992; Kellough & Lu, 1993; Kellough & Nigro, 2002; Perry, 1995; Risher, Fay, & Perry, 1997).

Pay-for-performance systems fall victim to the same criticisms made about performance evaluations noted in Chapter Nine, as well as additional complaints. Critics claim that the pay-for-performance evaluation process is subjective, that employees are rated by instruments that do not reflect their actual job competencies, that supervisors lack skills to develop performance standards and provide feedback, and that comparing individuals to one another sets up a competitive environment that can be destructive to department or unit cohesion (O'Donnell & O'Brien, 2000). An additional criticism is that adequate financial resources are not always allocated. For example, New York City recently signed a contract with the American Federation of State, County and Municipal Employees (AFSCME) District Council 37 that provides a pay raise of 8 percent and gives the mayor some merit pay flexibility. However, union officials recognize that since the contract was more generous than what city officials had originally planned for, the city would not be able to find much more in its budget for large merit payments on top of the across-the-board raises (Greenhouse & Saulny, 2001). Even when pay rewards are not restricted, the small percentage of difference between high and low performers typically found in merit systems does not encourage improved performance or reward outstanding employees (Heneman, 1992).

Merit pay systems have been condemned for focusing on compensation rather than on improved performance. Research has found that when pay and performance are discussed, employees fail to address the developmental issues and instead focus on not receiving a pay increase or on receiving a smaller increase than expected. When provided with constructive feedback in a training-and-development context, employees are likely to accept the information. When feedback is tied to pay increases, however, employees process the information differently. They tend to get defensive, believing that the rater is taking something away from them by not granting a pay increase. Other research indicates that when performance appraisal results determine pay, employees often set lower goals so that they can achieve them (Cascio, 1991; Lawler, 1989).

The concepts of procedural justice and distributive justice must be considered when developing and administering pay-for-performance systems. *Procedural justice* focuses on the perceived fairness of the evaluation procedures used to determine performance ratings or merit increases. For example, what procedures or instruments are used to guarantee a link between pay and performance? *Distributive justice* focuses on the perceived fairness of the rating and increases received relative to the work performed (Greenberg, 1986). For example, is the rating or increase congruent with performance inputs? Merit systems that are not developed with these principles in mind will lack the integrity and credibility necessary for employees to perceive that the system can discern and will reward differences in performance.

Research by Heneman (1992) indicates that for employees to accept the process as just, five components must exist: performance must be clearly defined, rewards must be communicated to employees, rewards must be made contingent on desired performance, opportunities to improve performance must exist, and the perceived relationship between rewards and performance should be regarded as just as important as the actual relationship.

To be successful, pay for performance must be linked to the strategic mission of the organization, and upper-level management must support the plan. Employees should participate in the development of the plan; this increases their understanding of, commitment to, and trust in the plan. Organizations must provide training to the raters and hold them accountable for the accuracy of their ratings (Healy & Southard, 1994; Heneman, 1992; Newlin & Meng, 1991; Perry, 1995; Risher, 2002).

Aurora, Colorado, failed in its attempt to introduce a merit pay plan. The city's supervisors were not trained in making evaluations, they were not sure what the standards were, and they did not know how to give performance feedback. The system produced uneven results and therefore lacked credibility among the employees. City manager Jim Griesemer acknowledged, "We hadn't made the investment in our supervisors that was necessary to give them the tools to do this as well as they were capable" (Witt, 1989, p. 33).

The less than favorable endorsement of merit pay programs has not discouraged the public sector from attempting to institute them, and there have been some successes. Schay (1997) reports that certain federal government demonstration projects—the Navy Demonstration Project at China Lake and a project at the National Institute of Standards and Technology (NIST)—appear to be successful. The pay-for-performance system introduced at China Lake was funded by money reserved for step increases, quality step increases, and promotions between grades included in a pay band. An additional 0.8 to 1.0 percent was reserved for cash bonuses.

Employees were evaluated on a five-level rating system linked to the system of pay increases. Evaluation of the China Lake project found that money was a motivator and that employees believed that good and bad performance was distinguished, good performance was rewarded, and the rewards and the process were fair.

The NIST program rated employees on a 100-point scale. Employees who received ratings at or above 40 points were eligible for an increase. Two summary rating categories were used (eligible or not eligible for a pay increase), but employee rankings on the 100-point scale determined the size of the pay increase.

Survey data completed by employees in both demonstration projects indicated that a majority of employees perceived that the ratings were fair, that meaningful performance appraisal sessions can take place between supervisors and subordinates, that supervisors are willing to explain and support the reward system, and that rewards can vary widely, depending on performance (Schay, 1997).

The city of Claremont, California, has implemented a pay-for-performance plan. The plan offers financial incentives to produce results and offer recognition to the top performers. The rewards vary from a raise that is a percentage of the employee's annual salary to a onetime lump-sum bonus. The city provides ongoing training for the managers who are responsible for implementing the plan. Managers and employees are expected to agree on a performance plan ahead of time, and the managers are expected to take notes throughout the year and provide developmental feedback to their employees.

Gainsharing

Gainsharing is a team bonus program that measures controllable costs, such as improved safety records or decreases in waste or units of output. Teamwork is encouraged, and all team members are rewarded for controlling costs or improving productivity. Formulas are used to measure costs that are controllable, and these costs are then compared to the costs of a historical base period. When performance improves relative to the base period, a bonus pool is funded. When performance falls short, no bonus pool is created. Employees keep a percentage of the bonus pool, and the organization keeps the rest. Charlotte, North Carolina, began a gainsharing program in 1994. Each year, the city manager sets a city-wide savings goal. If the goal is met, half of the savings are set aside to create an employee incentive pool and the balance is returned to the general fund (Risher, 1998). Half the pool is paid in equal shares to all employees, and payouts from the other half depend on the achievement of department goals. Each department establishes specific goals in two to all five of the following areas: customer satisfaction, productivity, quality, time standards, or safety. If a department has three goals and meets one, employees will receive 33 percent of the second half of their share of the pool.

Baltimore County established a gainsharing program that is based on cost-saving initiatives proposed by groups of county workers. It is a pilot program that began in two departments, the jail food preparation unit of the Bureau of Corrections and the parks and recreation maintenance division. Committees of employees and management first set goals to reduce costs and improve service and then implement them. Under the plan, half of the savings realized two years after a proposal's acceptance goes to employees in the departments, and the balance goes to the county. At the end of the second year, all savings go to the county. According to county officials, an additional benefit of gainsharing is that it gets employees involved in problem solving and developing solutions to work-related obstacles. Employees appreciate the additional training that comes with the implementation of gainsharing plans and feel that their involvement leads to greater job security, which in turn leads to improved morale. The success of the program has led county officials to believe that gainsharing will eventually be adopted by all departments (Boone, 1998). According to Charlotte's city manager, during 1999–2000, $49.6 million was returned to the general fund, and employees received payments of $2.6 million (Risher, 1999).

Zebulon, North Carolina, has adopted another type of gainsharing plan. Zebulon's plan involves the community from the inception of the budget cycle. Members of the community volunteer to serve on a focus committee for each department. Each committee develops survey questions for its department and forwards the questions to the town administrator to develop citizen surveys. Citizens evaluate the services and make comments or recommend improvements. The town administrator presents the results of the surveys to the town council, and department heads share the results with the employees within their units.

Organizational goals are also used. The town council and administrator plan the town direction for the coming fiscal year and determine goals. The goals and objectives must be met for gainsharing awards to be distributed. All of the departments work to meet the goals of their specific area. If a department is not meeting its goals, other departments can step in and help. Teamwork across departments is emphasized.

Employees are also expected to contribute to Zebulon's efficient operations. The employees' individual performance appraisals determine if they are eligible for an award. Employees who fail to score 2.95 or higher on a 5-point scale do not receive a gainsharing bonus. Any year-end budget savings are distributed to employees who are eligible (Patton & Daley, 1998).

Coral Springs, Florida, also has a gainsharing program that recognizes improvements in productivity and cost savings by city employees and departments. At the end of the fiscal year, any budget surplus gets distributed equally to each employee. In 2002, city employees each received approximately $400 (Pounds, 2003).

As these examples demonstrate, not all gainsharing plans are the same. The formulas and participative management features need to fit each other as well as the organization. Different situations require different designs. However, some common essential elements are necessary for any plan to succeed: (1) There must be a credible and trusted development process. (2) Employees must believe that improved performance and decreased costs will lead to bonuses; the bonuses must be understandable and large enough to influence performance, and employees must recognize how their behavior can influence the size of the bonus. (3) Employees need to be involved in the process; they must have influence over the measures used to calculate the bonus. (4) The measures must be appropriate and must focus on all of the controllable costs.

Measures such as units of output, materials, and supplies must all be addressed; otherwise employees may focus on one cost, leading to its reduction but also to increases in other costs. For example, data processing clerks may produce a greater number of records, but if the number of errors in the records has increased, the effort has been counterproductive. Or public works employees may be able to maintain and landscape more of the city's property in less time, but if the increased productivity results in equipment breakdowns and expensive repairs, that is counterproductive. The program must be maintained; because missions and environments change, gainsharing formulas and programs must change as well to stay relevant (Lawler, 1989, 2000).

Closing Thoughts on Equity

Despite an organization's best efforts to ensure equity, there are a number of factors outside an agency's control that affect compensation. For example, as positions demand higher skill requirements, organizations can expect to pay more for those skills. If skills are in abundance, employers can offer less even if those skills are crucial to the organization. For instance, schoolteachers are often paid less than electricians, despite the greater value of teachers to the school, because unions may restrict the number of qualified electricians, thus driving up their salaries, while there are plenty of applicants wishing to be teachers. Or jobs with unpleasant or hazardous working conditions, such as sanitation or public works, might demand higher salaries because the extra pay is necessary to attract individuals to those positions.

Developing a compensation system that meets employee and organizational goals requires fine tuning. Not all employees have the same priorities. Today, quality-of-life issues are also considered important by applicants and employees. To attract and retain employees, organizations need to offer either competitive wages or other benefits deemed important to employees and applicants, such as flexible work schedules, career mobility, a sense of purpose and the opportunity to use their skills, child care, or educational reimbursement programs.

An example of an organization that has made use of the many available options is Sheltering Arms, a nonprofit social service and welfare agency that provides assistance to abused and battered women. Sheltering Arms developed a compensation structure with three components to attract and retain employees. First, it compares its wage levels with industry standards and maintains parity with other voluntary agencies. Second, it provides greater emphasis on personal time off and other nonfinancial benefits. And third, it provides an incentive based payment plan in which a U.S.

savings bond is given to employees who contribute to agency goals (Kraten, 1995).

Executive Compensation and Benefits

The compensation and benefits provided to executives in public and nonprofit organizations are often different from the compensation and benefits other employees receive. In the public sector, executives are exempt from civil service protection and serve at the discretion of elected officials. In the nonprofit sector, executives serve at the discretion of the board of directors. Because in both sectors the positions lack security, executives are likely to have negotiated employment contracts that specify the level of compensation and benefits they will receive. Some common benefits found in executive employment contracts include severance protection; moving expenses; health, retirement, and disability insurance; professional association memberships and dues; and paid conference registration and associated expenses such as travel and accommodations.

Executives are hired for their professional experience and expertise. They must often make hard choices and unpopular decisions that run counter to the wishes of the policymaking and governing body. Severance protection allows executives to be free to make those decisions without having to worry about their financial situation if they are terminated. Severance protection usually includes a fixed amount of salary and the continuance of insurance benefits for a predetermined period of time.

Executives are typically recruited from the national labor market and often relocate to accept a position. Organizations that pay for moving expenses and in some cases provide a housing allowance in jurisdictions where housing is expensive find it easier to attract key executives. Executives will be less likely to relocate if they risk losing equity in their homes or if the costs associated with moving are prohibitive.

Because it is the responsibility of executives to guide as well as manage the organization, it is imperative that they have access to training and development activities such as attending conferences and belonging to professional associations. Organizations benefit when their executives are aware of the external forces affecting their agencies and changes in industry standards and practices. Agencies that maintain their competitive posture are led by proactive executives.

In both the public and nonprofit sectors, salaries are determined by surveying what relevant organizations in the external labor market pay for executive positions (Albert, 2000; Stene, 1980). Albert recommends that nonprofit executive salaries should be at the median or above the median of comparable organizations in the area. Board members should assess the agency's resources and offer the best salary and benefits package they can afford.

Concerns about some of the high salaries paid to nonprofit executives have been raised in light of the recent recession and nonprofit scandals. Senator Charles Grassly, a member of the Senate Finance Committee, has asked the Internal Revenue Service to do more to "help the public identify whether charities are spending donors' money on lavish salaries, expensive vacations, or other inappropriate items" (Lipman & Voelz, 2002, p. 34). However, nonprofit officials and consultants believe that while boards must be sensitive to public perception, they have an obligation to pay salaries high enough to allow them to recruit and retain talented executives who will help an organization operate its programs effectively. According to James Abruzzo, managing director of nonprofit practice for the executive search firm DHR International in Short Hills, New Jersey, "Some nonprofits are large and complex organizations and require the same kinds of skills and talents as does the private sector" (p. 34). The highest nonprofit salaries tend to be paid to the executives who run hospitals. Brian Gallagher, president of the United Way of America, notes that the nonprofit world needs to be conscious of the perception of executive compensation but that a segment of the public has unrealistic expectations about how much nonprofit executives should be paid. "For a lot of people, a charity is a charity, and the pay should be nothing or next to nothing. Once you hit $100,000, for most people that seems excessive" (p. 34).

Deciding the compensation of executives is difficult. Executives in public, nonprofit, and for-profit organizations may possess the same levels of responsibilities, administer budgets of similar size, and supervise similar-size staffs (as in public, nonprofit, and for-profit hospitals). The issue of federal executive pay was raised by the National Commission on the Public Service, which recommended raising the salaries of federal executives in the Senior Executive Service who oversee or direct federal programs so as to make them comparable to those in nonprofit organizations. A Congressional Budget Office report titled *Comparing the Pay of Federal and Nonprofit Executives: An Update* (2003) found that the median salary for chief executives at nonprofits with annual budgets of $25 million or more was about $176,800, while the median for federal executives was $138,200. However, when nonprofit organizations of all sizes are considered, the median salary of federal executives exceeds that of the nonprofit executives. The report cautions that the data were compiled by a consulting firm and may not be representative of all nonprofits. Wider ranges of data are needed before reaching conclusions on the adequacy of federal executive pay. The report also did not address any differences in the level of benefits (as for retirement or health care) between the two sectors. Likewise, if one looks at the *ICMA Newsletter*, salaries for city and county executives and other executive positions often exceed six figures.

All organizations must be careful that their executive salaries do not come at the expense of lower-level employees. All employees should be paid fair wages. In the nonprofit sector, low beginning salaries in agencies like the YMCA limit the number of college graduates who will enter the field of working with youth. YMCAs are willing to pay competitive salaries for executives, but junior staff are underpaid. After two or three years, the employees tend to leave, and the Y needs to recruit and train new staff (Vanneman, 1994). Similar examples can be found in the public sector.

Federal Laws Governing Compensation

All public and nonprofit employers are required to comply with two federal laws, the Fair Labor Standards Act (FLSA) and the Equal Pay Act.

The Fair Labor Standards Act

The FLSA was enacted in 1938. Minimum wage, overtime pay, equal pay, and child labor rules are its major provisions. The FLSA requires that employers keep records of the hours that employees have worked. Its overtime provision requires that employers pay one and one-half the regular rate of hourly pay for each hour worked in excess of forty hours per week.

The FLSA divides employees into "exempt" and "nonexempt" workers. Exempt employees are not covered by the overtime provisions. They can be expected to work more than forty hours per week without additional compensation. Title 29, Section 541, of the 1993 Code of Federal Regulations defines exempt employees as those who spend 80 percent of their working time performing administrative, executive, or professional duties.

Administrative employees' primary responsibilities consist of performing office-based duties related to the implementation of management policies or general business operations. They customarily and regularly exercise discretion and independent judgment.

Executive employees exercise discretionary decision-making powers and supervise two or more employees. They have the authority to hire and fire employees and to make recommendations as to the advancement and promotion and any other change of status of the employees they supervise.

Professional employees perform duties requiring advanced knowledge acquired through specialized intellectual instruction. Their work is predominantly intellectual and varied and is such that the output produced or the result accomplished cannot be standardized in relation to a given time period.

Employees are considered to be paid on a salary basis within the meaning of the FLSA if each pay period they receive a predetermined amount that constitutes all or part of their compensation and is not subject to reduction because of quality or quantity of the work performed. This means that employers are prohibited from making hourly deductions of pay from exempt employees.

Agencies with restricted budgets should not be tempted to classify employees as exempt as a way to avoid paying overtime. Louisiana State University (LSU) Health Science Center in Baton Rouge agreed to pay $396,997 in back overtime wages to 496 workers employed at nine hospitals throughout Louisiana. The back wages were the result of an investigation conducted by the New Orleans district office of the U.S. Department of Labor's Wage and Hour Division between January 2000 and June 2002. LSU misclassified certain salaried employees as exempt from the overtime provisions of the FLSA. The misclassified employees included medical, cafeteria, maintenance, security, and office personnel. Employees were either paid straight time for overtime hours worked or were credited with compensatory time at the rate of one hour of compensatory time for every hour of overtime worked instead of time-and-one-half as required by law. LSU was also assessed a civil monetary penalty of $8,250 for violating the law a second time. Previously, LSU had paid $29,093 in back overtime wages to twenty-two workers as a result of a two-year investigation between December 1996 and December 1998 (Employment Standards Administration, 2003).

In 1985, the Supreme Court ruled in *Garcia* v. *San Antonio Metropolitan Transit Authority* (488 U.S. 889) that the FLSA could be applied to state, county, and municipal employees. This meant that public employers could no longer use compensatory time in lieu of dollars and would have to pay overtime. Because of the financial burden this would impose, public agencies petitioned Congress for relief. Congress reacted by amending the FLSA with the Fair Labor Standards Amendments of 1985 (P.L. 99-150). Section 7(o) of the FLSA authorizes compensatory time off as a form of overtime. It applies only to public sector agencies. To be legal under the FLSA, compensatory time must be 1.5 hours for each hour worked; nonsworn personnel (public employees other than sworn officers such as police, fire, and corrections) may have no more than 240 hours of compensatory time on the books at any one time, and sworn personnel can accrue no more than 480 hours of compensatory time at any one time. Nonsworn and sworn personnel who reach the limits of 240 and 480 hours, respectively, must either receive cash for additional hours of overtime worked or use some compensatory time off before accruing further overtime compensation in the form of compensatory time off.

The 1985 amendment also has special provisions for hospital employees and for police and fire officials who typically work nontraditional shifts. Section 7(j) permits the use of a fourteen-day work period (instead of the usual seven-day workweek) in the computation of overtime provisions. Overtime is considered only if an employee works more than eighty hours during the fourteen-day period.

Section 7(k) provides for work periods up to twenty-eight days for public safety officials. They do not have to be paid overtime until they work more than 212 hours.

Nonprofit employers must comply with the FLSA overtime provision of one and one-half times an employee's normal hourly rate of pay for each hour beyond forty hours per week. Employees may elect compensatory time in lieu of overtime, but it must be their choice and not imposed by the employer.

In March 2003, the Department of Labor proposed a rule updating the current exemptions under the FLSA. Workers earning less than $22,100 per year will be entitled to overtime regardless of their duties. Workers earning more than $65,000 per year will be exempt from the minimum wage and overtime requirements if they meet any one of the requirements within the revised duties tests. At this writing, the changes had not yet been enacted.

Executive employees are exempt from overtime if their primary duty is managing the entire enterprise, a department, or a subdivision; if they customarily and regularly direct the work of two or more workers; and if they have authority to hire and fire other employees (or recommend hiring, firing, promotion, or other change of status of other employees).

Administrative employees are exempt if their primary duty is office or nonmanual work directly related to the management or general business operations of the employer or the employer's customers and if they hold a "position of responsibility" with the employer, defined as either performing work of substantial importance or requiring a high level of skill or training.

Learned professional employees are exempt if their primary duty is performing office or nonmanual work requiring knowledge of an advanced type in a field of science or learning that is customarily acquired by a prolonged course of specialized intellectual instruction but may also be acquired by alternative means such as an equivalent combination of intellectual instruction and work experience.

Creative professional employees are exempt if their primary duty of performing work requires invention, imagination, originality, or talent in a recognized field or artistic or creative endeavor.

Computer employees are exempt if their primary duties are (1) the application of systems analysis techniques and procedures, including consulting with users, to determine hardware, software, or system functional applications; (2) the design, development, documentation, analysis, creation, testing, or modification of computer systems or programs, including prototypes, based on and related to user or system design specifications; (3) the design, documentation, testing, creation, or modification of computer programs related to machine operating systems; or (4) a combination of the duties described in items 1 through 3, the performance of which requires the same level of skills. Workers are exempt if they are employed as a computer systems analyst, computer programmer, software engineer, or other similarly skilled worker in the computer field.

Outside sales employees are exempt if their primary duties are making sales or obtaining orders or contracts for services or for the use of facilities for which a consideration will be paid by the client or customer. Workers are exempt if they are customarily and regularly engaged away from the employer's place or places of business (U.S. Department of Labor, 2003b).

Equal Pay Act of 1963

In 1963, the FLSA was amended by the Equal Pay Act, which prohibits unequal pay differences for men and women who are performing equal work in jobs requiring equal skill, effort, and responsibility and performed in the same establishment under similar working conditions. Pay differences between equal jobs can, however, be justified when that differential is based on (1) a seniority system, (2) a merit system, (3) a piece-rate payment system that measures earnings by quality or quantity of production, or (4) any factor other than gender (for example, different experience or different work shifts).

Comparable Worth

Should sign painters and tree trimmers receive higher wages than emergency room nurses? What about state grain inspectors, who are at the same job evaluation level as administrative secretaries? In 2002, median weekly earnings for full-time female workers were 78 percent of the median earnings of their male counterparts. Women's pay is still behind the pay of men in virtually every sector of the economy (U.S. Bureau of Labor Statistics, 2003). If you think ER nurses should receive greater compensation than sign painters and tree trimmers, you are likely to favor *comparable worth* as an element to be considered in the development of compensation systems.

Comparable worth is the idea that each job has an inherent value or worth that can be compared to different types of positions across the organization. Jobs of greater inherent value to the organization should be paid more. Comparable worth has been defined as "equitable compensation relationships for jobs that, while not the same, have been evaluated as equivalent based on the composite skill, effort, responsibility, and working conditions required" (Dellion & Pearson, 1991). Comparable worth tries to eradicate the pay disparity between jobs that are traditionally female versus jobs that are traditionally male. Comparable worth argues that jobs associated with women tend to be undervalued and discriminated against in the marketplace—for example, when nurses are paid less than tree trimmers or when clerical employees, typically female, are paid less than physical plant employees, who are typically male (*Christensen* v. *State of Iowa*, 563 F.2d 353, 8th Cir., 1977; *Lemons* v. *City and County of Denver*, 620 F.2d 228, 19th Cir., 1980).

Opponents of comparable worth claim that pay disparities are the result of supply and demand, that market rates provide impartial values of labor (Taylor, 1989). In 1985, the Court of Appeals for the Ninth Circuit upheld that belief, ruling that salaries resulting from the market system do not amount to deliberate discrimination based on sex (*American Federation of State, County and Municipal Employees* v. *State of Washington*, 770 F.2d 1401, 1985; Gaston, 1986; Graham, 1992).

Advocates for comparable worth believe that labor market rates are not entirely objective. There is no going rate for any job. The determination of what wages to pay involves making value judgments and decisions. For example, to determine external equity, the agency decides which organizations should be compared; whether the data should be collected directly, purchased, or taken from government sources; and whether it wants to be a wage leader. It is also responsible for considering other forms of compensation. These decisions are rarely assessed for their discriminatory impact (Elliott, 1985; Taylor, 1989).

It has also been suggested that the compensable factors used during the job evaluation procedure to assign points or rankings often devalue women's work. Treiman and Hartman (1981), Elliott (1985), and Wittig and Lowe (1989) propose that sexual stereotypes and perceptions of gender differences combined with the expectations and experiences of work could influence the nature of job evaluation procedures and outcomes. Historically, female work was devalued, subject to the perception that a woman's income was secondary to her husband's. Blumrosen (1979, p. 435) states that "value systems and perceptions of the job analyst influence what information is collected and therefore what is available in later stages in the process."

Arvey (1986) and Elliott (1985) observe that subjectivity can play a major part in the evaluation process in determining the job factors that are considered important and in deciding their weights or points. For example, supervision is a compensable factor beneficial to men, while responsibilities such as planning, coordination, and scheduling (typically female tasks) are usually ignored. Physical strength (required for typically male tasks) is valued, while dexterity or handling multiple tasks simultaneously (required for jobs typically held by females) are not. Other characteristics and responsibilities, such as counseling and teaching, that are common in occupations heavily populated by women are often neglected as compensable factors. To eliminate these biases, compensable factors must be reevaluated; otherwise organizations risk incorporating these inequities into future job evaluation procedures.

The federal courts have not recognized comparable worth as a statutory requirement under the Equal Pay Act or Title VII of the Civil Rights Act of 1964. However, various legislative bodies have acted to remedy pay disparities across jobs of similar value to the organization. In 1984, Congress enacted the Pay Equity and Management Act, reflecting the federal government's interest in comparable worth. In 1987, the Federal Employee Compensation Study Commission Act examined and attempted to promote equitable pay practices within the federal workforce. This legislation was followed by the Federal Equitable Pay Practices Act of 1988, which directed a study to determine the extent to which wages are affected across the board by gender and to determine the role this influence may play in the formation of wage differentials between male- and female-dominated jobs (Kovach & Millspaugh, 1990).

Several states and local governments have passed legislation requiring that public jobs be paid according to their worth to the organization. An investigation by the state of Minnesota found that grain inspectors for the state were at the same job evaluation level as administrative secretaries but were paid $300 more per month. Each state job was evaluated using skill, effort, responsibility, and working conditions as the compensable factors. Despite similar internal value scores, men were paid more throughout state positions. To correct the disparity, the Minnesota legislature in 1982 passed a comparable worth law for state employees. The law required equitable compensation relationships between comparable male-dominated and female-dominated jobs.

In 1984, the Minnesota legislature enacted another law, which required other public employers, such as city and county governments, public utilities, libraries, hospitals, and school districts, to develop plans to institute pay equity and to implement those plans by 1987 (Aho, 1989; Watkins, 1992). Rhode Island followed in 1990, when it amended its classification and pay plan to authorize classification and pay increases for seventy job categories that were traditionally held by females. A study by the National Committee on Pay Equity revealed that more than fifteen hundred local governments, school districts, and community colleges have taken steps to identify and eliminate sex bias in public positions (Horrigan & Harriman, 1988).

While no federal legislation presently exists that mandates equal pay for comparable worth, the Fair Pay Act of 2003 and the Paycheck Fairness Act and were recently introduced in Congress. The Fair Pay Act of 2003 was introduced on April 9, 2003, by Representative Eleanor Holmes Norton (H.R. 1695) and Senator Tom Harkin (S. 841). The act would amend the Fair Labor Standards Act of 1938 to prohibit discrimination in the payment of wages on account of sex, race, or national origin and for other purposes. The bill seeks to end wage discrimination against people who work in female-dominated or minority-dominated jobs by establishing equal pay for equivalent work. The Fair Pay Act makes exceptions for different wage rates based on a seniority system, a merit system, or a system in which earnings are measured by quantity or quality of production, or differentials based on bona fide factors that the employer demonstrates are job-related or further legitimate business interests. It also contains a small business exemption.

The Paycheck Fairness Act was introduced by Congresswoman Rosa De Lauro (H.R. 781) and Senator Tom Daschle (S. 77), also to amend the Fair Labor Standards Act of 1938 to provide more effective remedies to victims of discrimination in the payment of wages on the basis of sex and for other purposes. The Paycheck Fairness Act would add nonretaliation requirements, increase penalties, and authorize the secretary of labor to seek additional compensatory or punitive damages. It requires the Equal Employment Opportunity Commission (EEOC) and the Office of Federal Contract Compliance Programs to train EEOC employees and affected individuals and entities on matters involving wage discrimination; directs the secretary of labor to provide for certain studies, information, a national summit, and guidelines, awards, and assistance for employer evaluations of job categories based on objective criteria; establishes the secretary of labor's National Award for Pay Equity in the Workplace; and amends the Civil Rights Act of 1964 to require the EEOC to collect certain pay information.

Summary

Compensation systems should be designed with the intent to attract, motivate, and retain proficient employees. A number of factors determine the salaries paid to public and nonprofit employees: the salaries paid in the external labor market, federal laws such as the FLSA and the Equal Pay Act, and the responsibilities and KSAOCs required to perform the jobs, as well as an agency's ability to pay competitive wages.

Equity refers to the perception by employees that they are being paid fairly. External, internal, and employee equity influence compensation systems. Market factors influence external equity, job evaluation or job worth influences internal equity, and employee equity is said to exist when employees performing similar jobs are compensated in a way that reflects their individual contributions. Broadbanding, skill-based pay or pay for knowledge, merit pay, and gainsharing are some of the innovations beginning to be seen in public and nonprofit sector compensation systems.

Public and nonprofit executives are hired for their professional experience and expertise. They lack job security and serve at the discretion of elected officials or board members. Because of this unique aspect of their employment, executives typically negotiate employment contracts that specify the level of compensation and benefits they will receive. Executives of some nonprofits also receive bonuses on their agency's performance.

Questions and Exercises

1. What type of equity (external, internal, or employee) is more important to you? Explain the reasons why.
2. Review current copies of the *ICMA Newsletter*, the *IPMA Newsletter*, the *Chronicle of Philanthropy*, or the *Nonprofit Times*. What positions receive the highest salaries? What factors do you think are most important in determining compensation?
3. In small groups, discuss the compensation policy in the organizations where you work. What is the basis for the policies? Does one organization have a more progressive policy than the others?
4. Go to the Office of Personnel Management (OPM) Web site (http://www.opm.gov). How many different salary schedules are there? For what positions?
5. Using the Internet, find salary schedules for two local governments, two state governments, and two nonprofit organizations. What are the similarities and differences across all six organizations?
6. Visit the AFL-CIO Web site (http://www.afl-cio.org). What is the union's position on the proposed changes to overtime pay? What are its concerns about executive compensation?

| Benefits

The preceding chapter on compensation provided an overview of salaries and wages, the direct financial compensation provided to employees for their contributions to the organization. But wages constitute only part of the compensation package. This chapter addresses indirect compensation, more commonly referred to as benefits.

The emphasis in compensating employees should be on the total compensation package, not just on direct wages or salary. Benefits are a crucial ingredient in creating an accurate compensation picture. The importance of benefits should not be underestimated; an attractive benefits package can assist in the recruitment and retention of qualified employees. Traditional benefits such as health insurance, retirement pensions, and paid time away from work, combined with less traditional benefits such as child and elder care, flexible scheduling, and educational assistance, are critical for attracting qualified applicants, encouraging loyalty and long-term employment, and motivating and rewarding incumbent employees.

Employee benefits often reach 40 percent of total compensation costs. Medical insurance premiums are the highest-cost single benefit. Research conducted by the Kaiser Family Foundation and the Health Research and Educational Trust found that premiums increased 13.9 percent between spring 2002 and spring 2003. On average, single premiums cost approximately $3,383 and family coverage approximately $9,068. The amount that employees pay for coverage has risen an average of 27 percent per year, and the employee share of premiums for family coverage rose an average of 16 percent per year. The study also found that in addition to paying more for health care coverage, employees are receiving fewer benefits (Kaiser Family Foundation, 2003). Paid time off, vacations, holidays, and sick leave combined account for about one-third of all benefits.

Employees often think of benefits as entitlements and not as compensation. In reality, the only entitlements are those benefits that are required by federal or state laws, such as employer contributions to Social Security or state pension plans, unemployment compensation, and workers' compensation. Aside from these, employers have tremendous discretion in deciding what types of benefits to provide. This chapter discusses the variety of benefits that organizations may choose to offer, as well as the quality-of-life and quality-of-work issues that are becoming more prevalent in today's workplaces.

Required Benefits

All employers are required to contribute to Social Security, unemployment compensation, and workers' compensation benefits. Public employers may be required by federal or state statutes to offer additional benefits, such as retirement or disability. The benefits provided by nonprofits are determined and approved by the board of directors.

Social Security

Social Security provides retirement, disability, death, survivor, and Medicare benefits for individuals beyond age sixty-five. The Social Security system was established in 1935; however, public and nonprofit employers and employees could decline to pay Social Security taxes and earn no credit toward Social Security benefits. The Social Security Amendments of 1983 made Social Security coverage mandatory for all employees of nonprofit organizations as of January 1, 1984. Coverage was extended to nonprofit employees working for organizations that had previously terminated coverage, as well as to employees who had never been covered by Social Security. The 1983 amendments included a special section that provided for nonprofit employees fifty-five years and older to be considered fully insured for benefits after acquiring at least twenty quarters of coverage.

The Social Security Act originally excluded state and local governments from coverage because of the concern that taxation of state and local governments by the federal government might be unconstitutional. The act was subsequently amended in the 1950s to permit state and local governments to choose coverage for employees not already covered under a retirement system. After five years of participating in the Social Security system, state and local governments could choose to repeal their action and terminate coverage of their employees. This was changed in 1983 by the Social Security Amendments Act, which eliminated the right of state and local government employers to withdraw from the system. Another change came in 1986. The Budget Reconciliation Act amended the Social Security Act and required all individuals hired by a state or local government to be covered by the Medicare segment of the program and subject to employer and employee payroll taxes. As of July 2, 1991, all state and local government employees (except police officers) not covered by a retirement program are required to participate in the full Social Security program. Federal employees hired on or after January 1, 1984, are covered by Social Security and are subject to full Social Security taxation.

Social Security provides four kinds of benefits: old-age or disability benefits, benefits for the dependents of retired or disabled workers, benefits for the survivors of a worker who dies, and a lump-sum death benefit.

Unemployment Compensation

Unemployment compensation was established as part of the Social Security Act of 1935. It was designed to provide a portion of wages to employees who have been laid off until they obtain another job. The employer pays into the unemployment compensation fund at a rate based on the average number of former employees who have drawn benefits from the fund. The fund is financed primarily through a payroll tax paid to the state and federal governments based on employees' wages. Each state determines its own waiting period for eligibility, level of benefits provided, and the length of time that benefits are paid.

Workers' Compensation

Workers' compensation is an employer-financed insurance program that provides compensation to employees who are unable to work because of job-related injuries or illness. Most states have their own workers' compensation laws and are responsible for administering their own programs. For this reason, the levels of protection and the costs of administering the programs vary from state to state. All of the programs have certain features in common (CCH Business Law Editors, 1992, p. 8):

- Workers receive benefits for accidental injury; wage-loss, medical, and death benefits are provided.
- Fault is not an issue; even if at fault in causing the injury, the employee still has the right to receive workers' compensation benefits.
- In exchange for the assurance of benefits, the employee (and the employee's dependent family members) gives up the right to sue the employer for damages for any injury covered by a workers' compensation law.

Responsibility for administering the system usually resides with a state board or commission. Employers are generally required to insure their workers' compensation liability through private insurance, state insurance funds, or self-insurance.

Independent contractors are not considered employees and do not have to be covered under the workers' compensation policy of the organization that hired them. Most state workers' compensation agencies apply the same test as the Internal Revenue Service (IRS) for determining whether a contractor is truly independent and not just so called by an employer who does not want to match the contractor's Social Security contributions or deduct and withhold income taxes. To decide whether a contractor is "independent," the IRS examines the relationship between the worker and the organization. Evidence of behavioral control, financial control, and the type of relationship are considered. *Behavioral control* covers facts that show whether the business has a right to direct and control how the work is done, through instructions, training, or other means. *Financial control* covers facts that show whether the organization has a right to control the business aspects of the worker's job. This includes the extent to which the worker has unreimbursed business expenses, the extent of the worker's investment in the business, the extent to which the worker makes services available to the relevant market, how the organization pays the worker, and the extent to which the worker can realize a profit or incur a loss. *Type of relationship* covers written contracts describing the relationship the parties intended to create; the extent to which the worker is available to perform services for other, similar businesses; whether the business provides the worker with employee benefits, such as insurance, a pension plan, vacation pay, or sick pay; and the permanence or impermanence of the relationship.

If the contractor can be fired or quit without any contractual liability; if the contractor is reimbursed for business and travel expenses; if the contractor performs the task in person, on company property, and during set hours; if the contractor is paid by the hour, week, or month rather than the job; and if the organization provides the contractor with tools or equipment, the contractor should probably be covered under the organization's workers' compensation policy. The state's workers' compensation agency should be contacted for verification.

In most states, unpaid volunteers are not considered employees and are typically not covered by workers' compensation. But in some states, there are exceptions for police and fire volunteers, and other volunteers may be covered under special circumstances.

Discretionary Benefits

Public and nonprofit employers recognize that to be competitive, they need to offer additional benefits beyond those mandated by law. Research indicates that integrated benefits programs can increase productivity, decrease turnover, increase the effectiveness of recruitment and retention programs, and assist in developing employee loyalty to the organizations (Cayer, 2003; Champion-Hughes, 2001; Daley, 1998; Durst, 1999; McCurdy, Newman, & Lovrich, 2002).

Pensions

Pensions provide retired or permanently disabled employees with income throughout the remainder of their lives. In the public sector, different classes of employees are often covered by different pension plans. For example, teachers, police, and firefighters have pension plans separate from those of other general employees. Some states have separate pension plans for judges and legislators.

Police and firefighters may retire with full benefits at a younger age and with fewer years of service than other employees.

Prior to 1984, the retirement plan covering most civilian federal employees was the Civil Service Retirement System (CSRS); employees covered by CSRS were excluded from paying Social Security taxes. The Social Security Amendments of 1983, however, required that federal employees hired after December 31, 1983, be covered by Social Security. A new retirement plan, the Federal Employees Retirement System (FERS), was established by Congress on June 6, 1986, and went into effect on January 1, 1987. Most federal employees hired after January 1, 1987, are covered by FERS, and employees covered under CSRS were given the opportunity to join FERS.

Like state and local government retirement systems, the federal government also has different age and years-of-service criteria that permit select groups of employees to retire early and with full benefits. Law enforcement officials, firefighters, air traffic controllers, military reserve technicians, and members of the defense intelligence Senior Executive Service (SES) and the senior cryptological SES are some of the positions eligible for early retirement.

A survey of 239 nonprofits across the country, conducted by the *Nonprofit Times* and Flynn Research, found that 87 percent of the respondents sponsored some type of pension plan for their employees (Clolery & Flynn, 2003). However, many smaller nonprofits such as grassroots or social justice organizations traditionally have not offered retirement plans. In an effort to give activists, advocates, and social justice organizers some future security, the National Organizers Alliance received start-up funds from the John D. and Catherine T. MacArthur Foundation, the Jessie Smith Noyes Foundation, the Unitarian Universalist Veatch Program at Shelter Rock, the Albert List Foundation, the Wieboldt Foundation, the Norman Foundation, and the Public Welfare Foundation to establish and implement a retirement program. Nonprofits that join the retirement program must contribute at least 5 percent of employees' total annual salary to the retirement plan, and workers must have a minimum of one year's employment at a social justice organization (Billitteri, 1999). "Observers say they hope the plan will focus attention on an issue they believe organized philanthropy has not taken seriously enough: the need for workers at small nonprofits to have at least minimal employment benefits. No reliable data exists on what percentage of small charities have retirement plans, but many experts believe it is low" (p. 27). The plan's advocates believe that social justice workers should not have to sacrifice their financial security as proof of devotion to a cause.

Defined-Benefit and Defined-Contribution Pension Plans

Two types of pension plans are common in the public and nonprofit sectors: defined-benefit and defined-contribution plans.

A *defined-benefit plan* is a pension plan that specifies the benefits or the methods of determining the benefits at the time of retirement but not the level or rate of contribution. The benefit amounts to be paid are determined by a formula that weighs the retiree's years of service, age, and salary history. Advantages of defined-benefit plans is that employees and employers can estimate the probable size of their pension benefits by assuming retirement dates and salary histories, and since public pensions are backed by taxpayers, they are guaranteed.

In *defined-contribution plans,* the employer guarantees that specified contributions, usually a percentage of annual salary, will be deposited in employees' accounts every year that they work. These accounts are invested. Employees are provided with a variety of investment options from which to choose. When employees retire, they receive lifetime payments or annuities, the size of which are determined by the amount on deposit, the interest rate earned on funds in the account, and the length of time during which the annuity is expected to be paid. The employee, the employer, or both may contribute to the pension plan.

A variety of employer-assisted defined-contribution pension plans are available to employees. The most common plans are 401(k), 403(b), and Section 457 plans, which are set up by employers and funded by employees. Employers design the plan and handle the automatic payroll deductions and paperwork. Employees make contributions and assume the investment risk and responsibility. Employers may match part or all of a worker's contribution. No federal agency guarantees the solvency of these plans. *401(k)* plans are used primarily in the private sector, although they are available to nonprofits. *403(b)* plans are typically used by nonprofit organizations that are exempt under Section 501(c)(3) of the Internal

Revenue Code, and public schools and colleges may also provide 403(b) retirement plans for employees. *Section 457* plans are offered to employees of state and local governments and nonprofit organizations as a supplement to other defined-benefit and defined-contribution plans. Contributions remain assets of the employer until distributed to the participant and are vulnerable to creditors if an employer goes bankrupt. Money is held in a trust, custodial account, or annuity contract.

Some employers will match an employee's contribution to a plan at a limited rate, such as 25 to 50 cents per dollar, or with matching stock options. The federal government provides a thrift savings plan for employees enrolled in FERS. The government will match up to 5 percent of the employees' contributions. Unfortunately, while most state and local governments have deferred compensation plans, they typically do not match the employee's contribution. TreeUtah, a Salt Lake City environmental group, offers its employees the opportunity to participate in a 403(b) plan, and according to its executive director, Meryl Redisch, should the agency's finances improve in the future, it will consider making contributions to each employee's account (Webber, 2003). Chicago's United Way administers a defined-benefit plan in which thirteen separate charities, including Lutheran Social Services and the Illinois Society for the Prevention of Blindness, participate, and the Nonprofit Coordinating Committee of New York offers its members participation in a 403(b) plan. As of September 2003, some 5,640 employees from 249 nonprofit groups had assets invested (Webber, 2003).

Defined-contribution pension plans are becoming more popular as more employers have realized the expense and long-term liabilities associated with funding defined-benefit plans. States such as Illinois and Florida are now providing state employees with the option of electing to enroll in a defined-contribution plan instead of requiring them to become part of the defined-benefit plan. In Florida, the annual employer contributions will be 9 percent for most employees, and members of law enforcement organizations will receive employer contributions of 20 percent due to their more generous pensions (Huntley, 2002).

An advantage of defined-contribution plans is that the money is portable if employees change jobs because there are no vesting requirements. In today's economy, workers tend to move from one organization to another and even between the public, nonprofit, and private sectors. One disadvantage of defined-contribution plans is that employees tend to be more conservative in selecting their investment options than professional investors. Conservative investment plans will lead to lower interest rates and fewer funds for retirement. Another potential disadvantage is that the money available at retirement is tied to the stock market. In the 1990s while the market soared, defined-contribution accounts looked attractive, but in the past few years, they have taken a hit, often dropping 30 percent or more. Employers who offer defined-contribution plans need to provide training and assist their employees with information on how to invest their money and plan for retirement.

Vesting

Vesting occurs when contributions made to a retirement plan belong to the employee. For most defined-benefit pension plans, if you leave the organization, you retain the nonforfeitable right to those benefits when you retire. However, you may be required to wait until you actually retire before receiving the benefits. Most defined-contribution pension plans allow you to take the accrued amount when you depart in a lump-sum payment that is taxable.

Vesting standards for nonprofit and private organizations were amended as part of the Tax Reform Act of 1986. New minimum standards went into effect in 1989 that enable employees to become fully vested in their pension plans after five years of service, or they may be 20 percent vested after three years of service, 20 percent for each year thereafter, and 100 percent vested after seven years of service.

In the public sector, wide variations exist as to when employees are entitled to vested benefits. In some plans, employees are required to work five years before benefits are guaranteed. Other plans require ten years of plan participation before vesting occurs. Employees considering employment in another organization covered by a different retirement system would want to find out whether they meet the minimum requirement for vesting.

As noted earlier, retirement systems at the federal, state, and local levels have special provisions for public safety officers. They can retire at an earlier age with full benefits after shorter working careers than employees in other fields.

The Employee Retirement Income Security Act of 1974 (ERISA) safeguards the pensions of nonprofit and private sector employees. ERISA sets minimum standards to ensure that employee benefit plans are financially sound so that employees receive the benefits promised by their employers. ERISA does not cover plans established or maintained by government entities or churches.

Insurance

Health insurance, life insurance, and long-term sickness and accident and disability insurance are also benefits provided to employees. Health insurance is the most frequently provided benefit and the benefit that receives the most attention. The types of insurance programs and the amount that employees and employers contribute to the plans vary.

The Consolidated Omnibus Budget Reconciliation Act of 1986 (COBRA) requires employers to offer laid-off or terminated employees the opportunity to continue their health insurance coverage. COBRA covers employers of twenty or more employees, except for federal government and religious organizations. Many states have their own versions of COBRA to cover small employers. COBRA enables former employees, spouses, and dependents to purchase insurance coverage for a limited amount of time after leaving the organization. COBRA also applies to divorced, separated, or widowed spouses. COBRA also extends Medicare coverage to state and local government employees.

The Health Insurance Portability and Accountability Act of 1996 (HIPPA) allows employees to switch their health insurance plan from one organization to another to get new health coverage, regardless of preexisting health conditions. The legislation also prohibits group insurance plans from dropping coverage for a sick employee and requires them to make individual coverage available to people who leave group plans. In April 2003, the privacy component of HIPPA became activated. Employees working for pharmacies, hospitals, clinics health insurance companies, and other health care organizations have an obligation to protect a patient's privacy, and organizations must make sure that health data are secure and private.

Mental Health Parity Act

One out of every five adults is diagnosed with a mental disorder in a given year. In 2001, some 44.3 million people were diagnosed with a mental disorder. Four out of the ten leading causes of disability in the United States are mental disorders (National Institute of Mental Health, 2001). Drug dependence and abuse, anxiety disorders, affective (mood) disorders, antisocial personality disorder, and schizophrenia are the most common (Schott, 1999). In an effort to encourage individuals to seek mental health treatment, the Mental Health Parity Act (MHPA; P.L. 104-204, 110 Stat. 2944) was passed in 1996. MHPA provided that beginning in January 1998, health insurance plans must provide the same coverage for mental illness as for physical disorders. It requires that group health plans provide parity for treatment of mental illness. It exempts employers with fewer than twenty-six employees.

More insurance programs are also beginning to offer dental, optical, and prescription drugs benefits in addition to traditional medical coverage.

Disability Benefits

Disability benefits are paid to employees who becomes disabled before qualifying for regular or early retirement benefits. Generally, disability benefit insurance provides a monthly benefit to employees who cannot work for an extended period of time due to injury or illness. Some employees, however, are not insured for long-term disability but are eligible for an immediate disability pension through their retirement plans. In most instances, long-term disability payments are a fixed percentage of predisability earnings. Most plans distinguish between disability attributed to an accident on the job, which pays higher benefits and has fewer requirements with respect to years of service, and disability that is not job-related.

Paid Time Away from Work

Most employers grant employees paid sick leave, vacation days, holidays, and personal days. Employers are not obligated to grant these benefits, and they vary across organizations.

In many public organizations, employees who accumulate their sick and vacation days are able to exchange them for cash compensation when they retire. This policy is meant to discourage capricious time away from work and to reward employees for their commitment to the organization. However, many organizations are rethinking this policy because accrued time becomes an unfunded liability. Reed and Swain (1997) cite an example of a midwestern community that provided this benefit but never costed it out. A city manager retired after twenty years of service and received $20,000 in sick leave benefits. After further examination, the city realized it had $1 million in unfunded liability. In Milwaukee County, Wisconsin, the retirements of the twenty-three employees in the county's highway operations department eligible to retire would cost $800,000 in sick leave payouts. The problem is that the budget doesn't include any money for payouts, and departments have to absorb the costs by not filling open positions. The sick leave payouts and pensions were part of an overall wage and benefits package that the county officials approved in 2001. Only now are the county supervisors realizing that the cost could reach $13 million in unfunded liabilities (Johnson, 2002).

Workers employed by the city of Tampa, Florida, may accumulate sick and vacation leave. When they retire, they are entitled to half of their accumulated sick leave, up to 240 hours of annual leave, and half of the rest of their accumulated annual leave. The amount of money they receive is based on the final hourly rate they were earning. Like many public employers, the city is facing numerous retirements. Payments to retirees of $50,000 or more are not unusual, and several payments surpassed $90,000. Between 2001 and 2003, the city will have paid $5.5 million to retiring employees in accrued vacation and sick leave (March, 2003). Other public employers permit employees to cash in unused sick days, but usually at a lower rate of pay or fewer number of days. For example, in Ohio, Cincinnati public schoolteachers and administrators are limited to a rate of 50 percent of their current pay (Swope, 1998), and in Illinois, the Edwardsville school district limits the cash-out rate to $50 per day for up to two hundred days, and the Belleville school district permits employees to receive compensation for ninety sick days at pay rates lower than their daily salaries (McDermott & Gillerman, 1995). Organizations that provide this benefit need to understand and plan for its financial implications when employees leave the organization.

Education Programs

Many public and nonprofit organizations provide tuition reimbursement to employees for additional education if the employee receives a B or better grade for the course. The Congress of National

Black Churches in Washington, D.C., offers employees in its national office a training allowance of $750 to $1,500 per person per year. The money can be used for job-related education and for training services and materials.

Unlike most other hospitals across the nation, Tampa General Hospital is not experiencing a nursing shortage, and its turnover rate is about half that of other hospitals. The hospital provides tuition for advanced training programs and will also reimburse nurses for time away from work (Varian, 2003). Education assistance is often combined with career and development programs.

Quality-of-Work and Quality-of-Life Issues

Changes in family structures and employee priorities have encouraged the evolution of a variety of employer-provided benefits. Employers wishing to compete for highly skilled employees believe that quality-of-work and quality-of-life issues can give them a competitive edge.

Flexible Benefits

As early as the 1970s, private sector organizations recognized that different family structures necessitated different employee benefits (Johnson, 1988; Wallace & Fay, 1988). Conventional employee benefit plans were designed to serve the needs of the family structure that was dominant during the 1940s and 1950s: a working father and his dependents (namely, a wife who stayed at home with small children). Today, families have changed, and so have their needs. Current family structures often include a single parent, multiple generations, and domestic partnerships. Continuing increases in dual-career and single-parent families will likely result in a continued demand for a variety of elder and child care services.

Studies conducted by the U.S. Merit Systems Protection Board and the General Accounting Office recognized this in the early 1990s. The U.S. Merit Systems Protection Board's report *Balancing Work Responsibilities and Family Needs: The Federal Civil Service Response* (1991) and the General Accounting Office's report *The Changing Workforce: Comparison of Federal and Nonfederal Work/Family Programs and Approaches* (1992) acknowledged the changing structure of American families and the need for evolving, flexible benefits.

Some solutions have been employer-sponsored group insurance plans that provide lower premiums or flexible spending accounts that enable greater flexibility in the types of services that benefits will pay for (Daley, 1998; Kossek, De Marr, Backman, & Kolar, 1993).

In the past, wives often took care of elderly parents or in-laws and children. Today, there are more single-parent families or families in which both spouses work full time, and they are unable to care for their children or parents. Thus many benefit plans now have provisions for elder care and child care. Employees with small children may need child care, employees with elderly or infirm parents may prefer elder care, and employees without any dependents might opt for a variety of other benefits such as dental care.

A recent study commissioned by MetLife that surveyed men and women in three Fortune 500 corporations indicates that today more men are providing assistance to their elderly parents and other relatives. Sandra Timmermann, director of the MetLife Mature Market Institute, the company's research group on issues related to aging, refers to men as the "hidden caregivers" (Jackson, 2003). "This isn't just a women's issue; it's really a societal issue." The findings recognize a need for more workplace support when employees care for the elderly. Such care costs companies an estimated $11.4 billion a year in lost productivity from absenteeism, turnover, and work interruptions (Jackson, 2003).

Child and elder care responsibilities have an impact on job performance. Research has found that caregiver responsibilities result in the excessive use of the phone at work, lateness, and unscheduled time off. Employee time spent on caregiver responsibilities affects productivity, absenteeism, turnover, and morale (Nelson-Horchler, 1989).

The concern about child care for parents who work is increasing. The Saint Petersburg, Florida, health network, which includes Bayfront Medical Center, Bayfront Medical Plaza, seven clinics, and an outpatient surgery center, has been recognized as one of the hundred "best companies for working mothers" in an annual rating by *Working Mother* magazine. It provides on-site day care and also has a clinic for ill children (Jackson, 2003). Employers who are cognizant of and sensitive to child care and family issues will have an advantage in recruiting and retaining employees.

An emerging issue in the public, nonprofit, and private sectors is the provision of domestic partnership benefits to employees. Such benefits extend workplace benefit coverage to unmarried heterosexual or same-sex couples. One way to support employees and make them feel part of the organization is to recognize and respect alternative families. Health insurance, sick leave, bereavement leave, pension plans, life insurance benefits, and access to employee assistance programs are some of the benefits that have been extended to domestic partners. Typically, couples qualify if they are living together and are jointly responsible for their financial well-being.

Employee Assistance Programs

Employee assistance programs (EAPs) are another important employer-provided benefit. Marital conflicts, alcohol and substance abuse, family stresses, AIDS, and other health-related concerns are some of the problems that come to work with employees. These problems often result in lower employee productivity and morale and may also lead to legal liabilities and high financial costs for the employer (Cayer, 2003; Daly, 2003).

EAPs provide counseling services for employees and their families. In the past, the focus of EAPs was on alcoholism and drug-related problems. The services of EAPs have since expanded to include counseling for marital problems, drug abuse, mental illness, financial stress, and the improvement of employer-employee communication.

EAPs also address such issues as prevention, health and wellness, employee advocacy, and the dysfunctional workplace. Employees with stressful lives are absent more often, resulting in lost productivity. Wellness programs are designed to improve employees' overall health, thus decreasing the occurrence and severity of medical problems and lowering the costs and number of medical claims (Hyland, 1990). Accident prevention classes, smoking cessation seminars, weight control programs, stress management workshops, and on-site exercise programs are also outgrowths of EAPs. The largest use of EAPs, however, is still for drug and alcohol addictions.

Alcohol and Drug Testing

Substance abuse is a pervasive problem in the American workforce. Alcohol and drug abuse are cited for decreases in productivity and increases in work-related accidents. To combat substance abuse in the workplace, legislators, judges, and regulatory agencies have passed laws or rendered decisions that regulate substance abuse testing in the workplace.

In 1986, President Ronald Reagan signed Executive Order 12564, which required federal agencies to set up programs to test workers in sensitive positions for illegal drug use and to establish a voluntary drug testing program for all other employees. In 1988, the Drug-Free Workplace Act was passed by Congress. The act required federal contractors and grantees who receive more than $25,000 in government business to certify that they would maintain drug-free workplaces. Organizations that did not comply with the requirements of the act could have their payments suspended and be excluded from consideration for government contracts for up to five years.

Nonprofit organizations that are the recipients of federal funds in excess of $25,000 are required to comply with the Drug-Free Workplace Act. State and local governments may also require government contractors to comply with drug abuse prevention efforts. In addition, nonprofits receiving state or local funds are expected to comply with state regulations.

Nonprofit employees employed under a collective bargaining agreement may be subject to an employer-imposed drug and alcohol testing policy. In 1989, the National Labor Relations Board (NLRB) ruled that the drug testing of current employees was a mandatory subject of collective bargaining but the drug testing of applicants was not (*Johnson-Bateman Company*, 295 NLRB 26, 1989). This decision was reversed by the Seventh Circuit Court in the case of *Chicago Tribune* v. *National Labor Relations Board* (974 F.2d 933, 7th Cir., 1992). The court held that the newspaper could rely on its broad management rights clause to implement a drug testing program on a unilateral basis. The management rights clause gave the employer the exclusive right "to establish and enforce reasonable rules and regulations relating to the operation of the facilities and employee conduct."

Public employees have been insulated from the capricious use of drug testing by the U.S. Constitution. They have challenged drug testing on grounds that it violates the Fourth Amendment's prohibition of reasonable searches and seizures. The Supreme Court rendered two decisions on this issue in 1989. In *Skinner* v. *Railway Labor Executives Association* (489 U.S. 602, 1989) and *National Treasury*

Employees Union v. *Von Raab* (489 U.S. 656, 1989), the Court ruled that public employers may require drug testing when a compelling government interest exists that overrides the employee's right to privacy. The court upheld drug testing when the public's health and safety is at risk or for law enforcement occupations that are involved in drug interdiction activities.

The Fourth Amendment is not applicable to nonprofit and private organizations, which may be restricted by state constitutional provisions, state and local laws regulating drug testing, collective bargaining obligations under the National Labor Relations Act, and federal and state laws prohibiting employment discrimination on the basis of disability. It is important that employers review these laws and regulations before instituting drug testing policies.

In 1991, the Omnibus Transportation Employee Testing Act (OTETA) was passed by Congress. OTETA requires the alcohol and controlled-substances testing of employees in safety-sensitive jobs in transportation, regardless of which sector they work in. Any employee required to hold a commercial driver's license or who performs other covered safety-sensitive functions is subject to testing. The law requires postaccident and random testing, as well as testing when there is a reasonable suspicion that an employee is under the influence of a controlled substance.

All organizations should establish alcohol and substance abuse policies, and supervisors should be trained to identify warning signs and instructed to refer employees to EAPs for further evaluation. Some of the common signs of alcohol and substance abuse are mood swings, slurred speech, memory loss, and drowsiness. There may be a decrease in productivity or an increase in absenteeism, tardiness, and workplace accidents. Supervisors should be educated in substance abuse issues; they should know how to identify problems and what assistance programs are available to employees.

Alcohol and drug testing policies should provide for written notice to employees that testing will be conducted, explain the procedures that will be used in the testing, employ a chain of custody so that samples are not lost or switched, confirm positive tests with more sensitive tests, and ensure confidentiality of test results. After an employee has completed rehabilitation and is ready to return to work, the organization should require written documentation from a health care professional that the employee is in recovery and is no longer using drugs or alcohol.

Flexible Job Environment

Changing family structures have focused attention not only on the need for variety in employer-provided benefits but also on the need for more flexible workplace policies. Employers must acknowledge that family life and work have changed, leading to increased stress on employees as they strive to balance the demands of both work and family life. Employees who cannot manage these conflicting demands are often less productive and, as noted earlier, are absent more often and have lower morale.

To better meet the needs of their employees, many organizations have developed flexible work structures. Flextime, voluntary shifts to part-time work, job sharing, flexible leaves, compressed work-weeks, and work-at-home or telecommuting opportunities are some of the strategies that are used to alleviate work and family conflicts.

Another issue affecting morale and motivation at work is career plateauing. As public and nonprofit agencies are confronted with fewer promotional opportunities, more employees have reached career plateaus. Career plateauing is the inability to move upward in the organization. To keep employees motivated, organizations must institute HRM policies that focus on the contributions employees can make to the organization without being promoted. Techniques such as job rotation, job enlargement, skill-based pay, and midcareer breaks have been used to maintain employee motivation.

Job rotation allows workers to diversify their activities. Employees perform a variety of tasks by moving to a new activity when their current tasks are no longer challenging or when the work schedule dictates it. They are thus provided with a range of experience that broadens their skills, provides them with a greater understanding of other activities within the agency, and prepares them to assume more responsibility. Job enlargement increases the scope of a job by increasing the number of different operations required in it. The job becomes more diverse and challenging because more tasks must be completed. Knowledge or skill-based pay can be used to keep employees motivated by keeping them engaged in learning new skills. Employees are not promoted to a higher-level position but are still able to perform new skills and assume new responsibilities.

Typically, midcareer breaks or sabbaticals have been considered one of the benefits of academia. However, many organizations have begun to realize the benefits of time spent away from work, and some foundations are willing to provide support for sabbaticals. The Durfee Foundation in Los Angeles began a program to underwrite sabbaticals in 1997. The Chicago Community Trust's Community Service Fellowship Program awards grants up to $100,000 to cover a twelve-month leave of absence, and the Annie E. Casey Foundation provides fellowships for nonprofit and government leaders to spend eighteen weeks in residence at the foundation's Baltimore headquarters, travel to seminars, and take temporary positions at other nonprofits to see how they operate. Claire Peeps, executive director of the Durfee Foundation, notes, "What fuels the nonprofit sector is human capital. Until we start paying better attention to that and supporting people in these simple and kind ways, we will burn them out and run the rubber off the tire" (Sommerfield, 2002, p. 52).

Not all organizations can afford to give paid leaves to employees, so some have developed alternatives, such as unpaid leave with a guarantee of a job upon return or unpaid leave but with tuition reimbursement to defray the costs of schooling.

Quality-of-life and quality-of-work benefits have become very important in organizations' ability to attract and motivate employees in tough economic times. Many nonprofits are unable to compete in benefits such as child care, dental care, or tuition reimbursement, so to remain competitive, they tend to offer health insurance and lots of flexibility as a way to assist their employees in balancing work and family. The director of human resources for Urban Peak, a charity in Denver that supports runaway and homeless youth, observed that offering benefits has become a necessity. "Look at the indirect costs of not having benefits, not just the direct costs. If people don't feel supported in their work environment, where they spend a good deal of their lives, it's going to affect the work" (Joslyn, 2002). The Southern Chester County Day Care Association in Avondale, Pennsylvania, offers its employees discounts on child care in its facility; other nonprofits are more liberal with time off and flextime or permit telecommuting. Big Brothers/Big Sisters of Central Arizona and the Girl Scouts of the USA both allow some of their employees to telecommute, which saves on rent and other workplace costs (Joslyn, 2002; Romero, 2003).

The American Federation for the Blind, in New York, has a paid leave policy that merges vacation days, sick days, and personal leave days into a common pot called "paid time off" that allows employees to take time off with the consent of their supervisors without having to explain why they are absent. The foundation also created a leave "donation bank" that allows employees to give unused leave to coworkers who need additional time off (Wellner, 2003).

United Jewish Communities in New York City offers flextime to all of its employees so that they can more effectively balance work and family. Employees are also allowed to work at home up to three days a week, are offered a generous vacation and holiday calendar, and are provided with learning opportunities and training programs in the office (Berger, 2001).

Preston (1990) found that the opportunity to perform a variety of work and to enhance one's skill development has been instrumental in attracting women to nonprofit organizations. Many women choose to work in nonprofits despite the often lower pay they provide in order to take advantage of the opportunities they offer. Organizations should not overlook the importance of quality-of-work and quality-of-life enhancements in motivating employees.

Military Leave

As a result of the war with Iraq and prolonged peacekeeping initiatives by the U.S. military, public and nonprofit employers need to be aware that Reserve and National Guard units called to active duty have rights with respect to the retirement and health benefits provided by their employers. The Uniformed Services Employment and Reemployment Rights Act of 1994 (USERRA) strengthens and clarifies the Veterans' Reemployment Right (VRR) statute. A fact sheet and interactive computer program, the USERRA Advisor, has been developed by the Department of Labor's Veterans' Employment and Training Service (VETS) to provide information as to the rights and responsibilities of individuals and their employers under the act (U.S. Department of Labor, 2003b).

Summary

Employer-provided benefits play an important role in strategic human resources management. Most organizations offer a variety of benefits, ranging from those mandated by law, such as Social Security, unemployment compensation, and workers' compensation, to those that are optional, such as pensions, health insurance, paid time away from work, educational programs, and a variety of quality-of-life and quality-of-work programs.

The types of benefits provided by employers are key to attracting quality applicants, to encouraging loyalty and long-term employment, and to motivating and rewarding incumbent employees. The literature on organizational culture and employee retention indicates that different human resources strategies result in different psychological climates that foster varying levels of commitment and retention among employees. In an analysis of voluntary turnover in state governments, Selden and Moynihan (2000) found that the most significant factor in reducing voluntary turnover is the provision of on-site child care. Flexible benefits that are sensitive to employee needs have the advantage of creating a work climate that is conducive to high levels of employee commitment, satisfaction, and morale.

Questions and Exercises

1. Why are benefits strategically important to employers?
2. You are to establish a benefits program for your employees. What things should you consider and why?
3. Visit the U.S. Department of Labor's Employee Benefits Security Administration Web site (http://www.dol.gov/ebsa). Share with the class information on three benefits that you were not familiar with and that are important to you.
4. Visit the Employee Benefit Research Institute's Web site (http://www.ebri.org). What should employers and employees know about employee benefits?
5. Each state has its own worker's compensation policy. Select two states, and compare and contrast their policies. For additional information on worker's compensation, visit http://www.law.cor nell.edu/topics/workers_compensation.html.
6. In the wake of corporate scandals, many private sector employees are finding their pensions at risk, and many public sector pension funds hit by declines in the stock market are underfunded. Visit the Web sites of the Pension Rights Center (http://www.pensionrights.org/index.htm) and the Pension Benefit Guaranty Corporation (http://www.pbgc.gov). Based on what you read there, develop a list of five questions to ask your pension administrator about the solvency of your future pension.

Chapter Twelve

Training and Development

The demands placed on public and nonprofit organizations keep changing. Agencies are threatened with budget cuts and reductions in staff, while citizens and clients are requesting increases in the level of services or new services. Changes in technology are requiring new skills. Jobs today are requiring employees to assume more challenging responsibilities. For example, the downsizing of managerial staff in many organizations has required that first-level supervisors possess conceptual and communication skills in addition to their technical and applied skills. Higher-level managers must develop skills that will enable them to scan the external environment and develop organizational strategies. Training and development are used by organizations to improve the skills of employees and enhance their capacity to cope with the constantly changing demands of the work environment. Agencies that wish to be viable must develop strategies to maximize their human resources.

Change has become an inevitable part of organizational life, and to remain viable, organizations must learn how to manage change. Public and nonprofit agencies need to help employees deal with change. Training and development activities are critical if agencies are going to survive.

Technology is being used to communicate with many people across large geographical areas, eliminating the need to be nearby for personal interactions. Demographics are changing; for example, senior citizens are now a significant percentage of the population, and there has been an increase in the number of racial and ethnic minorities employed in public and nonprofit agencies. Jobs have become less specialized, forcing employees to work in teams to deliver services, and productivity needs to be improved despite declining personnel and financial resources. Changes in goals, the purchase of new equipment, the enactment of new laws or regulations, fluctuations in the economy, increased pressures from stakeholders, and the actions of competitors are other variables that influence change. As the demands placed on public and nonprofit organizations keep changing, organizations must implement training and development activities to ensure that their staffs have the requisite knowledge, skills, abilities, and other characteristics (KSAOCs) to confront these new challenges. Training can be targeted to help employees learn new job-specific skills, improve their performance, or change their attitudes. Changes need to be anticipated; training and development needs should be identified for, and budgeted. Developing a comprehensive long-range training program requires a strategic human resources management (SHRM) plan and the recognition that in today's knowledge economy, employees are the most valuable resource. If knowledge is the primary economic enabler, workforce skills are the real capital (Harris, 2001). Agencies wishing to be viable must develop strategies to maximize their human capabilities. Training and development must be integrated into the core human resources management (HRM) functions.

Wexley and Latham (1991) define training and development as "a planned effort by an organization to facilitate the learning of job-related behavior on the part of its employees" (p. 3). Training and development programs seek to change the skills, knowledge, or attitudes of employees. Programs may be focused on improving an individual's level of self-awareness, increasing an individual's competency in one or more areas of expertise, or increasing an individual's motivation to perform his or her job well.

It is important to note the word *planned* in Wexley and Latham's definition. Training and development efforts need to be thought out, and the following questions need to be answered:

- How can you develop a comprehensive training plan to address the needs of managers, elected officials, support staff, direct service providers, volunteers, and board members?
- What methods can you use to assess your agency's training needs?

- How can you design and implement the training program?
- What training delivery methods will you use?
- How will you demonstrate that the training budget was well spent?

This chapter first presents the fundamental steps in training: assessing needs; developing objectives; developing the curriculum, including determining which methodologies and techniques to use; delivering the training, including a discussion of learning styles; and finally, evaluating training. Next, career development is defined, managerial and executive development are discussed, and examples of training and development efforts that have been implemented in public and nonprofit organizations are presented.

Needs Assessment

The first step in the training process is to determine the specific training needs. A need can be defined simply as the difference between what is currently being done and what needs to be done. This difference can be determined by conducting a needs assessment of the skills and knowledge currently required by the position and those anticipated as necessary for the future. A needs assessment is critical to discerning whether performance deficiencies can be eliminated by training. Without a needs assessment, it is impossible to design and implement a training program as the solution to a problem that is not related to a training deficiency.

For example, it comes to the attention of higher management that one supervisor rates women and minorities lower than he rates white males, and the ratings are not based on job-related performance criteria. The supervisor is sent to performance evaluation training, where he is exposed to common rating errors and the need for unambiguous performance standards, timely feedback, and so on. Despite the training, the supervisor refuses to use job-related performance criteria when he evaluates his female and minority staff. Performance evaluation training did not resolve the problem; the ratings were artificially lowered because of prejudice and not because the supervisor lacked knowledge of performance evaluation techniques.

A true needs assessment would have discovered that the problem was different than originally thought and that the solution may involve a different kind of training. In this case, the supervisor was not deficient in skills; rather, it was his attitude that needed to be modified. Multicultural diversity training or training on employment discrimination would have been more appropriate. It is very important for a needs assessment to be accurate if training is to be successful.

Organizations can determine training needs through a variety of techniques. A strategic job analysis performed prior to the needs assessment is useful. The job analysis should identify the KSAOCs that incumbents need to effectively perform their jobs. Surveys and interviews with incumbents and supervisors; performance evaluations that identify performance deficiencies; criticisms or complaints from clients, staff, or personnel in agencies working with your employees; changes in regulations or operating procedures; and requests for additional training by incumbents can all provide clues as to what training is needed.

The training required to provide the needed KSAOCs should be divided into training that can be learned on the job and training that requires formal instruction. For example, some jobs require certification or licenses mandated by state or federal regulations. More and more states are requiring, for instance, that substance abuse counselors be state-certified. In Missouri, paramedics are required to pass a state written exam and attend refresher courses every three years. In New York State, nonprofit residential facilities for delinquent or status offender youths are required to comply with a regulation that new employees must receive training on the HIV virus and AIDS within fifteen days of being hired. In these examples, training is provided by experts outside the agency. Training to acquire other KSAOCs can be provided on the job. Having supervisors explain new policies and procedures or train employees on how to use new equipment can be part of any training plan.

Developing Training Objectives

Training objectives are statements that specify the desired KSAOCs that employees will possess at the end of training. The objectives provide the standard for measuring what has been accomplished and for determining the level of accomplishment. For training objectives to be useful, they should be stated as specifically as possible. Here are some examples:

Recreation assistants will be able to apply basic first aid to injured participants such as cleaning and bandaging scraped knees and elbows.

Supervisors will be able to explain the agency's sexual harassment policy to employees.

Receptionists will be able to transfer and route calls on the new telephone communication system without disconnecting callers.

The development of training objectives should be a collaborative process incorporating input from management, supervisors, workers, and trainers to ensure that the objectives are reasonable and realistic.

Developing the Curriculum

After assessing the training needs and developing objectives, a training curriculum must be developed. Before developing the content and the manner of presenting the information, an analysis of the trainees must first be done. This step is crucial because the trainees often prescribe the kind of training that is likely to be effective. Some of the relevant issues to examine include the following:

- What are the participants' levels of education? For example, classroom instruction may be intimidating for employees with limited formal education.
- What are participants' expectations? Will all participants come to training with the same concerns?
- What are participants' knowledge levels, attitudes, and relationships with one another?
- Are participants prepared to receive technical instruction?
- Is the training voluntary or imposed from above?
- If the training is mandatory, will the participants be threatened by it?

The answers to these questions will provide some guidance to the trainers when developing the curriculum. The curriculum should provide the necessary information and be developed to maximize the imparting of KSAOCs.

One of the first decisions that needs to be made is whether to provide on-the-job instruction, off-the-job classroom instruction, or a combination of the two. On-the-job instruction takes place while the employee is actually working at the jobsite. It is usually provided by supervisors, who instruct subordinates in the correct way to perform a task, such as filling out new purchase order requisitions. Or a representative from the management information systems (MIS) department could demonstrate how to load and set up a new software package. On-the-job training is useful when employees are expected to become proficient at performing certain tasks or using equipment found at their workstations. Because the training is directly related to the requirements of the job, transferring skills is easier. Employees learn by actually doing the job, and they get immediate feedback as to their proficiency. Another type of on-the-job training is job rotation, in which employees move from job to job at planned intervals, either within their departments or across the organization. For example, many organizations train managers by placing them in different positions throughout the agency so that they end up with a comprehensive perspective of its operations.

Some KSAOCs are difficult to teach at the worksite, so off-site training will be necessary. For example, training probation officers in counseling and listening skills would be difficult to do at their desks because other employees not involved in the training would be distracted by the instruction. Off-site training provides an alternative to on-the-job training; employees receive training away from their posts or workstations. In addition to avoiding disruptions to the normal routine at the jobsite, off-site training also permits the use of a greater variety of training techniques. Discussion of some other common training techniques follows.

Lecture

In a lecture format, a trainer presents material to a group of trainees. Lectures have been criticized because the information in them flows in only one direction—from trainer to trainees. The trainees tend to be passive participants. Differences in the trainees' experiences, interests, expertise, and personalities are ignored. Lectures are limited to the transfer of cognitive material. Wexley and Latham (1991) report that lectures are beneficial when they are used to introduce new information or provide verbal directions for learning tasks that will eventually be developed through other techniques. Lectures are readily adaptable for use with other training techniques.

Experiential Exercises

Experiential exercises attempt to simulate actual job or work experiences. Learning can be facilitated without the cost and risks of making mistakes while actually on the job. For example, law enforcement agencies use experiential exercises to train officers in emergency and disaster planning.

Role Playing

Role playing gives trainees the opportunity to practice interpersonal and communication skills by applying them to lifelike situations. Participants are expected to act out the roles they would play in responding to specific problems that they may encounter in their jobs. Role playing can be used in a variety of contexts. Law enforcement academies use it when training officers how to interview crime victims, such as sexually abused children, or witnesses to a crime. Role playing is frequently used in supervisory training, in which participants are asked to counsel a subordinate who is suspected of having a substance abuse problem.

Case Studies

The use of case studies in training involves having participants analyze situations, identify problems, and offer solutions. Trainees are presented with a written description of a problem. After reading the case, they diagnose the underlying issues and decide what should be done. Then, as a group, the trainees discuss their interpretations and understanding of the issues and the proposed solutions.

Audiovisual Methods

Videos are often used for training in a variety of contexts. There are videos to educate employees on legal topics such as sexual harassment, hiring disabled applicants, and using progressive discipline; videos that focus on interpersonal and communication skills; and videos that simulate a grievance arbitration hearing, permitting trainees to view the process, hear witnesses testify, see the behavior of management and union representatives, and learn how arbitrators conduct proceedings. Videos can be used to demonstrate particular tasks, such as the procedures to follow when apprehending a suspect or extinguishing a chemical fire. Videos are often used in orientation sessions to present background information on the agency—history, purpose, and goals. This use eliminates the need for trainers or supervisors to repeat themselves for all new employees and ensures that the same information is presented every time.

Trainees may also be videotaped. They may be asked to make a presentation or to provide performance feedback to colleagues. They may then view the videotape to identify their strengths and weaknesses related to the topic.

An advantage of video is that it provides the opportunity to slow down, speed up, or stop the video to review specific activities and enable questions to be asked and answered. A disadvantage to the use of videos is that they can be expensive to purchase or make.

Programmed Instruction and Computer-Based Training

Programmed instruction and computer-based instruction are self-teaching methods designed to enable trainees to learn at their own pace. Training materials are developed about a specific content area, such as grant writing. Learning objectives and instructional goals are specified. Information and training materials are assembled for the employees to read and use for practice. At their own pace, employees read the materials or practice the competencies required by the training objectives. The employees are then asked to demonstrate what they have learned.

An example of programmed instruction is *Budgeting: A Guide for Local Governments*, a self-study course developed by the International City/County Management Association (Bland & Rubin, 1998). The course provides an overview of the basic principles of local government budgeting. Review questions and activities in the guide are designed to reinforce key concepts. Exercises encourage further thought about current practices. Students take unit tests and a final examination to assess their own progress. The Federal Law Enforcement Training Center (FLETC) has implemented a distance-learning program for law enforcement agencies. It provides access to more than seventeen hundred off-the-shelf courses and thirty-five courses in specific law enforcement topics such as electronic crime, DNA, vehicle searches, and roadblocks, as well as business skills, management, communication, and technology. The U.S. Capitol Police also offers an electronic training program to its staff. Some of the topics covered are emergency responder training for weapons of mass destruction, electronic crime scene investigation, DNA crime scene investigation, and professional development topics such as ethics, employee coaching, and management ("FLETC Program," 2003).

Computer-based training uses interactive exercises with computers to impart job skills. Training materials are on the Web or on CDs. Employees read information, instructions, and diagrams or other graphics on the computer screen and then respond accordingly.

Equipment Simulators

Anybody who has taken a driver's education course probably remembers the driving simulator that replicated a car's dashboard, gas, and brake pedals. Simulators are used to bring realism to training situations. For jobs like those in law enforcement, on-the-job training can be too dangerous, such as training police officers when to discharge firearms. So equipment and scenarios that replicate the shadows and noises of alleys are used to train police officers not to overreact. Fire departments use burn buildings, which are designed to withstand repeated fires, to give firefighters opportunities to practice rescue attempts while battling heat and smoke. It would be too expensive and dangerous to burn vacant or decayed buildings. New procedures can be attempted without the risk of endangering human lives. A recent innovation in firefighting training developed by the National Institute of Standards and Technology (NIST) is a virtual reality simulation of a fire situation that enables fire professionals to demonstrate how life-threatening conditions can develop in structures and to test firefighting tactics on computers. Firefighters will be able to learn the ramifications of opening a window, closing a door, or aiming a hose spray in a certain direction ("NIST Developing Virtual Reality," 2003).

Videoconferencing

Improvements in technology have made videoconferencing less expensive and more accessible to an increasing number of public and nonprofit organizations. Two-way video cameras and fiber-optic networks are able to transport interactive live images across large geographical distances. For example, firefighters in Tulsa, Oklahoma, are required to also be trained as emergency medical technicians (EMTs). To be certified as an EMT requires additional training hours added to the mandated 360 hours for each firefighter. To implement the necessary training, the fire department began offering training through streaming video on its network. The programming is comprised of live broadcasts from the fire department's own studio-recorded programs and satellite feeds from the Fire and EMT Network. Sixty percent of the training is conducted while the firefighters are working their shifts. To accommodate the different shifts, the shows are taped and broadcast three times on a given day and again three days later (Mariani, 2001).

BoardSource, formerly the National Center for Nonprofit Boards, offers teleconferencing seminars on topics of interest, such as board development and fundraising, to nonprofit board members and executives.

The advantages of video training include more flexibility in meeting training needs, a reduction in time lost in travel to training sites, and increased uniformity of training.

Community Resources

Nonprofit and public agencies should be aware of the many community resources that are often available to provide training at nominal cost or even free of charge. Many health care facilities offer workshops on topics that are targeted to specific clientele groups, such as depression among adolescents or the elderly, sex abuse, or substance abuse. Chapters of Planned Parenthood offer seminars on boosting self-esteem and preventing teen pregnancies. Hospice associations offer training on the issues associated with death and dying, and various professional associations also sponsor training classes. Managers and HRM departments need to be on the lookout for relevant community-based training opportunities. Each technique has its advantages and disadvantages, which need to be weighed in relation to time constraints, staff resources, finances, and desired outcomes.

Delivering Training

Other issues must be addressed in addition to curriculum. Should the training take place for short periods of time spread over many days, or should it encompass long periods over fewer days? What time of day should the training take place? What size group should be involved? There is no one right answer. It depends on the information being presented or the skills that need to be taught, as well as the aptitudes of the participants and the techniques that are used. Failing to consider any of these factors can negatively influence the results of training efforts. Most public sector and nonprofit employers cannot afford such waste.

The delivery of the training program is the stage where the trainers and the participants converge. At a well-organized worksite, the employees selected for training understand what the objectives of the training are and what they can expect. Patricia Murray, a trainer with the New York State Office of Children and Family Services, notes that one of the most common training errors is not to recognize that the participants are adults with life and work experiences. Murray recommends providing an agenda with training objectives so that participants will know where the training is headed and what methods and techniques will be used. She also recommends incorporating the group members' experience into the training (P. Murray, personal communication, 2003). A useful model to consider is that of Kolb (1984), which is based on adults learning from their experience. It is up to the trainers to create a climate in which individual learning styles are recognized and considered in the delivery of the content. This is especially important for employees who resist training or perceive it as a punishment and not as an opportunity.

Research on successful training programs shows that training programs should be designed to address not only substantive content or material but also how people learn and should therefore incorporate different learning strategies (Agochiya, 2002).

As the workforce becomes more diverse, there will be more variation in employees' ability to learn, in their learning styles, in their basic literacy skills, and in their functional life skills. It will be even more important for training to take into account individual backgrounds and needs. Adult learners see themselves as self-directed and expect to be able to answer some of their questions on the basis of their own experiences. Instruction tailored to adult learners allows the trainees the opportunity to participate in the process. The role of the training instructors is to facilitate learning; they use lots of questions, guide the trainees, and encourage two-way communication between the instructor and the class, as well as communication among the class's participants.

Evaluating Training

An evaluation of the training program is necessary to determine whether the training accomplished its objectives. Unfortunately, this is often the most neglected aspect of training, especially in the public sector (Bramley, 1996; Sims, 1998). Evaluation improves training programs by providing feedback to the trainers, participants, and managers, and it assesses employee skill levels. Evaluations can be used to measure changes in knowledge, in levels of skills, in attitudes and behavior, and in levels of effectiveness at both the individual and the agency level.

Kirkpatrick (1998) suggests that there are four primary levels at which training programs can be evaluated. The first level is measuring the participants' reactions to the training program. He refers to this step as a measure of customer satisfaction. Participants are asked to answer questions such as "Was the trainer knowledgeable?" "Was the material or information relevant?" "Will the information assist you in performing your job?" Data are gathered through the use of surveys distributed at the conclusion of the training session. Asking these questions provides data on the training program's content and the trainer's skill. (Trainers refer to this step as a "smile meter.")

According to Kirkpatrick (1998), learning has taken place when one or more of the following occurs: attitudes are changed, knowledge is increased, and skills are improved. The second level of evaluation measures whether learning has occurred as a result of attending the training. Did the participants acquire the skills or knowledge embodied in the objectives? Did the training impart the KSAOCs that were deemed important? To determine whether learning took place, participants can be tested on the information presented, follow-up interviews can be conducted, skill demonstrations can be required, or case studies can be developed that test the competencies that were intended to be taught. It is important to note that the methods used should be selected on the basis of the level of mastery desired.

The third level of evaluation attempts to measure the extent to which on-the-job behavioral change has occurred due to the participants' having attended the training program. Evaluation activities are aimed at determining whether the participants have been able to transfer to their jobs the KSAOCs they learned in training. Measurement at this stage is more difficult; it requires supervisors to collect work samples or observe employees' performance. Another technique would be to employ performance evaluations designed to measure the new competencies.

Kirkpatrick (1998) acknowledges that for change to occur, four conditions must be met: the employee must have a desire to change, must know what to do and how to do it, must work in the right climate, and must be rewarded for changing. Kirkpatrick notes that a training program can accomplish the first two requirements, but the right climate is dependent on the employee's immediate supervisor. Some supervisors may prevent their employees from doing what was taught in the training program; others may not model the behaviors taught in the training program, which discourages the employees from changing; some supervisors may ignore the fact that employees have attended the training program and thereby not support employees' efforts to change; others may encourage employees to learn and apply their learning on the job; and finally, some supervisors may know what the employees learned in the training and make sure that the learning transfers to the job. To assist in creating a positive climate so that learning transfers to the job, it is recommended that supervisors be involved in the development of the training program.

The fourth condition, that the employee be rewarded for changing, can include the feelings of satisfaction, achievement, proficiency, and pride that can occur with successful change. Extrinsic rewards such as praise from the supervisor, recognition from others, and possible merit rewards or promotions can also result.

If the training did not accomplish what it was intended to, the HRM department should assess the conditions the trainee returns to by trying to determine what the problem was and working with the line managers to make the necessary changes. Such an assessment could begin with the following questions: What gets in the way? Does the employee who just received training on a new computer system have to go back to the same old equipment? Does the employee reenter a crisis situation and have to revert to the way things were always done? Often so-called training problems are not training problems at all—they are environmental problems. For training to be most effective, the organization's culture must support training and hold its supervisors accountable for creating a climate in which employees can transfer what they have learned to their jobs.

The fourth level of evaluation attempts to measure the final results that occurred because employees attended the training. Ideally, training is linked to improved organizational performance. At this level, evaluation is concerned with determining what impact the training has had on the agency. Satisfactory final results can include such things as fewer grievances filed against supervisors, greater employee productivity, a reduction in the number of client complaints, a decrease in workplace accidents, larger amounts raised through fundraising, improved board relations, and less discrimination in the workplace. Some final results are easier to measure than others. For example, the dollars raised from fundraising activities, the number of workplace accidents, or the number of grievances filed can be easily quantified and compared to times before the training. Other final results, like eliminating discrimination, changing attitudes, and improving leadership and communication, are less quantifiable and more difficult to measure. Such results will have to be evaluated in terms of improved morale and attitudes. Although Kirkpatrick (1998) identifies only four levels of analysis, he emphasizes that as a final step, organizations must determine whether the benefits of the training outweigh its direct and indirect costs. Phillips and Stone (2002), in their book *How to Measure Training Results,* refer to this as level five, return on investment. The results from training programs should be converted to monetary values so that cost-benefit analyses can be conducted to determine if a training program should be continued. Examples of direct costs include expenses for instructor fees, facilities, printed materials, and meals. Indirect costs include the salaries of participants who are away from their regular jobs. Has there been a reasonable return on this investment? Basically, was the training worth its costs? Did it accomplish what it was designed to accomplish? Training evaluation reports should present a balance of financial and nonfinancial data.

The potential benefits from evaluating training programs include improved accountability and cost effectiveness for training programs, improved program effectiveness (are programs producing the intended results?), improved efficiency (are they producing the intended results with a minimum waste of resources?), and information on how to redesign current or future programs. Training must be tied to the strategic objectives of the organizations. With today's emphasis on outcome measurement, it is crucial that training programs be designed to enhance individual, unit, and organizational performance.

Career Development

Fitzgerald (1992) defines training as "the acquisition of knowledge and skills for present tasks, which help individuals contribute to the organization in their current positions. . . . To be successful, training must result in a change in behavior, such as the use of new knowledge and skills on the job" (p. 81). Career development, however, provides the employee with knowledge and skills that are intended to be used in the future. The purpose of career development is to prepare employees to meet future agency needs, thereby ensuring the organization's survival.

Career development is used to improve the skill levels of and provide long-term opportunities for the organization's present workforce. Career development programs provide incumbents with advancement opportunities within the organization so that they will not have to look elsewhere. Taking the time and spending resources to develop employees signals to them that they are valued by the agency. As a result, they become motivated and assume responsibility for developing their career paths (Fitz-enz, 1990).

The focus of career development plans is on where the agency is headed and where in the agency incumbents can find future job opportunities. Employees and supervisors should produce a development plan that focuses on employee growth and development. The plan should have measurable development objectives and an action plan. For example, supervisors should review their employees' skills with the job descriptions of higher-level positions within the same job family or of positions within the organization to which the employee might be able to cross over. By comparing employees' skills with the skill requirements of other positions, the employees and supervisors can determine what experience and training might still be needed for advancement or lateral movement. Supervisors should direct employees to relevant training opportunities and, when possible, delegate additional tasks and responsibilities to employees so that they may develop new competencies.

A number of career development programs can be found in the public and nonprofit sectors. Some of them focus on moving employees from clerical or paraprofessional positions into higher-paying administrative jobs. Others focus on developing supervisory and management skills. Examples of some of the programs follow.

Local 1199 of the Service Employees International Union (SEIU), New York's health and human services union, entered into a partnership with the City University of New York and has established a joint training program so that union members can take free courses to obtain nursing degrees or to upgrade their skills. The courses will range from nursing and precollege skills to continuing education and the training of laboratory and operating room technicians. The program is intended to help reduce the city's nursing shortage and to provide additional skills to Hispanic workers. It will be offered in the community where the health care workers live. All New Yorkers can participate in the program; however, only union members are able to attend free of charge. To accommodate the work schedules of the students, classes are offered from 8:00 A.M. to 9:00 P.M. Union members get free child care as well as free after-school programs for their older children (Greenhouse, 2002).

The state of Illinois instituted a career development program called the Upward Mobility Program as part of a master agreement between the American Federation of State, County and Municipal Employees and the state. Employees can work toward advancement in five major career paths: data processing, office services, accounting, human services, and medicine. Employees receive individual counseling to inform them of the career opportunities available and to guide them in developing their career plans. Participants take proficiency exams and complete required education and training programs designed to provide the skills and knowledge needed for advancement. The program covers all tuition costs and most mandatory registration fees for classes taken at public institutions and up to $310 per credit hour for undergraduate courses, $340 for master's courses, and $400 for Ph.D. courses at private schools. When all necessary training and education has been completed, employees are given special consideration when bidding on targeted titles.

Two career tracks are available: credential and certificate. The credential track is for positions that require specific degrees and licenses, such as social worker, licensed practical nurse, or child-protective associate investigator. Employees meet with Upward Mobility Program counselors to discuss the education required for the chosen position. When the employees obtain the necessary degree or license, they are issued a credential.

The certificate track is for positions that require employees to pass written proficiency exams before they can enroll in specific courses. The exam identifies which classes, if any, are required. Employees are required to take courses related to the sections of the exam in which they did not demonstrate proficiency. After employees complete the required coursework, they are retested. Once they have demonstrated proficiency in all segments of the exam, they are issued a certificate. The certificate gives the employee priority for the next vacancy in that job title in any agency, even if the title is in another bargaining unit job. Seniority prevails should two or more employees with certificates apply for the same position (State of Illinois, 2002).

Managerial and Executive Development

Problem-solving skills, initiative, the ability to function as a team player, interpersonal skills, and the creativity to seize opportunities are some of the critical skills that managers and executives of public and nonprofit agencies need to guide their agencies. Technical experience and competency are no longer enough; public and nonprofit organizations need leaders with the vision to direct and guide their agencies as city, state, and federal funding is cut.

One program in the public sector that emphasizes leadership development is provided by the Maine Leadership Institute (Maine Bureau of Human Resources, 2003). Maine, like many other states, is facing the retirement of significant numbers of top managers and executives. The impending loss of experience, combined with an outdated classification system and rules and the recognition that the leading cause of job dissatisfaction is employees' relationship with their manager, prompted Maine to develop a competency model for leadership for the Maine Management Service (see Exhibit 12.1). Participants in this program are exposed to ten core leadership competencies.

Exhibit 12.1. Leadership Competencies for Maine's State Government.

An Excellent Leader Is . . .

. . . INSPIRING

Visionary: Establishes and maintains a long-term, big picture perspective to move Maine State Government forward. Communicates the vision through Maine State Government in the form of distinctive strategies, policies, objectives, and action plans that maximize Maine State Government's ability to meet constituent needs.

A Supportive Coach: Monitors others' work efforts and follows through with constructive guidance and recommendations. Takes steps with employees to develop people with the necessary skills, abilities, and competencies. Acts as a mentor for others, particularly in Maine State Government.

An Effective Communicator: Articulates information clearly, adapting communication styles to match others. Creates an atmosphere in which timely and high quality information flows smoothly and effectively between self and others.

Models Integrity: Builds trust through demonstration of ethical behavior and personal authenticity. Demonstrates principles and values that model those of the organization. Follows through on stated vision regardless of difficulty. Sets standards for work, processes, and personal behavior; holds the organization accountable to those standards.

. . . A STEWARD

Customer Focused: Focuses efforts on discovering and meeting the customers' needs. "Customers" include internal colleagues, peers, team members, and Maine State citizens.

Results Oriented: Focuses efforts on attaining clear, concrete, timely, and measurable outcomes of importance to the organization. Uses time and resources on activities that will yield the greatest benefit by regularly evaluating and comparing work being done to goals, resulting in a sense of urgency.

Has Sound Judgment: Uses common sense and works collaboratively with others to create effective action plans based on appropriate information. Gains perspective from all available resources, develops an understanding of a situation, and reaches conclusions based on information gathered and applies intuition with sound analysis.

Exhibit 12.1. Leadership Competencies for Maine's State Government, Cont'd.

. . . AN EFFECTIVE PROBLEM SOLVER

An Analytical Thinker: Understands situations or complex issues or problems by breaking them down into smaller pieces or tracing the implications or impacts by using a step-by-step approach. Strives to understand causal relationships and to identify appropriate approaches or solutions.

Innovative: Acts as a creative resource for others by either offering new and novel ideas and approaches or facilitating an environment that encourages others to offer new or novel ideas and approaches. Consistently challenges current thinking, and always looks for ways to "take a different approach."

A Systems Thinker: Connects information, processes, and events by organizing divergent information and searching for common themes, patterns, and causal connections. Simultaneously sees the practical and political issues inherent in any situation.

Source: Maine Bureau of Human Resources, 2003. Used by permission of the Maine Management Service, Division of State Training and Development, Department of Government and International Affairs.

In 2000, the Federal Highway Administration (FHWA) realized that within ten years, 45 percent of its workforce would be eligible to retire. To position the agency to achieve the goals established in its strategic plan, the executive director set up the Work Force Planning and Professional Development Task Force. The task force was charged with developing a framework to ensure that the FHWA has trained, dedicated, and motivated employees who can deliver the agency vision, mission, and goals into the future. An analysis of the agency's future workforce needs revealed that there were talent, skill, and competency gaps. To close the gaps, the task force realized that the agency needed to have programs, processes, and employees who can adapt to continually changing needs as technology and program changes occur. Major changes were needed in the agency's culture, professional development, and business practices. To promote the necessary changes, the task force developed action plans for recruiting, hiring, and retention; internal resources management; quality-of-life; workforce and succession planning; and professional development.

In regard to professional development, the task force recommended that the opportunities available to employees for their development should be expanded and the agency should create an environment that encourages continuous learning. Specific action plans included the following (Federal Highway Administration, 2000):

- Integrate performance plan and workforce plan with training and development plans.
- Require individual development plans for all employees.
- Recognize employees who have become licensed, certified, or credentialed.
- Where appropriate, candidates for advancement in Technical Career Tracks who have professional registration or certification will be given higher consideration than those without.
- Use rotational and developmental assignments as professional developmental tools.
- Support and fund the formation and use of communities of practice.
- Evaluate professional development activities conducted by communities of practice for possible broader use.
- Encourage the movement of personnel between federal land and federal aid offices to enhance professional development.
- Expand the development of leadership, business, and professional skills to all levels of the organization including nonsupervisory positions.
- Expand and provide earlier leadership opportunities to shape future executives.
- Encourage a community of practice for secretarial and administrative assistant positions and identify champions to ensure its effective operation.
- Use vacancies in key position as opportunities for rotational or developmental assignments.
- Continue to invest at least 3 percent of salaries and benefits in training.
- Increase the use of FHWA employees as instructors for NHI [National Highway Institute] and other training.

- Expand the capacity to deliver training developed specifically for FHWA employees.
- Take greater advantage of local training opportunities.
- Expand the Academic Study Program to include nontechnical programs (e.g., leadership, generalists, administrative). Pursue legislation to allow the agency to fund advance degrees for employees.

San Diego County in California and Ramsey County in Minnesota developed leadership training programs (Goski, 2002; Green, 2002). The training and development programs in Hennepin County, Minnesota, and Broward County, Florida, were identified by the IPMA Benchmarking Committee for their "best practices." Both counties align training and development activities with organizational strategy. The impacts of training and development are evaluated. Responsibility for training and development throughout the organizations is shared with managers, supervisors, employees, and the departments of human resources management (Bjornberg, 2002).

Summary

Training is typically associated with improving the performance, knowledge, or skill of employees in their present positions. Career development is viewed as a continuous process consisting of evaluating abilities and interests, establishing career goals, and planning developmental activities that relate to the employees' and organization's future needs. Organizations must recognize the importance of both training and career development planning and provide career enhancement and developmental opportunities.

It is important that once their career development programs have been developed, organizations maintain their programs and revive them with new initiatives. Career development should be linked with other HRM strategies, such as succession planning, performance evaluations, quality management initiatives, and new-employee orientation. Managers should be held accountable for developing their individual employees. Providing feedback and coaching to their staff should be one of their main responsibilities.

Agencies that are serious about training and career development should continue to monitor, evaluate, and revise their training and career development programs. To be successful, training and career development programs need to be fully integrated with the organization's strategic focus and SHRM system. Increased skill acquisition will be effective only if agencies accurately identify and predict the types of KSAOCs and positions that will be required. If career paths are identified, training and development programs must be used to move employees along those paths. New approaches to training need to be considered, and organizational reward structures should encourage individual growth and development that benefits both the employee and the organization.

Questions and Exercises

1. Discuss why training must be a strategic imperative in today's organizations.
2. What kinds of analyses are required to determine the training needs of an organization, of individual employees, or of an entire unit?
3. In small groups, share your experiences with training. What are some advantages and disadvantages of the different training methods and delivery discussed in the chapter?
4. You are the head of a department. What methods of training and career development would you use with a talented employee?
5. Visit the American Society for Training and Development (ASTD) Web site (http://www.astd.org). What training topics are being discussed? Is there a need for a professional society devoted to training and development activities?
6. Visit the International City/County Management Association (ICMA) Web site (http://www.icma.org). What types of professional development opportunities is this organization promoting?
7. Visit the NPO Net: For and About Chicago Area Nonprofits Web site (http://www.npo.net). What kinds of training and professional development opportunities is this organization promoting?
8. Using the Internet, identify internship opportunities in federal, state, and local government and nonprofit organizations. How are the internships similar? How are they different? Explain.

Chapter Thirteen

Collective Bargaining in the Public and Nonprofit Sectors

The economic, technological, social, cultural, and legal changes affecting the workplace have also provoked changes in labor-management relations. The current economic distress leading to threats of downsizing and privatization, along with the public's concern about waste and inefficiency, requires that unions and employers reexamine their structure and systems to see how they can provide more effective services. To remain competitive, management and unions must adopt new approaches and attitudes for resolving conflicts. Together, management and unions must creatively resolve problems and develop solutions advantageous to both sides.

Collective bargaining has been defined as a process that obligates management and union representatives to negotiate in good faith in an attempt to reach an agreement concerning issues that affect employees. While many employers dislike having to recognize and negotiate with employee unions, other employers appreciate the continuity and stability that collective bargaining can bring to an organization. Issues that have been negotiated and that are part of a collective bargaining agreement are often resolved for the length of the contract. Collective bargaining includes the execution, interpretation, and enforcement of the negotiated contract.

This chapter presents the legal framework of collective bargaining, beginning with the history of private sector collective bargaining because the laws permitting public employee unionism are often patterned after the laws granting private sector employees the right to bargain; furthermore, nonprofit collective bargaining is governed by the same laws and rulings as collective bargaining in the private sector. This history is followed by an overview of the laws relevant to collective bargaining in the nonprofit and public sectors and then by discussion of the concepts and practices that constitute the collective bargaining process, including bargaining unit determination, the selection of a bargaining representative, unfair labor practices, the obligation to negotiate, union security devices, the scope of collective bargaining, management rights, impasse resolution, striking, and grievance arbitration. Distinctions between public and nonprofit labor relations are noted, and the chapter concludes with a discussion of the future of collective bargaining.

The History of Private Sector Collective Bargaining

Private sector labor-management relations were initially governed by the National Labor Relations Act of 1935 (NLRA). The NLRA permitted employees to organize and join unions for the purposes of collective bargaining. It addressed the rights of employees in the areas of union security agreements, picketing, and striking. Employer unfair labor practices were defined, as were the criteria for an appropriate bargaining unit, the selection of a bargaining representative, and the enforcement of the act. Under this law, employers were required to bargain in good faith with employee unions and could be cited for unfair labor practices if they attempted to interfere with the establishment of such unions. The NLRA established the National Labor Relations Board (NLRB) as the administrative agency responsible for enforcing the provisions of the act.

In 1947, Congress amended the NLRA with the passage of the Labor-Management Relations Act (LMRA). This act articulated union unfair labor practices. In 1959, the Labor-Management Reporting and Disclosure Act was passed by Congress. This act established a bill of rights for union members, specifying internal union election procedures and financial reporting disclosure requirements for unions and union officers. It also added restrictions on picketing, prohibiting "hot cargo" clauses, and closed certain loopholes in the LMRA. ("Hot cargo" agreements are contract provisions in which the employer promises not to handle products that the union finds objectionable because they have been produced by nonunion labor or at a plant on strike.) These three laws have been consolidated and are presently referred to as the Labor-Management Relations Act of 1947, as amended. Federal and state governments are excluded from coverage by the act. Nonprofits became covered in the 1970s.

The NLRB can direct elections and certify results only in the case of employers whose operations affect commerce. The LMRA applies to any employer or unfair labor practice affecting commerce. Therefore, the statute has a broad scope covering most employers (Feldacker, 1990).

Because the courts have broadly interpreted what practices "affect commerce," the NLRB could theoretically enforce the act for all employers whose operations involve trade of any kind. However, the board has chosen not to act in all cases. In 1950, the board decided to distinguish between businesses that interrupt the flow of interstate commerce and those that are so small that a dispute would probably have no impact on the flow of trade. It set monetary cutoff points, or standards, that limit the exercise of its power to cases involving employers whose effect on commerce is substantial. The board's requirements for exercising its power or jurisdiction are called "jurisdictional standards" or "jurisdictional yardsticks." These standards are based on the yearly amount of business done by the employer or on the yearly amount of its sales or purchases. The standards are stated in terms of total volume of business and are different for different kinds of enterprises (Commerce Clearing House, 1990; Feldacker, 1990; National Labor Relations Board, 1991). Exhibit 13.1 presents the board's current jurisdictional standards.

Collective Bargaining in Nonprofit Organizations

Originally, the NLRB excluded nonprofit employers from the NLRA's coverage. However, in the 1970s, the board asserted jurisdiction over nonprofits that had a "massive impact on interstate commerce" or those that met certain financial criteria—such as nursing homes with revenue over $100,000, visiting nurse associations, and similar facilities as applied to profit-making nursing homes (*Drexel Homes, Inc.,* 82 NLRB 151, 1970).

In August 1974, Congress amended the LMRA to bring nonprofit health care institutions under the law's coverage. At that

Exhibit 13.1. National Labor Relations Board Jurisdictional Standards in Effect Since July 1990.

Nonretail businesses	$50,000 total annual revenues
Office buildings	$100,000 total annual revenues
Retail enterprises	$500,000 total annual volume of business
Public utilities	$250,000 total annual volume of business or $50,000 direct or indirect outflow or inflow
Newspapers	$200,000 total annual volume of business
Radio, telegraph, television, and telephone enterprises	$100,000 total annual volume of business
Hotels, motels, and residential apartment houses	$500,000 total annual volume of business
Transportation enterprises, links and channels of interstate commerce	$50,000 total annual income
Transit systems	$250,000 total annual volume of business
Taxicab companies	$500,000 total annual volume of business
Private universities and colleges	$1 million gross annual revenues
Symphony orchestras	$1 million gross annual revenues
Law firms and legal assistance programs	$250,000 gross annual revenues
Employers that provide social services	$250,000 gross annual revenues
Privately operated health care institutions[a]	$250,000 total annual volume of business
Nursing homes, visiting nurse associations, and related facilities and associations	$100,000 total annual volume of business[b]
Enterprises in the Territories and the District of Columbia	Jurisdictional standards apply in the Territories; *all* businesses in the District of Columbia come under NLRB jurisdiction.
National defense	Jurisdiction is asserted over all enterprises affecting commerce when their operations have a substantial impact on national defense, whether or not the enterprises satisfy any other standard.

[a]Defined as hospitals, convalescent hospitals, health maintenance organizations, health clinics, nursing homes, extended care facilities, or other institutions devoted to the care of the sick, infirm, or aged.

[b]

time, Congress added Section 2(14), which defines "health care institutions" as hospitals, nursing homes, and other health care facilities without regard to whether they are operated for profit. The health care amendments indicated that Congress had no objection to bringing nonprofit employers under federal labor law. Two years later, in 1976, the NLRB began to treat nonprofit and charitable institutions the same way it treated businesses operated for profit. If a nonprofit employer was sufficiently involved in the interstate flow of money or goods that a labor dispute might disrupt the flow of commerce, the board would assume jurisdiction. The board established a jurisdictional standard of $250,000 annual revenue for all social service agencies other than those for which there is another specific standard application for the type of activity in which the organization is engaged. For example, the specific $100,000 standard would still apply for a nursing home (Feldacker, 1990).

The NLRB asserts jurisdiction over nonprofit service organizations that provide services to or for an exempt governmental agency such as Head Start, child care services, and medical clinics that are supported by state or federal funds (Feldacker, 1990). Some of these agencies have argued that they are excluded by the NLRA by the exemption for government agencies. The board holds that such agencies are covered by the act, even though government-funded, if they retain independence in labor-management matters, such as establishing wages, hours, and working conditions for their employees. The sole standard for taking jurisdiction is whether the contractor has "sufficient control over the employment conditions of its employees to enable it to bargain with labor organization as its representative." The board looks closely at the nature of the relationship between the government institution and the contractor.

An interesting issue of jurisdiction surfaced in *National Labor Relations Board* v. *Catholic Bishop of Chicago* (440 U.S. 490, 100 LRRM 2913, 1979). The Supreme Court held that the NLRB cannot assert jurisdiction over church-operated schools because such jurisdiction would violate the First Amendment guarantee of freedom of religion and the separation of church and state. The Court held that the religious and secular purposes of church-sponsored schools are so intertwined that the board's jurisdiction would unconstitutionally introduce the board into the operations and policies of the church. The board does, however, assert jurisdiction over church-operated nonprofit social agencies such as nursing homes, hospitals, and child care centers because they function essentially the same as their secular counterparts: they receive government financial support, they are regulated by the state along with other nonprofit social agencies, and their activities only tangentially relate to the sponsoring organization's religious mission (Feldacker, 1990).

Collective Bargaining in the Federal Government

The Civil Service Reform Act of 1978 (CSRA) and Executive Order 12871 issued on October 1, 1993, govern labor relations in the federal sector. The CSRA covers most employees of the executive agencies of the United States, including the Library of Congress and the Government Printing Office. The exclusions include federal employees working for the Government Accounting Office (GAO), Federal Bureau of Investigation (FBI), National Security Agency (NSA), Central Intelligence Agency (CIA), Federal Labor Relations Authority, Federal Service Impasses Panel, Tennessee Valley Authority (TVA), Foreign Service of the United States, Department of State, United States Information Agency, and Agency for International Development and its successor agency or agencies, the United States Postal Service, and employees engaged in administering a labor-management relations law. TVA employees and postal employees are covered by other statutes. TVA employees are covered by the Employment Relationship Policy Act of the New Deal and have been covered since 1935. The Postal Recognition Act of 1970 granted collective bargaining rights to postal employees under the NLRA. However, unlike private sector employees, postal employees are denied the right to strike. Employees working for the GAO, FBI, NSA, and CIA have no statutory authority to engage in collective bargaining.

With the creation in 2003 of the Department of Homeland Security, many federal employees who had collective bargaining rights saw those rights slip away. Inspectors working for the Bureau of Alcohol, Tobacco, Firearms and Explosives (ATF) may become exempt from collective bargaining, and on January 7, 2002, President George W. Bush issued Executive Order 13252, which prevented unions from organizing certain subdivisions in the Department of Justice, citing national security concerns. Exempted from organizing are employees in the United States Attorneys' Offices, Criminal Division, INTERPOL–U.S. Central Bureau, the National Drug

Intelligence Center, and the Office of Intelligence Policy and Review. James M. Loy, the head of the Transportation Security Administration (TSA), successfully blocked attempts to unionize airport screeners, also stating that collective bargaining rights could jeopardize national security. The American Federation of Government Employees (AFGE) has sued the TSA in federal court in an attempt to overturn the order.

Title VII of the CSRA enacted the provision known as the Federal Service Labor-Management Relations Statute (LMRS). This statute created the Federal Labor Relations Authority (FLRA) to administer and enforce the CSRA. The FLRA is governed by three bipartisan members who are appointed by the president with the advice and consent of the Senate. The members are appointed for staggered five-year terms.

Dissatisfied parties may appeal rulings made by the FLRA to the U.S. Court of Appeals. The authority of the FLRA is similar to that of the NLRB. The FLRA determines appropriate bargaining units, supervises and conducts union elections, conducts hearings and resolves allegations of unfair labor practices, prescribes criteria for and resolves issues relating to determining compelling need for agency rules or regulations, resolves exceptions to arbitrators' awards, and takes such other actions as are necessary and appropriate to effectively administer the provisions of Title VII of the CSRA.

Federal employees may not bargain over wages and benefits or prohibited political activities. Executive Order 12871 modified the scope of bargaining, requiring agencies to negotiate "the numbers, types, and grades of employees or positions assigned to any organizational subdivision, work project, or tour of duty, and the technology, methods and means of performing work" (5 USC7 106, 1993). Despite this change, the scope of negotiable issues is still more restrictive for federal employees than for employees at other levels of government, for nonprofits, and for the private sector. For example, federal employees may not strike. You may recall that in 1980, President Ronald Reagan fired striking air traffic controllers.

Collective Bargaining in State and Local Governments

Many states have passed laws that grant state and local government employees the right to participate in collective bargaining with their employers. Other states only permit public employees the right to "meet and confer" with a public employer. In Alabama, Georgia, and Nebraska, teachers' collectives may meet and confer, but all other employees may bargain; in California, local employees may meet and confer, while all other employees may use collective bargaining; in Texas, teachers may meet and confer, but there is no coverage for state employees; and local government public employees in Missouri may meet and confer. Still other states lack statutes that permit or recognize the right of public employees to join unions or bargain with public employers. The duty to meet and confer provides unions with the right to discuss with the public employer proposals establishing the terms and conditions of employment. However, employers are free to ignore the views of the unions and make unilateral decisions as to the terms and conditions of employment.

Many state statutes are very complete and are referred to as comprehensive statutes. These statutes are modeled after the Labor-Management Relations Act of 1947, as amended. Like the LMRS, they guarantee public employees the right to join or form labor unions or to refrain from joining unions; they also establish procedures for the selection of employee representatives, define the scope of bargaining and unfair labor practices, address union security provisions, permit or prohibit strikes, prescribe remedies to resolve contract negotiation impasses, provide mechanisms for contract grievance resolution, and establish an administrative agency to oversee the law. These statutes are referred to as public employee relations acts, or PERAs.

Concepts and Practices of Collective Bargaining

What follows are explanations of the issues introduced in the overview, along with specific examples to illustrate the concepts of collective bargaining as they are applied in the federal, state, and local governments and in the nonprofit sector. For purposes of this discussion, all of the labor-management collective bargaining acts—private or nonprofit (LMRA), federal (LMRS), and state (PERAs)—will be referred to generically as labor-management relations acts.

Labor-management relation acts designate or create agencies to provide oversight of the acts and to administer relations among employers, employees, and unions. The NLRB governs private and nonprofit labor relations, the FLRA provides oversight for the federal government, and although the names of these administrative agencies tend to vary across the states (New Jersey's version is the Public Employment Relations Commission, the Illinois version is known as the Illinois State Labor Relations Board, and Florida calls its board the Public Employee Relations Commission), they are often referred to as public employee relations boards, or PERBs.

Unit Determination

The labor-management relations acts generally define the procedures for designating the employees' representative or union. Before a union can represent a group of employees, the constituency of the group must be determined. The group of employees that can potentially be represented by one representative at the bargaining table is called the *appropriate bargaining unit.* The acts contain guidelines for both the determination of the appropriate unit and the procedures to be used for such determination.

The labor-management relation's acts exclude some general categories of employees from a bargaining unit. For example, managerial and confidential employees are excluded as a matter of policy because their interests are more closely aligned with management than with the bargaining unit. Managerial employees are individuals employed by an agency in positions that require or authorize them to formulate, determine, or influence the policies of the agency. Confidential employees are those who assist the individuals who formulate, determine, or execute labor policy. Included in this category are employees who have access to information about labor relations or who participate in deliberations of a labor relations nature and are required to keep that information confidential from the labor organization representing a bargaining unit. Professional and technical employees, and in some cases supervisors, may also be excluded from an overall bargaining unit, but they are still entitled to representation as their own units. Professional employees perform work of a predominantly intellectual, nonstandardized nature. The work must require the exercise of discretion and independent judgment and make use of knowledge that is customarily acquired through college or university attendance. Technical employees perform work of a technical nature that requires the use of independent discretion and special training. They may have acquired their training in college, in technical schools, or on the job. A supervisor is an individual who has the authority, in the interests of the agency, to hire, direct, assign, promote, reward, transfer, furlough, lay off, recall, suspend, discipline, or remove employees and to adjust their grievances or effectively recommend such action.

Public safety officers often receive special treatment. Some states have separate statutes for police officers and firefighters, while others include them in municipal or general statutes. Fourteen states have statutes that require police officers to be in units composed only of police officers, and twelve states require the same for firefighters. This special treatment is meant to ensure the community's safety. The state of Delaware has separate police and firefighter units "to protect the public by assuring the orderly and uninterrupted operations and functions of public safety services" (Police Officers' and Firefighters' Employment Relations Act, 1986).

Selection of a Bargaining Representative

The labor-management relations acts also contain specific procedures for the selection of an exclusive bargaining representative. *Exclusive recognition* is the term applied when one union has the right and responsibility to speak on behalf of all employees in the bargaining unit. Voluntary recognition by the employer is the easiest way of designating a union. It is available only if the union can demonstrate support by a majority of employees in the unit. This is usually achieved by having employees sign recognition cards authorizing the union to represent them in collective bargaining.

If voluntary recognition is not achieved, or if it is challenged by a claim of majority representation by another representative organization, a secret-ballot election may be held to select the exclusive bargaining representative. The administrative agencies have the authority to regulate these representation elections, which are also subject to judicial review. Some states, such as Delaware, Hawaii, Iowa, Rhode Island, and Wisconsin, insist that a secret-ballot election be held to determine employee representation. A union that has been voluntarily recognized by the employer as the exclusive representative possesses the same rights as a union that has been certified through a formal certification election.

The procedures for a certification election are similar across ←
the nonprofit, federal, and state sectors. Unions must request that
employees in the proposed unit sign recognition cards authorizing the union to represent them. The union must obtain a "show
of interest" by the unit members. The required show of interest is
not less than 30 percent of employees for nonprofits, the federal
government, and the majority of states. However, if the employer
chooses not to voluntarily recognize a union, an election will be
held. If the union receives 51 percent of the votes, it will be recognized as the exclusive representative.

Union Security

Labor-management relations acts contain provisions for union security devices. Union security provisions address the degree to
which unions can compel union membership or mandate the pay- ←
ment of dues to support their activities. Most contracts in the nonprofit and private sectors contain some kind of union security
provision, and union security provisions are articulated in each
state's public employee relations act. Neither the LMRS nor the
Postal Reorganization Act of 1970 permits any form of required
membership as a condition of employment. Federal employees are
free not to join unions. The different types of union security provisions are explained in the following paragraphs.

Closed shop. Under a closed shop agreement, an employer was
not permitted to hire anyone who was not already a member of the
union. Closed-shop arrangements became illegal in the private sector under Section 8(a)(3) of the Labor-Management Relations Act
of 1947, as amended. Closed-shop arrangements have always been
prohibited in the public sector because they infringe on the employer's prerogative in determining employment standards, as well
as restrict the selection of new employees.

Union shop. Under a union shop provision, all unit employees
are required to join the exclusive bargaining representative after
being hired. An employer operating under a union shop agreement
may hire employees who are not members of the union. However,
the nonunion employees must join the union within the period
specified in the agreement, which is usually thirty days, and remain
a member of the union as a condition of continued employment.

Compulsory membership by a certain date after employment prevents "free riders," employees who are not union members but who benefit from union negotiations without paying their share of the union's operating expenses. Free riders are a particular problem in the federal government, where union shops are prohibited.

Agency shop. Under an agency shop agreement, all of the unit employees are required to pay a service fee to the exclusive bargaining representative, whether or not they are union members. The service fee is designed to make nonmembers pay their share of the expense of representing all of the unit employees.

Fair share. The fair-share provision resembles the agency shop provision in that employees must pay a proportion of regular union dues to cover the exclusive representative's costs for collective bargaining. However, unlike agency shops, nonbargaining activities are not funded by nonunion members.

Maintenance of membership. Under maintenance-of-membership provisions, employees are not required to become union members. However, employees who join a union must remain members and pay membership dues to the union until the contract expires.

Dues checkoff. Because unions depend for their support on the fees collected from employees, they must have a reliable and continuous system for collecting membership dues. A dues checkoff mechanism permits unions to collect fees from employers, who withhold the union dues from the employees' paychecks and forward the funds to the union. This is a more efficient process than collecting fees from individual members. Dues checkoff is typically combined with one of the other union security provisions.

Right-to-work states. Many states are known as "right-to-work" states (Alabama, Arizona, Arkansas, Florida, Georgia, Idaho, Iowa, Kansas, Louisiana, Mississippi, Nebraska, North and South Carolina, North and South Dakota, Tennessee, Texas, Utah, Virginia, and Wyoming). According to right-to-work laws, individuals cannot be forced to join or pay dues to a labor union. Furthermore, no worker need be a union member to acquire or retain employment. In the nonprofit and private sectors, Section 14(b) of the LMRA permits states to outlaw various forms of union security provisions: "Nothing in this Act shall be construed as authorizing the execution or application of agreements requiring membership in a labor organization as a condition of employment in any State or

Territory in which such execution or application is prohibited by State or Territorial law." This provision means that an employer can reject a union's demands for the recognition of union security arrangements that are illegal under state law.

Unfair Labor Practices

Labor-management relations acts enumerate specific unfair labor practices that may be engaged in by the employer, union, or both. Unfair labor practices are actions by either the employer or the union that interfere with the employees' exercise of statutory rights. The administrative agencies generally have exclusive jurisdiction to hear unfair labor practice suits filed by an employee, the employer, or the union, which is subject to limited judicial review.

Unfair labor practice provisions are intended to protect the rights of employees, unions, and employers by prohibiting discrimination, interference, and coercion by both employers and unions. For unions, unlawful activities would constitute interference with the employer's management duties and rights. Charges of employer discrimination, interference, and coercion often pertain to the rights of employees to engage in union activity and the rights of unions to represent their members.

The Scope of Collective Bargaining

The scope of collective bargaining constitutes which subjects are negotiable. Specific topics have generally been classified on a case-by-case basis into three types: mandatory, permissive, and illegal.

Mandatory topics of bargaining are topics that the laws (whether private, nonprofit, federal, or state) require management and labor to bargain over. Either side can bargain to impasse on a mandatory topic if they can demonstrate that they made a good-faith effort to reach agreement on it. Mandatory topics in both the nonprofit and for-profit sectors typically include wages, salaries, fringe benefits, and working conditions. Mandatory topics for federal employers and employees are restricted to conditions of employment that affect working conditions, including personnel policies, practices, and matters, whether established by rule, by regulation, or otherwise. Federal employees may not bargain over wages or fringe benefits.

The statutes that permit collective bargaining by public employees vary in what they consider mandatory topics of bargaining. For example, Massachusetts has a requirement that

> the employer and the exclusive representative shall meet at reasonable times, including meetings in advance of the employer's budget-making process, and shall negotiate in good faith with respect to wages, hours, standards or productivity and performance, and any other terms and conditions of employment, including without limitation, in the case of teaching personnel employed by a school committee, class size and workload but such obligation shall not compel either party to agree to a proposal or make a concession; provided however that in no event shall the right of any employee to run as a candidate for or to hold elective office be deemed to be within the scope of negotiation.

Notice that this law requires negotiation over standards of performance and productivity, and class size and workload for teachers, as well as the more standard issues. Some states, such as Nevada, are even more explicit in defining and articulating mandatory subjects.

A *permissive topic* is a matter related to optional policy that may be bargained over if there is mutual agreement between labor and management, but neither side may unilaterally insist on such bargaining. Neither management nor labor has to bargain over permissive topics. In many states, permissive topics of bargaining include insurance benefits, retirement benefits, productivity bargaining, and grievance and discipline procedures. Permissive topics in the federal sector under Section 7106 of Title 5 of the U.S. Code include, at the election of the agency, work projects, tour of duty, or the technology, methods, and means of performing work. Education benefits could be considered a permissive topic. Because they are not wages, hours, or working conditions, they would not be considered mandatory topics. However, the employer and union could elect to negotiate them.

Deciding whether an issue is mandatory or permissive has generally been accomplished on a case-by-case basis. Administrative agencies and the courts have devised varying and flexible tests rather than fixed rules. The decision is difficult because many issues affect both the terms and conditions of employment and management policymaking. Examples of this dilemma surface frequently in teaching and social work. Teachers want to negotiate issues such as class size, curriculum, teaching loads, and nonteaching duties and responsibilities. Social workers want to bargain over caseload, treatment alternatives, or the process of deciding what services are appropriate for clients. These issues address working conditions, but they are also dimensions of management policy.

Illegal topics cannot be bargained and any agreement to bargain with respect to illegal topics will be void and unenforceable. Instead, illegal topics must typically be resolved through the legislative process. Examples of illegal or prohibited subjects of bargaining at the federal and state levels are the negotiation of the organization's objectives, how the objectives should be implemented, the agency's organizational structure, and employment standards. Issues regarding retirement, job qualifications, selection, placement, promotion criteria, and the functions of the civil service commission or merit system are often excluded from bargaining in the public sector. The Iowa Public Employee Relations Act specifically excludes the public retirement system from the scope of mandatory bargaining. Other states exclude the merit system. Illegal topics for nonprofit and private organizations could include a closed-shop union security provision or contract terms in violation of state or federal laws. For example, contract clauses that permit unions to discriminate against persons of color or against members of certain religious groups would be illegal because they violate Title VII of the 1964 Civil Rights Act and many state fair employment practice acts.

Employer-Management Rights

The missions of public sector organizations are decided by legislative bodies. The managers responsible for the performance of these functions are accountable to those legislative bodies and ultimately to the people. Major decisions made in bargaining with public employees are inescapably political because they involve critical policy choices. The matters debated at the bargaining table are not simply questions of wages, hours, and vacations. Directly at issue are questions of the size and allocation of the budget, the tax rates, the level of public services, and the long-term obligation of the government. These decisions are political in the sense that they are to be made by elected officials who are politically responsible to the voters. They are generally considered legislative decisions and not subject to delegation (Edwards, Clark, & Craver, 1979). Therefore, public sector employers tend to have more discretion than nonprofit or private sector employers in exercising their management rights.

Impasse Resolution

When management and labor are unable to agree to contract terms, an impasse occurs. Third-party intervention often becomes necessary to help resolve their differences. Three procedures are commonly used to resolve impasses: mediation, fact-finding, and arbitration.

Mediation. When a bargaining impasse occurs, either one or both of the parties may request mediation. Mediation involves the introduction of a neutral third party into the negotiation process to assist the bargaining parties in resolving their differences. Mediators often meet with the parties individually at first to discover the conflict. They then encourage the parties to resume bargaining. Mediators may suggest compromise positions that bridge the gap in negotiations, or they may act as intermediaries to persuade the parties that their proposals are unrealistic. Mediators serve only an advisory role. They have no power to compel the settlement of disputes. Mediation findings are not binding unless approved by both parties in the dispute.

Fact-finding. Fact-finding involves holding an adversarial hearing, at which each side presents its position on the issues involved in the dispute. The fact-finding body studies the evidence that was presented at the hearing and then makes recommendations for a final settlement.

Fact-finder recommendations are not binding on the parties. However, fact-finder recommendations are often made public, and the threat of unfavorable publicity often makes both sides more willing to reach a negotiated settlement. Fact-finding is grounded in the belief that public opinion will encourage the parties to accept the fact-finder's report so as not to appear unreasonable.

Interest arbitration. Interest arbitration is the procedure used when mediation or fact-finding has not resolved a bargaining impasse. An arbitrator will hold an adversarial hearing and, based on the evidence presented, determine the terms of the final agreement. Arbitration resolves conflicts without the use of a strike. State and local governments typically use arbitration as a substitute for permitting the right to strike. Only statutes may compel the use of arbitration to conciliate contract disputes. The courts lack jurisdiction to compel arbitration in the absence of statutory authority. To discourage routine reliance on arbitration, many statutes impose the cost of arbitration on the parties.

Interest arbitration has been criticized for intruding on local government sovereignty. The third party is unaccountable to the voters or elected officials yet makes decisions that affect the employer-employee relationship. To avoid this concern, many statutes require that arbitration decisions be approved by a majority of the appropriate legislative body.

Public sector arbitration varies across the states, and there are several forms. Compulsory binding arbitration requires that any dispute not settled during negotiations must end in arbitration. Arbitrators are free to make awards based on the evidence presented. The arbitrator is free to take any reasonable position and is usually inclined to make a decision that accommodates the positions of both parties in order to arrive at a realistic and effective agreement.

Final-offer arbitration permits each party to submit proposals, or final offers, to arbitration. There are two types of final-offer arbitration: final offer by issue and final offer by package. In final-offer-by-package arbitration, the arbitrator must select either the union's or the employer's final offer on all of the disputed issues. The arbitrator may not modify the proposals or compromise on the two offers. This procedure assumes that each side will make reasonable offers to prevent the arbitrator from selecting the other party's final package. In final-offer-by-issue arbitration, the arbitrator selects either side's final offer on an issue-by-issue basis. The arbitrator is free to select the most reasonable position on each issue. The arbitrator's decision may reflect a combination of employer and union offers. Arbitration by issues gives the arbitrator more flexibility in developing an agreement, because the award may incorporate proposals from both sides. This method has been criticized for possibly producing compromise awards that eliminate some of the risk by going to arbitration.

An arbitrator's decision tends to be final and is limited to issues within the permissible scope of collective bargaining. The determination of an issue outside the scope of bargaining will be viewed as a decision made beyond the jurisdiction of the arbitrator and will therefore be reversed. All mandatory topics of bargaining are considered to be within the scope of compulsory arbitration. Nonmandatory topics of bargaining are generally not considered to be within the scope of arbitration unless both parties agree to submit the topic. Most arbitration statutes contain specific criteria that arbitrators must consider in making their decisions. In addition to guiding arbitrators, these criteria facilitate judicial review.

Strikes

It is illegal for federal employees to go on strike. Nonprofit employees are permitted to strike, and presently ten states—Alaska, Hawaii, Illinois, Minnesota, Montana, Ohio, Oregon, Pennsylvania, Vermont, and Wisconsin—have laws that permit some public employees the right to strike. However, there is little consistency across the states in which employees are covered and in the conditions that permit them to strike.

Among states that permit strikes by public employees, a clear delineation is made between employees who are permitted to strike and those who are prohibited from striking. Most states limit permission to employees who are not responsible for the public's welfare. The state of Alaska, for example, divides its employees into two groups: those who provide essential services, such as police and fire protection, and employees who provide services that will not seriously affect the public, such as sanitation. Police and firefighters are prohibited from striking due to the threat to the public's safety that their absence would impose. Sanitation, public utility, and snow removal employees, however, may engage in strikes if there has first been an attempt at mediation with the employer and if a majority of employees in the unit vote by secret ballot to authorize the strike.

In most states that permit strikes by public employees, a set of stipulations must be adhered to before a strike is considered allowable. For example, Hawaii's statutes permit strikes for nonessential employees in a bargaining unit if the unit has no process for binding arbitration. Before these employees may strike, they must first comply with impasse procedures, sixty days must be allowed to elapse after the fact-finding board publishes its recommendations, and the unit must give a ten-day notice of intent to strike. Still, the Hawaii Labor Relations Board retains the right to set requirements to avoid danger to public health or safety.

In Montana, nurses in public health care facilities are permitted to strike only if a written notice is given thirty days in advance and no other health care facility within a 150-mile radius intends to strike or is engaged in a strike. These limitations to strike allowance permits the public employer to take action to prevent the strike or to prepare for the absence of public workers. If the restrictions concerning strikes are not adhered to, public employers have the right to take certain disciplinary actions against the union and the striking employees.

Even where strikes are permitted, many state statutes grant the courts the authority to issue injunctions or restraining orders if the strike presents a danger to public health or safety. If a strike is enjoined by the courts, violation of the court order could result in civil contempt penalties for the union and employees.

Grievance Arbitration

Grievance arbitration occurs when labor believes that management has violated the terms of a labor contract and files a grievance. In grievance arbitration, a neutral third party is asked to resolve the disagreement that could not be settled by the involved parties. A hearing is held that enables the parties to present evidence and testimony that support their respective positions on the case. After reviewing all of the evidence presented, the arbitrator then renders a decision based on the merits of the case. The arbitrator's decision tends to be final and legally binding on both parties.

The scope of an arbitrator's authority is usually negotiated and stated in the collective bargaining agreement. A commonly negotiated clause authorizes the arbitrator to resolve all disputes concerning the application or interpretation of the contract, but it prohibits the arbitrator from adding to or subtracting from the express terms of the agreement in formulating an award.

Grievance arbitration is undertaken as the last resort in settling disputes because it is an expensive process. Direct costs involve the expenses associated with preparing the case and the arbitrator's fee. Indirect costs involve all the time spent away from work by the grievant, supervisor, union representative, witnesses, and other associated employees. The contract usually specifies which party will be responsible for paying the arbitrator's fee. It is common for labor and management to equally share the cost of an arbitration proceeding. Because sharing the costs makes it less expensive for the union to extend the grievance and appeal process until arbitration, some agreements require that the losing party pay all of the fees associated with arbitration. Holding the losing party responsible for all of the costs should provide the party whose grievance is weak with an incentive to settle at a lower level in the proceedings, and it should encourage the union to screen cases more carefully.

Grievance arbitration is expressly authorized by statute for the nonprofit and private sectors. The LMRA requires that all contracts contain a grievance resolution procedure. This requirement is also found in Section 7121 of the Federal Service Labor-Management Relations Statute and in most state statutes.

Public Sector Distinctions

Public sector collective bargaining has been influenced by underlying beliefs and organizational structures not found in the private sector. The principle of government sovereignty and the doctrine of illegal separation of powers are two examples of such beliefs. The *sovereignty doctrine* holds that employees have only the rights that government permits them to have. The *doctrine of illegal separation of powers* forbids a government to share its powers with others. It has been used most frequently to limit the scope of mandatory topics of bargaining. Opponents of public sector collective bargaining have noted that there is a fundamental conflict between collective bargaining and these doctrines because government has a responsibility to act on behalf of all citizens, not just union members, and the public interest should not be subjugated to the political struggles between unions and government.

Another belief unique to public sector collective bargaining is that public employees have no right to withhold services from their fellow citizens. For many public sector jobs, such as police and firefighting, no competitive market exists. Machines cannot provide those services, and consumers cannot turn to other suppliers.

Public sector contract negotiations tend to be more difficult due to the diffusion of authority that exists in the public sector. The executive branch of government is responsible for the day-to-day administration of public organizations and contract negotia- ← tions. It is the legislative branch that has responsibility for the budget and the final authority to legitimize a settlement. Because members of public unions are also voters, they often attempt to influence the collective bargaining process by lobbying the people who are dependent on them for reelection.

For these ideological and structural reasons, and because many people did not see the need for unionization, the legal framework for public sector collective bargaining lagged behind that of the private sector. Job protection was granted to public employees through civil service systems. Selection, retention, and promotion were based on merit qualifications. Over the years, civil service systems expanded to include job classification, salary administration, and the administration of grievance procedures, training, and safety. Public sector employees had protections usually not found in the private sector. The impetus for change surfaced when proponents for bargaining contended that civil service systems were often inflexible and were unable or unwilling to respond to demands for wage and fringe benefit adjustments and changes in working conditions that typically required legislative adjustment (Kearney & Carnevale, 2001).

Changes in the Legal Framework

In 1959, Wisconsin enacted the first state statute permitting municipal employees the right to form, join, and be represented by labor organizations. Three years later, President John Kennedy issued Executive Order 10988, which granted federal employees the right to join and form unions and to bargain collectively. The order established a framework for collective bargaining and encouraged the expansion of collective bargaining rights to state and local government employees. Kearney and Carnevale (2001) outlined the demise of the sovereignty doctrine: beginning in 1967, the federal courts have ruled that the First Amendment's freedom of association prohibits states from interfering with public sector employees' right to join and form unions (*Atkins* v. *City of Charlotte*, U.S. Dist.Ct. 296 F.Supp., 1969; *Keyeshian* v. *Board of Regents*, 385

U.S. 589, 1967; *Letter Carriers* v. *Blount,* 305 F.Supp. 546, D.D.C., 1969; *McLaughlin* v. *Tilendis,* 398 F.2d 287, 1968). These decisions invalidated the sovereignty doctrine, contributing to the growth of unions.

The Supreme Court held in *Smith* v. *Arkansas State Highway Employees Local 1315* (441 U.S. 463, 1979), however, that nothing in the Constitution requires public employers to either recognize or collectively bargain with public employee unions. Employees can form and join unions without the benefit of protective legislation, but public employers are not compelled to recognize or bargain with unions (Dilts, 1993). Public employers are required to bargain only under laws that mandate bargaining. The duty to bargain can be imposed only by statute.

Collective bargaining does occur, however, in states that do not provide statutory protection and procedures. For example, in Arizona, local governments have passed protective ordinances to permit de facto bargaining. Indiana permits de facto bargaining, and in Louisiana and West Virginia, state courts have in effect permitted collective bargaining in limited applications (Dilts, Boyda, & Scherr, 1993).

Limitations of Civil Service

With the growth of government, public agencies became larger, more impersonal, and more dominated by civil service regulations and boards. This depersonalization of public service helped isolate and alienate individual employees. Employees looked to unions for support. Civil service and merit systems were no longer perceived as neutral advocates for employees. In many cases, merit systems were viewed as alternative forms of favoritism, reifying employers' subjective biases.

The need to reconcile collective bargaining and the merit system has been recognized by public sector unions. Jerry Wurf, former president of the American Federation of State, County and Municipal Employees (AFSCME), saw both the merit system and collective bargaining as legitimate in government labor-management relations. AFSCME's international constitution lists among the union's central objectives "to promote civil service legislation and career service in government" (Wurf, 1974). In fact, the early years of AFSCME's history were part of the movement to reform government and advocate for the enactment of civil service laws. Merit systems existed in only eleven states. Civil service was viewed as a means to end political kickbacks and protect members who might be fired because of political behavior.

Today, it is common to find both unions and civil service systems in public organizations. As noted earlier, however, many statutes have management rights clauses that limit the scope of mandatory topics of bargaining. Some statutes state that when in conflict, civil service regulations take precedence over contract terms.

To regain their influence, the unions have refocused their energies on issues of the new and diverse workforce. The number of females and minority members in the public workforce has increased. Issues such as pay equity, comparable worth for equitable job classifications, health and safety protection, training and retraining, quality of work life, job enlargement, and broader job classifications in many contracts have replaced the previous emphasis on wages, seniority, and work rules.

Nonprofit Sector Distinctions

Unions and nonprofit organizations are not typically linked in most people's thoughts. That may be because many nonprofits are small and do not meet the NLRB's jurisdictional standards. Another reason may be because nonprofit agencies often respond to new social needs and thus become desirable places to work even if salaries are lower and working conditions are less comfortable than in more established institutions. Initiatives such as rape crisis and domestic violence centers, agencies that provide support and respite services to parents of special needs children, hospices for the terminally ill, and homes for people with AIDS are some of the services provided by voluntary agencies. Other nonprofit organizations that often pay their employees lower salaries include cultural, social, and educational institutions, day care centers, social welfare agencies, and health care facilities.

The research on unionization and nonprofits has tended to focus on social workers and health care professionals. The dismantling of human services programs under President Reagan in the 1980s resulted in less job security and a decline in real wages. During this time, changes in working conditions also occurred.

Pressure toward greater productivity has increased, and influence in policymaking has decreased, leading to declines in professional autonomy (Benton, 1993; Hush, 1969; Sherer, 1994; Tambor, 1973). For human services professionals, unionization has been viewed as a vehicle for defending professional autonomy and improving working conditions. Unions have sought to expand the scope of bargaining to include such issues as agency-level policymaking, agency missions, standards of service, and concerns about job satisfaction, as well as malpractice and professional liability insurance, legal representation of workers, sabbatical leaves, minimum required training, workload issues, advance training sessions, in-service training, conferences, degree programs, licensing examination assistance, and remuneration for enhanced education (Tambor, 1988).

Human services workers are not the only employees of the nonprofit sector who have joined unions. The International Brotherhood of Teamsters represents nonprofit bargaining units that include hospitals, nursing homes, and health care facilities, as well as Masonic homes, retirement communities, Goodwill Industries, and the Association for Advancement of the Blind and Retarded. Bargaining unit employees include social workers, teachers, secretaries, housekeepers, nurses, dieticians, cooking staff, dishwashers, groundskeepers, maintenance activity aids, stock clerks, paramedics, emergency medical technicians, X-ray technicians, accountants, receptionists, cashiers, mechanics, painters, electricians, youth care workers, vehicle drivers, and dispatchers. The Communications Workers of America also represents a large number of workers employed by such nonprofit agencies as museums, housing authorities, social service and health care agencies, libraries, and philanthropic foundations. AFSCME represents more than sixty thousand nonprofit agency employees who work in the areas of health, social, community, and educational services, and the Service Employees International Union (SEIU) represents thousands of employees working in health care and public services. In 2001, SEIU was able to organize 80,000 new members, including 10,000 employees at Catholic Healthcare West hospitals in California, 11,700 home care workers in Oregon, 1,400 probation and parole officers in Missouri, and 10,000 building services workers.

Nonprofit Agency Employees (AFSCME, 1988), a publication that promotes unionization, addresses the similarities between public and private nonprofit employees: both look for recognition, for dignity and respect, and for decent wages and improved benefits. Private nonprofit employees work in highly stressful occupations, yet they receive salaries that may not be commensurate with the responsibilities and complexities of their jobs. Employees of nonprofits share many of the same desires as their public sector counterparts: better pay and benefits, contract language protection, career mobility, and safer work environments. Yet the vast majority of these workers have no union representation. AFSCME has taken the position that to win better working conditions and benefits, nonprofits need the clout of union representation.

Hush (1969) and Tambor (1973) observed that the unionization of nonprofits challenges the traditions that voluntary agencies have defined for themselves: altruistic roles and the denial of self-interest as wage earners. The impact of a union contract operating as the authority in place of the board of directors, personnel committee, or administrative staff members seems to contradict the values of openness, dignity, and communication often associated with nonprofits. For the boards and administrators of volunteer agencies, union interest among staff represents a threat to existing relationships. Nevertheless, more and more nonprofit employees are seeking union support. Nonprofit administrators, boards of directors, and personnel committee members must work with their staff to develop progressive and relevant human resources management policies.

While unionization in the for-profit sector has decreased due in part to the downward shift in the number of manufacturing, construction, and transportation employees, there has been an increase in the number of professional employees and service industry employees who are joining unions. Professional employees such as medical doctors, legal aid attorneys, archivists and assistant curators at museums, social workers, nurses, and orchestra musicians are examples of some occupational groups that have unionized in nonprofit organizations. Many employees have viewed unionization as a way to defend their professional autonomy, improve working conditions, and maintain or improve their economic security.

Professional and service sector workers are turning to the old-line blue-collar trades to protect their interests. These unions have experience in contract negotiations as well as substantial financial and technical resources, and they realized that if they want to remain viable, they must follow the job growth. Job growth is in the service sector, for both higher-paid technical and professional positions and low-paid service workers such as custodians, nursing assistants, and child care workers. Twenty-nine different unions are actively involved with the AFL-CIO's Department for Professional Employees. Actors, doctors, engineers, journalists, librarians, musicians, nurses, performing artists, athletes, teachers, university faculty, and attorneys are some of the professional employees represented by unions (Shostak, 1991). United Auto Workers (UAW) Local 2110, in New York City, represents employees in more than twenty workplaces. Local 2110 represents professional employees in a variety of non-profit organizations such as the Museum of Modern Art, the New York Historical Society, Mercy College, Columbia University, Union Theological Seminary, Teachers College, and Barnard College. The Professional and Administrative Staff Association (PASTA) of the Museum of Modern Art in New York represents 250 administrative assistants, archivists, curatorial staff, conservators, graphic artists, librarians, salespeople, secretaries, visitor assistants, and writers. PASTA is affiliated with Local 2110 of the United Auto Workers. Other arts groups associated with the UAW are the National Writers Unions and the Graphic Artists Guild. The staffs at the New York Historical Society, the Whitney Museum, the Guggenheim, and the San Francisco Museum of Modern Art are also unionized (see Exhibits 13.2 and 13.3).

The impact of competition and organizational restructuring has become an issue in nonprofit organizations. Contracts have called for employers to notify employees of impending layoffs and to offer voluntary leaves of absences to employees before reducing their hours. In other circumstances, unions have been called on to defend professional autonomy and improve working conditions. Collective bargaining has expanded the scope of labor negotiations to include such issues as agency-level policymaking, agency missions, standards of service, and professional judgment. Other negotiated topics have included coverage for malpractice and professional liability insurance, legal representation of workers, workload issues,

Exhibit 13.2. The Museum of Modern Art's Primer on Unions.

How does a union work?

A union is a group of employees who want to have a say in their working conditions, wages, and benefits. Even if you've never been in a union job before, perhaps you've had a contract or a letter of agreement with an employer. Such agreements typically state your wages, your fringe benefits, and the basic duties for your job. In a union, workers negotiate their salaries and other working conditions together. By bargaining collectively, they are able to establish far better terms than if each person attempted to negotiate alone.

What are the unions at MoMA?

The Museum has collective bargaining agreements (i.e., contracts) with unions that represent five groups at MoMA: Our group, PASTA, represents the professional and administrative employees. Other union groups at the Museum are the operating engineers/art preparators, film projectionists, security, and housekeeping.

Are unions common in the museum world?

Though people often associate unions with blue-collar jobs, many professional and administrative employees are unionized, from journalists and teachers to social workers and attorneys. In fact, the rate of white-collar unionization has greatly accelerated in recent years. While it may seem unusual for the staff of an arts institution to be organized in a union, the staff of the New York Historical Society is in the same union as PASTA; some workers at the Metropolitan Museum, the Whitney, and the Guggenheim are also unionized. The professional staff of the San Francisco Museum of Modern Art organized several years ago and acknowledges PASTA as a model for its union.

How is PASTA organized?

Much of the actual work of PASTA is accomplished by its Program Committee, a seven-person group elected from the PASTA rank and file. The committee's prime responsibility is to see that our contract with the Museum is properly carried out. To that end, it meets regularly as a group and with management, monitors working conditions, conducts grievances when necessary, and regularly reports to members. At contract renewal time, a Negotiating Committee is elected from the membership. Other groups may from time to time be formed from the membership.

Exhibit 13.2. The Museum of Modern Art's Primer on Unions, Cont'd.

PASTA constitutes one shop of the New York City–based Local 2110. The local comprises roughly thirty shops from companies in publishing, higher education, finance, law, and other fields. Our union has taken a lead in organizing women as well as workers in nonprofits that have never been organized before. We have broken new ground in winning benefits such as childcare, flex-time, job classification, domestic partner benefits, and family leave. Local 2110 is in turn affiliated with the United Auto Workers (UAW), an international union. Finally, the UAW is a member of the American Federation of Labor-Congress of Industrial Organizations (AFL-CIO).

Hey, I'm not an auto worker. Why the UAW?

Tens of thousands of UAW members have never been in an auto plant! The UAW, one of the largest and most powerful unions in the country, provides our local union with resources and expertise to assist us in negotiations, organizing, civil rights and political activities, and health and safety work. Among the arts groups affiliated with the UAW are the National Writers Union and the Graphic Artists Guild.

How is my contract negotiated?

After consulting with and polling the members of PASTA, an elected Negotiating Committee of 5–7 members meets along with union officials from the local and representatives of the Museum. In meetings scheduled over several months, they negotiate details such as:

- length of the contract
- wage minimums for each of 14 job classifications
- salary increases for each year of the contract
- the terms of health and other benefits

Throughout the bargaining, they keep the membership informed of progress. When they feel they have achieved a satisfactory package, they present it to members for a vote.

Over the years, PASTA negotiators have successfully established benefits such as tuition reimbursement of up to $1,300 per employee annually, improvements in medical and dental coverage, increased job security measures as MoMA undergoes expansion, and the recent introduction of a 403(b) retirement plan.

**Exhibit 13.2. The Museum of Modern Art's
Primer on Unions, Cont'd.**

Who decides on accepting a contract or going out on strike?

You do. All contract proposals are voted on by the entire membership in the workplace. You elect the negotiating committee and decide whether to accept or reject a contract. Before a strike is even considered, members vote whether to authorize it and also elect a strike committee.

What else does the union do?

Safe working conditions are a prime concern of any union, and a PASTA committee is organized to see that all members enjoy a safe and sanitary workplace.

Through the Consortium for Workers Education, Local 2110 offers opportunities for education such as free Spanish classes and computer training.

We hope that you never have a disagreement with your supervisor at MoMA. But if you are treated unjustly, the union is here to help. By law, you have the right to request the presence of a union representative at any disciplinary hearing. If you and your union representative feel you have been treated unfairly, the union can file a grievance on your behalf. If the situation cannot be settled within the workplace, the union can bring your case to arbitration, in which an outside, impartial arbitrator hears the case and issues a binding decision.

What do these union benefits cost me?

Union dues are 1.15% of your salary. All employees hired into PASTA positions after September 9, 2000, must either join the union and pay dues or pay the equivalent amount as an agency fee. Once you choose your option, the Payroll department automatically makes the appropriate deduction from your biweekly paycheck. New employees must inform the union of their choice within 30 days of starting work. There is no initiation fee for PASTA, nor any charge for services like conducting grievances or arbitration.

Playing an active role in your union strengthens your voice in the workplace and affords an opportunity to meet and work with employees from a wide variety of fields at the Museum. We encourage you to join with your colleagues in the union, attend union meetings, and take part in elections and other union activities.

**Exhibit 13.2. The Museum of Modern Art's
Primer on Unions, Cont'd.**

Other shops in Local 2110: Addison Wesley Longman; American Civil Liberties Union; Ames & Rollinson; Amsco School Publications; Aspira of NY; Barnard College; C&S Delivery Service; Columbia University; Dormitory Authority; Feminist Press; Good Old Lower East Side; HarperCollins Publishers; Housing Finance Agency; Levy, Ratner & Behroozi; Mercy College; Monthly Review; National Council of Churches; National Jewish Hospital; New York Association for New Americans; New York Civil Liberties Union; New York Historical Society; New York University; Rabinowitz, Boudin; Stamford Advocate; State Bank of India; State of New York Mortgage Agency; Teachers College; Technical Career Institutes; Union Theological Seminary; and The Village Voice.

Source: Courtesy of the Professional and Administrative Staff Association, Museum of Modern Art (PASTA-MoMA).

the provision of in-service training, financial assistance for licensing examinations, and remuneration for enhanced education. Professional employees in both the public and nonprofit sectors are joining unions due to changes brought about by privatization and the shift toward managed care, not only in the health care field but also in the provision of social welfare services. As more public services become privatized and former public employees enter nonprofit agencies, nonprofit managers can expect to see an increase in union activity.

Privatization of Public Services

The movement toward the privatization of public services was acknowledged by AFL-CIO President John Sweeney back in 1995 when he spoke to the California Association of Public Hospitals. He projected that 1.7 million health care workers could lose their jobs as a result of the proposed cuts in Medicare and Medicaid. He expressed concern that an increasing number of public sector service workers such as technicians, nurse aides, and nurses working in hospitals, nursing homes, home health agencies, ambulatory clinics, blood banks, public health programs, and health maintenance organizations could lose their jobs as more health care services become privatized.

Exhibit 13.3. Museum of Modern Art Strike Notice.

MoMA Staff on Strike

Who are we?

We are the Professional and Administrative Staff Association (PASTA) of The Museum of Modern Art, representing 250 administrative assistants, archivists, curatorial staff, conservators, graphic artists, librarians, salespeople, secretaries, visitor assistants, and writers. Our union is Local 2110, UAW.

Why are we on strike?

After seven months of negotiations, MoMA management has forced a strike by leaving the bargaining table without seriously addressing these issues:

- *Salaries* at the Museum remain deplorably low. The median wage for employees in our union is $28,000 a year. Forty employees in our union earn the starting salary at MoMA of $17,000. Management proposes to grant raises of only 3% in the coming years, at a time when MoMA's investments have never been so profitable.

- *Healthcare* is a prime concern. Management refuses to maintain our health insurance over the life of the contract, opening the door to increased costs to the staff. Other benefits would face similar cutbacks.

- *Layoffs* at MoMA are a certainty in the near future. Next year the Museum will begin construction of a $650 million expansion project. Exhibitions, research facilities, and administration will be relocated to Queens. We are seeking a fair severance plan and the right to resume our jobs when the new building opens.

- *Ten unfair labor practice charges* against MoMA are pending with the National Labor Relations Board. Among other tactics, the Museum has refused to bargain in good faith, threatened union supporters, and illegally removed employees from the bargaining unit.

What can you do?

Please honor our picket line. Do not visit MoMA or its stores today. A list of other New York museums and retail stores is [provided].

Contact Glenn Lowry, director of the museum, and express support for our cause: (212) 708-9773. Fax: (212) 708-9744, E-mail: glenn_lowry@moma.org or comments@moma.org. Address: 11 West 53 St., New York, NY 10019

Wear our stickers and sign our petitions.

Contribute to the MoMA Striker Hardship Fund: Send contributions to MoMA Striker Hardship Fund, c/o Local 2110 UAW, 113 University Place, NY, NY 10003. Checks should be payable to the MoMA Striker Hardship Fund.

Exhibit 13.3. Museum of Modern Art Strike Notice, Cont'd.

ALTERNATE DESTINATIONS
Please visit these other museums and stores. Thank you for your support.

ART MUSEUMS
Brooklyn Museum/200 Eastern Parkway, Brooklyn/closed Mon. and Tues.
Cooper-Hewitt National Design Museum, Smithsonian Institute/2 East 91st Street/closed Mon.
Dahesh Museum/601 Fifth Avenue/closed Sun. & Mon.
Drawing Center/35 Wooster St. (between Grand & Broome)/closed Sun. and Mon.
Frick Collection/1 East 70th Street at Fifth Avenue/closed Mon.
Guggenheim Museum/1071 Fifth Avenue at 89th Street/closed Thurs.
International Center of Photography/1130 Fifth Avenue at 94th St./closed Mon.
Metropolitan Museum of Art/Fifth Avenue at 82nd Street/closed Mon.
Museo del Barrio/1230 Fifth Avenue at 105th Street/closed Mon. and Tues.
Museum of the City of New York/Fifth Avenue at 103rd Street/closed Mon. and Tues.
Museum of Television and Radio/25 West 52nd Street/closed Mon.
New Museum of Contemporary Art/583 Broadway/closed Mon. and Tues.
Studio Museum in Harlem/144 West 125th Street/closed Mon. and Tues.
Whitney Museum of American Art/945 Madison (between 74th and 75th Streets)/closed Mon.

BOOKSTORES
Barnes & Noble/Fifth Avenue at 48th Street
Coliseum Books/57th Street at Broadway
Hacker Art Books/45 West 57th Street (between Fifth and Sixth Avenues)
Rizzoli/31 West 57th Street (between Fifth and Sixth Avenues)
Urban Center Architectural Books/457 Madison Avenue

DESIGN STORES
Felissimo/10 West 56th Street
Mikasa/28 West 23rd Street
Moss/146 Greene Street (Soho)
The Museum Company Store/Fifth Avenue at 53rd Street
The Sharper Image/4 West 57th Street
Takashimaya/693 Fifth Avenue (between 54th and 55th Streets)
Whitney Museum Store Next Door/943 Madison Avenue (between 74th and 75th Streets)

Source: Courtesy of the Professional and Administrative Staff Association, Museum of Modern Art (PASTA-MoMA).

Regardless of whether public health services become privatized, many unions have already adopted an aggressive posture to organize public, private, and nonprofit health care facilities. Not only is the American Nurse Association actively organizing health care employees, but so are unions not typically associated with health care, such as the United Auto Workers; United Food and Commercial Workers; Retail, Wholesale and Department Store Unions; American Federation of State, County and Municipal Employees' International Union; and the American Federation of Teachers.

The increasing privatization of social and human services will also affect the growth of unions in nonprofit organizations. As more and more public services become privatized and former public employees enter nonprofit agencies, nonprofit managers can expect to see an increase in union activities. In the San Francisco Bay area, five SEIU locals have formed a Bay Area task force known as United Community Workers to coordinate organizing drives among nonprofits (Peters & Masaoka, 2000).

Former state and local government employees such as social workers, case managers, mental health therapists, psychologists, and juvenile justice workers are attractive targets for union organizing activities. Workers in these positions are often responsible for caseloads that exceed the recommended maximums stated in professional standards, confront stressful situations daily, are required to work overtime on a regular basis, and often do not have adequate health and retirement benefits.

Summary

Union contracts with public and nonprofit agencies recognize that new issues have emerged and that labor-management understanding and cooperation are important. The uncertainty of many workplace changes has shaken the confidence of many employees that their jobs are secure and that their wages will remain competitive. Uncertain economic times, decreases in health care benefits for many workers, an increase in the temporary workforce, and reduced and lost pensions have all contributed to an insecurity in the labor market that is now affecting many public and nonprofit organizations. Changes in the labor market coupled with ineffective and sometimes arbitrary and unfair management often lead employees to unionize when they feel threatened.

The future of the labor movement will hinge on its ability to reach out to new constituencies and collectively develop a new agenda for political action. Women, persons of color, and new immigrants typically work in the service sector and might benefit by joining a union. The AFL-CIO and other unions have reframed their platforms to emphasize issues such as wage stagnation, employment insecurity, and the growing economic inequality between workers and owners. They are talking about corporate responsibility, democracy in the workplace, and worker rights. Other important issues being discussed are universal health care, continuing education and retraining, and making child care available to low wage earners. Unions have begun to emphasize the need for greater racial, gender, and class equality and improving the political and economic status of workers and their communities. Moving beyond the traditional subject matters of collective bargaining—wages, hours, and working conditions—these new issues focus attention on the needs for affordable and safe day care, maternal leave benefits, an increased ability to work flexible hours, the elimination of sexual harassment and discrimination in the workplace, and eliminating the exploitation of immigrant workers. There are more than twenty thousand home health aides in New York City. Most are paid $6 or $7 an hour. Nearly all of them are women, and most of them do not receive health care, sick pay, or vacations. They bathe clients, feed and dress them, and administer their medication. They provide critical services but are not recognized by market wages. Insecurity is also felt by workers in other positions seen as socially useful, such as teaching, social work, nursing, child care, and case management, but are financially underrewarded despite their importance and their stressful working conditions.

According to the American Hospital Association, hospitals around the country have 126,000 nursing vacancies, and the vacancy rate could triple over the next decade as baby boomers age. Hospital mergers, continuous cost-cutting, and heavy workloads, combined with an aging workforce, have contributed to the nursing shortage. Fewer people are entering nursing programs to replace those who are leaving. Incumbent nurses report a growing dissatisfaction with heavy staffing levels, unreasonable workloads, increased use of overtime, lack of sufficient support staff, and adequate wages (General Accounting Office, 2001b).

Unions have sought to expand the scope of bargaining to include such issues as agency-level policymaking, agency missions, standards of service, coverage for malpractice and professional liability insurance, legal representation of workers, workload issues, the provision of in-service training, financial assistance for licensing examination, and remuneration for enhanced education. New employee benefits, including the introduction of labor-management committees, the provision of mental health and substance abuse benefits, child care benefits, employee individual development plans, incentive awards, counseling for tests, alternative work schedules, safety precautions such as guidelines covering the use of video display terminals, and tax-sheltered annuities are also finding their way in collective bargaining agreements.

When employees choose to join unions, increased compensation and benefits are not the only reasons. Often there are concerns about effective management and the quality of the workplace climate. Clark, Clark, Day, and Shea (2000) found that market-based health care reforms are having a negative impact on the environment in which registered nurses (RNs) work. RNs have been replaced with less qualified and less expensive personnel—such as licensed practical nurses (LPNs) and technicians. Patient staffing ratios have also been increased. Some of the reforms, many nurses believe, threaten the quality of patient care, and many nurses believe that joining a union will help them gain greater control over patient care. Collective bargaining gives professionals the ability to demand that the standards of their profession be respected and enforced. The threat of losing control over their environment factors into the decision to vote for union representation. Nurses with a negative perception of the climate are more likely to vote for a union than nurses who perceive their work climate positively.

Registered nurses are not the only nonprofit employees who view unionization as a way to have input in decision making. Research by Peters and Masaoka (2000) found that nonprofit staffs have an expectation of participatory management. Prounion staff were concerned about the lack of professional human resources management practices, a lack of effective supervision, unfairness in the assignment of workloads, and the lack of diversity in their organizations. Some of the respondents believed that unionization was a way to call attention to inexperienced and unqualified management as well as to bring about more effective leadership.

For public and nonprofit organizations that are not yet unionized, it is important to have a progressive human resources management system in place that respects employees. Examinations, performance appraisals, promotions, and merit pay systems must be administered in an equitable and consistent manner. Jobs must be enriched to eliminate tasks that are routine and boring, and career enrichment opportunities must be provided. Employees must feel that their jobs are important and that they are contributing to the mission of the agency. Whether or not workers join unions depends on their perceptions of the work environment and on their desire to participate in or influence employment conditions. Organizations that provide employees with the opportunity to participate in the decision-making process are less likely to be the targets of unionization.

Questions and Exercises

1. From an employee perspective, what are some advantages of working in a unionized organization? What are some disadvantages?
2. From a management perspective, what are some advantages of a unionized organization? What are some disadvantages?
3. Why is unionization growing in the public and nonprofit sectors and retracting in the private for-profit sector?
4. Identify three issues that unions have been fighting for during contract negotiations in recent years. Were they successful? How do you explain those outcomes?
5. Visit the National Labor Relations Board's Web site (http://www.nlrb.gov). Why is it important for public employees and employers to understand the National Labor Relations Act as amended?
6. Visit the American Arbitration Association's Web site (http://www.adr.org). What are some of the requirements needed to become a labor arbitrator? Do you possess those characteristics and training?
7. Visit the Web sites of the American Federation of State, County and Municipal Employees (AFSCME) (http://www.afscme.org)

and the Service Employees International Union (SEIU) (http://www.seiu.org). Identify three issues that health care workers are concerned about and three issues that public employees in general are concerned about. Are these issues important to you as well? Explain.

8. Visit the Web site of the National Public Employers Labor Association (NPELRA) (http://www.npelra.gov). Identify three issues of concern to public employers. Are you concerned about those issues? Explain.

Conclusion: Challenges for Public and Nonprofit Organizations

The chapters in Part One of this book addressed how society and workplaces have changed and what the human resources management (HRM) implications of those changes are for public and nonprofit organizations. The chapters in Part Two have focused on seven HRM techniques and practices: job analysis, recruitment and selection, performance evaluation, compensation, benefits, training and development, and collective bargaining. This chapter will summarize the main points addressed in earlier chapters and discuss how strategic human resources management (SHRM) can be used to help organizations cope with the challenges that lie ahead.

What to Expect

As noted earlier in the book, public and nonprofit organizations are facing and will continue to be confronted with reduced budgets that lowered funding for social services, health care, education, legal services, and arts and culture programs. Instead of expanding programs and hiring new employees, organizations are facing reductions in force. To cope, they must be prepared to invest time and money in training their present staff. For many agencies, there is likely to be an increase in the use of contingency workers, of workers employed on a temporary or part-time basis, and of specific services contracted out to independent contractors.

New cultural and social changes are affecting the workplace. The numbers of female, minority, disabled, and older workers have increased substantially. Not only have the public and nonprofit workforces become more demographically diverse, but employees' values have also changed. They want challenging jobs, and they want to exercise discretion in those jobs.

Jobs are changing, and with those changes arise quality-of-life and quality-of-work issues. Employees want to satisfy important personal needs by working in the organization. In addition to the desire for more autonomy, employees are looking for a better fit between work and family responsibilities. They are seeking alternative work schedules such as flextime, compressed schedules, and part-time employment opportunities so that they can spend more time with their families.

The legal environment has also changed. Public and nonprofit agencies must comply with federal, state, and local laws; with executive orders; with the rules and regulations promulgated by administrative agencies such as the Equal Employment Opportunity Commission and the U.S. Department of Labor; and with federal and state court decisions. Equal employment opportunity, compensation, labor relations, and employer contributions to benefits such as retirement plans and pensions, workers' compensation, and unemployment insurance are regulated by law. The legal environment must be monitored because it is always changing. Some of the legislation that was pending before Congress and in state and federal courts at the time this book was written may have become law by now and have further changed the legal environment.

Technology has changed many jobs and has led to new skill requirements and organizational structures. Changes in information technology have led to modifications in job knowledge and responsibilities. Earlier chapters provided some examples of the uses of technology and its effects on the workplace. The increased use of information technology has changed the way organizations are structured and the way work is organized and managed. For example, the city of Tampa has installed an online "message center" that lets citizens follow their questions, complaints, and requests for information as they move through the city's e-mail system. Once an e-mail is sent, the system responds with a tracking number. The tracking number allows the citizen to see who has read the e-mail and what those individuals have done with it (Karp, 2003).

While the use of technology can be exciting, there are some caveats of which employers need to be aware. To eliminate any gaps in gender, race, or age, employers should require technology training for all employees in appropriate job categories. The training programs should be monitored to ensure that all eligible employees participate. Training in computer skills is not enough, and stereotypes that suggest that women, persons of color, individuals with disabilities, and older workers are incapable of learning new technology should be purged from the workplace (Wooldridge, 1994).

All of these forces have implications for managing public and nonprofit organizations. Many jobs have been changed or eliminated, and employees must constantly upgrade their knowledge, skills, abilities, and other characteristics (KSAOCs). In some instances, upgrading incumbent employees' KSAOCs is not enough; organizations must recruit and hire people with advanced skills. For public and nonprofit organizations to survive, they need employees who can help them provide high-quality mission-related services. To be assured of this, organizations must link their HRM functions to the short- and long-term priorities of the organization.

Public and nonprofit organizations are subject to the capriciousness of funding, financial support, and market positions, in addition to public and political support, which also often vacillates. The demands placed on public and nonprofit organizations keep changing. Across both sectors, there is the recognition that organizations need to restructure their HRM systems because they are often unable to attract and retain energetic and competent personnel. They need to reengineer management systems to make best use of their workforces to facilitate improvements in the quality and productivity of their outputs.

Alternative service delivery programs require new skills. Employees and organizations can no longer afford tunnel vision or overspecialization. To be effective requires a breadth of knowledge, an interest in learning, and a willingness to tap the knowledge of others (Bozeman & Straussman, 1990). The immediate SHRM implication is that agencies must identify the KSAOCs needed both now and in the future, and they must audit their organizations to determine whether those KSAOCs are possessed by current employees or can be obtained through training and development activities. If neither of these is the case, HRM departments must work with department managers and line personnel to develop recruitment and selection strategies. Managers and employees need to think about the future and prepare for impending changes.

The requirement for flexibility and speed of response to market changes is likely to continue. This has implications for the practice of SHRM. Agencies need to invest in their workforces and ensure that their members have sufficient security. Employees who fear losing their jobs will resist new innovations. Instead, agencies should provide learning environments, invest in development opportunities, and train and retrain their employees when dictated by changes in technology or demands for service.

As noted by Cohen and Eimicke (2002, p. 11), the "effective public manager of the twenty-first century will need to be creative, innovative, and entrepreneurial, as well as a lifelong learner. Stability, complacency, and routine will increasingly be replaced by change, new problems, and new solutions. Get used to it."

Challenges of Strategic Human Resources Management

The demographic characteristics of the labor force have changed. As noted in earlier chapters, there have been increases in the number of women, racial and ethnic minorities, older employees, disabled workers, and homosexuals. Organizations must recognize underlying attributes, or nonobservable characteristics, such as different learning styles, different working styles and values, and different types of personalities, as well as differences in culture, socioeconomic background, educational background, occupational background, and professional orientation.

To accommodate the changing workforce and to minimize conflict, organizations should promote a greater awareness of diversity issues and cultural differences. It is also important that they audit their human resources functions to ensure that they are free of bias. Recruitment selection, training and development, performance evaluation, and compensation and benefits should be administered in an equitable fashion. To avoid discriminating against the disabled, the essential functions of positions and the KSAOCs necessary for successful performance must be identified.

Under the Age Discrimination in Employment Act, employers can no longer force employees to retire when they reach a certain age, as long as they are still capable of performing their jobs. In fact, the U.S. Congress is encouraging individuals to work longer and delay retirement (thereby delaying when they will begin to receive Social Security benefits). Fewer employees retiring at early ages combined with flatter organizational structures results in fewer promotional opportunities and career plateauing. To retain a motivated and energetic workforce, new types of career enhancement opportunities need to be developed to challenge incumbent employees. To older employees who are reluctant to retire, organizations may want to offer part-time work, phased retirements, or early retirement buyouts.

Families are another characteristic that differentiate workers. Many employees in the public and nonprofit sector are parents who need greater flexibility in work schedules and work patterns to accommodate family responsibilities. Flexible work arrangements are needed for parents to care for young children or in some cases for employees to care for their parents. More opportunities should be available for part-time work, and there should be greater variety in benefits programs, such as child care and elder care. Benefits packages should recognize alternative families and different priorities.

Alternative scheduling, now being used in many public and nonprofit organizations, includes job sharing, flextime, and a compressed workweek, in which a full week's work is compressed into fewer than five days. Working at home or telecommuting are other options.

Changes in Skill Requirements

Today, more and more jobs in the public and nonprofit sectors are of a professional nature, requiring higher levels of education, and fewer jobs involve routine tasks. Technology has taken over much of the workplace's mentally and physically repetitive tasks. Jobs today require employees to possess greater skills as they assume more challenging responsibilities. Organizations need to acquire the skills necessary for coping with the challenges brought on by today's competitiveness.

Accompanying the change in competitiveness are changes in the way organizations are evaluated. The new performance standards are *efficiency*, defined as the ability to produce higher volume with the same or fewer resources; *quality*, defined as matching products or services to a human need with a consistent conformance to standards; *variety*, defined as providing choices to suit diverse tastes and needs; *customization*, defined as tailoring goods and services to individual clienteles; *convenience*, defined as developing user-friendly products and services and delivering them with high levels of customer satisfaction; and *timeliness*, defined as delivering innovations to customers, making continuous improvements, and developing new applications quickly (Carnevale & Carnevale, 1993).

These new performance standards require improved skills and competencies for employees throughout the organization, regardless of position. Skills deemed to be necessary include the academic basics, including proficiency in reading, writing, and computation; self-management skills, such as self-esteem, motivation, goal-setting ability, and a willingness to participate in career development activities; social skills, such as interpersonal, negotiation, and teamwork skills; communication skills, such as the ability to listen and communicate clearly; and influencing skills or leadership abilities (Carnevale & Carnevale, 1993).

Today's jobs require a more educated workforce with advanced knowledge. Training needs to be continuous; alternative training methods, such as interactive videos and individual training modules, can be used. Employees need to be trained not just for their present positions but also for future jobs and KSAOCs. Training must be available for all employees regardless of their level in the organization.

As skill requirements increase, job tasks often become less specific. In such situations, job requirements become more flexible and overlapping, making the development of standardized examinations more difficult. Due to changes in the workplace and the rapid changes in technology that necessitate a high degree of adaptation and evolution, it will become necessary to develop selection examinations that capture a variety of KSAOCs. More accurate selection techniques need to be used, employing many of the advanced techniques identified in Chapter Eight, to evaluate not only technical skills but also interpersonal and leadership skills. Selection techniques will have to assess many of the skills associated with organizational citizen behaviors, adaptability, and flexibility. Employees will need to possess initiative, judgment, decision-making skills, leadership abilities, interpersonal skills, and other competencies often neglected during the selection process.

Summary

The underlying belief of SHRM is the conviction that public and nonprofit employees are important assets to an organization and critical for the organization's success. Human resources representatives should be part of the strategic planning process, along with representatives from other departments. After strategies are formulated, human resources specialists, department directors, line managers, employees, and in unionized organizations, union representatives should collaborate to develop programs, policies, job tasks, and responsibilities that are compatible with the organization's overall strategies.

References

Adams, L. E. (1992, February). Securing your HRIS in a microcomputer environment. *HR Magazine*, pp. 56–61.

Agochiya, D. (2002). *Every trainer's handbook.* New Delhi, India: Sage.

Aho, K. (1989). Achieving pay equity. *American City and County, 104,* 14–15.

Albert, S. (2000). *Hiring the chief executive: A practical guide to the search and selection process* (Rev. ed.). Washington, DC: National Center for Nonprofit Boards.

Alexander, G. D. (1991, February). Working with volunteers: No pain, no gain. *Fund Raising Management,* pp. 62–63.

American Federation of State, County, and Municipal Employees. (1988). *Nonprofit agency employees: Working for people, not for profit.* Washington, DC: AFL-CIO.

American Psychological Association, Division of Industrial and Organizational Psychology. (1987). *Principles for the validation and use of personnel selection procedures* (3rd ed.). Washington, DC: Author.

Ammons, D. N., & Glass, J. J. (1989). *Recruiting local government executives: Practical insights for hiring authorities and candidates.* San Francisco: Jossey-Bass.

Andersen, D. F., Belardo, S., & Dawes, S. S. (1994). Strategic information management: Conceptual frameworks for the public sector. *Public Productivity and Management Review, 17,* 335–353.

Anderson, L. M., & Baroody, N. B. (1992, August). Managing volunteers. *Fund Raising Management,* pp. 43–45.

Andrews, M., & Molzhon, C. (1999, Summer). Kansas offers new training academy. *Newsletter of the National Association of State Personnel Executives,* pp. 5–6.

Anft, M. (2002, June 13). New leader sets sights on rebuilding Hale House. *Chronicle of Philanthropy,* p. 44.

Arvey, R. D. (1986). Sex bias in job evaluation procedures. *Personnel Psychology, 39,* 315–335.

Arvey, R. D., & Faley, R. H. (1988). *Fairness in selecting employees* (2nd ed.). Reading, MA: Addison-Wesley.

Arvey, R. D., Nutting, S. M., & Landon, T. E. (1992). Validation strategies for physical ability testing in police and fire settings. *Public Personnel Management, 21,* 301–312.

Ashbaugh, S., & Miranda, R. (2002). Technology for human resources management: Seven questions and answers. *Public Personnel Management, 31*(1), 7–20.

Avery, G. (2000). Outsourcing public health laboratory services: A blueprint for determining whether to privatize and how. *Public Administration Review, 60*(4), 330–337.

Axelrod, N. R. (2002). *Chief executive succession planning: The board's role in securing your organization's future.* Washington, DC: BoardSource.

Baker, A. (2002, August 7). New York City facing exodus of firefighters. *New York Times.*

Baker, J. R. (1994). Government in the twilight zone: Motivations of volunteers to small city boards and commissions. *State and Local Government Review, 26,* 119–128.

Ball, A. (2003, June 23). Charities get a new kind of volunteer: Jobless professionals keep skills sharp by giving them away. *Austin-American Statesman.*

Ban, C., & Riccucci, N. (1993). Personnel systems and labor relations: Steps toward a quiet revolution. In F. J. Thompson (Ed.), *Revitalizing state and local public service: Strengthening performance, accountability, and citizen confidence* (pp. 71–103). San Francisco: Jossey-Bass.

Barrett, G., Phillips, J., & Alexander, R. (1981). Concurrent and predictive validity designs: A critical reanalysis. *Journal of Applied Psychology, 66,* 1–6.

Barrick, M. R., & Mount, M. K. (1991). The big five personality dimensions and job performance: A meta-analysis. *Personnel Psychology, 44,* 1–26.

Barrick, M. R., Mount, M. K., & Judge, T. A. (2001). Personality and performance at the beginning of the new millennium: What do we know and where do we go next? *International Journal of Selection and Assessment Performance, 9*(1–2), 9–29.

Beatty, R. W., Craig, E., & Schneier, C. E. (1997). "New HR roles to impact organizational performance: From "partners" to "players." *Human Resource Management, 36*(1), 29–37.

Becker, B. E., Huselid, M. A., & Ulrich, D. (2001). *The HR scorecard: Linking people, strategy, and performance.* Boston: Harvard Business School Press.

Bennett, B. (2001, March 13). Lauderdale police hire Creole-speaking officer. *Miami Herald,* pp. 1B–2B.

Benton, T. (1993). Union negotiating. *Nursing Management, 23,* 70–72.

Berger, J. (2001, January). NPO workers taking more unscheduled days off. *Nonprofit Times, 15,* 1, 6.

Bernardin, H. J. (1986). Subordinate appraisal: A valuable source of information about managers. *Human Resources Management, 25,* 421–439.

Bernstein, N. (2001a, May 13). At Hale House, broken bonds and pain for a little girl lost. *New York Times.*

Bernstein, N. (2001b, April 25). Some jailed mothers say Hale House didn't keep promises. *New York Times.*

Billitteri, T. J. (1999, February 11). A safety net for aging activists: Coalition sets up first pension plan designed for social-justice crusaders. *Chronicle of Philanthropy,* pp. 27–28.

Billitteri, T. J. (2000, January 27). 1 in 10 foundations offers domestic-partner benefits, survey finds. *Chronicle of Philanthropy,* p. 27.

Bjornberg, L. (2002). Training and development: Best practices. *Public Personnel Management, 31*(4), 507–516.

Bland, R. L., & Rubin, I. S. (1998). *Budgeting: A guide for local governments self-study course.* Washington, DC: International City/County Management Association.

Blumrosen, R. G. (1979). Wage discrimination, job segregation, and Title VII of the Civil Rights Act of 1964. *University of Michigan Law Review, 12,* 397–502.

Boone, M. (1998). Gainsharing in Baltimore County, Maryland. *Pioneer Institute of Public Policy Research,* pp. 51–57.

Borman, W. C., & Motowidlo, S. M. (1993). Expanding the criterion domain to include elements of contextual performance. In N. Schmitt and W. C. Borman (Eds.), *Personnel selection* (pp. 71–98). San Francisco: Jossey-Bass.

Borman, W. C., Penner, L. A., Allen, T. D., & Motowidlo, S. J. (2001). Personality predictors of citizenship performance. *International Journal of Selection and Assessment, 9,* 52–69.

Bowen, W. G. (1994, September-October). When a business leader joins a nonprofit board. *Harvard Business Review,* pp. 38–43.

Bozeman, B., & Straussman, J. D. (1990). *Public Management Strategies: Guidelines for Managerial Effectiveness.* San Francisco: Jossey-Bass.

Bradley, B., Jansen, P., & Silverman, L. (2003, May). The nonprofit sector's $100 billion opportunity. *Harvard Business Review,* pp. 94–103.

Bramley, P. (1996). *Evaluating training effectiveness* (2nd ed.). London: McGraw-Hill.

Bromwich, M. R. (2002, June 2). The hard work of transforming the FBI. *New York Times.*

Brown, J. (2003a, May). COMPASS find the way. *Government Technology,* pp. 50–52.

Brown, J. (2003b, May). Let your fingers do the talking: Hiring new school employees in Florida is faster thanks to a new statewide digital fingerprinting system. *Government Technology,* pp. 44–48.

Brudney, J. L. (1990). The availability of volunteers: Implications for local governments. *Administration and Society, 21,* 413–424.

Brudney, J. L. (1993). *Fostering volunteer programs in the public sector.* San Francisco: Jossey-Bass.

Brudney, J. L. (1999). The effective use of volunteers: Best practices for the public sector. *Law and Contemporary Problems, 62*(4), 219–255.

Brudney, J. L. (2001). Volunteer administration. In J. S. Ott (Ed.), *Understanding nonprofit organizations: Governance, leadership, and management* (pp. 329–338). Boulder, CO: Westview Press.

Brudney, J. L., & Kellough, E. (2000). Volunteers in state government: Involvement, management, and benefits. *Nonprofit and Voluntary Sector Quarterly, 29,* 111–130.

Bullard, A. M., & Wright, D. S. (1993). Circumventing the glass ceiling: Women executives in American state government. *Public Administration Review, 53,* 189–202.

Campion, M. A., Pursell, E. D., & Brown, B. K. (1988). Structured interviewing: Raising the psychometric properties of the employment interview. *Personnel Psychology, 41,* 25–42.

Carnevale, A. P., & Carnevale, D. G. (1993). Public administration and the evolving world of work. *Public Productivity and Management Review, 17*(1), 1–14.

Carpenter, C. (2002, November 1). PBS stations cut staffs, budgets are off millions: Fundraising, sponsorships both decline. *Nonprofit Times,* pp. 1, 10, 12.

Carroll, J. B., & Moss, D. A. (2002, October). *State employee worker shortage: The impending crisis.* Lexington, KY: Council of State Governments.

Caruso, D. B. (2003, June 18). Philly scales back school privatization. *Washington Post.*

Carver, J. (1990). *Boards that make a difference: A new design for leadership in public and nonprofit organizations.* San Francisco: Jossey-Bass.

Cascio, W. F. (1991). *Applied psychology in personnel* (4th ed.). Englewood Cliffs, NJ: Prentice Hall.

Cascio, W. F. (2000). *Costing human resources: The financial impact of behavior in organizations* (4th ed.). Cincinnati, OH: South-Western College.

Cayer, N. J. (2003). Public employee benefits and the changing nature of the workforce. In S. W. Hays & R. C. Kearney (Eds.), *Public personnel administration: Problems and prospects* (4th ed., pp. 167–179). Upper Saddle River, NJ: Prentice Hall.

CCH Business Law Editors. (1992). *Workers' compensation manual: For managers and supervisors.* Chicago: Commerce Clearing House.

Champion-Hughes, R. (2001). Totally integrated employee benefits. *Public Personnel Management, 30*(3), 287–302.

Clark, D., Clark, P., Day, D., & Shea, D. (2000). The relationship between health care reform and nurses' interest in union representation: The role of workplace climate. *Journal of Professional Nursing, 16*(2), 92–97.

Clark, P. B., & Wilson, J. Q. (1961). Incentive systems: A theory of organizations. *Administrative Science Quarterly, 6,* 129–166.

Clemetson, L. (2002, May 17). Treasury Dept. faces suit by minority agents. *New York Times.*

Clolery, P., & Flynn, P. (2003, February 15). Nonprofits outpace business in pension offerings. *Nonprofit Times,* pp. 1, 4–5.

Cnaan, R. A., & Goldberg-Glenn, R. S. (1991). Measuring motivation to volunteer in human services. *Journal of Applied Behavioral Science, 27,* 269–284.

Coggburn, J. D. (1998). Subordinate appraisals of managers: Lessons from a state agency. *Review of Public Personnel Administration, 18*(1), 68–79.

Cohen, S., & Eimicke, W. (2002). *The effective public manager: Achieving success in a changing government* (3rd ed). San Francisco: Jossey-Bass.

Cohn, D. (2003, March 13). Live-ins almost as likely as marrieds to be parents. *Washington Post,* p. A1.

Columbia University Graduate Program in Public Policy and Public Administration, School of International and Public Affairs. (1993, March). *New York City solutions II: Transforming the public personnel system.* New York: Columbia University.

Commerce Clearing House. (1990). *Employment relations.* Chicago: Author.

Congressional Budget Office. (2003, July). *Comparing the pay of federal and nonprofit executives: An update.* Washington, DC: Author.

Cook, M. E., La Vigne, M. F., Pagano, C. M., Dawes, S. S., & Pardo, T. A. (2002, July). *Making a case for local e-government.* Albany, NY: Center for Technology in Government.

Cornwell, C., & Kellough, J. E. (1994). Women and minorities in federal government agencies: Examining new evidence from panel data. *Public Administration Review, 54,* 265–270.

Cox, T., Jr. (2001). *Creating the multicultural organization: A strategy for capturing the power of diversity.* San Francisco: Jossey-Bass.

Dailey, R. C. (1986). Understanding organizational commitment for volunteers: Empirical and managerial implications. *Journal of Voluntary Action Research, 15,* 19–31.

Daley, D. (1998). An overview of benefits for the public sector: Not on the fringe anymore. *Review of Public Personnel Administration, 19*(3), 5–22.

Daly, J. L. (2003). Government and the utilization of employee assistance. In W. G. Emener, W. S. Hutchison, Jr., & M. A. Richard (Eds.), *Employee assistance programs: Wellness/enhancement programming* (3rd ed., pp. 271–281). Springfield, IL: Thomas.

Davenport, T. H., & Short, J. E. (1990, Summer). The new industrial engineering: Information technology and business process redesign. *Sloan Management Review,* pp. 11–27.

Davis, R. (2001, March 5). To keep a pledge, scouts pay. *St. Petersburg Times,* pp. 1B, 7B.

Deal, T., & Kennedy, A. (1982). *Corporate culture.* Reading, MA: Addison-Wesley.

Dellion, H., & Pearson, R. (1991, September 14). Edgar vetoes comparable worth. *Chicago Tribune,* p. 13.

Denhardt, K. G., & Leland, P. (2003, February 6–8). *Incorporating issues of spirituality into the MPA curriculum.* Paper presented at the 26th Annual Teaching Public Administration Conference, Dayton, OH.

Detling, D. G. (2002, March). Innovative use of HR technology at the city of Medford, OR. *IPMA News,* p. 9.

Dilts, D. A. (1993). Labor-management cooperation in the public sector. *Journal of Collective Negotiations in the Public Sector, 22,* 305–311.

Dilts, D. A., Boyda, S. W., & Scherr, M. A. (1993). Collective bargaining in the absence of protection legislation: The case of Louisiana. *Journal of Negotiations in the Public Sector, 22,* 259–265.

Dixon, M., Wang, S., Calvin, J., Dineen, B., & Tomlinson, E. (2002). The panel interview: A review of empirical research and guidelines for practice. *Public Personnel Management, 31*(3), 397–428.

Dobbins, G. H., Lin, T. R., & Farh, J. L. (1992). A field study of race and age similarity effects on interview ratings in conventional and situational interviews. *Journal of Applied Psychology, 77,* 363–371.

Downey, K. (2003, March 20). Muslim men settle suit over workplace abuse. *Washington Post,* p. E2.

Duer, T. (2002, May). An online employment system: The big view. *IPMA News,* p. 27.

Durst, S. (1999). Assessing the effect of family-friendly programs on public organizations. *Review of Public Personnel Administration, 19*(3), 19–33.

Edwards, H. T., Clark, R. T., Jr., & Craver, C. B. (Eds.). (1979). *Labor relations law in the public sector* (3rd ed.). New York: Bobbs-Merrill.

Elliott, R. H. (1985). *Public personnel administration: A values perspective.* Reston, VA: Reston.

Ellis, S. J. (1995). *The board's role in effective volunteer involvement.* Washington, DC: National Center for Nonprofit Boards.

Ellis, S. J. (2002, May 1). Your Web site: Does it welcome prospective volunteers? *Nonprofit Times,* p. 18.

Employment Standards Administration, Wage and Hour Division. (2003, March). *LSU health sciences center to pay $396,997 in back overtime wages to workers in Louisiana.* Retrieved July 15, 2003, from the U.S. Department of Labor Web site, http://www.dol.gov/esa/media/press/whd/whdpressVB.asp?pressdoc=dallas/2003040.

Equal Employment Opportunity Commission. (1989, July 1). Sexual Harassment, 29 C.F.R., Ch. xiv, Sec. 1604, 197–198.

Ewoh, A.I.E. (1999). An inquiry into the role of public employees and managers in privatization. *Review of Public Personnel Administration 19*(1), 8–27.

Farr, C. A. (1983). *Volunteers: Managing volunteer personnel in local government.* Washington, DC: International City/County Management Association.

Federal Highway Administration. (2000, December). *Workforce planning and professional development task force: Positioning FHWA for the future.* Retrieved on August 22, 2003, from the Federal Highway Administration Web site, http://www.fhwa.dot.gov/reports/workforce/execsumm.htm.

Feldacker, B. S. (1990). *Labor guide to labor law* (3rd ed.). Englewood Cliffs, NJ: Prentice-Hall.

Feuer, D. (1987). Paying for knowledge. *Training, 24,* 57–66.

Fine, M. G., Johnson, F. L., & Ryan, M. S. (1990). Cultural diversity in the workplace. *Public Personnel Management, 19,* 305–319.

Fisher, J. C., & Cole, K. M. (1993). *Leadership and management of volunteer programs: A guide for volunteer administrators.* San Francisco: Jossey-Bass.

Fitz-enz, J. (1990). Getting and keeping good employees. *Personnel, 67,* 25–28.

Fitz-enz, J. (1996). *How to measure human resources management* (2nd edition). New York: McGraw-Hill.

Fitz-enz, J. (2000). *The ROI of human capital: Measuring the economic value of employee performance.* New York: AMACOM.

Fitzgerald, W. (1992). Training versus development. *Training and Development Journal, 5,* 81–84.

FLETC program brings e-learning to new levels. (2003, June). *IPMA-HR News,* pp. 1, 7.

Gael, S. (1988). *The job analysis handbook for business, industry, and government* (Vols. 1 and 2). New York: Wiley.

Gardner, H. (1993). *Multiple intelligences: The theory in practice.* New York: Basic Books.

Gardner, H. (1999). *Intelligence reframed: Multiple intelligences for the 21st century.* New York: Basic Books.

Gardner, H., & Hatch, T. (1989). Multiple intelligences go to school. *Educational Researcher, 18,* 4–10.

Gaston, C. L. (1986). An idea whose time has not come: Comparable worth and the market salary problem. *Population Research and Policy Review, 5,* 15–29.

General Accounting Office. (1992, April). *The changing workforce: Comparison of federal and nonfederal work/family programs and approaches.* Washington, DC: Government Printing Office.

General Accounting Office. (2001a). *Federal employee retirements: Expected increase over the next 5 years illustrates need for workforce planning.* (GAO Publication No. GAO-01-509). Washington, DC: Government Printing Office.

General Accounting Office. (2001b). *Nursing workforce: Emerging nurse shortages due to multiple factors.* (GAO Publication No. GAO-01-944). Washington, DC: Government Printing Office.

General Accounting Office. (2001c). *Security and Exchange Commission: Human capital challenges require management attention.* (GAO Publication No. GAO-01-947). Washington, DC: Government Printing Office.

General Accounting Office. (2002a). *HUD human capital management: Comprehensive strategic workforce planning needed.* (GAO Publication No. GAO-02-839). Washington, DC: Government Printing Office.

General Accounting Office. (2002b). *A model of strategic human capital management.* (GAO Publication No. GAO-02-373SP). Washington, DC: Government Printing Office.

General Accounting Office. (2003). *Enhanced agency efforts needed to improve diversity the senior corps turns over.* (GAO Publication No. GAO-03-34). Washington, DC: Government Printing Office.

Gibelman, M. (2000). The nonprofit sector and gender discrimination: A preliminary investigation into the glass ceiling. *Nonprofit Management and Leadership, 10*(2), 251–269.

Gilbert, J. A., & Ivancevich, J. M. (2000). Valuing diversity: A tale of two organizations. *Academy of Management Executives, 14*(1), 93–105.

Gilmore, T. N. (1993). *Finding and retaining your next chief executive: Making the transition work.* Washington, DC: National Center for Nonprofit Boards.

Goleman, D. (1995). *Emotional intelligence: Why it can matter more than IQ.* New York: Bantam.

Goleman, D. (1998). *Working with emotional intelligence.* New York: Bantam.

Goski, J. (2002). A model of leadership development. *Public Personnel Management, 31*(4), 517–522.

Governor's Human Resources Advisory Council. (1993). *Recommendations for change in Illinois.* Springfield: Illinois Department of Central Management Services.

Graham, M. (1992). The drive for comparable worth: Has it sputtered out? *P.A. Times, 15,* 8.

Green, M. E. (2002). Ensuring the organization's future: A leadership development case study. *Public Personnel Management, 31*(4), 431–439.

Greenberg, J. (1986). Determinants of perceived fairness of performance evaluations. *Journal of Applied Psychology, 71,* 340–342.

Greenhouse, S. (2002). CUNY and union join a Bronx program to train nurses and improve health care skills. *New York Times.*

Greenhouse, S., & Saulny, S. (2001, April 12). City's municipal workers on contract and 8% raise. *New York Times,* p. A1.

Gupta, N. (1997). Rewarding skills in the public sector. In H. Risher & C. H. Fay (Eds.), *New strategies for public pay: Rethinking government compensation programs.* San Francisco: Jossey-Bass.

Gupta, N., Jenkins, G. D., Jr., & Curington, W. P. (1986). Paying for knowledge: Myths and realities. *National Productivity Review, 5,* 107–123.

Guy, M. E. (1993). Three steps forward, two steps backward: The status of women's integration into public management. *Public Administration Review, 53,* 285–292.

Harris, B. (2001). Training for light speed. *Government and Information Technology, 8,* 46–47.

Hass, N., (1993, August 3). Buy a bridge? *Financial World,* pp. 31–35.

Hays, S. W., & Kearney, R. C. (2001). Anticipated changes in human resource management: Views from the field. *Public Administration Review, 61*(5), 585–597.

Healy, B., & Southard, G. D. (1994). *Pay for performance: Administrative policy manual, Policy No. 30–19.* Claremont, CA: City of Claremont.

Henderson, R. (1989). *Compensation management* (5th ed.). Englewood Cliffs, NJ: Prentice Hall.

Heneman, R. D. (1992). *Merit pay: Linking pay increases to performance ratings.* Reading, MA: Addison-Wesley.

Henriques, D. B. (2003, July 3). Edison stays afloat by altering course. *New York Times.*

Herman, R. D., & Heimovics, R. D. (1989). Critical events in the management of nonprofit organizations: Initial evidence. *Nonprofit and Voluntary Sector Quarterly, 18,* 119–132.

Herzlinger, R. E. (1994, July-August). Effective oversight: A guide for nonprofit directors. *Harvard Business Review,* pp. 52–60.

Hinden, D. R., & Hull, P. (2002). Executive leadership transition: What we know. *Nonprofit Quarterly, 9*(4), 24–29.

Horrigan, J., & Harriman, A. (1988). Comparable worth: Public sector unions and employers provide a model for implementing pay equity. *Labor Law Journal, 39,* 704–711.

Houle, C. O. (1989). *Governing boards: Their nature and nurture.* San Francisco: Jossey-Bass.

Hughes, M. A., Ratliff, R. A., Purswell, J. L., & Hadwiger, J. (1989). A content validation methodology for job related physical performance tests. *Public Personnel Management, 18,* 487–504.

Hunger and homelessness on the rise in major U.S. cities. (2003, January). *P.A. Times*, p. 2.

Hunter, J. E. (1986). Cognitive ability, cognitive aptitude, job knowledge, and job performance. *Journal of Vocational Behavior, 29*, 340–362.

Huntley, H. (2002, March 24). State employees get retirement plan choice. *St. Petersburg Times*, p. 4H.

Hush, H. (1969). Collective bargaining in voluntary agencies. *Social Casework, 50*, 210–213.

Hyland, S. L. (1990, September). Helping employees with family care. *Monthly Labor Review*, pp. 22–26.

Ingraham, P. W., & Rosenbloom, D. H. (1990). *The State of Merit in the Federal Government*. Washington, DC: National Commission on the Public Service.

Ingram, R. T. (1988). *Ten basic responsibilities of nonprofit boards*. Washington, DC: National Center for Nonprofit Boards.

Inocencio, M., & Gravon, C. (2002). Leading change: Planned Parenthood of Rhode Island. *Nonprofit Quarterly, 9*(2), 36–40.

Jackson, M. (2003, June 15). More sons are juggling jobs and care for parents. *New York Times*, sec. 3.9.

Jacobs, J. A., & Gerson, K. (1998). Who are the overworked Americans? *Review of Social Economy, 56*(4), 442.

Jamison, I. B. (2003). Turnover and retention among volunteers in human service agencies. *Review of Public Personnel Administration, 23*(2), 114–132.

Janofsky, M. (2003, February 5). States' budget gaps widen nearly 50% in two months. *New York Times*.

Johnson, M. (2002, January 10). Fallout will be fewer services, more vacant jobs, officials say. *Milwaukee Journal Sentinel*.

Johnson, R. E. (1988). Flexible benefit plans. In J. Matzer Jr. (Ed.), *Pay and benefits: New ideas for local government* (pp. 72–86). Washington, DC: International City/County Management Association.

Jones, J. (2003, February 1). Women gaining on men, as nonprofits' salaries steadily increase. *Nonprofit Times*, pp. 21–23.

Joslyn, H. (2002, February 21). Balancing work and family: Charities face new challenges over what benefits to provide. *Chronicle of Philanthropy*, pp. 7–13.

Joslyn, H. (2003, March 20). Charity's glass ceiling. *Chronicle of Philanthropy*. Retrieved March 17, 2003, from http://philanthropy.com/premium/articles/v15/i11/11004701.html.

Kaiser Family Foundation. (2003, September). *New survey shows workers are paying more and getting less for their health coverage*. Retrieved on September 9, 2003, from the Kaiser Family Foundation Web site, http://www.kaisernetwork.org.

Kanter, R. M., & Summers, D. V. (1987). Doing well while doing good: Dilemmas of performance measurement in nonprofit organizations and the need for a multiple-constituency approach. In W. W. Powell (Ed.), *The nonprofit sector: A research handbook* (pp. 154–165). New Haven, CT: Yale University Press.

Kaplan, R. S., & Norton, D. P. (1996). *The balanced scorecard: Translating strategy into action.* Boston: Harvard Business School Press.

Karp, D. (2003, October 19). Service keeps City Hall on track. *St. Petersburg Times,* pp. 1B, 7B.

Kearney, R. C., & Carnevale, D. G. (2001). *Labor relations in the public sector* (3rd ed.). New York: Dekker.

Kellough, J. E., & Lu, H. (1993). The paradox of merit pay in the public sector. *Review of Public Personnel Administration, 13,* 45–64.

Kellough, J. E., & Nigro, L. G. (2002). Pay for performance in Georgia state government: Employee perspectives on Georgia gain after 5 years. *Review of Public Personnel Administration, 22,* 146–166.

Kerkman, L. (2003, October 30). Salary gap is shrinking for female charity CEO's, survey finds. *Chronicle of Philanthropy,* pp. 57–59.

Kettl, D. F. (2002). *The transformation of governance: Public administration for twenty-first century America.* Baltimore: Johns Hopkins University Press.

Kim, P. S. (1993). Racial integration in the American federal government: With special reference to Asian Americans. *Review of Public Personnel Administration, 13,* 52–66.

Kim, P. S., & Lewis, G. B. (1994). Asian Americans in the public service: Success, diversity, and discrimination. *Public Administration Review, 54,* 285–290.

Kirkpatrick, D. L. (1998). *Evaluating training programs: The four levels* (2nd ed.). San Francisco: Berrett-Koehler.

Knauft, E. B., Berger, R. A., & Gray, S. T. (1991). *Profiles of excellence: Achieving success in the nonprofit sector.* San Francisco: Jossey-Bass.

Kolb, D. A. (1984). *Experiential learning: Experience as a source of learning and development.* Englewood Cliffs, NJ: Prentice Hall.

Kossek, E. E., De Marr, B. J., Backman, K., & Kolar, M. (1993). Assessing employees' emerging elder care needs and reactions to dependent care benefits. *Public Personnel Management, 22,* 617–638.

Kovach, K. A., & Millspaugh, P. E. (1990). Comparable worth: Canada legislates pay equity. *Academy of Management Executives, 4,* 92–101.

Kramer, R. M., & Grossman, B. (1987). Contracting for social services: Process management and resource dependencies. *Social Service Review, 61,* 32–55.

Kraten, M. (1995, June). HR policies in the nonprofit arena. *Nonprofit Times,* p. 29.

Lane, P. (1995, March 13). Partners in public service. *Nation's Cities Weekly*, p. 12.

Lawler, E. E., III. (1989). Pay for performance: A strategic analysis. In L. R. Gomez-Mejia (Ed.), *Compensation and benefits* (pp. 136–181). Washington, DC: Bureau of National Affairs.

Lawler, E. E., III. (2000). *Rewarding excellence: Pay strategies for the new economy*. San Francisco: Jossey-Bass.

Leonhardt, D. (2003, February 6). U.S. economy in worst hiring slump in 20 years. *New York Times*.

Lewis, G. B. (1988). Progress toward racial and sexual equality in the federal civil service? *Public Administration Review, 48*, 389–397.

Lewis, G. B. (1994). Women, occupations, and federal agencies: Occupational mix and interagency differences in sexual inequality in federal white-collar employment. *Public Administration Review, 54*, 271–276.

Light, P. C. (1998). *Sustaining innovation: Creating nonprofit and government organizations that innovate naturally*. San Francisco: Jossey-Bass.

Light, P. C. (1999). *The true size of government*. Washington, DC: Brookings Institution.

Light, P. C. (2000a). The empty government talent pool. *Brookings Review, 18*(1), 20–23.

Light, P. C. (2000b). *Making nonprofits work: A report on the tides of nonprofit management reform*. Washington, DC: Brookings Institution.

Light, P. C. (2003). *In search of public service*. Washington, DC: Brookings Institution.

Lipman, H. (2002, February 4). D.C. United Way moves to quell complaints. *Chronicle of Philanthropy*. Retrieved February 7, 2002, from http://philanthropy.com/premium/articles/v14/i08/08004201.htm.

Lipman, H., & Voelz, M. (2002, October 3). Big pay rise in pay for CEOs: Charity and foundation heads see 7.5% median gain in salary. *Chronicle of Philanthropy*, pp. 33–47.

Lipsky, M., & Smith, S. R. (1989–1990). Nonprofit organizations, government, and the welfare state. *Political Science Quarterly, 104*, 625–648.

Liptak, A. (2002, December 21). California may bar judges from joining the Boy Scouts. *New York Times*.

Loden, M. (1996). *Implementing diversity*. Chicago: Irwin.

Long, K. H. (2003, September 1). Bush policy sparks "revolt" by ex-park officers. *Tampa Tribune*, pp. 1, 10.

Longenecker, C., & Ludwig, D. (1990). Ethical dilemmas in performance appraisal revisited. *Journal of Business Ethics, 9*, 961–969.

Maine Bureau of Human Resources. (2003). *Maine Leadership Institution: Preparing mangers to lead*. Retrieved on February 12, 2004, from the Government of Maine Web site, http://www.maine.gov/bhr/mms/leadership/index.html.

March, W. (2003, May 25). Accrued sick, vacation pay costs Tampa big bucks. *Tampa Tribune.*

Mariani, M. (2001). The training channel. *Governing, 14*(10), 38–39.

Marquis, C. (2003, March 13). Total of unmarried couples surged in 2000 U.S. census. *New York Times.*

Masterson, S. S., & Taylor, M. S. (1996). Total quality management and performance appraisal: An integrative perspective. *Journal of Quality Management, 1,* 67–89.

McCabe, B. C., & Stream, C. (2000). Diversity by the numbers: Changes in state and local government workforces, 1980–1995. *Public Personnel Management, 29*(1), 93–106.

McCurdy, A. H., Newman, M. A., & Lovrich, N. P. (2002). Family-friendly workplace policy adoption in general and special-purpose local governments: Learning from the Washington State experience. *Review of Public Personnel Administration, 22*(1), 27–51.

McCurley, S. (1993, January–February). How to fire a volunteer and live to tell about it. *Grapevine,* pp. 8–11.

McDaniel, M. A., Finnegan, E. B., Morgenson, F. P., Campion, M.A., & Braverman, E. P. (1997, April). *Predicting performance from common sense.* Paper presented at the 12th Annual Society for Industrial Organizational Psychology Conference, Saint Louis, MO.

McDaniel, M. A., Finnegan, E. B., Morgenson, F. P., Campion, M.A., & Braverman, E. P. (2001). Use of situational judgment tests to predict job performance: A clarification of the literature. *Journal of Applied Psychology, 86*(4), 730–740.

McDermott, K., & Gillerman, M. (1995, June 14). Retiring East St. Louis educators can cash in unused sick days repaid generously. *St. Louis Post-Dispatch,* pp. 1, 10.

McEvoy, G. M. (1990). Public managers' reactions to appraisals by subordinates. *Public Personnel Management, 19,* 201–212.

McIntosh, S. S. (1990). Clerical jobs in transition. *Human Resources Magazine, 35,* 70–72.

McKay, J. (2003a, May). Crunch time: Outsourcing and other options are back on the table as states scramble for answers to a dire budget situation. *Government Technology,* pp. 18–21.

McKay, J. (2003b, August). Full court press: Stanislaus County's superior court aggressively pursues information integration. *Government Technology,* pp. 44–46.

Mergenbagen, P. (1991, June). A new breed of volunteer. *American Demographics,* pp. 54–55.

Milliken, F. J., & Martins, L. L. (1996). Searching for common threads: Understanding the multiple effects of diversity in organizational change. *Academy of Management Review, 21,* 402–433.

Montjoy, R. S., & Brudney, J. L. (1991). Volunteers in the delivery of public services: Hidden costs . . . and benefits. *American Review of Public Administration, 21,* 327–344.

Morrison, E. K. (1994). *Leadership skills: Developing volunteers for organizational success* (3rd ed.). Tucson, AZ: Fisher Books.

Murphy, C. (2002, October 31). Much of the business of state government has gone private. *St. Petersburg Times.*

Murphy, C. (2003, February 5). Contractors get a close look. *St. Petersburg Times,* p. 10A.

Murphy, K. R. (1996). Individual differences and behavior in organizations: Much more than *g.* In K. R. Murphy (Ed.), *Individual differences in organizations* (pp. 3–30). San Francisco: Jossey-Bass.

Muson, H. (1989, March). The nonprofit prophet. *Across the Board,* pp. 24–38.

Naff, K. C., & Kellough, J. E. (2002). A changing workforce: Understanding diversity programs in the federal government. In M. A. Abramson & N. W. Gardner (Eds.), *Human capital, 2002* (pp. 355–410). Lanham, MD: Rowman & Littlefield.

Nason, J. W. (1993). *Board assessment of the chief executive: A responsibility essential to good governance* (4th ed.). Washington, DC: National Center for Nonprofit Boards.

National Academy of Public Administration. (2000). *The case for transforming public-sector human resources management.* Washington, DC: Author.

National Association of Counties. (2003). *Acts of caring award winners.* Retrieved on February 12, 2004, from the National Association of Counties Web site, http://www.naco.org/Template.cfm?Section= Acts_of_Caring_Awards&Template=/cffiles/awards/acts_srch.cfm& YearSelected=2003.

National Commission on the Public Service. (1989). *Leadership for America: Rebuilding the public service.* Washington, DC: Author.

National Commission on the State and Local Public Service. (1993). *Hard truths/tough choices: An agenda for state and local reform.* Albany, NY: Nelson A. Rockefeller Institute of Government.

National Governors Association. (2002). *A governor's guide to creating a 21st-century workforce.* Washington, DC: Author.

National Governors Association & National Association of State Budget Officers. (2002). *The fiscal survey of states.* Washington, DC: Authors.

National Institute of Mental Health, National Institutes of Health. (2001). *The numbers count.* Retrieved on August 25, 2003, from the National Institute of Mental Health Web site, http://www.nimh.nih.gov/ publicat/numvers.cfm.

National Labor Relations Board. (1991). *A guide to basic law and procedures under the NLRA.* Washington, DC: Government Printing Office.

National Park Service. (2003). *Volunteers-In-Parks.* Retrieved on February 12, 2004, from the National Park Service Web site, http://www.nps.gov/volunteer.

National Partnership for Women and Families. (1998). *Family matters: A national survey of women and men.* Retrieved August 23, 1999, from the National Partnership Web site, http://www.nationalpartnership.org/survey/survey8.htm.

National Performance Review. (1993). *Creating a government that works better and costs less.* Washington, DC: Author.

Nelson, W. R. (1982). Employment testing and the demise of the PACE examination. *Labor Law Journal, 35,* 729–750.

Nelson-Horchler, J. (1989). Elder care comes of age. *Industry Week, 238,* 54–56.

Newcombe, T. (2001, October 22). Racing to replace retirees. *Government Technology,* p. 24.

Newcombe, T. (2002, January). Electronic empowerment: Growing child support caseloads and fewer resources have led some states to begin using the Internet for service delivery and case management. *Government Technology,* pp. 50–51.

Newlin, J. G., & Meng, G. J. (1991). The public sector pays for performance. *Personnel Journal, 70,* 110–114.

NIST developing virtual reality training tool for firefighters. (2003, August 19). *Government Technology.* Retrieved on August 26, 2003, from the *Government Technology* Web site, http://www.govtech.net/news/news.phtml?docid=2003.08.19–64605.

O'Connell, B. (1988). *Finding, developing, and rewarding good board members.* Washington, DC: INDEPENDENT SECTOR.

Odendahl, T., & Youmans, S. (1994). Women on nonprofit boards. In T. Odendahl & M. O'Neill (Eds.), *Women and power in the nonprofit sector* (pp. 183–221). San Francisco: Jossey-Bass.

O'Donnell, M., & O'Brien, J. (2000). Performance-based pay in the Australian public service. *Review of Public Personnel Administration, 20*(2), 20–34.

Office of National Drug Control Policy. (2001). *The economic costs of drug abuse in the U.S., 1992–1998.* (Publication No. NCJ-190636). Washington, DC: Author.

Office of Personnel Management. (1993). *Revisiting civil service, 2000: New policy direction needed.* Washington, DC: Author.

Office of Personnel Management. (1994). *Toward reinvention: A guide to HRM reform.* Washington, DC: Author.

Office of Personnel Management. (1999a). *Federal human resources employment trends (An Occupation in Transition, Part 1).* Washington, DC: Author.

Office of Personnel Management. (1999b). *Looking to the future: Human resources competencies (An Occupation in Transition, Part 2)*. Washington, DC: Author.

Office of Personnel Management. (2000). *The HR workforce: Meeting the challenge of change (An Occupation in Transition, Part 3)*. Washington, DC: Author:

Office of Personnel Management. ((2003). Retrieved July 15, 2003, from the U.S. Office of Personnel Management Web site, http://www.opm.gov/oca/03tables/html/gs.asp.

O'Neill, M. (1994). The paradox of women and power in the nonprofit sector. In T. Odendahl & M. O'Neill (Eds.), *Women and power in the nonprofit sector* (pp. 1–16). San Francisco: Jossey-Bass.

Organ, D. W. (1988). *Organizational citizenship behavior: The good soldier syndrome*. Lexington, MA: Lexington Books.

Ospina, S., & O'Sullivan, J. F. (2003). Working together: Meeting the challenge of workplace diversity. In S. W. Hays & R. C. Kearney (Eds.), *Public personnel administration: Problems and prospects* (4th ed.). Upper Saddle River, NJ: Prentice Hall.

Page, P. (1994). African-Americans in executive branch agencies. *Review of Public Personnel Administration, 14*(1), 24–51.

Pagno, M. A. (2002). *City fiscal conditions in 2002*. Washington, DC: National League of Cities.

Patton, K. R., & Daley, D. M. (1998). Gainsharing in Zebulon: What do workers want? *Public Personnel Management, 27*(1), 117–131.

Pearce, J. L. (1993). *Volunteers: The organizational behavior of unpaid workers*. New York: Routledge.

Perry, J. L. (1995). Compensation, merit pay, and motivation. In S. W. Hays & R. C. Kearney (Eds.), *Public personnel administration: Problems and prospects* (3rd ed., pp. 121–317). Englewood Cliffs, NJ: Prentice Hall.

Perry, J. L., & Kramer, K. L. (1993). The implications of changing technology. In F. J. Thompson (Ed.), *Revitalizing state and local public service: Strengthening performance, accountability, and citizen confidence* (pp. 225–245). San Francisco: Jossey-Bass.

Peters, J. B., and Masaoka, J. (2000). A house divided: How nonprofits experience union drives. *Nonprofit Management and Leadership, 10*(3), 305–317.

Phillips, J. J., & Stone, R. D. (2002). *How to measure training results*. New York: McGraw-Hill.

Phillips, P. P. (Ed.). (2002). *Measuring ROI in the public sector*. Alexandria, VA: ASTD.

Phillips, P. P., & Phillips, J. J. (2002). The public sector challenge: Developing a credible ROI Process. In P. P. Phillips (Ed.), *Measuring ROI in the public sector* (pp. 1–32). Alexandria, VA: ASTD.

Pierson, J., & Mintz, J. (1995). *Assessment of the chief executive: A tool for governing boards and chief executives of nonprofit organizations.* Washington, DC: National Center for Nonprofit Boards.

Pincus, F. L. (2003). *Reverse discrimination: Dismantling the myth.* Boulder, CO: Rienner.

Podsakoff, P. M., Mackenzie, S. B., Paine, J. B., & Bachrach, D. G. (2000). Organizational citizenship behaviors: A critical review of the theoretical and empirical literature and suggestions for future research. *Journal of Management, 26,* 513–563.

Pogrebin, R. (2003, February 11). City's arts budget being cut in money pinch. *New York Times.*

Police Officers' and Firefighters' Employment Relations Act. 19 Delaware Laws c. 16, §1601–1623.

Pounds, M. H. (2003, October 26). Coral Springs is known for being run like a business: City earns two Florida Sterling Quality awards. *South Florida Sun-Sentinel,* p. 1F.

Praeger, J. (1994). Contracting out government services: Lessons from the private sector. *Public Administration Review, 54,* 176–183.

Preston, A. E. (1990). Women in the white-collar nonprofit sector: The best option or the only option? *Review of Economics and Statistics, 72,* 560–568.

Primoff, E. S. (1975, June). *How to prepare and conduct job-element examinations.* Washington, DC: U.S. Civil Service Commission, Personnel Research and Development Center.

Pristin, T. (2001, May 8). Facing scrutiny, president of Hale House will resign. *New York Times.*

Pulakos, E. D., Arad, S., Donovan, M. A., & Plamondon, K. E. (2000). Adaptability in the workplace: Development of a taxonomy of adaptive performance. *Journal of Applied Psychology, 85,* 612–624.

Pynes, J. E. (2003). "Strategic human resources management." In S. W. Hays & R. C. Kearney (Eds.), *Public personnel administration: Problems and prospects* (4th ed., pp. 93–105). Upper Saddle River, NJ: Prentice Hall.

Ragavan, C. (2003, May 26). Mueller's mandate: The FBI chief has a little job to do—overhaul the agency from top to bottom. *U.S. News and World Report.*

Reed, B. J., & Swain, J. W. (1997). *Public finance administration* (2nd ed). Thousand Oaks, CA: Sage.

Rehfuss, J. A. (1986). A representative bureaucracy? Women and minority executives in California career service. *Public Administration Review, 46,* 454–460.

Reinke, S. J. (2003). Does the form really matter? Leadership, trust, and acceptance of the performance appraisal process. *Review of Public Personnel Administration, 23*(1), 23–37.

Riccucci, N. M. (2002). *Managing diversity in public sector workforces.* Boulder, CO: Westview Press.

Riccucci, N. M., & Lurie, I. (2001). Employee performance evaluation in social welfare offices. *Review of Public Personnel Administration, 21*(1), 27–37.

Rimer, S. (2003, July 3). Boy Scouts under fire; ban on gays is at issue. *New York Times,* p. 19A.

Risher, H. (1998). Can gainsharing help to reinvent government? *Public Management, 80*(5), 17–21.

Risher, H. (1999). Are public employers ready for a "new pay" program? *Public Personnel Management, 28*(3), 323–343.

Risher, H. (2002). Pay-for-performance: The keys to making it work. *Public Personnel Management, 31*(3), 317–332.

Risher, H., Fay, C. H., & Perry, J. L. (1997). Merit pay: Motivating and rewarding individual performance. In H. Risher & C. H. Fay (Eds.), *New strategies for public pay: Rethinking government compensation programs* (pp. 253–271). San Francisco: Jossey-Bass.

Risher, H., & Schay, B. W. (1994). Grade banding: The model for future salary programs? *Public Personnel Management, 32*(3), 187–199.

Robbins, S. P. (1994). *Essentials of organizational behavior* (4th ed.). Englewood Cliffs, NJ: Prentice Hall.

Rocheleau, B. (1988). New information technology and organizational context: Nine lessons. *Public Productivity Review, 12,* 225–236.

Romero, C. L. (2003, July 20). Working from home a win-win situation: Telecommuting is cheap, easy. *Asheville Citizen-Times,* pp. D1–D2.

Ruderman, M. N., Ohlott, P. J., Panzer, K., & King, S. N. (2002). Benefits of multiple roles for managerial women. *Academy of Management Journal, 45*(2), 369–386.

Ryan, W. P. (1999, January-February). The new landscape for nonprofits. *Harvard Business Review,* pp. 127–136.

Saidel, J. R., & Cour, S. (2003). Information technology and the voluntary sector workplace. *Nonprofit and Voluntary Sector Quarterly, 32*(1), 5–24.

Salamon, L. M. (1995). *Partners in the public service.* Baltimore: Johns Hopkins University Press.

Salamon, L. M. (1999). *America's nonprofit sector: A primer* (2nd ed.). New York: Foundation Center.

Same sex couples earn death benefit. (2002, June 26). *St. Petersburg Times,* pp. 1A, 8A.

Sanchez, J. I., & Levine, E. L. (1999). Is job analysis dead, misunderstood, or both? New forms of work analysis and design. In A. I. Kraut & A. K. Korman (Eds.), *Evolving practices in human resource management* (pp. 43–68). San Francisco: Jossey-Bass.

Sanecki, K. (2000, January-February). Hands and hearts in government services. *Quality Cities,* pp. 53–54.

Santaniello, G. (2003, April 20). For charities, the taxman cometh. *New York Times.*

Schay, B. W. (1997). Paying for performance: Lessons learned in fifteen years of federal demonstration projects. In H. Risher & C. H. Fay (Eds.), *New strategies for public pay: Rethinking government compensation programs* (pp. 207–230). San Francisco: Jossey-Bass.

Schmidt, F. L. (1988). The problem of group differences in ability test scores in employment selection. *Journal of Vocational Behavior, 33,* 272–292.

Schmidt, F. L., & Hunter, J. E. (1998). The validity and utility of selection methods in personnel psychology: Practical and theoretical implications of 85 years of research findings. *Psychological Bulletin, 124,* 262–274.

Schock, S. (1998–1999, Winter). "Update on Nebraska's Information Technology Training Program." *Newsletter of the National Association of State Personnel Executives,* p. 4.

Schott, R. L. (1999). Managers and mental health: Mental illness and the workplace. *Public Personnel Management, 28*(2), 161–183.

Scott, M. (2003, April 29). Like a good neighbor, Oldsmar is there. *St. Petersburg Times,* p. 4B.

Selby, C. C. (1978). Better performance from nonprofits. *Harvard Business Review,* pp. 92–98.

Selden, S. C., & Moynihan, D. P. (2000). A model of voluntary turnover in state government. *Review of Public Personnel Administration, 20*(2), 63–74.

Shareef, R. (1994). Skill-based pay in the public sector. *Review of Public Personnel Administration, 14*(3), 60–74.

Shareef, R. (1998). A midterm case study of skill-based pay in the Virginia Department of Transportation. *Review of Public Personnel Administration, 18*(1), 5–22.

Shareef, R. (2002). The sad demise of skill-based pay in the Virginia Department of Transportation. *Review of Public Personnel Administration, 22*(3), 233–240.

Sherer, J. L. (1994, March). Can hospitals and organized labor be partners in redesign? *Hospitals and Health Networks, 68,* 56–58.

Shostak, A. B. (1991). *Robust unionism: Innovations in the labor market movement.* Ithaca, NY: ILR Press.

Sidberry, T. B. (2002). Building diversity in organizations. *Nonprofit Quarterly, 9*(2), 28–33.

Siegel, G. B. (1994). Three federal demonstration projects: Using monetary performance awards. *Public Personnel Management, 23,* 243–255.

Sims, R. R. (1998). *Reinventing training and development*. Westport, CT: Quorum.

Sisneros, A. (1992). Hispanics in the senior executive service: Continuity and change in the decade 1980–1990. *Review of Public Personnel Administration, 12,* 5–25.

Slack, J. D. (1987). Affirmative action and city managers: Attitudes toward recruitment of women. *Public Administration Review, 47,* 199–206.

Smith, C. A., Organ, D. W., & Near, J. P. (1983). Organizational citizenship behavior: Its nature and antecedents. *Journal of Applied Psychology, 68,* 655–663.

Smith, K. C., & McDaniel, M. A. (1997, April). *Criterion and construct evidence for a measure of practical intelligence.* Paper presented at the 12th Annual Society for Industrial Organizational Psychology Conference, Saint Louis, MO.

Smith, M. (1999, October). Broadbanding: Is it right for your organization? *IPMA News,* pp. 10–11.

Snelling, B. W., & Kuhnle, J. H. (1986). When should a nonprofit organization use an executive search firm and when not? In INDEPENDENT SECTOR (Ed.), *Aiming high on a small budget: Executive searches and the nonprofit sector* (pp. 1–8). Washington, DC: INDEPENDENT SECTOR.

Sommerfield, M. (2000, March 23). A break between good deeds: Sabbaticals give charity executives chance to hone skills—or just unwind. *Chronicle of Philanthropy,* pp. 51–53.

Starling, G. (1986). *Managing the public sector* (3rd ed.). Chicago: Dorsey Press.

State of Illinois, Central Management Services. (2002). *Upward Mobility Program.* Retrieved on August 22, 2003, from the State of Illinois Web site, http://www.state.il.us/cms/persnl/ump/default.htm.

States plunging into red. (2003, February 3). *St. Petersburg Times.*

Steinberg, R. J., & Jacobs, J. A. (1994). Pay equity in nonprofit organizations: Making women's work visible. In T. Odendahl & M. O'Neill (Eds.), *Women and power in the nonprofit sector* (pp. 79–120). San Francisco: Jossey-Bass.

Stene, E. O. (1980). *Selecting a professional administrator: A guide to municipal councils* (2nd ed.). Washington, DC: International City/County Management Association.

Sternberg, R. J. (1985). *Beyond IQ.* New York: Cambridge University Press.

Stowers, G.N.L., & Melitski, J. (2003). Introduction to symposium. *Public Performance and Management Review, 26*(4), 321–324.

Sweeney, J. (1995, December 8). Speech to the California Association of Public Hospitals. Retrieved from the AFL-CIO Web site, http://www.aflcio.org.

Swift, E. W. (1992–1993). Glass ceilings and equity. *Public Manager, 21,* 34–36.

Swiss, J. E. (1992). Adapting total quality management (TQM) to government. *Public Administration Review, 52,* 356–362.

Swope, C. (1998). Cincinnati schools are afflicted by sick pay. *Governing, 11*(9), 54.

Tambor, M. (1973). Unions and voluntary agencies. *Social Work, 18,* 41–47.

Tambor, M. (1988). Collective bargaining in the social services. In P. R. Keys & L. H. Ginsberg (Eds.), *New management in human services* (pp. 81–101). Silver Springs, MD: National Association of Social Workers.

Taylor, S. (1989). The case for comparable worth. *Journal of Social Issues, 45,* 23–37.

Thompson, J. R., & Le Hew, C. W. (2000). Skill-based pay as an organizational innovation. *Review of Public Personnel Administration, 20*(1), 20–40.

Towers Perrin. (1992). *Why did we adopt skill-based pay?* New York: Towers Perrin.

Treiman, D. J., & Hartman, H. (1981). *Women, work, and wages.* Washington, DC: National Academy of Sciences.

Tremain, K. (2003, September-October). Pink slips in the parks: The Bush administration privatizes our public treasures. *Sierra,* pp. 27–35, 52.

Ulrich, D. (1997). *Human resource champions.* Boston: Harvard Business School Press.

Ulrich, D. (1998, January-February). A new mandate for human resources. *Harvard Business Review,* pp. 125–134.

Ulrich, D., Losey, M. R., & Lake, G. (Eds.). (1997). *Tomorrow's HR management: 48 thought leaders call for change.* New York: Wiley.

Uniform Guidelines on Employee Selection Procedures. (1978, August 25). *Federal Register,* pp. 38290–38315.

U.S. Bureau of Labor Statistics. (2001). *Contingent and alternative employment arrangements.* Retrieved on June 17, 2003, from the Bureau of Labor Statistics FTP site, ftp://ftp.bls.gov/pub/news.release/conemp.txt.

U.S. Bureau of Labor Statistics. (2003). *Highlights of women's earnings in 2002.* (BLS Report No. 972). Retrieved on October 29, 2003, from the Bureau of Labor Statistics Web site, http://www.bls.gov/cps/cpswom2002.pdf.

U.S. Census Bureau. (2003a, March 13). Census bureau releases census 2000 report on married and unmarried couples. *Department of Commerce News.* Retrieved on April 1, 2003, from the Census Bureau Web site, http://www.census.gov/Press-Release/www/2003/cb03cn05.html.

U.S. Census Bureau. (2003b, January 21). Census bureau releases population estimates by age, sex, race and Hispanic origin. *Department of*

Commerce News. Retrieved on May 2, 2003, from the Census Bureau Web site, http://www.census.gov/Press-Release/www/2003/cb03–16.html.

U.S. Conference of Mayors. (2002, December). *A status report on hunger and homelessness in America's cities, 2002.* Washington, DC: Author.

U.S. Department of Labor. (2003a). *E-government strategic plan: Transforming into a digital department.* Washington, DC: Author.

U.S. Department of Labor. (2003b). *U.S. Department of Labor proposal to strengthen overtime protection: Side-by-side comparison.* Retrieved on July 15, 2003, from the Department of Labor Web site, http://www.dol.gov/_sec/media/speeches/541_Side_By_Side.htm.

U.S. Merit Systems Protection Board. (1991). *Balancing work responsibilities and family needs: The federal civil service response.* Washington, DC: Government Printing Office.

U.S. Merit Systems Protection Board. (1992). *A question of equity: Women and the glass ceiling in the federal government.* Washington, DC: Government Printing Office.

U.S. Merit Systems Protection Board. (1993). *The changing face of the federal workforce: A symposium on diversity.* Washington, DC: Government Printing Office.

U.S. Merit Systems Protection Board. (2003a). *The federal selection interview: Unrealized potential.* Washington, DC: Government Printing Office.

U.S. Merit Systems Protection Board. (2003b). *Help wanted: A review of federal vacancy announcements.* Washington, DC: Government Printing Office.

Unspoken rule: Real men don't take paternity leave. (2000, June 6). *Tampa Tribune,* Business & Finance, p. 9.

Van Slyke, D. (2003). The mythology of privatization in contracting for social services. *Public Administration Review, 63*(3), 296–315.

Vanneman, A. (1994, July-August). Youth worker salaries: Going nowhere, slowly. *Youth Today,* pp. 4–5.

Varian, B. (2003, June 29). Tampa hospital finds its pulse. *St. Petersburg Times,* pp. 1A, 11A.

Wald, M. L. (2003a, June 30). Congress and Bush split on privatizing at FAA. *New York Times.*

Wald, M. L. (2003b, August 3). Controller dispute threatens FAA, budget for coming year. *New York Times.*

Wallace, M. J., Jr., & Fay, C. H. (1988). *Compensation theory and practice* (2nd ed.). Boston: PWS-Kent.

Wallace, N. (2001, February 22). A virtual army of volunteers: Charities find new ways to let people do good works online. *Chronicle of Philanthropy,* pp. 37–39.

Walsh, E. (2003a, May 30). OMB details "outsourcing" revisions. *Washington Post.*

Walsh, E. (2003b, June 20). Union sues OMB over policy on outsourcing. *Washington Post.*

Walters, J. (2000a). The employee exodus. *Governing, 12*(6), 36–38.

Walters, J. (2000b). Reckoning with rewards. *Governing, 13*(3), 36–37.

Washington State Department of Personnel. (2000). *State of Washington workforce planning guide: Right people, right jobs, right time.* Retrieved on January 27, 2003, from the State of Washington Web site, http://hr.dop.wa.gov/workforceplanning.

Watkins, B. (1992). Reassessing comparable worth: The Minnesota experience. *P.A. Times,* p. 8.

Watts, A. D., & Edwards, P. K. (1983). Recruiting and retaining human services volunteers: An empirical analysis. *Journal of Voluntary Action Research, 12,* 9–22.

Webber, M. (2003, May 29). Taking care of tomorrow: Small charities find ways to offer retirement plans to employees. *Chronicle of Philanthropy.*

Weitzman, M. S., Jalandoni, N. T., Lampkin, L. M., & Pollak, T. H. (2002). *The new nonprofit almanac and desk reference: The essential facts and figures for managers, researchers, and volunteers.* San Francisco: Jossey-Bass.

Wellner, A. S. (2003, October 30). A new paid-leave system makes a charity's workers less harried. *Chronicle of Philanthropy,* p. 59.

Wexley, K. N., & Latham, G. P. (1991). *Developing and training human resources in organizations* (2nd ed.). New York: HarperCollins.

Wheeland, C. M. (1994). Evaluating city manager performance: Pennsylvania managers report on methods their councils use. *State and Local Government Review, 26,* 153–160.

Whelan. D. (2003, February 6). Packard Foundation announces grantmaking cuts of $50 million. *Chronicle of Philanthropy,* p. 11.

Whitaker, B. (2003, January 25). Deficit tripled, Los Angeles archdiocese says. *New York Times.*

Widmer, C. (1985). Why board members participate. *Journal of Voluntary Action Research, 14,* 8–23.

Wilson, J. Q. (1989). *Bureaucracy: What government agencies do and why they do it.* New York: Basic Books.

Wise, L. R. (2002). Public management reform: Competing drivers of change. *Public Administration Review, 62*(5), 555–567.

Witt, E. (1989). Sugarplums and lumps of coal. *Governing, 2*(2), 28–33.

Wittig, M. A., & Lowe, R. H. (1989). Comparable worth theory and policy. *Journal of Social Issues, 45,* 1–21.

Wooldridge, B. (1994). Changing demographics of the workforce: Implications for the use of technology as a productivity improvement strategy. *Public Productivity and Management Review, 17,* 371–386.

Wurf, J. (1974). Merit: A union view. *Public Administration Review, 34,* 431–434.

Wyatt, K. (2000, October 22). Girl Scouts' recruiting drive tells old image to take a hike. *Tampa Tribune,* p. 23.

Zedeck, S. (1996). Foreword. In K. R. Murphy (Ed.), *Individual differences in organizations* (p. 12). San Francisco: Jossey-Bass.

Zernike, K. (2000, August 29). "Policy on gays costing Scouts allies, money." *New York Times,* pp. 1, 3.

Name Index

Subject Index

Southwest Florida Water Management District (SWFWMD), workflow system, 59
Southwood Psychiatric Hospital,
Healey v., 75
Sovereignty doctrine, 324, 325–326
Split-half reliability, 186–187
The Spring of Tampa Bay, Inc, 142
Staffing systems, HRIS used for managing, 65–66
Stanislaus County Superior Court,
information use by, 55–56
State equalization factor, 228
State governments: ADA and ADEA
violations by, 14; broadbanding
adopted by, 242; collective bargaining in, 311–312, 325–326;
comparable worth regulations of,
259; expected workforce losses
in, 22, 25, 26–27; fiscal conditions
in, 5–6; glass ceiling in, 97; IT
worker shortage and, 27–28; privatization by, 15; Social Security
participation by, 264; workforce
planning by, 25–26, 27–28, 29,
30–31. See also Public sector
State laws: on collective bargaining,
312, 313, 318, 319, 322–323; on
pregnancy discrimination, 77;
on sexual orientation discrimination, 113; on workers' compensation, 265–266
State of Illinois, 299
State of Iowa, Christensen v., 257
The State of Merit in the Federal
Government (Ingraham and
Rosenbloom), 18
State of Rhode Island, Department
of Mental Health, Retardation,
and Hospitals, Cook v., 89
State of Texas et al., Hopwood et al.
v., 92
State of Washington, American
Federation of State, County, and
Municipal Employees (AFSCME)
v., 257

State of Washington Workforce Planning
Guide (Washington State Department of Personnel), 25
"States Plunging into Red," 6
Stotts, Firefighters of Local Union
1784 v., 87, 92
Strategic human resources management (SHRM): challenges for,
345–346; defined, 23; human resources information as basis of,
22–23; implementing, 31–32, 35;
obstacles to implementing, 32,
34–35, 42; rationale for, 17
Strategic human resources plan:
of Clearwater, Florida, 35, 36–41;
sample, 33–34
Strategic job analysis, 161–163
Strategic planning, 23–24
Strategic-level information systems,
60–61
Strikes, 322–323, 333, 335–336
Structured checklists, job analysis
data collected in, 157, 158–159
Structured oral exams, 177, 195
Subject matter experts (SMEs): and
designing strategic job analyses,
162; and job analysis data collec-
tion, 155, 161; and Job Element
Method (JEM) of job analysis, 165
Subjective measures, 213
Subordinate evaluations, 205
Succession analyses, 29
Succession planning, 29–30
Sundowner Offshore Services, Inc.,
Oncale v., 111
Supervisors: performance evalua-
tions reviewed by, 210; as perfor-
mance evaluators, 204, 205, 206,
211; sexually harassing behavior
by, 112–113, 118–119

T

Tampa Bay Make-a-Wish Foundation, 208
Tampa, Florida, sick and vacation
leave payouts at retirement, 273